World Economic and Financial Surveys

World Economic Outlook
October 2018

Challenges to Steady Growth
· ·

I N T E R N A T I O N A L   M O N E T A R Y   F U N D

©2018 International Monetary Fund

Cover and Design: Luisa Menjivar and Jorge Salazar
Composition: AGS, An RR Donnelley Company

Cataloging-in-Publication Data

Joint Bank-Fund Library

Names: International Monetary Fund.
Title: World economic outlook (International Monetary Fund)
Other titles: WEO | Occasional paper (International Monetary Fund) | World economic and
    financial surveys.
Description: Washington, DC : International Monetary Fund, 1980- | Semiannual | Some
    issues also have thematic titles. | Began with issue for May 1980. | 1981-1984: Occasional
    paper / International Monetary Fund, 0251-6365 | 1986-: World economic and financial
    surveys, 0256-6877.
Identifiers: ISSN 0256-6877 (print) | ISSN 1564-5215 (online)
Subjects: LCSH: Economic development—Periodicals. | International economic relations—
    Periodicals. | Debts, External—Periodicals. | Balance of payments—Periodicals. |
    International finance—Periodicals. | Economic forecasting—Periodicals.
Classification: LCC HC10.W79

HC10.80

ISBN 978-1-48437-679-9 (paper)
        978-1-48437-719-2 (Web PDF)
        978-1-48437-735-2 (ePub)
        978-1-48437-736-9 (Mobi)

The *World Economic Outlook* (WEO) is a survey by the IMF staff published twice a
year, in the spring and fall. The WEO is prepared by the IMF staff and has benefited
from comments and suggestions by Executive Directors following their discussion of the
report on September 20, 2018. The views expressed in this publication are those of the
IMF staff and do not necessarily represent the views of the IMF's Executive Directors
or their national authorities.

Recommended citation: International Monetary Fund. 2018. *World Economic Outlook:
Challenges to Steady Growth.* Washington, DC, October.

Publication orders may be placed online, by fax, or through the mail:
International Monetary Fund, Publication Services
P.O. Box 92780, Washington, DC 20090, USA
Tel.: (202) 623-7430 Fax: (202) 623-7201
E-mail: publications@imf.org
www.imfbookstore.org
www.elibrary.imf.org

CONTENTS

Tables

Online Tables

Figures

Online Figures

ASSUMPTIONS AND CONVENTIONS

A number of assumptions have been adopted for the projections presented in the *World Economic Outlook* (WEO). It has been assumed that real effective exchange rates remained constant at their average levels during July 17 to August 14, 2018, except for those for the currencies participating in the European exchange rate mechanism II (ERM II), which are assumed to have remained constant in nominal terms relative to the euro; that established policies of national authorities will be maintained (for specific assumptions about fiscal and monetary policies for selected economies, see Box A1 in the Statistical Appendix); that the average price of oil will be $69.38 a barrel in 2018 and $68.76 a barrel in 2019 and will remain unchanged in real terms over the medium term; that the six-month London interbank offered rate (LIBOR) on US dollar deposits will average 2.5 percent in 2018 and 3.4 percent in 2019; that the three-month euro deposit rate will average –0.3 percent in 2018 and –0.2 percent in 2019; and that the six-month Japanese yen deposit rate will yield on average 0.0 percent in 2018 and 0.1 percent in 2019. These are, of course, working hypotheses rather than forecasts, and the uncertainties surrounding them add to the margin of error that would in any event be involved in the projections. The estimates and projections are based on statistical information available through September 18, 2018.

The following conventions are used throughout the WEO:

. . .   to indicate that data are not available or not applicable;

–   between years or months (for example, 2017–18 or January–June) to indicate the years or months covered, including the beginning and ending years or months; and

/   between years or months (for example, 2017/18) to indicate a fiscal or financial year.

"Billion" means a thousand million; "trillion" means a thousand billion.

"Basis points" refers to hundredths of 1 percentage point (for example, 25 basis points are equivalent to ¼ of 1 percentage point).

Data refer to calendar years, except in the case of a few countries that use fiscal years. Table F in the Statistical Appendix lists the economies with exceptional reporting periods for national accounts and government finance data for each country.

For some countries, the figures for 2017 and earlier are based on estimates rather than actual outturns. Table G in the Statistical Appendix lists the latest actual outturns for the indicators in the national accounts, prices, government finance, and balance of payments indicators for each country.

What is new in this publication:

- *Argentina*'s consumer prices, which were previously excluded from the group composites because of data constraints, are now included starting from 2017 onward.

- Data for *Aruba* are included in the data aggregated for the emerging market and developing economies.

- *Egypt*'s forecast data, from which the nominal exchange rate assumptions are calculated, were previously excluded because the nominal exchange rate was a market sensitive issue; they are now made public.

- *Swaziland* is now called *Eswatini*.

- *Venezuela* redenominated its currency on August 20, 2018, by replacing 100,000 bolívares Fuertes (VEF) with 1 bolívar Soberano (VES). Local currency data, including the historical data, for Venezuela are expressed in the new currency beginning with the October 2018 WEO database.

In the tables and figures, the following conventions apply:

- If no source is listed on tables and figures, data are drawn from the WEO database.

- When countries are not listed alphabetically, they are ordered on the basis of economic size.

- Minor discrepancies between sums of constituent figures and totals shown reflect rounding.

As used in this report, the terms "country" and "economy" do not in all cases refer to a territorial entity that is a state as understood by international law and practice. As used here, the term also covers some territorial entities that are not states but for which statistical data are maintained on a separate and independent basis.

Composite data are provided for various groups of countries organized according to economic characteristics or region. Unless noted otherwise, country group composites represent calculations based on 90 percent or more of the weighted group data.

The boundaries, colors, denominations, and any other information shown on the maps do not imply, on the part of the International Monetary Fund, any judgment on the legal status of any territory or any endorsement or acceptance of such boundaries.

Corrections and Revisions

The data and analysis appearing in the *World Economic Outlook* (WEO) are compiled by the IMF staff at the time of publication. Every effort is made to ensure their timeliness, accuracy, and completeness. When errors are discovered, corrections and revisions are incorporated into the digital editions available from the IMF website and on the IMF eLibrary (see below). All substantive changes are listed in the online tables of contents.

Print and Digital Editions

Print copies of this *World Economic Outlook* can be ordered at https://www.bookstore.imf.org/books/title/world-economic-outlook-october-2018.

The WEO is featured on the IMF website at http://www.imf.org/publications/WEO. This site includes a PDF of the report and data sets for each of the charts therein.

The IMF eLibrary hosts multiple digital editions of the *World Economic Outlook*, including ePub, enhanced PDF, Mobi, and HTML: http://elibrary.imf.org/OCT18WEO.

Copyright and Reuse

Information on the terms and conditions for reusing the contents of this publication are at http://www.imf.org/external/terms.htm.

This version of the *World Economic Outlook* (WEO) is available in full through the IMF eLibrary (www.elibrary. imf.org) and the IMF website (www.imf.org). Accompanying the publication on the IMF website is a larger compilation of data from the WEO database than is included in the report itself, including files containing the series most frequently requested by readers. These files may be downloaded for use in a variety of software packages.

The data appearing in the WEO are compiled by the IMF staff at the time of the WEO exercises. The historical data and projections are based on the information gathered by the IMF country desk officers in the context of their missions to IMF member countries and through their ongoing analysis of the evolving situation in each country. Historical data are updated on a continual basis as more information becomes available, and structural breaks in data are often adjusted to produce smooth series with the use of splicing and other techniques. IMF staff estimates continue to serve as proxies for historical series when complete information is unavailable. As a result, WEO data can differ from those in other sources with official data, including the IMF's International Financial Statistics.

The WEO data and metadata provided are "as is" and "as available," and every effort is made to ensure their timeliness, accuracy, and completeness, but these cannot be guaranteed. When errors are discovered, there is a concerted effort to correct them as appropriate and feasible. Corrections and revisions made after publication are incorporated into the electronic editions available from the IMF eLibrary (www.elibrary.imf.org) and on the IMF website (www.imf.org). All substantive changes are listed in detail in the online tables of contents.

For details on the terms and conditions for usage of the WEO database, please refer to the IMF Copyright and Usage website (www.imf.org/external/terms.htm).

Inquiries about the content of the WEO and the WEO database should be sent by mail, fax, or online forum (telephone inquiries cannot be accepted):

World Economic Studies Division
Research Department
International Monetary Fund
700 19th Street, NW
Washington, DC 20431, USA
Fax: (202) 623-6343
Online Forum: www.imf.org/weoforum

PREFACE

The analysis and projections contained in the *World Economic Outlook* are integral elements of the IMF's surveillance of economic developments and policies in its member countries, of developments in international financial markets, and of the global economic system. The survey of prospects and policies is the product of a comprehensive interdepartmental review of world economic developments, which draws primarily on information the IMF staff gathers through its consultations with member countries. These consultations are carried out in particular by the IMF's area departments—namely, the African Department, Asia and Pacific Department, European Department, Middle East and Central Asia Department, and Western Hemisphere Department—together with the Strategy, Policy, and Review Department; the Monetary and Capital Markets Department; and the Fiscal Affairs Department.

The analysis in this report was coordinated in the Research Department under the general direction of Maurice Obstfeld, Economic Counsellor and Director of Research. The project was directed by Gian Maria Milesi-Ferretti, Deputy Director, Research Department; and Oya Celasun, Division Chief, Research Department.

The primary contributors to this report were Rudolfs Bems, Christian Bogmans, Francesca Caselli, Wenjie Chen, Francesco Grigoli, Bertrand Gruss, Zsóka Kóczán, Toh Kuan, Weicheng Lian, Akito Matsumoto, Mico Mrkaic, Malhar Nabar, Natalija Novta, Andrea Pescatori, and Petia Topalova.

Other contributors include Michal Andrle, Gavin Asdorian, Luisa Calixto, Yan Carrière-Swallow, Federico Diez, Angela Espiritu, Rachel Yuting Fan, Gregg Forte, Meron Haile, Mandy Hemmati, Benjamin Hilgenstock, Ava Yeabin Hong, Benjamin Hunt, Deniz Igan, Christopher Johns, Lama Kiyasseh, Jungjin Lee, Daniel Leigh, Daniela Muhaj, Susanna Mursula, Cynthia Nyanchama Nyakeri, Emory Oakes, Rafael Portillo, Evgenia Pugacheva, Adrian Robles Villamil, Susie Xiaohui Sun, Suchanan Tambunlertchai, Nicholas Tong, Julia Xueliang Wang, Shan Wang, Jilun Xing, Juan Yépez, Yuan Zeng, Qiaoqiao Zhang, Candice Huiyuan Zhao, Caroline Chenqi Zhou, and Jillian Zirnhelt.

Joseph Procopio from the Communications Department led the editorial team for the report, with production and editorial support from Christine Ebrahimzadeh and Linda Kean and editorial assistance from James Unwin, Lucy Scott Morales, Sherrie Brown, and Vector Talent Resources.

The analysis has benefited from comments and suggestions by staff members from other IMF departments, as well as by Executive Directors following their discussion of the report on September 20, 2018. However, both projections and policy considerations are those of the IMF staff and should not be attributed to Executive Directors or to their national authorities.

A typical foreword to the *World Economic Outlook* (WEO) highlights how data since the previous projection alter our baseline growth assumptions. It pays detailed attention to the most recent developments and interprets the implications for policies going forward. This WEO foreword—my last—will instead situate the current conjuncture in a broader historical context, the better to draw out lessons for the future.

The occasion justifies my unusual approach. This WEO is appearing shortly after the 10th anniversary of the Lehman Brothers collapse and, moreover, at a time of mounting uncertainties—not only over economic policies but also over the global framework of international relations within which policies are made.

The decade since the global financial crisis of 2008–09 has indeed brought dramatic economic and political developments, a trend that seems unlikely to recede any time soon. How can policymakers guide their economies through the troubled waters ahead? How can they strengthen and modernize the post–World War II multilateral system, which supported an unparalleled 70 years of peace and prosperity? To answer, we must consider not only the impact of the crisis itself but also the years just before, when some key patterns that have defined the post-crisis period first emerged.

The Precrisis Decade

It was in the period before the crisis when some of our current economic vulnerabilities first came to be. The chart tracks real global growth since 1980, along with the contributions of advanced economies and of emerging market and developing economies. After the Asian crisis (1997–98) and the collapse of the dot-com bubble (2000–01), the growth of emerging market and developing economies accelerated significantly while advanced economies, even though recovering, grew at rates below prior levels.

Two things stand out. First, advanced economies' growth has generally trended downward since the mid-2000s. This long-term decline stems from aging workforces and slower productivity growth, which coincide with falling economic dynamism and rising

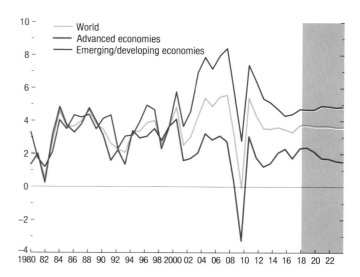

Figure 1. Real GDP Growth, by Country Group
(Year over year)

Source: IMF, *World Economic Outlook*, October 2018.
Note: Grey area denotes projections.

market concentration. Notably, the longer-term future growth rates that the WEO projects for advanced economies are below current levels.

Second, the start of the new millennium brought a growth surge in emerging market and developing economies that decisively placed them ahead of advanced economies' growth. Rapid Chinese growth was responsible for some, but clearly not all, of this decoupling, because the pattern remains even after subtracting China's algebraic growth contribution (as well as India's, for that matter). The growth acceleration is a robust consequence of stronger policy frameworks in many emerging market and developing economies, including their embrace of more open trade. Because it also derives from the greater weight of these fast-growing economies in the world economy, their distinct growth advantage over advanced economies looks likely to continue unless advanced economies can meet their structural economic challenges.

The Asian crisis and the dot-com collapse—and intervening events like the forced bailout of Long-Term Capital Management (LTCM) in 1998, which avoided a possible systemic financial meltdown—illustrate pointedly how balance-sheet weaknesses and asset-price bubbles can bring down financial institutions and entire economies. In his 1998 Henry L. Stimson Lecture at Yale University, Alexandre Lamfalussy wrote presciently of the US market turmoil that followed that year's Russian default: "If such developments can take place in the model market of the world, what is the practical value of recommending that emerging markets copy this model?"

Many emerging market and developing economies did draw and act on lessons from these crises, for example, by embracing inflation targeting, adopting more flexible exchange rate regimes, and implementing macroprudential policies—lessons well worth remembering today. Advanced economies, however, were more complacent, often viewing financial crises as problems to which only emerging market and developing economies were susceptible—notwithstanding the contradictory evidence from several near-misses, including LTCM. The result was the global financial crisis, which ended the mid-decade global boom. As a group, emerging market and developing economies generally weathered that crisis well, given its severity, and they have continued to grow more quickly than during the 1980s and 1990s.

The Postcrisis Decade

World growth took a rarely precedented tumble in 2009, but all regions of the world experienced a bounce back in 2010–11, supported by vigorous countercyclical responses throughout the Group of Twenty countries. Many advanced economies reduced policy interest rates to the zero lower bound and began to experiment with unconventional monetary policies.

After 2010–11, however, a succession of shocks—the euro area crisis, reversals of fiscal stimulus in major economies, wobbles in Chinese growth, and falling commodity prices—all prevented continued strong and synchronized growth. Relatively favorable economic fundamentals in the United States made it likely that the Federal Reserve would be the first among major central banks to normalize monetary policy, and the dollar strengthened starting in the summer of 2014. Global markets were spooked a year later when China, feeling the resulting pressure on its heavily managed exchange rate, began to allow its currency to fall against the dollar. The tensions did not recede quickly. Within a month of the Federal Reserve's first interest-rate hike in nearly 10 years at the end of 2015, global financial markets swooned

and commodity prices fell further. The 2016 global growth rate of 3.3 percent was the lowest since 2009.

Economic optimism began to return midway through 2016, despite any effects from the surprise outcome of the UK Brexit referendum in June. Late that year, manufacturing activity surged and growth picked up broadly around the world, leading to the most evenly balanced global upswing since 2010. Global trade, which had grown unusually slowly during 2012–16, also rebounded as investment began to recover. As of the April 2018 WEO, we projected global growth to rise to 3.9 percent in both 2018 and 2019, and for the first time in a while, assessed short-term risks to our growth forecast to be evenly balanced between potential positive and negative surprises.

Now, in October 2018, the outlook is one of less balanced and more tentative expansion than we hoped for last April. Growth in the United States remains exceptionally robust for now, powered by a procyclical fiscal expansion that may, however, weigh on US and global growth later. But we have downgraded near-term growth prospects for the euro area, Korea, and the United Kingdom. Our reassessment is more dramatic for emerging markets as a group, where we see growth easing in Latin America (notably Argentina, Brazil, Mexico), the Middle East (notably Iran), and emerging Europe (notably Turkey). Our 2019 growth projection for China is also lower than in April, given the latest round of US tariffs on Chinese imports, as are our projections for India. Owing to these changes, our international growth projections for both this year and next are downgraded to 3.7 percent, 0.2 percentage point below our last assessments and the same rate achieved in 2017. At the global level, recent data show weakening in trade, manufacturing, and investment. Overall, world economic growth is still solid compared with earlier this decade, but it appears to have plateaued.

These more moderate growth numbers and the weaker incoming data that underpin them owe, in part, to a sharp rise in policy uncertainty over the past year—a development yet to be reflected in advanced economy financial markets but evident in news-based uncertainty measures. Uncertainty over trade policy is prominent in the wake of US actions (or threatened actions) on several fronts, the responses by its trading partners, and a general weakening of multilateral consultation on trade issues. The possible failure of Brexit negotiations poses another risk. Amid the trade uncertainties, financial conditions are tightening for emerging market and developing economies as they adjust to progressive interest rate hikes by the Federal Reserve and an impending end of asset purchases by the European Central Bank. Compared with 10 years ago, many of these economies have higher levels of corporate and sovereign debt, leaving them more vulnerable. With geopolitical tensions also relevant in several regions, we judge that, even for the near future, the possibility of unpleasant surprises outweighs the likelihood of unforeseen good news.

Policy Challenges

Perhaps the biggest secular challenge for many advanced economies centers on the slow growth of workers' incomes, perceptions of lower social mobility, and, in some countries, inadequate policy responses to structural economic change. Not only has the trend in long-term advanced economy growth been downward; in many countries, the more meager gains have gone primarily to the relatively well-off. In the United States, for example, median real household income was about the same in 2016 as in 1999. This pattern clearly predates the global financial crisis and the euro area crisis. But the crises themselves, along with aspects of the policy response, further soured the public mood. Such discontent in turn helped give rise to current tensions over trade policy as well as a broader skepticism toward centrist policies and leaders, who have traditionally supported global cooperation as the proper response to shared challenges.

Policymakers must take a long-term perspective to address this malaise. Inclusive fiscal policies, educational investments, and ensuring access to adequate health care can reduce inequality and are key priorities. So too are more secure social safety nets that can help workers adjust to a range of structural shocks, whether from globalization, technological change, or (in some countries) climate change. Policies to promote labor force participation and the economic inclusion of women and youth are especially important. Structural reform priorities differ by country, but in general, addressing them will raise output and growth over the medium term. That said, due consideration must be given to those who are already disadvantaged but might lose out further. Support for research and development and basic and applied scientific research offers the promise of raising growth rates, as many studies have shown. These policy priorities are also relevant to emerging market and developing economies.

Most countries also need to build fiscal buffers to make room for policy responses to the next recession when it comes and to reduce the long-term tax costs of servicing high public debts. Several emerging market and developing economies must undertake fiscal reforms to ensure the sustainability of public finances and improve market sentiment. Global and national actions have buttressed financial stability since the crisis, but the work remains incomplete in several respects, including, for example, safeguarding the nonbank financial sector and resolution in insolvency, especially for systemically important international banks, where a cooperative global framework is urgently needed. Some financial oversight measures that grew out of the crisis could be simplified, but a wholesale rollback would risk future instability. Even piecemeal deregulation must be cautious and carefully considered, because a sequence of smaller actions could eventually weaken the system enough to leave it fragile. Indeed, precisely because monetary policy will need to remain accommodative where inflation is below target levels and will need to proceed cautiously elsewhere, effective macro- and microprudential levers must remain available.

The growing weight of emerging market and developing economies in the global economy means that advanced economies internalize fewer of the global gains from their own support of multilateral cooperation. They perceive the leakage of benefits to other countries to be relatively larger now than in the past, compared with their own benefits. This change may tempt some to retreat into an imagined self-sufficiency. But economic interdependence is greater than ever—through trade, finance, knowledge spillovers, migration, and environmental impacts, to name a few channels—and that makes cooperation in areas of common concern more important than ever too, including for advanced economies.

Multilateralism must evolve so that every country views it to be in its self-interest, even in a multipolar world. But that will require *domestic* political support for an internationally collaborative approach. Inclusive policies that ensure a broad sharing of the gains from economic growth are not only desirable in their own right; they can also help convince citizens that international cooperation works for them. I am proud that during my tenure, the IMF has increasingly championed such policies while supporting multilateral solutions to global challenges. Without more inclusive policies, multilateralism cannot survive. And without multilateralism, the world will be a poorer and more dangerous place.

Maurice Obstfeld
Economic Counsellor

EXECUTIVE SUMMARY

The steady expansion under way since mid-2016 continues, with global growth for 2018–19 projected to remain at its 2017 level. At the same time, however, the expansion has become less balanced and may have peaked in some major economies. Downside risks to global growth have risen in the past six months and the potential for upside surprises has receded.

Global growth is projected at 3.7 percent for 2018–19—0.2 percentage point lower for both years than forecast in April. In the United States, momentum is still strong as fiscal stimulus continues to increase, but the forecast for 2019 has been revised down due to recently announced trade measures, including the tariffs imposed on $200 billion of US imports from China. Growth projections have been marked down for the euro area and the United Kingdom, following surprises that suppressed activity in early 2018. Among emerging market and developing economies, the growth prospects of many energy exporters have been lifted by higher oil prices, but growth was revised down for Argentina, Brazil, Iran, and Turkey, among others, reflecting country-specific factors, tighter financial conditions, geopolitical tensions, and higher oil import bills. China and a number of Asian economies are also projected to experience somewhat weaker growth in 2019 in the aftermath of the recently announced trade measures. Beyond the next couple of years, as output gaps close and monetary policy settings continue to normalize, growth in most advanced economies is expected to decline to potential rates—well below the averages reached before the global financial crisis of a decade ago. Slower expansion in working-age populations and projected lackluster productivity gains are the prime drivers of lower medium-term growth rates. US growth will decline as fiscal stimulus begins to unwind in 2020, at a time when the monetary tightening cycle is expected to be at its peak. Growth in China will remain strong but is projected to decline gradually, and prospects remain subpar in some emerging market and developing economies, especially for per capita growth, including in commodity exporters that continue to face substantial fiscal consolidation needs or are mired in war and conflict.

Risks to global growth skew to the downside in a context of elevated policy uncertainty. Several of the downside risks highlighted in the April 2018 World Economic Outlook *(WEO)—such as rising trade barriers and a reversal of capital flows to emerging market economies with weaker fundamentals and higher political risk—have become more pronounced or have partially materialized. While financial market conditions remain accommodative in advanced economies, they could tighten rapidly if, for example, trade tensions and policy uncertainty were to intensify. Monetary policy is another potential trigger. The US economy is above full employment, yet the path of interest rate increases that markets anticipate is less steep than that projected by the Federal Reserve. Unexpectedly high inflation readings in the United States could therefore lead investors to abruptly reassess risks. Tighter financial conditions in advanced economies could cause disruptive portfolio adjustments, sharp exchange rate movements, and further reductions in capital inflows to emerging markets, particularly those with greater vulnerabilities.*

The recovery has helped lift employment and income, strengthened balance sheets, and provided an opportunity to rebuild buffers. Yet, with risks shifting to the downside, there is greater urgency for policies to enhance prospects for strong and inclusive growth. Avoiding protectionist reactions to structural change and finding cooperative solutions that promote continued growth in goods and services trade remain essential to preserve and extend the global expansion. At a time of above-potential growth in many economies, policymakers should aim to enact reforms that raise medium-term incomes to the benefit of all. With shrinking excess capacity and mounting downside risks, many countries need to rebuild fiscal buffers and strengthen their resilience to an environment in which financial conditions could tighten suddenly and sharply.

In advanced economies, economic activity lost some momentum in the first half of 2018 after peaking in the second half of 2017. Outcomes fell short of projections in the euro area and the United Kingdom; growth in world trade and industrial production declined; and some high-frequency indicators moderated. Core inflation remains very different across advanced economies—well below objectives in the euro area and Japan, but close to target in the United

Kingdom and the United States. Across emerging market and developing economies, activity continued to improve gradually in energy exporters but softened in some importers. Activity slowed more markedly in Argentina, Brazil, and Turkey, where country-specific factors and a souring of investor sentiment were also at play. Inflation has generally increased in emerging market and developing economies, in part reflecting the pass-through of currency depreciations. While financial conditions have tightened in many emerging market and developing economies, they remain supportive in advanced economies, despite continued federal funds rate increases in the United States.

Global growth is forecast at 3.7 percent for 2018–19, 0.2 percentage point below the April 2018 WEO projection, and is set to soften over the medium term. Global financial conditions are expected to tighten as monetary policy normalizes; the trade measures implemented since April will weigh on activity in 2019 and beyond; US fiscal policy will subtract momentum starting in 2020; and China will slow, reflecting weaker credit growth and rising trade barriers. In advanced economies, marked slowdowns in working-age population growth and lackluster productivity advances will hold back gains in medium-term potential output. Across emerging market and developing economies, medium-term prospects are mixed. Projections remain favorable for emerging Asia and emerging Europe, excluding Turkey, but are tepid for Latin America, the Middle East, and sub-Saharan Africa, where—despite the ongoing recovery—the medium-term outlook for commodity exporters remains generally subdued, with a need for further economic diversification and fiscal adjustment. Prospects for 2018–19 were marked down sharply for Iran, reflecting the impact of the reinstatement of US sanctions. For Turkey, market turmoil, sharp currency depreciation, and elevated uncertainty will weigh on investment and consumer demand, likewise justifying a sharp negative revision in growth prospects. Growth for China and a number of Asian economies have also been revised down following the recently announced trade measures. Some 45 emerging market and developing economies—accounting for 10 percent of world GDP in purchasing-power-parity terms—are projected to grow by less than advanced economies in per capita terms over 2018–23, and hence to fall further behind in living standards.

The balance of risks to the global growth forecast is tilted to the downside, both in the short term and beyond. The potential for upside surprises has ebbed, given diminished growth momentum and tighter financial conditions in emerging market and developing economies. At the same time, several of the downside risks highlighted in the April 2018 WEO—such as rising trade barriers and a reversal of capital flows to emerging market economies with weaker external positions, such as Argentina and Turkey—have become more pronounced or have partially materialized.

Escalating trade tensions and the potential shift away from a multilateral, rules-based trading system are key threats to the global outlook. Since the April 2018 WEO, protectionist rhetoric has increasingly turned into action, with the United States imposing tariffs on a variety of imports, including on $200 billion of imports from China, and trading partners undertaking or promising retaliatory and other protective measures. An intensification of trade tensions, and the associated rise in policy uncertainty, could dent business and financial market sentiment, trigger financial market volatility, and slow investment and trade. Higher trade barriers would disrupt global supply chains and slow the spread of new technologies, ultimately lowering global productivity and welfare. More import restrictions would also make tradable consumer goods less affordable, harming low-income households disproportionately.

Still-easy global financial conditions could tighten sharply, triggered by more aggressive monetary policy tightening in advanced economies or the materialization of other risks that shift market sentiment. Such developments would expose vulnerabilities that have accumulated over the years, dent confidence, and undermine investment (a key driver of the baseline growth forecast). In the medium term, risks stem from a potential continued buildup of financial vulnerabilities, the implementation of unsustainable macroeconomic policies amid a subdued growth outlook, rising inequality, and declining trust in mainstream economic policies. A range of other noneconomic risks are also relevant. If any of these risks materializes, the likelihood of other adverse developments will rise.

The environment of continued expansion offers a narrowing window of opportunity to advance policies and reforms—both multilaterally and at the country level—that extend the momentum and raise medium-term growth for the benefit of all, while building buffers for the next downturn and strengthening resilience to an environment where financial conditions could tighten suddenly and sharply.

Foster cooperation. Countries need to work together to tackle challenges that extend beyond their own borders. To preserve and broaden the gains from decades of rules-based global trade integration, countries should cooperate to reduce trade costs further and resolve disagreements without raising distortionary barriers. Cooperative efforts are also essential for completing the financial regulatory reform agenda, strengthening international taxation, enhancing cybersecurity, tackling corruption, and mitigating and coping with climate change.

Bring inflation to target, build buffers, curb excess imbalances. Monetary accommodation needs to continue where inflation is weak, but cautious, well-communicated, data-dependent normalization should proceed where inflation is close to target. Fiscal policy should aim to rebuild buffers for the next downturn, and the composition of public spending and revenues should be designed to bolster potential output and inclusiveness. In countries at or close to full employment, with an excess current account deficit and an unsustainable fiscal position (notably the United States), public debt needs to be stabilized and eventually reduced, and procyclical stimulus, which is contributing to rising global imbalances and heightened risks to the US and global economies, should be withdrawn. Countries with both excess current account surpluses and fiscal space (for example, Germany) should increase public investment to boost potential growth and reduce external imbalances.

Strengthen the potential for higher and more inclusive growth. All countries should grasp the opportunity to adopt structural reforms and policies that raise productivity and ensure broad-based gains—for instance, by encouraging technological innovation and diffusion, increasing labor force participation (especially by women and youth), supporting those displaced by structural change, and investing in education and training to enhance job opportunities.

Build resilience. Macro- and microprudential policies face the challenges of building financial buffers, curtailing rising leverage, limiting excessive risk taking, and containing financial stability risks (including threats to cybersecurity). In the euro area, balance sheet repair needs to continue. Emerging market economies should aim to keep contingent liabilities and balance sheet mismatches in check. Building on recent efforts, China should continue to rein in credit growth and address financial risks, even if growth temporarily slows. Among the main findings of Chapter 2 is that countries with stronger fiscal positions before the global financial crisis, and those with more flexible exchange rate regimes, experienced smaller output losses. Underscoring the importance of macroprudential policies and effective supervision, countries with greater financial vulnerabilities before the global financial crisis suffered larger output losses. The analysis in Chapter 3 highlights important ways in which emerging market and developing economies can reap the benefits from stronger institutions. In the current juncture where global financial conditions are normalizing, more credible monetary policy frameworks that effectively anchor inflation expectations can make the economy more resilient to adverse external shocks by improving the tradeoff between inflation and output.

Improve convergence prospects for low-income developing countries. Continued progress toward the 2030 United Nations Sustainable Development Goals is imperative to foster greater economic security and better living standards for a rising share of the world's population. Given their generally high levels of public indebtedness, low-income developing countries need to make decisive progress to strengthen their fiscal positions while prioritizing well-targeted measures to reduce poverty. They must also boost the resilience of their financial systems. Investing in human capital, improving access to credit, and reducing infrastructure gaps can promote economic diversification and improve the capacity to cope with climate shocks.

CHAPTER 1

GLOBAL PROSPECTS AND POLICIES

Global growth for 2018–19 is projected to remain steady at its 2017 level, but its pace is less vigorous than projected in April and it has become less balanced. Downside risks to global growth have risen in the past six months and the potential for upside surprises has receded.

Global growth is projected at 3.7 percent for 2018–19—0.2 percentage point lower for both years than forecast in April. The downward revision reflects surprises that suppressed activity in early 2018 in some major advanced economies, the negative effects of the trade measures implemented or approved between April and mid-September, as well as a weaker outlook for some key emerging market and developing economies arising from country-specific factors, tighter financial conditions, geopolitical tensions, and higher oil import bills. Beyond the next couple of years, as output gaps close and monetary policy settings begin to normalize, growth in most advanced economies is expected to decline to potential rates well below the averages reached before the global financial crisis of a decade ago. Medium-term prospects remain generally strong in emerging Asia but subpar in some emerging market and developing economies, especially for per capita growth, including in commodity exporters that continue to face substantial fiscal consolidation needs or are mired in war and conflict.

The balance of risks to the global growth forecast has shifted to the downside in a context of elevated policy uncertainty. Several of the downside risks highlighted in the April 2018 World Economic Outlook *(WEO)—such as rising trade barriers and a reversal of capital flows to emerging market economies with weaker fundamentals and higher political risk—have become more pronounced or have partially materialized. Meanwhile, the potential for upside surprises has receded, given the tightening of financial conditions in some parts of the world, higher trade costs, slow implementation of reforms recommended in the past, and waning growth momentum. While financial market conditions remain accommodative in advanced economies, they could tighten rapidly if trade tensions and policy uncertainty intensify, or unexpectedly high inflation in the United States triggers a stronger-than-anticipated monetary policy response. Tighter financial conditions*

in advanced economies could cause disruptive portfolio adjustments, sharp exchange rate movements, and further reductions in capital inflows to emerging markets, particularly those with greater vulnerabilities.

The recovery has helped lift employment and income, has strengthened balance sheets, and has provided an opportunity to rebuild buffers. However, with risks shifting to the downside, there is greater urgency for policies to enhance prospects for strong and inclusive growth. Avoiding protectionist reactions to structural change and finding cooperative solutions that promote continued growth in goods and services trade remain essential to preserving and extending the global expansion. At a time of above-potential growth in many economies, policymakers should aim to enact reforms that raise medium-term incomes for the benefit of all. With shrinking excess capacity and mounting downside risks, many countries need to rebuild fiscal buffers and strengthen their resilience to an environment in which financial conditions could tighten suddenly and sharply.

Recent Developments and Prospects
Softer, More Uneven Momentum

In the first half of 2018, global growth shed some of the strong momentum registered in the second half of last year, and the expansion became less synchronized across countries. Activity moderated more than expected in some large advanced economies from its strong pace last year, while the emerging market and developing economy group continued to expand at broadly the same pace as in 2017 (Figure 1.1).

Among advanced economies, growth disappointed in the euro area and the United Kingdom. Slower export growth after a strong surge in the final quarter of 2017 contributed notably to the euro area slowdown. Higher energy prices helped dampen demand in energy importers, while some countries were also affected by political uncertainty or industrial actions. In the United Kingdom, growth moderated more than anticipated, partly because of weather-related

Figure 1.1. Global Activity Indicators

Global growth moderated in the first half of 2018, with negative surprises to activity in several large advanced economies. After rapid growth in 2017, world trade volumes and industrial production have slowed, and some high-frequency indicators have softened.

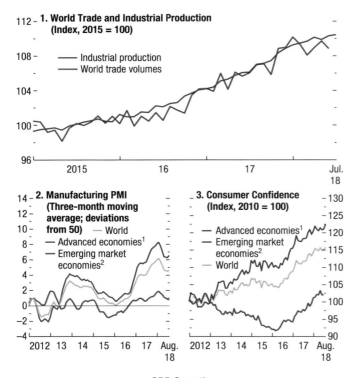

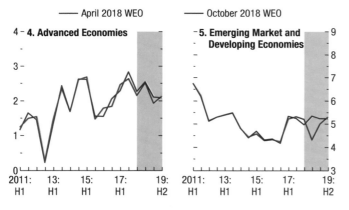

Sources: CPB Netherlands Bureau for Economic Policy Analysis; Haver Analytics; Markit Economics; and IMF staff estimates.
Note: CC = consumer confidence; PMI = purchasing managers' index; WEO = *World Economic Outlook*.
[1]Australia, Canada (PMI only), Czech Republic, Denmark, euro area, Hong Kong SAR (CC only), Israel, Japan, Korea, New Zealand (PMI only), Norway (CC only), Singapore (PMI only), Sweden (CC only), Switzerland, Taiwan Province of China, United Kingdom, United States.
[2]Argentina (CC only), Brazil, China, Colombia (CC only), Hungary, India (PMI only), Indonesia, Latvia (CC only), Malaysia (PMI only), Mexico (PMI only), Philippines (CC only), Poland, Russia, South Africa, Thailand, Turkey, Ukraine (CC only).

disruptions in the first quarter. Set against these developments, the US economy maintained robust growth, particularly in the second quarter, with private sector activity buoyed further by sizable fiscal stimulus.

Aggregate growth in the emerging market and developing economy group stabilized in the first half of 2018. Emerging Asia continued to register strong growth, supported by a domestic demand-led pickup in the Indian economy from a four-year-low pace of expansion in 2017, even as activity in China moderated in the second quarter in response to regulatory tightening of the property sector and nonbank financial intermediation. Higher oil prices lifted growth among fuel-exporting economies in sub-Saharan Africa and the Middle East. The recovery in Latin America continued, though at a more subdued pace than anticipated as tighter financial conditions and a drought weighed on growth in Argentina and a nationwide truckers' strike disrupted production in Brazil.

Trade Tensions

Since January, a sequence of US tariff actions on solar panels, washing machines, steel, aluminum, and a range of Chinese products, plus retaliation by trading partners has complicated global trade relations.[1] While the preliminary agreement between the United States and Mexico on some bilateral trade issues has been a step forward, the future of the trilateral North American Free Trade Agreement (NAFTA) remains uncertain as the United States and Canada work to resolve remaining issues. Moreover, the potential for escalating trade tensions looms.[2]

Although sentiment has generally remained strong despite the intensification of trade disputes, and headline high-frequency data point to continued momentum, some of the more trade-sensitive data

[1]Following tariff increases in early 2018 on washing machines, solar cells, steel, and aluminum, the United States on June 15 announced a 25 percent tariff on imports from China worth $50 billion; China announced retaliation on a similar scale. On September 17, the United States announced a 10 percent tariff—rising to 25 percent by year end—on an additional $200 billion in imports from China. In response, China, announced tariffs on a further $60 billion of US imports.
[2]The United States has also suggested that a further $267 billion of Chinese goods—covering nearly all remaining Chinese imports—may be hit with tariffs, and it has separately raised the possibility of tariffs on the automotive sector that would affect many other countries (see Scenario Box 1).

Figure 1.2. Commodity and Oil Prices
(Deflated using US consumer price index; index, 2014 = 100)

The commodity price index has risen in the past six months, driven by higher energy prices. Food prices fell amid rising trade tensions, while the price of metals softened because of weaker demand from China.

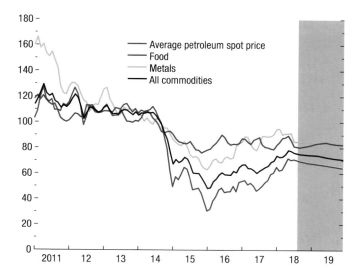

Sources: IMF, Primary Commodity Price System; and IMF staff estimates.

have weakened since the start of the year. Surveys of purchasing managers in China, the euro area, Japan, and the United States point to softer growth in export orders. Sector-specific sentiment indicators for auto-makers in Germany and Japan suggest more pessi-mism about the outlook than at the start of the year. Industrial production subindices for the United States, Japan, and Germany indicate greater moderation in capital-goods-producing sectors than for the rest of manufacturing, which could signal weaker capital spending. German manufacturing orders fell by about 4 percent on a monthly basis in June (contributing to a 6½ percent drop in the second quarter on a quar-terly, annualized basis) followed by a close to 1 percent decline in July. Consistent with the evidence from the production side, international trade in goods appears to have slowed since early 2018 after very rapid growth late in 2017 (Figure 1.1). Growth in import volumes in some of the main advanced economies (United States, euro area, Japan) has declined. The trade slowdown could reflect a combination of factors, such as some payback from the very strong trade growth in late 2017 and weaker capital spending in a more uncertain global environment.

Commodity Index Rising on Higher Energy Prices

The IMF's Primary Commodities Price Index rose 3.3 percent between February 2018 and August 2018—that is, between the reference periods for the April 2018 and the current WEO—driven by higher energy prices (Figure 1.2). As discussed in the Com-modities Special Feature, the energy subindex rose 11.1 percent. Food prices were down 6.4 percent, and the metals subindex declined 11.7 percent.

Oil prices rose to more than $76 a barrel in June—the highest level since November 2014—reflecting the collapse in Venezuela's production, unexpected outages in Canada and Libya, and expectations of lower Ira-nian exports following US sanctions. Prices dropped to about $71 a barrel by August following a decision by the Organization of the Petroleum Exporting Coun-tries (OPEC) and the non-OPEC oil exporters (includ-ing Russia) to increase oil production. The coal price index—an average of Australian and South African prices—increased 9.8 percent from February 2018 to August 2018, reflecting tight supply conditions. Strong demand for liquefied natural gas in China and India as well as higher oil prices kept the spot price for lique-fied natural gas close to its highest level in three years.

The decline in the IMF's agricultural price index between the reference periods reflects, to a large extent, trade tensions and concerns about global growth. Moreover, weather-related supply shortfalls of cocoa, cotton, and wheat are smaller than previously antici-pated. Among commodities affected by trade tensions, soybean prices fell in June as China announced retalia-tory import tariffs on US soybeans.

The softening of metals prices between February and August 2018 was largely due to weaker demand from China. Metals markets also experienced high volatility, reflecting, in part, implemented tariff actions, US sanctions on aluminum giant Rusal, and higher trade policy uncertainty. The price of iron ore, the primary input in steel manufacture, dropped 12.4 per-cent between the reference periods. Aluminum prices reached a seven-year high in May after the Rusal sanc-tions, before declining more than 10 percent in June and July as tariff hikes were implemented.

Rising Headline Inflation, but Core Remains Subdued

Higher energy prices have lifted headline year-over-year inflation rates in advanced and emerging market and developing economies over the past six

Figure 1.3. Global Inflation

(Three-month moving average; annualized percent change, unless noted otherwise)

Higher fuel prices have lifted headline inflation over the past six months, and, in emerging market and developing economies, core inflation has also inched up. Wage growth, however, remains muted despite continued declines in unemployment rates.

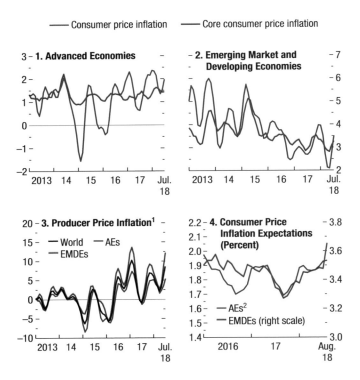

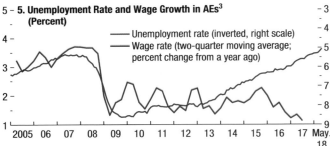

Sources: Consensus Economics; Haver Analytics; Organisation for Economic Co-operation and Development; US Bureau of Labor Statistics; and IMF staff calculations.
Note: AEs = advanced economies (AUT, BEL, CAN, CHE, CZE, DEU, DNK, ESP, EST, FIN, FRA, GBR, GRC, HKG, IRL, ISR, ITA, JPN, KOR, LTU, LUX, LVA, NLD, NOR, PRT, SGP, SVK, SVN, SWE, TWN, USA); EMDEs = emerging market and developing economies (BGR, BRA, CHL, CHN, COL, HUN, IDN, IND, MEX, MYS, PER, PHL, POL, ROU, RUS, THA, TUR, ZAF). Country list uses International Organization for Standardization (ISO) country codes.
[1]AEs exclude HKG, ISR, and TWN. EMDEs include UKR; exclude IDN, IND, PER, and PHL.
[2]AEs include AUS; exclude LUX.
[3]Blue line includes AUS and NZL; excludes BEL. Red line includes AUS and MLT; excludes HKG, SGP, and TWN.

months. Core inflation—that is, excluding food and energy—remains below central banks' targets in most advanced economies. Among emerging market and developing economies, excluding Venezuela's hyperinflation, core inflation remains below the average of recent years but has inched up in recent months (Figure 1.3).

Among advanced economies, core annual consumer price inflation in the United States, where unemployment hovers around multidecade lows, has exceeded 2 percent since March. The Federal Reserve's preferred price index of personal consumption expenditure has also risen close to the target 2 percent. Core inflation in the United Kingdom averaged slightly more than 2 percent in the first half of 2018, lower than last year, as the effects of the large sterling depreciation of 2016–17 on domestic prices have gradually faded. In the euro area and Japan, core inflation remains weak at about 1 percent in the euro area and 0.3 percent in Japan.[3]

Real wage growth in most advanced economies remains muted, even as labor markets tighten and output gaps close (and, in some cases, as the gap turns positive with the economy operating above potential). In the United States and Japan, for example, where unemployment rates are the lowest since 2000 and 1993, respectively, wages have risen only moderately, reflecting, in part, weak productivity growth and possibly greater labor market slack than reflected in headline unemployment numbers.

In the emerging market and developing economy group, core inflation remains contained at about 2 percent in China, where domestic demand has slowed in response to financial regulatory tightening. In India, core inflation (excluding all food and energy items) has risen to about 6 percent as a result of a narrowing output gap and pass-through effects from higher energy prices and exchange rate depreciation. Core inflation has declined in Brazil and Mexico (to about 2½ percent and 3½ percent, respectively), reflecting moderations in activity and improved anchoring of expectations. In Russia, core inflation dropped this year (averaging less than 2 percent until May, and rising slightly in June), consistent with moderately tight monetary policy, declining inflation expectations, and low exchange rate pass-through.

[3]For Japan, the core consumer price index excludes fresh food and energy.

Financial Conditions Marginally Tighter, Localized Pressures

As discussed in the October 2018 *Global Financial Stability Report* (GFSR), global financial conditions have marginally tightened over the past six months. Although they remain accommodative and generally supportive of growth, significant differences have emerged between advanced and emerging market economies. In advanced economies, after spiking in the early months of the year, market volatility has subsided and risk appetite remains relatively strong. The widening growth differential between the United States and other advanced economies, together with associated divergences in monetary policy stances and long-term yields, have contributed to US dollar appreciation since April. Against this backdrop, localized pressure points have emerged in countries with weaker macroeconomic fundamentals and greater political uncertainty. The financial market impact of trade tensions has so far been contained to specific sectors, such as automobiles and aluminum, and some trade-sensitive currencies.

As expected by markets, the Federal Reserve raised the target range of the federal funds rate to 1.75–2 percent in June. With economic expansion in the United States gaining momentum, and a sizable fiscal stimulus anticipated to amplify already-buoyant private sector activity, the Federal Reserve signaled two additional rate hikes in 2018 and three in 2019. Also, in June, the European Central Bank announced an extension of its asset purchase program through the end of the year, while indicating it would reduce monthly purchases from €30 billion to €15 billion in October. The central bank also committed to maintaining rates at current levels at least through the summer of 2019. In July the Bank of Japan modified its yield curve control policy to allow a wider deviation band for the benchmark 10-year yield around an unchanged target of about zero percent. The Bank of Japan also introduced forward guidance on maintaining ultralow policy rates for an extended period of time. Among other advanced economies, the Bank of Canada raised its policy rate by 25 basis points in July, as did the Bank of England in August (marking only its second rate hike in a decade).

Long-term bond yields have diverged among advanced economies since February–March (Figure 1.4). As of mid-September, the 10-year US Treasury yield has risen to about 3.0 percent, while yields on German 10-year bunds have dropped 25

basis points to 0.45 percent and yields on UK gilts have remained at about 1.5 percent. Italian sovereign spreads have widened considerably since late May, initially owing to difficulties in the formation of a government and, more recently, because of uncertainty about the forthcoming budget. As of mid-September, they stood at about 250 basis points. In contrast, other euro area sovereign spreads have remained compressed. Corporate spreads have increased slightly since April, particularly among non-investment-grade credits (Figure 1.4, panel 4). With advanced economies' corporate profits remaining generally healthy, equity indices in the United States are slightly higher. Elsewhere, they are at broadly the same level (Figure 1.4, panel 5). As noted in the October 2018 GFSR, US equity prices now appear modestly higher than their model-based values, based on alternative measures of S&P 500 earnings expectations as well as proxies for both the discount factor and the equity risk premium. Price-to-earnings ratios are little changed relative to April (Figure 1.4, panel 6).

As of mid-September, the US dollar has strengthened by about 6½ percent in real effective terms since February (the reference period for the April 2018 WEO), consistent with the widening interest rate and expected growth differentials (Figure 1.5, panel 1). The euro, the yen, and the pound sterling have weakened vis-à-vis the US dollar but remain broadly unchanged in real effective terms, reflecting the depreciation of emerging market currencies discussed below.

Among emerging market economies, Argentina and Turkey have come under severe market pressure in recent weeks. In Argentina, tighter global financial conditions, together with a domestic corruption scandal and persistent uncertainty over the success of the stabilization plan underlying the program with the IMF, have contributed to financial market volatility. Despite a 2,000-basis-point hike in the short-term policy rate and several increases of reserve requirements, the Argentinean peso depreciated by over 40 percent in real effective terms between February and mid-September, equity valuations fell further, and sovereign spreads rose to above 700 basis points. In Turkey, concerns about underlying fundamentals and political tensions with the United States triggered a sharp depreciation of the currency (27 percent between February and mid-September in real effective terms), declining asset prices, and widening spreads. In response, the authorities released some foreign exchange liquidity by lowering reserve require-

Figure 1.4. Advanced Economies: Monetary and Financial Market Conditions
(Percent, unless noted otherwise)

Despite monetary policy tightening in the United States, financial conditions remain generally supportive of growth in advanced economies. Since earlier this year, long-term government bond yields have diverged: a steeper path of expected policy rates has modestly lifted US 10-year government bond yields, while yields on German and UK long-term bonds have fallen.

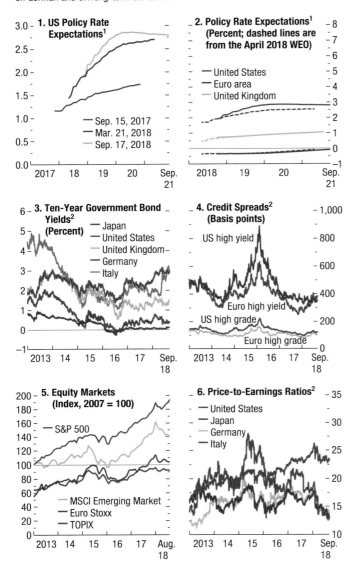

Sources: Bloomberg Finance L.P.; Thomson Reuters Datastream; and IMF staff calculations.
Note: MSCI = Morgan Stanley Capital International; S&P = Standard & Poor's; TOPIX = Tokyo Stock Price Index; WEO = *World Economic Outlook*.
[1]Expectations are based on the federal funds rate futures for the United States, the sterling overnight interbank average rate for the United Kingdom, and the euro interbank offered forward rate for the euro area; updated September 17, 2018.
[2]Data are through September 17, 2018.

Figure 1.5. Real Effective Exchange Rate Changes, February–September 2018
(Percent)

The US dollar has appreciated in real effective terms by about 6.5 percent since February on the back of widening interest rate and growth differentials. Emerging market currencies have generally weakened, with very large depreciations in Turkey and Argentina on growing concerns about macroeconomic imbalances and a notable weakening of the South African rand—after its strong rally in previous months—and of the Brazilian *real*.

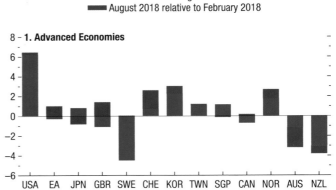

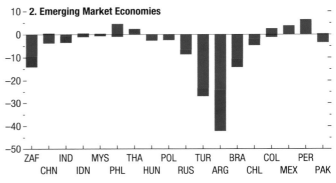

Source: IMF staff calculations.
Note: EA = euro area. Data labels use International Organization for Standardization (ISO) country codes. Latest data available are for September 14, 2018.

ments and limited the capacity of banks to engage in cross-currency swap and forward transactions. The effective rate was increased first by providing liquidity to banks at the higher overnight lending rate rather than the weekly repo rate, and, in early September, by a 625 basis point hike in the benchmark policy rate.

Several other central banks (India, Indonesia, Mexico, Philippines) have also raised policy rates in recent months as headline inflation has risen and, in some cases, currencies have come under pressure (Figure 1.6). In China, the central bank maintained its policy rate while lowering banks' required reserve ratio in two separate moves (targeted to certain banks in April, followed by a more general cut in July) to support lending. Long-term yields have generally increased and sovereign spreads have widened, reflecting a reduction in bond flows to emerging markets in recent months. However, markets appear to be discriminating across countries, as spreads have widened to a much larger extent for countries with greater external financing needs (Figure 1.6, panel 4). Equity indices in emerging market and developing economies have generally declined, reflecting rising trade tensions and tighter external financial conditions (Figure 1.7). In some cases (for example, China), domestic regulatory tightening has contributed to a retreat in equity prices.

Currency movements for other emerging market and developing economies have mostly reflected developments in underlying fundamentals and perceptions of future policy direction (Figure 1.5, panel 2). Between February and mid-September, the Brazilian *real* declined 14 percent as domestic activity slowed and external financial conditions became tighter, while the Chinese renminbi depreciated by 3.5 percent as macro policies shifted to a more accommodative stance in recent months, and as trade tensions with the United States rose. The South African rand depreciated by some 14 percent on weaker-than-expected activity in the first half of the year and slow reform progress, unwinding some of the earlier gains associated with the change in the leadership. In contrast, the Mexican peso has appreciated by over 3½ percent since February after concerns about postelection shifts in policy direction began to fade, counteracting some of the negative sentiment stemming from US tariff actions and uncertainty surrounding NAFTA's future prior to the August agreement.

Tracking indicators and early data releases suggest that, after a buoyant start to the year, capital flows to emerging markets weakened considerably in the second quarter and beyond (Figure 1.8). In particular, evidence from investment fund flows and other high-frequency data sources suggests that nonresident portfolio flows, which were strong during 2017 and early 2018, turned negative in May–June of 2018, consistent with foreign exchange market pressures on several emerging market economies. While portfolio flows appeared to have stabilized during July, alongside currency valuations, outflows have resumed in August amid weakening investor sentiment following the depreciation of the Turkish lira and the Argentinean peso.

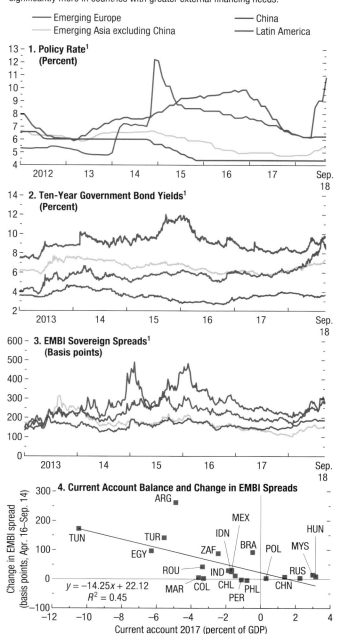

Figure 1.6. Emerging Market Economies: Interest Rates and Spreads

Among emerging markets, policy rates have generally increased since the spring (the sharp increase for emerging Europe reflects the policy rate hikes in Turkey). Long-term government bond yields have also generally increased, and sovereign spreads have widened over the past six months. Spreads have widened significantly more in countries with greater external financing needs.

Sources: Bloomberg Finance L.P.; Haver Analytics; IMF, *International Financial Statistics;* Thomson Reuters Datastream; and IMF staff calculations.
Note: Emerging Asia excluding China comprises India, Indonesia, Malaysia, the Philippines, and Thailand (except EMBI spread); emerging Europe comprises Poland, Romania, Russia, and Turkey; Latin America comprises Brazil, Chile, Colombia, Mexico, and Peru. EMBI = J.P. Morgan Emerging Markets Bond Index. Data labels use International Organization for Standardization (ISO) country codes.
[1]Data are through September 14, 2018.

Figure 1.7. Emerging Market Economies: Equity Markets and Credit

Equity indices have declined amid rising trade tensions and somewhat tighter external financial conditions.

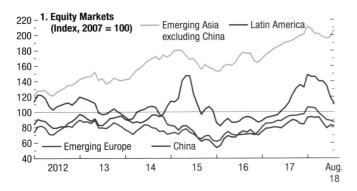

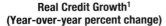

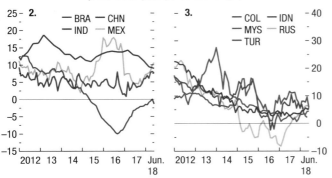

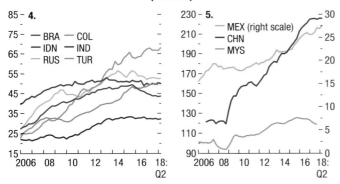

Sources: Bloomberg Finance L.P.; Haver Analytics; IMF, *International Financial Statistics* (IFS); and IMF staff calculations.
Note: Data labels use International Organization for Standardization (ISO) country codes.
[1] Credit is other depository corporations' claims on the private sector (from IFS), except in the case of Brazil, for which private sector credit is from the Monetary Policy and Financial System Credit Operations published by Banco Central do Brasil, and China, for which credit is total social financing after adjusting for local government debt swaps.

Figure 1.8. Emerging Market Economies: Capital Flows

Capital flows to emerging markets appear to have weakened considerably in the second quarter of 2018, with nonresident portfolio flows turning negative in May–June 2018.

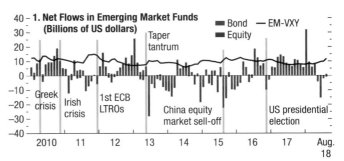

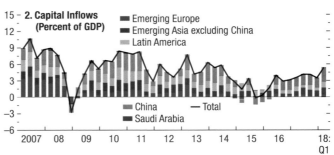

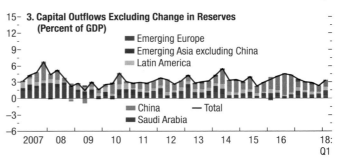

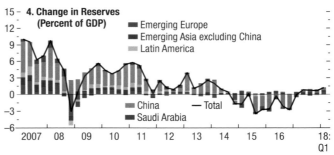

Sources: Bloomberg Finance L.P.; EPFR Global; Haver Analytics; IMF, *International Financial Statistics*; and IMF staff calculations.
Note: Capital inflows are net purchases of domestic assets by nonresidents. Capital outflows are net purchases of foreign assets by domestic residents. Emerging Asia excluding China comprises India, Indonesia, Malaysia, the Philippines, and Thailand; emerging Europe comprises Poland, Romania, Russia, and Turkey; Latin America comprises Brazil, Chile, Colombia, Mexico, and Peru.
ECB = European Central Bank; EM-VXY = J.P. Morgan Emerging Market Volatility Index; LTROs = long-term refinancing operations.

Forces Shaping the Outlook

Diverging Cyclical Positions

While the global expansion is projected to continue in 2018 and 2019, it is becoming less synchronized. Compared with 2017, which saw the most widely shared pickup in country annual growth rates since 2010, a smaller share of countries, particularly among advanced economies, is expected to experience an acceleration of activity for 2018 and beyond.[4] In part, this reflects diverging cyclical positions, with expansions peaking in some countries while others continue to emerge from deep recession. Recent fuel price increases also have varying impacts on short-term prospects for fuel exporters and importers.

Following a stretch of above-trend growth in advanced economies during 2015–17, output gaps have closed or are set to close in most cases. As remaining slack diminishes and high capacity utilization begins to constrain supply, the growth rate of output is projected to start declining toward its potential, particularly among some euro area countries and in Japan. The US economy is an important exception to the pattern. It is expected to continue to grow above potential until 2020, helped by sizable fiscal stimulus. The pace of expansion is expected to dip below the economy's potential growth rate thereafter as the stimulus reverses and reinforces the effects of ongoing monetary tightening.

The Impact of Commodity Price Increases

Most nonfood commodities have registered price increases since mid-2017. Most notable has been the increase in oil prices—about $30 a barrel, or 70 percent, since June 2017. Some of this increase is expected to dissipate over the medium term because of higher US shale production and OPEC+ supply. Nonetheless, as shown in the Commodities Special Feature, oil futures curves are notably higher than a year ago.

The improved outlook for oil prices contributes to revisions to growth prospects for fuel exporters and importers—with a more notable impact on the

exporters, given the implied magnitude of the changes in disposable income (Figure 1.9). A comparison of forecast revisions between the April 2018 WEO and the current report shows an upward revision of about 0.1 and 0.3 percentage point for 2018 and 2019, respectively, for a group of fuel exporters, excluding countries whose prospects are heavily conditioned by domestic strife, geopolitical tensions, or outright macroeconomic collapse. In contrast, growth prospects for the same period have been revised downward by about 0.1–0.3 percentage point for the rest of the world, a group dominated by fuel importers (Figure 1.9, panel 3).

Investment, Trade, and the Global Expansion

A core element of the 2017 upsurge in global growth and trade was the pickup in investment in advanced economies and an end to investment contractions in some large, stressed commodity exporters. Overall, both global imports and investment growth, at about 5 percent, were the highest since the 2010–11 rebound from the global financial crisis. This pace of expansion in investment is projected to ease in 2018 and 2019 compared with 2017, with a more notable decline in trade growth (Figure 1.10).

Despite this easing, investment growth in emerging market and developing economies is projected to remain robust over the next five years at about 5½ percent, accounting for well over one-third of their GDP growth rate during that period (Figure 1.11). Medium-term prospects for investment growth are much weaker in advanced economies, with capital spending projected to slow considerably as growth declines toward its lower potential rate and the fiscal stimulus in the United States begins to unwind.

At the same time, rising trade tensions and policy uncertainty—discussed in more detail below—raise concerns about global economic prospects. These factors could lead firms to postpone or forgo capital spending and hence slow down growth in investment and demand. This slowdown would also weaken trade growth, as capital and intermediate goods account for an important share of global trade. As mentioned earlier, high-frequency data point to a slowdown in global trade and industrial production, somewhat weaker manufacturing purchasing managers' indices, and especially weaker export orders, but the extent to which these factors have affected capital spending and trade are still unclear. Consistent with signs of slower production of capital

---

[4]In 2017, 58 percent of countries, accounting for 75 percent of world GDP in purchasing-power-parity terms, experienced a pickup in year-over-year growth rates. In 2018, 52 percent of economies, accounting for 47 percent of world GDP, are projected to register a pickup in annual growth rates. For 2019, the corresponding numbers are 54 percent of economies, accounting for 32 percent of global GDP.

Figure 1.9. Impact of Commodity Price Changes

Higher oil prices have led to a sizable increase in the projected terms-of-trade windfall gains and losses in 2018–19. This is reflected in growth forecast revisions relative to the April 2018 *World Economic Outlook*: Nonstressed fuel exporters are expected to grow faster in 2018–19 than previously projected, while growth prospects for oil importers were revised downward.

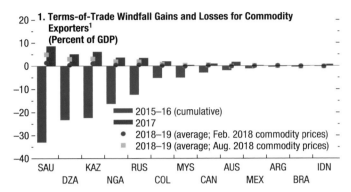

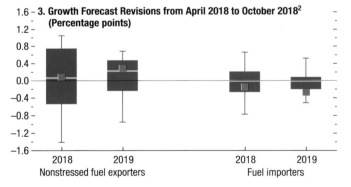

Source: IMF staff estimates.
Note: Data labels in the figure use International Organization for Standardization (ISO) country codes.
[1]Gains (losses) for 2018–19 are simple averages of annual incremental gains (losses) for 2018 and 2019. The windfall is an estimate of the change in disposable income arising from commodity price changes. The windfall gain in year t for a country exporting x US dollars of commodity A and importing m US dollars of commodity B in year $t-1$ is defined as $(\Delta p_t^A x_{t-1} - \Delta p_t^B m_{t-1}) / Y_{t-1}$, in which Δp_t^A and Δp_t^B are the percentage changes in the prices of A and B between year $t-1$ and year t, and Y is GDP in year $t-1$ in US dollars. See also Gruss (2014).
[2]The yellow horizontal line inside each box represents the median; the upper and lower edges of each box show the top and bottom quartiles; the red markers denote the top and bottom deciles; and the gray square indicates the purchasing-power-parity-weighted mean. Stressed fuel exporters include Iran, Iraq, Libya, South Sudan, Venezuela, and Yemen.

Figure 1.10. Global Investment and Trade
(Percent change)

The pace of expansion of global investment is projected to ease in 2018 and 2019 compared with 2017, with a more notable decline in trade growth.

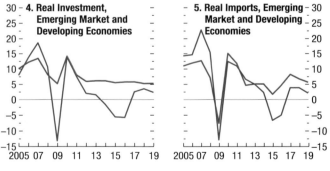

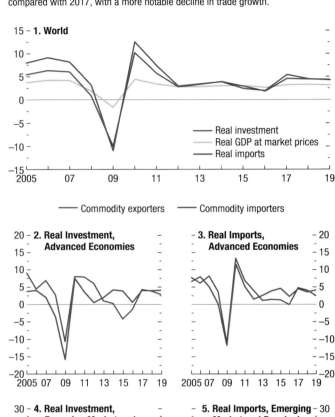

Source: IMF staff calculations.
Note: World and advanced economies exclude Ireland. Commodity exporters include fuel and nonfuel primary products exporters listed in Table D of the Statistical Appendix, as well as Australia, Brazil, Canada, Colombia, New Zealand, Norway, and Peru.

goods, the forecast for fixed investment growth in 2018 was revised downward in advanced economies by about 0.4 percentage point relative to the April 2018 WEO, particularly in advanced Asia and the United Kingdom. This downward revision was accompanied by downward revisions to export growth (by over 1 percentage point) and especially import growth (by 1.4 percentage point). The forecast for investment and trade growth in 2019 is also weaker. For emerging market and developing economies, trade growth was revised down modestly for 2018 and more substantially for 2019. The forecast for investment growth for 2018–19 is weaker than in April, despite higher capital spending in India, on account of contracting investment in economies under stress, such as Argentina and Turkey, which is also reflected in a downward revision for import growth, particularly for 2019.

Structural Headwinds

The cyclical upsurge in global growth that began in mid-2016—and is now extended by procyclical fiscal stimulus in the United States and associated favorable spillovers to trading partners—has helped overcome powerful structural headwinds acting on potential growth. After the cyclical boost in demand and the US stimulus run their course, and as growth in China continues to slow in line with the necessary rebalancing of the economy, global growth is set to moderate, weighed down by structural drags. The increase in trade costs would also depress medium-term prospects by hindering efficient resource allocation, investment, and productivity.

- Among advanced economies, the subdued outlook for potential growth reflects, to a large extent, slower labor force growth due to population aging (as discussed in Chapter 2 of the April 2018 WEO). While labor productivity growth is expected to improve in the medium term, the slight acceleration will only partially offset the slower increases in labor input. Box 1.1 discusses the rise in corporate market power in advanced economies, a trend that could be a further drag on business dynamism, investment, and productivity. Some policy measures that are supporting short-term activity in some economies (such as larger US fiscal deficits) are not sustainable—and hence come at the cost of lower future growth because they will need to be reversed.

- Among emerging market and developing economies, prospects for many economies to close income gaps relative to advanced economies appear weaker than in the past (Figure 1.12). Some 45 emerging market

Figure 1.11. Contributions to GDP Growth
(Percent)

In the medium term, investment growth is projected to remain robust in emerging market and developing economies, accounting for well over one-third of their GDP growth. In advanced economies, investment growth is expected to weaken significantly over the next five years.

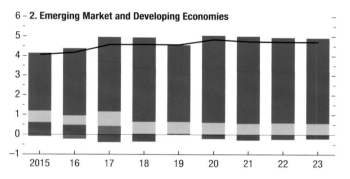

Source: IMF staff calculations.

and developing economies—accounting for 10 percent of world GDP in purchasing-power-parity terms—are projected to grow by less than advanced economies in per capita terms over 2018–23, and hence to fall further behind in living standards. Commodity prices, despite their recent increase, are projected to remain below the levels seen before 2011–13. Commodity exporters face a difficult adjustment to structurally lower revenues than in the past, requiring diversification of their economies away from commodity dependence and mobilization of noncommodity sources of revenue to finance pressing development needs. The adjustment costs associated with this transition will weigh on the medium-term growth outlook for this group of economies.

Figure 1.12. Per Capita Real GDP Growth
(Percent)

Prospects for emerging market and developing economies to narrow gaps in living standards relative to advanced economies are uneven.

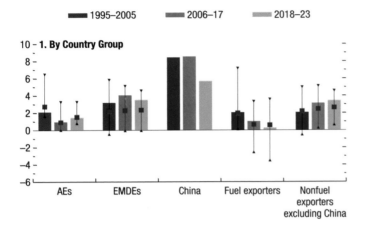

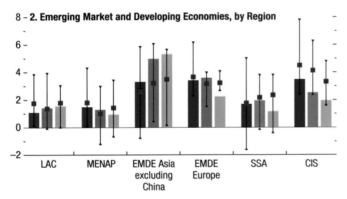

Source: IMF staff estimates.
Note: AEs = advanced economies; CIS = Commonwealth of Independent States; EMDE = emerging market and developing economy; LAC = Latin America and the Caribbean; MENAP = Middle East, North Africa, Afghanistan, and Pakistan; PPP = purchasing power parity; SSA = sub-Saharan Africa. Bars denote PPP GDP-weighted averages, red markers indicate the medians, and black markers denote the top and bottom deciles of per capita GDP growth in the country groups. The fuel and nonfuel exporter subgroups are defined in Table D of the Statistical Appendix and cover EMDEs only.

The Forecast

Policy Assumptions

The WEO baseline forecast assumes an expansionary fiscal policy stance for advanced economies in 2018, owing largely to US fiscal stimulus, turning neutral in 2019 (Figure 1.13).[5] From 2020 onward, fiscal

[5]The revision to the expected fiscal policy stance for advanced economies in 2019 relative to the April 2018 WEO reflects smaller-than-previously anticipated declines in the structural primary balances of the United States and France, which outweigh the

policy is expected to be contractionary in advanced economies as the US fiscal stimulus begins to unwind. The fiscal stance is assumed to be broadly neutral in emerging market and developing economies through the forecast horizon.

Monetary policy stances are projected to diverge among advanced economies. The US federal funds target is expected to increase to about 2.5 percent by the end of 2018 and about 3.5 percent by the end of 2019 (the forecast assumes a total of eight rate hikes during 2018–19). The policy target rate is expected to decline to 2.9 percent in 2022. Policy rates are projected to remain negative in the euro area until mid-2019 and close to zero in Japan through the end of 2019. They are expected to rise gradually thereafter but to remain very low through the forecast horizon in both cases. For emerging market economies, monetary policy stances are assumed to vary, based on the economies' cyclical positions.

The baseline forecast incorporates the impact of tariffs that had been announced by the United States as of mid-September, namely a 10 percent tariff on all aluminum imports, a 25 percent tariff on all steel imports, a 25 percent tariff on $50 billion of imports from China imposed in July and August, and a 10 percent tariff on an additional $200 billion of imports from China imposed in late September, rising to 25 percent by year end, as well as the retaliatory measures taken by trading partners.[6] The forecast assumes that part of the negative effect of these trade measures will be offset by policy stimulus from China (and possibly other economies as well). The forecast does not incorporate the impact of further tariffs on Chinese and other imports threatened by the United States, but not yet implemented, due to uncertainty about their exact magnitude, timing, and potential retaliatory response. Scenario Box 1 discusses the potential economic consequences of further escalation in trade tensions and rising trade barriers.

Assumptions about Financial Conditions and Commodity Prices

The baseline forecast assumes that global financial conditions will tighten gradually as the expansion

more expansionary-than-previously projected stance of Germany, Greece, and Italy.

[6]In particular, the Chinese authorities have announced tariffs ranging from 5–10 percent on $60 billion of imports from the United States in response to the US tariffs imposed in September.

continues in 2018–19, but remain generally supportive of growth. A well-communicated, data-dependent normalization of monetary policy in the United States and the United Kingdom is expected to continue, leading to a steady increase in long-term interest rates. Financial market volatility is assumed to remain low. The increase in advanced economy long-term sovereign bond yields is expected to generate some rebalancing of global portfolios. Nonetheless, barring some cases in which macroeconomic and financial imbalances have increased in recent years, sovereign bond spreads for most emerging market economies are assumed to remain contained.

The IMF's Primary Commodity Price Index is projected to increase about 18 percent in 2018 from its 2017 average (a cumulative increase from 2016 of about 36 percent) and then to fall marginally in 2019. Oil prices are expected to average $69.38 a barrel in 2018 (higher than the April 2018 WEO projection of $62.30 and the 2017 price of $52.80 a barrel). Global oil supply is expected to gradually increase over the forecast horizon, lowering oil prices to $68.76 a barrel in 2019, and further to about $60 a barrel in 2023. Metal prices are expected to increase by about 5.3 percent in 2018, before declining by 3.6 percent in 2019 as the effects of recent tariff actions take hold and trade policy uncertainty weighs on metals demand.

Global Growth Outlook

Global growth is projected at 3.7 percent in 2018 and 2019, 0.2 percentage point below the April 2018 WEO, even though well above its level during 2012–16. Differences in the outlook across countries and regions are notable (Table 1.1, Annex Tables 1.1.1–1.1.7, and Boxes 1.2 and 1.3 provide details of country projections). Global growth is expected to remain steady at 3.7 percent in 2020, as the decline in advanced economy growth with the unwinding of the US fiscal stimulus and the fading of the favorable spillovers from US demand to trading partners is offset by a pickup in emerging market and developing economy growth. Thereafter, global growth is projected to slow to 3.6 percent by 2022–23, largely reflecting a moderation in advanced economy growth toward the potential of that group.

Growth in advanced economies will remain well above trend at 2.4 percent in 2018, before softening to 2.1 percent in 2019. The forecast for both years is 0.1 percentage point weaker than in the April 2018

Figure 1.13. Fiscal Indicators
(Percent of GDP, unless noted otherwise)

The fiscal policy stance in advanced economies is assumed to be expansionary in 2018, before turning neutral in 2019. In emerging market and developing economies, the fiscal policy stance is assumed to be broadly neutral.

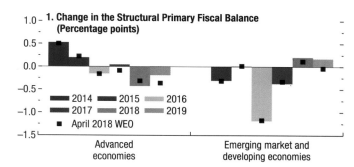

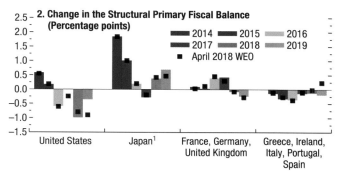

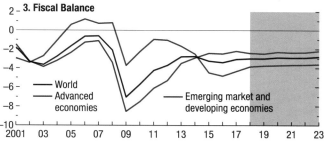

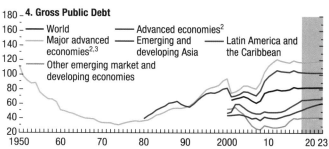

Source: IMF staff estimates.
Note: WEO = *World Economic Outlook*.
[1]Japan's latest figures reflect comprehensive methodological revisions adopted in December 2016.
[2]Data through 2000 exclude the United States.
[3]Canada, France, Germany, Italy, Japan, United Kingdom, United States.

Table 1.1. Overview of the *World Economic Outlook* Projections
(Percent change, unless noted otherwise)

	2017	Projections		Difference from July 2018 *WEO Update*[1]		Difference from April 2018 WEO[1]	
		2018	2019	2018	2019	2018	2019
World Output	**3.7**	**3.7**	**3.7**	**−0.2**	**−0.2**	**−0.2**	**−0.2**
Advanced Economies	**2.3**	**2.4**	**2.1**	**0.0**	**−0.1**	**−0.1**	**−0.1**
United States	2.2	2.9	2.5	0.0	−0.2	0.0	−0.2
Euro Area	2.4	2.0	1.9	−0.2	0.0	−0.4	−0.1
Germany	2.5	1.9	1.9	−0.3	−0.2	−0.6	−0.1
France	2.3	1.6	1.6	−0.2	−0.1	−0.5	−0.4
Italy	1.5	1.2	1.0	0.0	0.0	−0.3	−0.1
Spain	3.0	2.7	2.2	−0.1	0.0	−0.1	0.0
Japan	1.7	1.1	0.9	0.1	0.0	−0.1	0.0
United Kingdom	1.7	1.4	1.5	0.0	0.0	−0.2	0.0
Canada	3.0	2.1	2.0	0.0	0.0	0.0	0.0
Other Advanced Economies[2]	2.8	2.8	2.5	0.0	−0.2	0.1	−0.1
Emerging Market and Developing Economies	**4.7**	**4.7**	**4.7**	**−0.2**	**−0.4**	**−0.2**	**−0.4**
Commonwealth of Independent States	2.1	2.3	2.4	0.0	0.2	0.1	0.3
Russia	1.5	1.7	1.8	0.0	0.3	0.0	0.3
Excluding Russia	3.6	3.9	3.6	0.3	−0.1	0.4	0.0
Emerging and Developing Asia	6.5	6.5	6.3	0.0	−0.2	0.0	−0.3
China	6.9	6.6	6.2	0.0	−0.2	0.0	−0.2
India[3]	6.7	7.3	7.4	0.0	−0.1	−0.1	−0.4
ASEAN-5[4]	5.3	5.3	5.2	0.0	−0.1	0.0	−0.2
Emerging and Developing Europe	6.0	3.8	2.0	−0.5	−1.6	−0.5	−1.7
Latin America and the Caribbean	1.3	1.2	2.2	−0.4	−0.4	−0.8	−0.6
Brazil	1.0	1.4	2.4	−0.4	−0.1	−0.9	−0.1
Mexico	2.0	2.2	2.5	−0.1	−0.2	−0.1	−0.5
Middle East, North Africa, Afghanistan, and Pakistan	2.2	2.4	2.7	−1.1	−1.2	−1.0	−1.0
Saudi Arabia	−0.9	2.2	2.4	0.3	0.5	0.5	0.5
Sub-Saharan Africa	2.7	3.1	3.8	−0.3	0.0	−0.3	0.1
Nigeria	0.8	1.9	2.3	−0.2	0.0	−0.2	0.4
South Africa	1.3	0.8	1.4	−0.7	−0.3	−0.7	−0.3
Memorandum							
European Union	2.7	2.2	2.0	−0.2	−0.1	−0.3	−0.1
Low-Income Developing Countries	4.7	4.7	5.2	−0.3	−0.1	−0.3	−0.1
Middle East and North Africa	1.8	2.0	2.5	−1.2	−1.3	−1.2	−1.1
World Growth Based on Market Exchange Rates	3.2	3.2	3.1	−0.1	−0.2	−0.2	−0.2
World Trade Volume (goods and services)	**5.2**	**4.2**	**4.0**	**−0.6**	**−0.5**	**−0.9**	**−0.7**
Imports							
Advanced Economies	4.2	3.7	4.0	−0.8	−0.4	−1.4	−0.5
Emerging Market and Developing Economies	7.0	6.0	4.8	0.0	−0.9	0.0	−0.8
Exports							
Advanced Economies	4.4	3.4	3.1	−0.8	−0.6	−1.1	−0.8
Emerging Market and Developing Economies	6.9	4.7	4.8	−0.6	−0.3	−0.4	−0.5
Commodity Prices (US dollars)							
Oil[5]	23.3	31.4	−0.9	−1.6	0.9	13.4	5.6
Nonfuel (average based on world commodity export weights)	6.8	2.7	−0.7	−3.3	−1.2	−2.9	−1.2
Consumer Prices							
Advanced Economies	1.7	2.0	1.9	−0.2	−0.3	0.0	0.0
Emerging Market and Developing Economies[6]	4.3	5.0	5.2	0.3	0.7	0.2	0.7
London Interbank Offered Rate (percent)							
On US Dollar Deposits (six month)	1.5	2.5	3.4	−0.1	−0.1	0.1	0.0
On Euro Deposits (three month)	−0.3	−0.3	−0.2	0.0	−0.1	0.0	−0.2
On Japanese Yen Deposits (six month)	0.0	0.0	0.1	0.0	0.0	0.0	0.0

Note: Real effective exchange rates are assumed to remain constant at the levels prevailing during July 17–August 14, 2018. Economies are listed on the basis of economic size. The aggregated quarterly data are seasonally adjusted. WEO = *World Economic Outlook*.
[1]Difference based on rounded figures for the current, July 2018 *World Economic Outlook Update*, and April 2018 *World Economic Outlook* forecasts. The differences are also adjusted to include Argentina's consumer prices since the July 2018 Update.
[2]Excludes the Group of Seven (Canada, France, Germany, Italy, Japan, United Kingdom, United States) and euro area countries.
[3]For India, data and forecasts are presented on a fiscal year basis and GDP from 2011 onward is based on GDP at market prices with fiscal year 2011/12 as a base year.
[4]Indonesia, Malaysia, Philippines, Thailand, Vietnam.

Table 1.1 *(continued)*

	Year over Year				Q4 over Q4[7]			
			Projections				Projections	
	2016	2017	2018	2019	2016	2017	2018	2019
World Output	**3.3**	**3.7**	**3.7**	**3.7**	**3.2**	**4.0**	**3.5**	**3.8**
Advanced Economies	**1.7**	**2.3**	**2.4**	**2.1**	**2.0**	**2.5**	**2.3**	**1.9**
United States	1.6	2.2	2.9	2.5	1.9	2.5	3.1	2.3
Euro Area	1.9	2.4	2.0	1.9	2.0	2.7	1.7	1.9
Germany	2.2	2.5	1.9	1.9	1.9	2.8	1.9	1.6
France	1.1	2.3	1.6	1.6	1.2	2.8	1.3	1.7
Italy	0.9	1.5	1.2	1.0	1.0	1.6	0.8	1.3
Spain	3.2	3.0	2.7	2.2	2.9	3.0	2.5	2.1
Japan	1.0	1.7	1.1	0.9	1.5	2.0	1.0	−0.3
United Kingdom	1.8	1.7	1.4	1.5	1.7	1.3	1.5	1.4
Canada	1.4	3.0	2.1	2.0	2.0	3.0	2.1	1.9
Other Advanced Economies[2]	2.3	2.8	2.8	2.5	2.6	2.9	2.8	2.4
Emerging Market and Developing Economies	**4.4**	**4.7**	**4.7**	**4.7**	**4.4**	**5.2**	**4.6**	**5.3**
Commonwealth of Independent States	0.4	2.1	2.3	2.4	1.0	1.7	2.2	2.3
Russia	−0.2	1.5	1.7	1.8	0.8	1.2	2.1	1.9
Excluding Russia	2.0	3.6	3.9	3.6	...	...	...	...
Emerging and Developing Asia	6.5	6.5	6.5	6.3	6.3	6.7	6.2	6.5
China	6.7	6.9	6.6	6.2	6.8	6.8	6.4	6.2
India[3]	7.1	6.7	7.3	7.4	6.1	7.7	6.5	7.9
ASEAN-5[4]	4.9	5.3	5.3	5.2	4.8	5.4	5.1	5.6
Emerging and Developing Europe	3.3	6.0	3.8	2.0	3.8	6.1	0.9	4.0
Latin America and the Caribbean	−0.6	1.3	1.2	2.2	−0.8	1.7	0.5	2.8
Brazil	−3.5	1.0	1.4	2.4	−2.4	2.2	1.7	2.5
Mexico	2.9	2.0	2.2	2.5	3.3	1.6	2.2	3.0
Middle East, North Africa, Afghanistan, and Pakistan	5.1	2.2	2.4	2.7	...	...	...	...
Saudi Arabia	1.7	−0.9	2.2	2.4	2.1	−1.4	3.5	2.1
Sub-Saharan Africa	1.4	2.7	3.1	3.8	...	...	...	...
Nigeria	−1.6	0.8	1.9	2.3	...	...	...	...
South Africa	0.6	1.3	0.8	1.4	1.0	1.9	0.5	0.9
Memorandum								
European Union	2.0	2.7	2.2	2.0	2.1	2.8	1.9	2.1
Low-Income Developing Countries	3.6	4.7	4.7	5.2	...	...	...	...
Middle East and North Africa	5.2	1.8	2.0	2.5	...	...	...	...
World Growth Based on Market Exchange Rates	2.5	3.2	3.2	3.1	2.7	3.4	3.0	3.0
World Trade Volume (goods and services)	**2.2**	**5.2**	**4.2**	**4.0**	...	...	...	...
Imports								
Advanced Economies	2.4	4.2	3.7	4.0	...	...	...	...
Emerging Market and Developing Economies	1.8	7.0	6.0	4.8	...	...	...	...
Exports								
Advanced Economies	1.8	4.4	3.4	3.1	...	...	...	...
Emerging Market and Developing Economies	3.0	6.9	4.7	4.8	...	...	...	...
Commodity Prices (US dollars)								
Oil[5]	−15.7	23.3	31.4	−0.9	16.2	19.6	19.6	−3.6
Nonfuel (average based on world commodity export weights)	−1.5	6.8	2.7	−0.7	10.3	1.9	1.3	1.9
Consumer Prices								
Advanced Economies	0.8	1.7	2.0	1.9	1.2	1.7	2.1	1.9
Emerging Market and Developing Economies[6]	4.2	4.3	5.0	5.2	4.2	3.7	4.6	4.1
London Interbank Offered Rate (percent)								
On US Dollar Deposits (six month)	1.1	1.5	2.5	3.4	...	...	...	...
On Euro Deposits (three month)	−0.3	−0.3	−0.3	−0.2	...	...	...	...
On Japanese Yen Deposits (six month)	0.0	0.0	0.0	0.1	...	...	...	...

[5]Simple average of prices of UK Brent, Dubai Fateh, and West Texas Intermediate crude oil. The average price of oil in US dollars a barrel was $52.81 in 2017; the assumed price, based on futures markets, is $69.38 in 2018 and $68.76 in 2019.

[6]Excludes Venezuela but includes Argentina starting from 2017 onward. See country-specific notes for Argentina and Venezuela in the "Country Notes" section of the Statistical Appendix.

[7]For World Output, the quarterly estimates and projections account for approximately 90 percent of annual world output at purchasing-power-parity weights. For Emerging Market and Developing Economies, the quarterly estimates and projections account for approximately 80 percent of annual emerging market and developing economies' output at purchasing-power-parity weights.

WEO. In 2018, weaker-than-expected outturns in the first half of the year have led to downward revisions for the euro area and the United Kingdom. In 2019, recent trade measures are expected to weigh on economic activity, especially in the United States, where the 2019 growth forecast was revised down by 0.2 percentage point. Growth is expected to decline to 1.8 percent in 2020 as the US fiscal stimulus begins to unwind and euro area growth moderates toward its medium-term potential. Growth is projected to fall to 1.4 percent later on as working-age population growth continues to slow and productivity growth remains moderate.

With emerging Asia continuing to expand at a strong pace—despite a 0.3 percentage point downward revision to the 2019 growth forecast mostly driven by recently announced trade measures—and activity in commodity exporters firming, growth in the emerging market and developing economy group is set to remain steady at 4.7 percent in 2018–19. Over the medium term, growth is projected to rise to slightly less than 5 percent. Beyond 2019, the aggregate growth rate for the group reflects offsetting developments as growth moderates to a sustainable pace in China, while it improves in India (owing to structural reforms and a still-favorable demographic dividend), commodity exporters (though to rates below the average of recent decades), and some economies experiencing macroeconomic stress in 2018–19. In comparison with the April 2018 WEO, the growth forecast for emerging market and developing economies was marked down for 2018 and 2019 by 0.2 percentage point and 0.4 percentage point, respectively, and for 2020–23 by about 0.2 percentage point. For 2018–19, the main sources of the downward revision are the negative expected impact of the trade measures implemented since the April 2018 WEO on activity in China and other economies in emerging Asia, much weaker activity in Iran following the reimposition of US sanctions, a sharp projected slowdown in Turkey following the ongoing market turmoil, and a more subdued outlook for large economies in Latin America (Argentina, Brazil, Mexico). Over 2020–23, the revisions primarily reflect a downward reassessment of the still-strong growth prospects for India and a lower growth forecast for Pakistan and Turkey, in addition to continued weaker growth in Iran.

Inflation Outlook

Largely reflecting recent increases in commodity prices, inflation is expected to rise this year across both advanced and emerging market and developing economies. In advanced economies, it is projected to pick up to 2 percent in 2018, from 1.7 percent in 2017. Inflation in emerging market and developing economies excluding Venezuela is expected to increase to 5.0 percent this year from 4.3 percent in 2017 (Box 1.4 provides details of the inflation outlook for individual countries).

Among advanced economies, core inflation will rise over the forecast horizon, with differentiation across countries mostly based on cyclical positions. In the United States, for example, core personal consumption expenditure price inflation, the Federal Reserve's preferred measure, is expected to rise to 2.1 percent in 2018 and 2.3 percent in 2019 (from 1.6 percent in 2017), as the sizable, procyclical fiscal stimulus lifts output above potential. Core inflation is assumed to gradually decline to 2 percent thereafter, with a monetary policy response that ensures expectations remain well anchored. In the euro area, core harmonized index of consumer prices inflation is projected to increase slowly to 2 percent by 2022, reflecting the influence of backward-looking elements in the inflation processes.

Within the group of emerging market and developing economies, core inflation rates are expected to be more dispersed than among advanced economies. To a large extent, the dispersion reflects variation in cyclical positions, anchoring of inflation expectations, and inflation targets.

External Sector Outlook

Current Account Positions

After remaining broadly stable in 2017, current account deficits and surpluses in 2018 are, on the whole, forecast to widen slightly from 2017 (Figure 1.14). The most notable drivers of predicted current account changes for 2018 are the increase in oil prices, which is expected to result in an improvement in the current account balance of oil exporters of about 3 percent of their GDP, and strong growth in the United States, which is projected to lead to a modest widening of the US current account deficit for this year. Given that most fuel exporters were already running surpluses in 2017, both factors will lead to some widening of global current account imbalances.

Forecasts for 2019 and beyond indicate a gradual decline in the current account balances of oil exporters (because average oil prices are projected to decline compared with their current levels), as well as an initial further widening of the US current account deficit, driven by expansionary fiscal policy. Over the medium term, current account balances should narrow again, with a stabilization in the US current account deficit as the expansionary effects of fiscal policy wane, coupled with some narrowing of surpluses in China and, to a lesser extent, in Europe. The recently imposed trade measures by the United States and retaliatory actions by trading partners are expected to have a limited impact on external imbalances (see 2018 *External Sector Report* for a discussion of the relation between trade costs and external imbalances).

As highlighted in the IMF's 2018 *External Sector Report*, many countries' current account imbalances in 2017 were too large in relation to country-specific norms consistent with underlying fundamentals and desirable policies. It is therefore interesting to document how current account balances are projected to evolve in coming years. As shown in panel 1 of Figure 1.15, current account balances in 2018 are projected to move in a direction consistent with some reduction in those excess imbalances (despite a larger deficit in the United States and a larger surplus in Germany). Medium-term projections suggest, on average, further movement of current account balances in the same direction, but also feature a widening of the US current account deficit and persistent large surpluses in many advanced European and Asian economies (Figure 1.15, panel 2).[7] At the same time, given that changes in macroeconomic fundamentals relative to 2017 affect not only current account balances but also their equilibrium values, the path of future excess imbalances cannot be precisely inferred from this exercise.[8]

International Investment Positions

Changes in international investment positions reflect both net financial flows and valuation changes arising from fluctuations in exchange rates and asset prices. Given that WEO projections assume broadly stable real effective exchange rates and limited variation in asset prices, changes in international investment positions are driven by projections for net external bor-

---

[7]The change in the current account balance over 2018 would offset, on average, about one-fifth of the 2017 current account gap, while the change between 2017 and 2023 would offset about half of the 2017 gap.

[8]For instance, an improvement in the terms of trade is typically associated with a larger equilibrium current account balance and a more appreciated equilibrium exchange rate.

Figure 1.14. Global Current Account Balance
(Percent of world GDP)

After a slight widening in 2018, current account balances are expected to narrow marginally over the medium term as the surpluses of oil exporters decline and the US current account deficit stabilizes with the fading of the expansionary effects of fiscal policy.

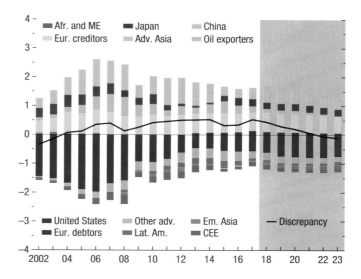

Source: IMF staff estimates.
Note: Adv. Asia = advanced Asia (Hong Kong SAR, Korea, Singapore, Taiwan Province of China); Afr. and ME = Africa and the Middle East (Democratic Republic of the Congo, Egypt, Ethiopia, Ghana, Jordan, Kenya, Lebanon, Morocco, South Africa, Sudan, Tanzania, Tunisia); CEE = central and eastern Europe (Belarus, Bulgaria, Croatia, Czech Republic, Hungary, Poland, Romania, Slovak Republic, Turkey, Ukraine); Em. Asia = emerging Asia (India, Indonesia, Pakistan, Philippines, Thailand, Vietnam); Eur. creditors = European creditors (Austria, Belgium, Denmark, Finland, Germany, Luxembourg, Netherlands, Norway, Sweden, Switzerland); Eur. debtors = European debtors (Cyprus, Greece, Ireland, Italy, Portugal, Spain, Slovenia); Lat. Am. = Latin America (Argentina, Brazil, Chile, Colombia, Mexico, Peru, Uruguay); Oil exporters = Algeria, Azerbaijan, Iran, Kazakhstan, Kuwait, Nigeria, Oman, Qatar, Russia, Saudi Arabia, United Arab Emirates, Venezuela; Other adv. = other advanced economies (Australia, Canada, France, Iceland, New Zealand, United Kingdom).

---

rowing and lending (in line with the current account balance), with their ratios to domestic and world GDP affected by projected growth rates for individual countries and for the world economy as a whole.[9],[10]

---

[9]WEO forecasts include projections of 10-year government bond yields, which would affect bond prices going forward, but the impact of those changes in bond prices on the valuation of external assets and liabilities is typically not included in international investment position forecasts.

[10]Exchange rate changes can affect the evolution of international investment positions. For instance, according to estimates by the United States Bureau of Economic Analysis, the 7 percent depreciation of the US dollar in nominal effective terms between the end of 2016 and the end of 2017 improved the US net international investment position by about 6 percent of GDP by increasing the domestic currency value of foreign currency assets held by US residents.

Figure 1.15. Current Account Balances in Relation to Economic Fundamentals

Current account balances in 2018 are projected to move in a direction consistent with some reduction in excess imbalances. Medium-term projections suggest further modest movement of current account balances in the same direction.

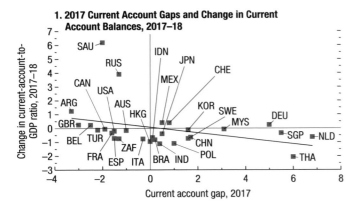

1. 2017 Current Account Gaps and Change in Current Account Balances, 2017–18

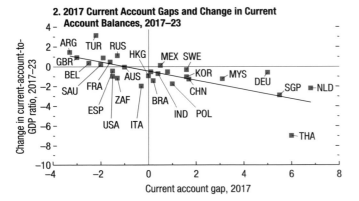

2. 2017 Current Account Gaps and Change in Current Account Balances, 2017–23

Source: IMF staff calculations.
Note: Data labels use International Organization for Standardization (ISO) country codes.

Figure 1.16. Net International Investment Position

Creditor and debtor net international investment positions are projected to widen slightly over the medium term.

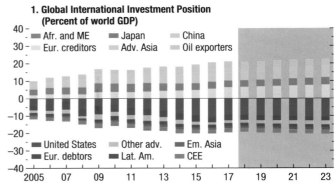

1. Global International Investment Position (Percent of world GDP)

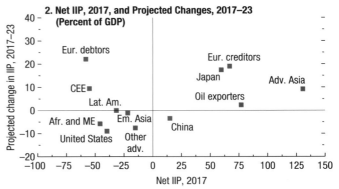

2. Net IIP, 2017, and Projected Changes, 2017–23 (Percent of GDP)

Source: IMF staff estimates.
Note: Adv. Asia = advanced Asia (Hong Kong SAR, Korea, Singapore, Taiwan Province of China); Afr. and ME = Africa and the Middle East (Democratic Republic of the Congo, Egypt, Ethiopia, Ghana, Jordan, Kenya, Lebanon, Morocco, South Africa, Sudan, Tanzania, Tunisia); CEE = central and eastern Europe (Belarus, Bulgaria, Croatia, Czech Republic, Hungary, Poland, Romania, Slovak Republic, Turkey, Ukraine); Em. Asia = emerging Asia (India, Indonesia, Pakistan, Philippines, Thailand, Vietnam); Eur. creditors = European creditors (Austria, Belgium, Denmark, Finland, Germany, Luxembourg, Netherlands, Norway, Sweden, Switzerland); Eur. debtors = European debtors (Cyprus, Greece, Ireland, Italy, Portugal, Spain, Slovenia); IIP = international investment position; Lat. Am. = Latin America (Argentina, Brazil, Chile, Colombia, Mexico, Peru, Uruguay); Oil exporters = Algeria, Azerbaijan, Iran, Kazakhstan, Kuwait, Nigeria, Oman, Qatar, Russia, Saudi Arabia, United Arab Emirates, Venezuela; Other adv. = Other advanced economies (Australia, Canada, France, Iceland, New Zealand, United Kingdom).

As panel 1 of Figure 1.16 shows, over the next five years, creditor and debtor positions as a share of world GDP are projected to widen slightly. On the creditor side, this is explained primarily by the growing creditor positions of a group of European advanced economies, a result of large projected current account surpluses. On the debtor side, this reflects some increase in the debtor position of the United States and other advanced economies (a group including Canada, France, and the United Kingdom, among others), partially offset by a further sizable improvement in the position of euro area debtor countries.

Similar trends are highlighted in panel 2 of Figure 1.16, which shows projected changes in net international investment positions as a percentage of domestic

GDP across countries and regions between 2017 and 2023, the last year of the WEO projection horizon. The net creditor position of advanced European economies is projected to exceed 85 percent of GDP and of Japan to exceed 75 percent of GDP, while the net debtor position of the United States is projected to approach 50 percent of GDP, some 9 percentage points above the 2017 estimate. In contrast, the net international investment position of a group of euro area debtor countries, including Italy and Spain, is expected to improve by more than 20 percentage points of their collective GDP, and by 2023, net foreign liabilities would be about half their level a decade earlier.

Domestic and External Contributions to GDP Growth

Another way to look at the prospects for global rebalancing is to examine the domestic and external contributions to GDP growth in creditor and debtor countries. Growth in domestic demand was faster in creditor countries than in debtor countries in 2017, as in previous years, primarily reflecting high growth in China (Figure 1.17). At the same time, the net external contribution to growth was again positive for creditors, driven this time by positive contributions from China, creditor Europe, and Japan. For 2018, the net external contribution to growth is slightly negative for creditors, with a positive contribution from creditor Europe, Japan, and other advanced Asian economies broadly offset by negative contributions from China and oil exporters. Among debtor countries, the net external contribution to growth is forecast to be positive for Latin American debtor countries and to remain negative for the United States because of expansionary fiscal policy.

Implications of Imbalances

Sustained excess external imbalances in the world's key economies and policy actions that threaten to widen such imbalances pose risks to global stability. The fiscal easing under way in the United States is leading to a tightening of monetary conditions, a stronger US dollar, and a larger US current account deficit. These trends risk aggravating trade tensions and may result in a faster tightening of global financing conditions, with negative implications for emerging market economies, especially those with weak external positions. Over the medium term, widening debtor positions in key economies could constrain global growth and possibly result in sharp and disruptive currency and asset price adjustments.

As discussed in the section titled "Policy Priorities," the US economy, which is already operating beyond full employment, should implement a medium-term plan to reverse the rising ratio of public debt, accompanied by fiscal measures to gradually boost domestic capacity. This would help ensure more sustainable growth dynamics as well as contain external imbalances. Stronger reliance on demand growth in some

Figure 1.17. Growth for Creditors and Debtors
(Percent)

In 2017 and 2018, domestic demand growth was faster in creditor countries than in debtor countries.

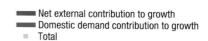

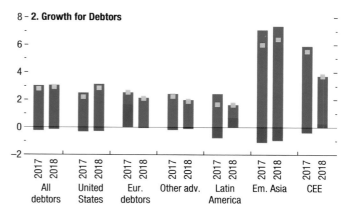

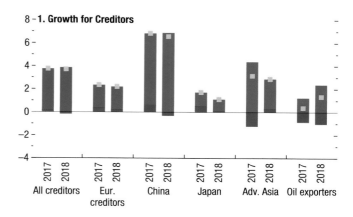

Source: IMF staff calculations.
Note: Adv. Asia = advanced Asia (Hong Kong SAR, Korea, Singapore, Taiwan Province of China); CEE = central and eastern Europe (Belarus, Bulgaria, Croatia, Czech Republic, Hungary, Poland, Romania, Slovak Republic, Turkey, Ukraine); Em. Asia = emerging Asia (India, Indonesia, Pakistan, Philippines, Thailand, Vietnam); Eur. creditors = European creditors (Austria, Belgium, Denmark, Finland, Germany, Luxembourg, Netherlands, Norway, Sweden, Switzerland); Eur. debtors = European debtors (Cyprus, Greece, Ireland, Italy, Portugal, Spain, Slovenia); Latin America = Argentina, Brazil, Chile, Colombia, Mexico, Peru, Uruguay; Other adv. = other advanced economies (Australia, Canada, France, Iceland, New Zealand, United Kingdom); Oil exporters = Algeria, Azerbaijan, Iran, Kazakhstan, Kuwait, Nigeria, Oman, Qatar, Russia, Saudi Arabia, United Arab Emirates, Venezuela.

creditor countries, especially those with policy space to support it, such as Germany, would help facilitate domestic and global rebalancing while sustaining world growth over the medium term.

Risks

The balance of risks to the short-term global growth forecast has now shifted to the downside. The potential for upside surprises has receded, given the tightening of financial conditions in some parts of the world, the rise in trade costs, slow implementation of reforms recommended in the past, and waning growth momentum, reflected in worse-than-anticipated outturns in several large economies, weakening growth of industrial production, and a softening of some high-frequency indicators. At the same time, several of the downside risks highlighted in the April 2018 WEO have become more pronounced or have partially materialized—such as rising trade barriers and a reversal of capital flows to emerging market economies with weaker fundamentals and higher political risk. With protectionist rhetoric increasingly turned into action with the United States imposing tariffs on a wide range of imports and retaliatory actions by trading partners, escalation of trade tensions to an intensity that carries systemic risk is a distinct possibility without policy cooperation. And global financial conditions, while still generally easy, could tighten sharply, triggered by faster-than-anticipated monetary policy tightening in advanced economies or the emergence of other risks that would cause market sentiment to deteriorate suddenly. With public and corporate debt near record levels in many countries, such developments would expose vulnerabilities that have built up over the years, dent confidence, and undermine investment—a key driver of the baseline growth forecast.

In the medium term, risks to the growth outlook remain skewed to the downside as they were in April. These risks stem from a continued buildup of financial vulnerabilities, the implementation of unsustainable macroeconomic policies in the face of a subdued growth outlook, rising inequality, and declining trust in mainstream policies. A range of other noneconomic factors continue to cloud the outlook. If any of these risks materializes, the likelihood of other destabilizing developments could increase, amplifying negative growth consequences. The limited policy space to counteract downturns in advanced and emerging market economies further exacerbates concerns about these undesirable possibilities.

Trade Tensions and Policy Uncertainty

Escalating trade tensions and the potential shift away from a multilateral, rules-based trading system are key threats to the global outlook. Discontent with trade practices and the rules-based trading system has led to a range of trade actions since January, as noted in the section titled "Recent Developments." A cooperative approach to reduce trade costs and resolve disagreements without raising tariff and nontariff barriers has so far proved elusive, with the United States imposing tariffs on a variety of imports and trading partners undertaking retaliatory measures. As discussed in the 2018 *External Sector Report*, widening external imbalances in some large economies, such as the United States—where the fiscal expansion will likely increase the country's current account deficit—could further fuel protectionist sentiments. The proliferation of trade actions and threats, and the ongoing renegotiations of major free trade agreements, such as NAFTA and the economic arrangements between the United Kingdom and the rest of the European Union, have created pervasive uncertainty about future trade costs.[11] An intensification of trade tensions and the associated further rise in policy uncertainty could dent business and financial market sentiment, trigger financial market volatility, and slow investment and trade. An increase in trade barriers would disrupt global supply chains, which have become an integral part of production processes in the past decades, and slow the spread of new technologies, ultimately lowering global productivity and welfare. It would also make tradable consumer goods less affordable, harming low-income households disproportionately. In addition to their negative effects on domestic and global growth, protectionist policies would likely have very limited effect on external imbalances, as discussed in the 2018 *External Sector Report*.

Scenario Box 1 discusses the potential economic consequences of further escalation in trade tensions and rising trade barriers. Illustrative simulations suggest that a combination of higher import tariffs by the United States (along the lines threatened by the US administration so far) and retaliatory measures

---

[11]As discussed in the 2016 United Kingdom IMF Article IV Selected Issues paper and the 2018 Euro Area IMF Article IV Selected Issues paper, the rise in trade barriers between the United Kingdom and the European Union would imply sizable losses for the UK economy and, to a lesser extent, for its trading partners, with negative impacts concentrated in countries with the largest trade links with the United Kingdom.

by its trading partners could inflict significant costs on the global economy, especially through its impact on confidence and financial conditions. According to model simulations, global GDP would fall by more than 0.8 percent in 2020 and remain roughly 0.4 percent lower in the long term compared with a baseline without trade tensions. The disruption caused by an escalation of trade restrictions could be particularly large in the United States and China, with GDP losses of more than 0.9 percent in the United States and over 1.6 percent in China in 2019, and in the NAFTA trading partners, where GDP is simulated to be more than 1.6 percent lower in 2020 than in the absence of tariff measures.

As discussed in the July 2018 Group of Twenty Surveillance Note and the October 2016 WEO, such illustrative scenarios likely understate the negative repercussions of rising trade tensions on the global economy. Inward-looking trade policies could come together with tighter restrictions on the cross-border flows of factors of production. Curbs to migration would prevent aging economies from taking advantage of demographic trends in other parts of the world to ease labor supply pressures (Chapter 2 of the April 2018 WEO). The disruption to international economic links would also make it harder for countries to tackle cooperatively, and in a coordinated manner, the other multilateral challenges they face, now or in the future.

Beyond trade, recent and forthcoming elections have raised the prospect of realigned policy agendas. Political and policy uncertainty could deter private investment and weaken economic activity in several countries by raising the possibility of slower reform or of significant change to policy objectives. For example, the recent difficulties with forming a government in Italy and the possibility of reversal of reforms or the implementation of policies that would harm debt sustainability triggered a sharp widening in spreads. In Turkey, growing concerns about the credibility of the policy agenda, underlying fundamentals, and political tensions with the US were the main factors behind the sharp depreciation of the Turkish lira, the decline in asset prices, and widening spreads in August. In China, the recent shift to a more accommodative macro policy stance, while fine-tuning the pace of deleveraging, has brought renewed attention to the difficult trade-off between growth and stability that policymakers face. These developments are consistent with an overall increase in global economic policy uncertainty since the start of this year (Figure 1.18). IMF staff analysis

suggests that 2019 and 2020 growth forecast revisions compared with the April 2018 WEO are slightly more negative for countries that trade extensively with the United States—which could serve as a proxy for the global repercussions of the uncertain direction of US trade policy (Figure 1.18, panel 2).

Financial Tensions

After years of an extremely supportive financial environment, the global economy remains vulnerable to a sudden tightening of financial conditions. As discussed in the April and October 2018 GFSRs, measures of equity valuations appear stretched in some markets, investors have moved into riskier asset classes in search of yield, and the share of firms with low investment-grade ratings in advanced economy bond indices has increased significantly. Across many economies, government and corporate debt is substantially higher than before the global financial crisis (April 2018 *Fiscal Monitor*). In some emerging markets, there are concerns about rising contingent liabilities and increasing balance sheet mismatches. A surprise tightening of global financial conditions could expose these vulnerabilities and derail the expansion.

As discussed in previous WEOs, various factors could trigger a sudden change in global financial conditions. Signs of firmer-than-expected inflation in the United States (for example, as capacity constraints become more binding) could lead to a shift in market expectations of US interest rate hikes, which are currently well below those assumed in the WEO baseline forecast. A negative shock could trigger a sudden deterioration of risk appetite, which in turn could lead to disruptive portfolio adjustments, accelerate and broaden the reversal of capital flows from emerging markets, and lead to further US dollar appreciation, straining economies with high leverage, fixed exchange rates, or balance sheet mismatches. Rising trade tensions and political and policy uncertainty could also make market participants abruptly reassess fundamentals and risks. The recent turmoil in Turkey, exacerbated by political tensions with the United States against the backdrop of deteriorating fundamentals, including a belated monetary policy response to increasing inflation, exemplifies the increased salience of this risk for other vulnerable emerging markets. In an environment of gradually tightening global interest rates and rising uncertainty, the likelihood of contagion from such episodes to other economies has also

Figure 1.18. Policy Uncertainty and Trade Tensions

Global economic policy uncertainty has increased sharply since the beginning of the year. Growth forecast revisions for 2019 and 2020 are slightly more negative for countries with larger trade exposure to the United States.

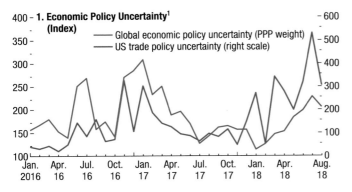

1. Economic Policy Uncertainty[1] (Index)

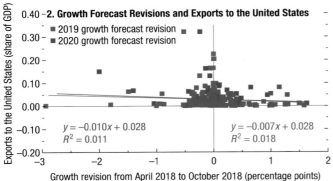

2. Growth Forecast Revisions and Exports to the United States

Sources: Baker, Bloom, and Davis (2016); United Nations COMTRADE database; and IMF staff calculations.
Note: PPP = purchasing power parity. Baker-Bloom-Davis index of Global Economic Policy Uncertainty (GEPU) is a GDP-weighted average of national EPU indices for 20 countries: Australia, Brazil, Canada, Chile, China, France, Germany, Greece, India, Ireland, Italy, Japan, Korea, Mexico, the Netherlands, Russia, Spain, Sweden, the United Kingdom, and the United States.
[1]Mean of global economic policy uncertainty index from 1997 to 2015 = 100; mean of US trade policy uncertainty index from 1985 to 2010 = 100.

risen. The increase in Italian sovereign yields since May is another case in point. A significant further decline in sovereign bond prices, with possible contagion effects, would impose valuation losses on investors, worsen public debt dynamics, and weaken bank balance sheets, reigniting concerns about sovereign-bank feedback loops in the euro area.

Financial tensions could also arise from regulatory actions. In China, where the authorities are taking welcome steps to slow credit growth, uncoordinated financial and local government regulatory action could have unintended consequences that trigger disorderly repricing of financial assets, increase rollover risks, and

lead to stronger-than-forecast negative effects on activity. More broadly, an indiscriminate rollback of postcrisis regulatory reform and oversight—both domestically and internationally—could encourage excessive risk taking, leading to a further buildup of financial vulnerabilities.

Cybersecurity breaches and cyberattacks on critical financial infrastructure represent an additional source of risk because they could undermine cross-border payment systems and disrupt the flow of goods and services. Continued rapid growth of crypto assets could create new vulnerabilities in the international financial system.

Other Factors

A range of other factors continues to influence the medium-term outlook in various regions. Geopolitical risks (Figure 1.19) and domestic strife are weighing on the outlook in several economies, especially in the Middle East and sub-Saharan Africa. Box 1.5 documents the depth of macroeconomic distress in several countries (such as Libya, Venezuela, and Yemen) and compares it to other cases of large GDP collapses in recent history. While the baseline forecast assumes a gradual easing of existing strains, an intensification of conflicts in the Middle East and Africa not only would have large negative domestic repercussions (Box 1.1 of the April 2017 WEO), but could trigger a rise in migrant flows into Europe, potentially deepening political divisions. In several systemically important economies, declining trust in national and regional institutions may increase the appeal of politically popular but unsustainable policy measures, which could harm confidence, threaten medium-term sustainability, and, in the case of Europe, undermine regional cohesion. Furthermore, many countries remain vulnerable to the economic and humanitarian costs of extreme weather events and other natural disasters, with potentially significant cross-border ramifications through migration flows.

Fan Chart Analysis

A fan chart analysis—based on equity and commodity market data as well as the dispersion of inflation and term spread projections of private forecasters—shows a downward shift in the balance of risks relative to the October 2017 WEO, as shown in Figure 1.20. The shift is broad based—with all indicators showing a decline in the current year extending into 2019. The worsening of the risk profile mostly reflects anticipated exacerbation of global trade tensions, which will weigh on investment and growth. These measures already

Figure 1.19. Geopolitical Risk Index
(Index)

Geopolitical risks continue to trend upward.

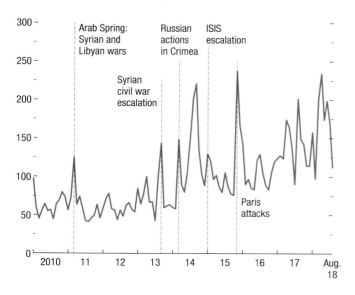

Source: Caldara and Iacoviello (2018).
Note: ISIS = Islamic State.

appear, at least in part, to be priced into US equities, whose risk profile has worsened. A greater likelihood of higher energy prices adds to downside risks. Box 1.6 discusses the challenges of predicting recessions.

As discussed in the October 2018 GFSR, growth-at-risk analysis suggests a slight increase in short-term downside risks to global financial stability compared with the April 2018 GFSR, and continued risks to medium-term growth that are well above historical norms.

Policy Priorities

With risks shifting to the downside, domestic and multilateral policies have a vital role to play in sustaining the global expansion and enhancing prospects for strong and inclusive growth. Global growth remains above trend but, with momentum appearing to peak, strengthening resilience and tackling long-standing challenges become more urgent.

Policies—Advanced Economies

In *advanced economies*, the macroeconomic policy stance should be tailored to the maturing cyclical

Figure 1.20. Risks to the Global Outlook

The risks around the central global growth forecast for 2018 and 2019 have tilted to the downside.

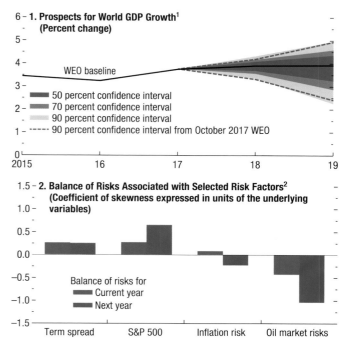

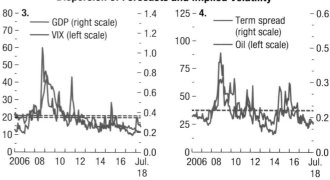

Sources: Bloomberg Finance L.P.; Chicago Board Options Exchange (CBOE); Consensus Economics; Haver Analytics; and IMF staff estimates.
[1]The fan chart shows the uncertainty around the October 2018 *World Economic Outlook* (WEO) central forecast with 50, 70, and 90 percent confidence intervals. As shown, the 70 percent confidence interval includes the 50 percent interval, and the 90 percent confidence interval includes the 50 and 70 percent intervals. See Appendix 1.2 of the April 2009 WEO for details. The 90 percent intervals for the current-year and one-year-ahead forecasts from the October 2017 WEO are shown.
[2]The bars depict the coefficient of skewness expressed in units of the underlying variables. The values for inflation risks and oil market risks enter with the opposite sign since they represent downside risks to growth.
[3]GDP measures the purchasing-power-parity-weighted average dispersion of GDP growth forecasts for the Group of Seven economies (Canada, France, Germany, Italy, Japan, United Kingdom, United States), Brazil, China, India, and Mexico. VIX is the CBOE Standard & Poor's (S&P) 500 Implied Volatility Index. Term spread measures the average dispersion of term spreads implicit in interest rate forecasts for Germany, Japan, the United Kingdom, and the United States. Oil is the CBOE crude oil volatility index. Forecasts are from Consensus Economics surveys. Dashed lines represent the average values from 2000 to the present.

position. While rising oil prices are largely responsible for higher headline inflation, core inflation has also been firming in the context of narrowing or closing output gaps. Where inflation is close to or above target, data-dependent and well-communicated monetary normalization is appropriate. In cases where inflation is still significantly below target, continued accommodative monetary policy remains appropriate. As much as possible, countries should use this period of sustained growth to rebuild fiscal buffers. Structural reforms aimed at increasing labor productivity, labor force participation, and flexibility of the labor market would be welcome. Investments in physical and digital infrastructure, as well as reduced barriers to entry in services markets, could boost growth potential in the medium term.

Monetary Policy: Data Dependent, Well Communicated, Country Specific

In the *United States*, the monetary policy stance should be gradually tightened as inflation pressures emerge amid solid growth and historically low unemployment. The large and procyclical fiscal stimulus places an additional burden on the Federal Reserve to raise policy rates to keep inflation expectations anchored around the target and prevent the economy from overheating. In this context, the Federal Reserve's continued adherence to data-dependent policymaking and clear communication will be vital to ensuring a smooth adjustment—both domestically and abroad.

In the *United Kingdom*, where the output gap is closed and unemployment is low, a modest tightening of monetary policy may be warranted, although at a time of heightened uncertainty, monetary policy should remain flexible in response to changing conditions associated with the Brexit negotiations.

In the *euro area* and *Japan*, accommodative monetary policies remain appropriate. In the *euro area*, positive output gaps and tightening labor markets should eventually lift inflation, but the increase is projected to happen slowly over the forecast horizon, given a strong backward-looking element in the inflation process. The European Central Bank's expectation that policy rates will remain low through the summer of 2019, and beyond, if necessary, together with the net asset purchases until the end of the year (and the sizable stock of acquired assets and the associated reinvestments), are therefore vital. In *Japan,* where inflation is not expected to reach the target over the next five years, a sustained accommodative monetary stance is also a necessity. The Bank of Japan recently reinforced

its commitment to reflate the economy by introducing forward guidance on policy interest rates and increasing flexibility of market operations to make the accommodative monetary stance more sustainable.

Fiscal Policy: Rebuild Buffers, Enhance Inclusiveness, and Boost Medium-Term Potential

Above-trend growth in many advanced economies offers a chance to build fiscal buffers and prepare for the next downturn. Figure 1.21 highlights that, while public debt is projected to decline in many of the largest advanced economies over the next five years, projected changes in public debt are uncorrelated with initial debt levels.[12] Procyclical fiscal stimulus should be avoided and rolled back (for example, in the United States), while further steps should be taken by countries with fiscal space and excess external surpluses to boost domestic growth potential and address global imbalances (for example, in Germany). In cases where fiscal consolidation is appropriate, the pace of fiscal tightening should depend on economic conditions and avoid exerting sharp drags on demand, and efforts should be made to reorient the composition of spending and revenues to enhance inclusiveness and protect vulnerable people. Fiscal spending should prioritize areas that can support growth, such as investing in physical and digital infrastructure, boosting labor force participation where aging threatens future labor supply, and enhancing workforce skills.

In the *United States*, the tax overhaul and higher spending will widen the fiscal deficit, which was already set to deteriorate over the long term because of aging-related spending. Against the backdrop of record low unemployment rates, the deficit expansion is providing a short-term boost to activity in the United States and many of its trading partners, but at the cost of elevated risks to the US and global economies. The larger deficit not only will leave fewer budget resources to invest in supply-side reforms, but will add to an already-unsustainable public debt and contribute to a rise in global imbalances. With the US economy already operating above potential, expansionary fiscal policy could lead to an inflation surprise, which may trigger a faster-than-currently anticipated rise in US interest rates, a tightening of global financial conditions, and further US dollar appreciation, with potentially negative

---

[12]The October 2018 *Fiscal Monitor* discusses the evolution of public sector balance sheets, which provide a more comprehensive view of the state of public finances.

spillovers for the global economy. The preferred policy course would be to increase the revenue-to-GDP ratio through greater reliance on indirect taxes.

In the *United Kingdom*, the fiscal targets—which envisage the cyclically adjusted public sector deficit falling below 2 percent of GDP and public debt beginning to decline by 2020–21—provide an anchor for medium-term objectives while allowing for flexibility in the short term. The pace of fiscal consolidation can be eased if risks materialize and growth slows sharply.

In *Japan*, the debt trajectory needs to be anchored by a credible medium-term fiscal consolidation plan, which should be based on gradual increases in the consumption tax rate beyond the 2 percentage-point increase envisaged for October 2019. However, in the short term, premature fiscal tightening should be avoided to support growth momentum and reflation.

In the *euro area*, countries with currently limited fiscal space (for example, *France, Italy, Spain*) should use this period of above-potential growth and accommodative monetary policy to rebuild fiscal buffers, which would help alleviate bank-sovereign strains. France's plan to restrain spending is a welcome step. Countries with fiscal space, such as *Germany*, should fund measures that would raise potential output and facilitate external rebalancing, for example, by increasing public investment in physical and human capital.

Structural Policies: Boost Potential Growth

Low productivity and an aging workforce weigh heavily on the medium-term growth prospects of advanced economies. Reforms of product and labor markets could boost medium-term productivity, labor supply, and growth potential and are especially important when fiscal and monetary policy are constrained. Reforms that strengthen education and health care would help tackle poverty and inequality and prepare workers for challenges arising from rapid progress in labor-saving technologies and globalization.

In the *euro area*, structural reforms have attracted much discussion in individual countries, but progress has been mixed. *France* has made welcome strides in improving labor market flexibility, and, more recently, in legislating measures to better align workforce skills with business needs to boost employment. Continued progress with planned reforms that aim to ease corporate administrative burdens would also benefit long-term growth. In *Germany*, policies to increase labor supply and investment, as well as to support entrepreneurship and advance digital transformation,

Figure 1.21. Projected Change in Public Debt

Public debt in most major advanced economies is projected to decline over 2017–23, while it is projected to increase in some of the largest emerging market and developing economies. But there is no clear relationship between the projected change in debt ratios and the level of debt prevailing in 2017.

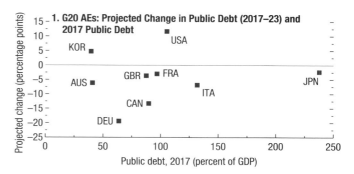

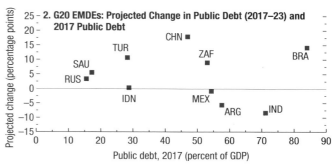

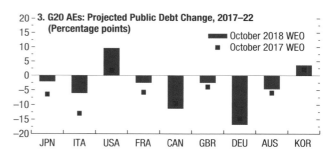

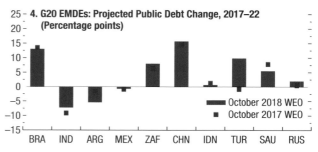

Source: IMF staff calculations.
Note: AEs = advanced economies; EMDEs = emerging market and developing economies; G20 = Group of Twenty; WEO = *World Economic Outlook*.

would all be beneficial, and should be supported with available fiscal space—particularly in contexts such as the current year in which the budget is in surplus. In *Italy*, past pension and labor market reforms should be preserved, and further measures should be pursued, such as decentralizing wage bargaining to align wages with labor productivity at the firm level. In *Spain*, the structural reform agenda, which aims to raise the effectiveness of active labor market policies and reduce labor market segmentation, needs new impetus.

In *Japan*, the foremost priority should be labor market reform that could help lift productivity and wage inflation. For example, the government's Work Style Reform appropriately focuses on reducing labor market duality via the "equal pay for equal work" pillar. Boosting labor force participation rates among women and older workers, and allowing more use of foreign labor, would help support an aging population, but might add to deflationary pressures in the short term and should be tackled after the Work Style Reform.

In the *United States*, labor supply could be incentivized among lower-income households by increasing the generosity of the Earned Income Tax Credit and raising the federal minimum wage. Education reforms could focus on expanding apprenticeships and vocational programs to offer attractive noncollege career paths, designing new federal financing options for tertiary education, reducing funding differences across districts, and offering more support to low-income areas.

In the *United Kingdom*, where goods and labor markets are already flexible, reforms should focus on easing planning restrictions to boost housing supply, improving the quality of transport infrastructure, and raising human capital among the lower skilled (such as by raising the basic skills of high school graduates). Active labor market policies should facilitate the relocation of workers in industries that are likely to be more affected by higher trade barriers after Brexit.

Financial Sector Policies: Complete Balance Sheet Cleanup, Increase Resilience to Shocks

The potential for greater financial market volatility requires fortifying financial systems and avoiding a rollback of the postcrisis regulatory reforms. As discussed in the October 2018 GFSR, macroprudential tools need to be developed and deployed, and macroprudential policy buffers need to be rebuilt, including by raising capital buffers, to provide insurance against a future tightening of financial conditions. In the *euro area*, completing the banking union remains a prior-

ity. Continued progress with balance sheet cleanup is essential to strengthen credit intermediation in several economies. There is also a general need to improve euro area banks' cost efficiency and profitability through proactive supervision, greater use of digitization, and revamped business models. In *Japan*, the drag on bank profitability from low interest rates and demographic headwinds could be remedied by increasing fee-based income and diversifying revenue sources, together with consolidation. In the *United States*, rising leverage, a weakening of underwriting standards for corporate credit, the growth of passively managed investment products, and cyber risks bear close monitoring. Changes to financial oversight should continue to ensure that the current risk-based approach to regulation, supervision, and resolution is preserved (and strengthened in the case of nonbanks).

Policies—Emerging Market Economies

With advanced economy interest rates expected to increase from current still-accommodative levels and with trade tensions rising, emerging market and developing economies need to be prepared for an environment of higher volatility. Many need to enhance resilience through an appropriate mix of fiscal, monetary, exchange rate, and prudential policies to lessen their vulnerability to tightening global financial conditions, sharp currency movements, and reversals in capital flows. Given subdued medium-term prospects for per capita incomes in many countries and mounting downside risks to growth, reforms need to be enacted to bolster growth potential and ensure that all segments of society have access to opportunities.

Managing Trade-Offs and Enhancing Resilience

Although global financial conditions remain generally supportive from a historical perspective, continued monetary policy normalization in the United States and a stronger US dollar, coinciding with country-specific factors, have put pressure on the exchange rates and funding costs of some emerging market economies (for example, *Brazil, India, Indonesia, Mexico, South Africa,* and especially *Argentina and Turkey*), and have led to further reductions in capital inflows. Policy reactions have been varied. In addition to allowing the exchange rate to adjust, albeit to varying degrees, countries resorted to interest rate hikes (such as in *Argentina, Indonesia, Mexico, Turkey*), the activation of official financing (for example, in *Argentina*), and intervention in the foreign exchange market (*Argentina* and *Brazil*). The challenges that Turkey faces will require a comprehensive policy package comprising monetary, fiscal, quasi-fiscal, and financial sector policies.

Monetary policy in emerging market economies will need to manage the trade-off between supporting activity should external financial conditions tighten further, and keeping inflation expectations anchored. As Chapter 3 demonstrates, firmer anchoring of inflation expectations—fostered, for example, by credible fiscal and monetary policy frameworks—reduces inflation persistence and limits the pass-through of currency depreciations to domestic prices, allowing greater leeway for monetary policy to support output.

Turning to individual countries, monetary policy should be tightened to reanchor expectations where inflation continues to be high (as recently done in *Argentina*), where it is increasing further in the wake of a sharp currency depreciation (*Turkey*), or where it is expected to pick up (*India*). Monetary policy should instead remain accommodative in *Brazil*, where unemployment remains high and inflation is gradually increasing toward the inflation target. In *Mexico*, conditional on expectations remaining anchored, monetary policy may become accommodative to support activity once inflation is firmly on a downward path. Given the inflation outlook, monetary policy could also be adjusted from its moderately tight stance toward a neutral stance in *Russia*. Recent tightening in *Indonesia* was broadly appropriate to tackle risks to inflation from exchange rate depreciation and rising inflation expectations. Given external uncertainty, monetary policy may stay on hold in the immediate future, while the impact of recent actions is assessed. In *South Africa*, possible exchange rate pressures amid US monetary policy tightening, rising risk aversion, and higher oil prices pose upside risks to inflation.

Exchange rate flexibility can help economies absorb external shocks, although the effects of exchange rate depreciations on private and public sector balance sheets and on domestic inflation expectations require close monitoring. Under floating exchange rate regimes, foreign exchange interventions should be limited to addressing disorderly market conditions while protecting reserve buffers (for example, in *Argentina, Brazil, India, Indonesia, Mexico, South Africa, Turkey*). As highlighted in Chapter 2, countries with flexible exchange rate regimes and those with lower financial vulnerabilities experienced less damage to output in the aftermath of the global financial crisis.

Long-standing advice on the importance of reining in excess credit growth where needed, supporting healthy bank balance sheets, containing maturity and currency mismatches, and maintaining orderly market conditions has become even more relevant in the face of renewed market volatility. In *China*, it will be important, despite growth headwinds from slower credit growth and trade barriers, to maintain the focus on deleveraging and continue regulatory and supervisory tightening, greater recognition of bad assets, and more market-based credit allocation to improve resilience and boost medium-term growth prospects. In *India*, reform priorities include reviving bank credit and enhancing the efficiency of credit provision by accelerating the cleanup of bank and corporate balance sheets and improving the governance of public sector banks.

Considerable progress was made in *Russia* in recent years to shore up financial stability, including by closing weak banks, introducing reforms to the resolution framework, enacting measures to reduce dollarization, and increasing the risk weights of unsecured consumer and mortgage loans. However, efficiency, competition, and governance in the banking system should still be improved. In *Turkey*, where significant stress is emerging in bank and corporate balance sheets, further progress should be made in strengthening bank supervision and enhancing the crisis management framework.

In *Brazil*, the financial sector has proved resilient, despite the severity of the 2015–16 recession, yet bank credit is lagging, especially for nonfinancial firms. Key reforms have strengthened supervision and regulation but remaining vulnerabilities, including related-party exposures and transactions, large exposures, country and transfer risk, and restructured loans, still need to be addressed and the safety net strengthened. *Mexico* remains exposed to bouts of financial volatility in global markets, given its open capital account and deep financial integration with the rest of the world. The exchange rate should remain the main shock absorber, and foreign exchange intervention should only be used to guard against disorderly market conditions. The Flexible Credit Line provides additional insurance in case of tail events.

South Africa has a range of buffers, including a floating exchange rate, deep financial markets, contained foreign currency exposures, and long debt maturities. However, significant vulnerabilities arise from large gross external financing needs. Deepening reforms to improve governance and the business environment would help reduce such vulnerabilities.

In *Saudi Arabia*, further financial development and inclusion should be pursued while maintaining financial stability. Increased finance for small and medium-sized enterprises; more developed debt markets; and improved financial access, especially for women; will support growth and equality. Reforms should focus on removing structural impediments that may dissuade financial institutions from entering these markets. In *Egypt*, while healthy foreign reserves and a flexible exchange rate leave the economy well positioned to manage any acceleration in outflows, maintenance of sound macroeconomic frameworks and consistent policy implementation, which have led to a successful macroeconomic stabilization, is important.

Rebuilding Fiscal Buffers

Public debt has increased in emerging markets over the past decade, and is projected to increase further in many of the largest economies over the next five years (Figure 1.21). This highlights the need to preserve and rebuild buffers. The composition of spending and revenues should be growth friendly and protect the most vulnerable. As shown in Chapter 2, strong fiscal positions before the global financial crisis helped lessen damage to GDP in its aftermath.

A gradual fiscal consolidation is needed in *China* to preserve policy space and ensure broader macroeconomic sustainability. The composition of fiscal policy should support the needed rebalancing from investment to private consumption, and reverting to infrastructure stimulus to boost slowing growth should be avoided. In *India*, a high interest burden and risks from rising yields also require continued focus on debt reduction to establish policy credibility and build buffers. These efforts should be supported by further reductions in subsidies and enhanced compliance with the Goods and Services Tax. Fiscal policy is appropriately geared toward rebuilding fiscal buffers in *Indonesia*, but untargeted subsidies should continue to be reduced, and a medium-term strategy should be put in place to increase the tax ratio, which is low by international standards.

Fiscal consolidation is a key priority in *Brazil* as well. Pension reform is essential for securing fiscal sustainability and ensuring fairness, given that pension expenditures are high and rising and pensions are unduly generous for some segments of the population. While recent measures to increase transparency are welcome, the fiscal framework needs to be strengthened, including by increasing budget flexibility. It will also be

necessary to continue restraining the government wage bill, harmonizing the federal and state tax regimes, and improving subnational government finances, while protecting effective social programs. A more ambitious medium-term fiscal target in *Mexico* would help ensure continued market confidence, rebuild fiscal space, and prepare the country to better deal with long-term demographics-related spending pressures. Significant upfront fiscal adjustment is needed in *Argentina* to lessen the federal financing burden and put public debt on a firm downward trajectory.

Further fiscal consolidation is needed over the medium term in *Russia*, and should continue in line with the fiscal rule, to rebuild fiscal buffers in the short term; the recent relaxation of the fiscal rule could weaken the hard-won credibility of the authorities' macroeconomic framework. To finance increased spending on health, education, and infrastructure, other spending could be reduced, alongside raising the main value-added tax rate, strengthening tax compliance, and broadening the tax base. Parametric pension reform could provide some fiscal space as well. Fiscal and quasi-fiscal consolidation is also needed as part of *Turkey*'s policy package. Specific measures are needed to secure Turkey's stated medium-term program targets, and, on the quasi-fiscal side, public-private partnership activity needs to be managed carefully, and state loan guarantees should be gradually reduced and limited to cases of clear market failures. In *South Africa*, a gradual and growth-friendly fiscal consolidation will be needed to strengthen public finances, focusing on wage savings and complemented by measures to boost efficiency of other current spending, including through better targeting of education subsidies and the rationalization of transfers to public entities.

Structural Reforms to Boost Growth

Structural reforms remain essential to raising growth potential and spreading its benefits more widely, including through streamlining regulations and enhancing competitiveness, investing in infrastructure and human capital, and increasing labor market efficiencies.

Despite a growing emphasis in *China* on the quality rather than the speed of growth, tensions persist between stated development goals and intentions to reduce leverage and allow market forces to play a larger role in the economy. An overarching priority is to continue with reforms, even if the economy slows down, and to avoid a return to credit- and investment-driven stimulus. Key elements of the reform agenda should include strengthening financial regulation and tightening macroprudential settings to rein in the rapid increase in household debt; deepening fiscal structural reforms to foster rebalancing (making the personal income tax more progressive and increasing spending on health, education, and social transfers); tackling income inequality by removing barriers to labor mobility and strengthening fiscal transfers across regions; more decisively reforming state-owned enterprises; and fostering further market liberalization, particularly in services. Addressing the distortions that affect trade and cross-border flows is also needed.

In *India*, important reforms have been implemented in recent years, including the Goods and Services Tax, the inflation-targeting framework, the Insolvency and Bankruptcy Code, and steps to liberalize foreign investment and make it easier to do business. Looking ahead, renewed impetus to reform labor and land markets, along with further improvements to the business climate, are also crucial. In *Indonesia*, the priorities are to enhance infrastructure, streamline regulations to boost competition and competitiveness, improve education quality, and ease labor market regulation to support employment.

In *Brazil*, recent advances in trade facilitation and reforms of the labor and subsidized credit markets are welcome, but more reforms are needed to boost productivity, including by improving financial intermediation, investing in infrastructure, and effectively implementing anti–money laundering and anticorruption measures. In *Argentina*, reforms will need to ensure that the benefits from stronger, sustained growth extend to all parts of society by strengthening the social safety net, including through a redesign of assistance programs.

Priority areas in *Russia* include improving property rights and governance, enhancing the institutional infrastructure, reforming labor markets, and investing in innovation and infrastructure. Structural reforms in *Turkey* should focus on increasing labor market flexibility to help lower unemployment and the output costs of disinflation, and strengthening the business climate to help improve the composition of external inflows and enhance resilience.

Recent reforms in *South Africa*, such as measures adopted to tackle corruption, to strengthen procurement, and in the intention to eliminate wasteful expenditure, are welcome. However, further reforms are needed to increase policy certainty, improve the efficiency of state-owned enterprises, enhance flexibility

in the labor market, improve basic education, and align training with business needs.

Policies—Low-Income Developing Countries

Despite an uptick in growth in 2017–18, many low-income countries continue to face substantial risks, including from a tightening of global financial conditions, heightened trade tensions, and domestic policy slippages. Many continue to grapple with noneconomic challenges, such as rising temperatures, natural disasters, and internal conflict. Low-income countries therefore need to take advantage of the growth recovery to enact reforms that help build resilience, raise potential growth and its inclusiveness, and move closer toward achieving the Sustainable Development Goals.

Rebuilding Fiscal Buffers and Enhancing Financial Resilience

Despite recent narrowing of fiscal deficits as a result of stronger fuel revenues and some fiscal consolidation efforts, public debt burdens have risen in many low-income countries in the past several years. For oil exporters in *sub-Saharan Africa*, foreign-currency-denominated public debt has increased by as much as 80 percent from 2010–13 to 2017, while for non-resource-intensive countries the increase is about 18 percent over the same period (April 2018 *Regional Economic Outlook: Sub-Saharan Africa*). Many low-income countries are increasingly shifting away from traditional multilateral and bilateral sources of debt toward bond issuances and non–Paris Club bilateral creditors, resulting in higher debt-service costs.

Strengthening of fiscal positions is necessary to reduce debt vulnerabilities. Fuel exporters should guard against the temptation to let higher oil prices delay reforms. Despite their recent recovery, oil prices are projected to remain below the 2013 peak. Boosting non-oil revenues and continuing fiscal consolidation plans remain key goals for oil exporters. The focus should be on growth-friendly fiscal adjustment, with a shift in spending toward productive and social outlays accompanied by frontloaded domestic revenue mobilization, through, for example, broadening the tax base and strengthening revenue administration. Moreover, enhancing financial resilience through proactive banking supervision, ensuring adequate provisioning for losses by banks, and improving resolution frameworks to keep expensive public bailouts at bay can help foster a financial system supportive of growth.

Figure 1.22. Change in the Working-Age Population (15–64) Relative to 2015 Levels
(Millions)

By 2035 the number of people in low-income countries reaching working age (15–64) will exceed that of the rest of the world combined.

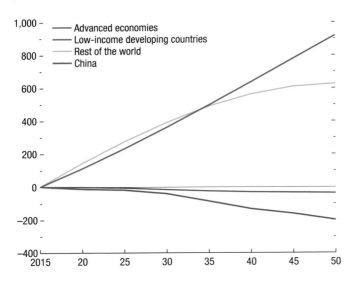

Sources: UN (2017); and IMF staff calculations.

Building More Robust and Diverse Economies

Under current policies in many low-income countries, per capita income growth is projected to remain sluggish and below past averages. Many low-income countries are also facing pressure to accommodate a rapid increase in the working-age population. It is estimated that by 2035, the number of people in low-income countries reaching working age (15–64) will exceed that of the rest of the world combined (Figure 1.22). Creating enough jobs to absorb the new entrants will be vital for welfare and social and political stability. In this regard, economic diversification into labor-intensive activities outside agriculture, and away from excessive dependence on commodities for resource-intensive exporters, is critical. While the manufacturing sector has traditionally served as a source of well-paying jobs for low- to middle-skilled workers in developing economies, market services sectors such as retail, transport, telecommunications, and financial and business services can be viable alternatives (Chapter 3 of the April 2018 WEO). Facilitating private sector development—including by strengthening investor rights and the rule of law, reducing the cost of doing business, and enhancing infrastructure and openness to trade—would help strengthen investment and growth.

Improving education standards will be essential to ensure that the growing pool of workers has the necessary skills.

Achieving robust growth will also require enhancing the macroeconomic resilience of low-income countries, including against climate change. Stronger buffers and sound macroeconomic policy frameworks, alongside policies and institutions that make it easier for labor and capital to move across economic sectors and geographic regions, are essential to that end. To reduce adverse consequences from climate change, countries could also invest in specific adaptation strategies that reduce exposure and vulnerability to weather shocks, such as climate-smart infrastructure, the adoption of appropriate technologies and regulations, and putting in place well-targeted social safety nets that can promptly deliver support (Chapter 3 of the October 2017 WEO).

Fostering Inclusive Growth

Although inequality has declined since 2000 across sub-Saharan Africa, Asia, and Latin America, low-income countries continue to experience significant inequality (October 2017 *Fiscal Monitor*). Policies to address inequality include ensuring macroeconomic stability to improve the sustainability of growth; investing in physical infrastructure, especially in poor regions; and creating an enabling environment for competition and trade, for instance through product market reforms that treat all market entrants equally. Other policies entail enabling access to financial services for low-income households and small and medium-sized enterprises, for example by leveraging recent developments in fintech. Finally, investments in accessible and good-quality education, including early childhood development, and broad-based health care are essential.

Multilateral Policies

Avoiding protectionist reactions to structural change and finding cooperative solutions that promote continued growth in goods and services trade will be essential to preserve and extend the global expansion. Global cooperation remains vital to dealing with challenges that transcend countries' borders and resolving disagreements that threaten the gains from international economic integration. To preserve and broaden these gains, countries need to work together in several areas.

- *Trade*: Trade openness under a rules-based, multilateral trading system has helped diffuse innovation, lift productivity, and expand the variety of goods and services available globally. Policymakers should aim to reduce trade costs further and resolve disagreements without raising tariff and nontariff barriers while facilitating the adjustment of those displaced by trade and technology. Such efforts could significantly raise global welfare, as documented in Chapter 2 of the October 2016 WEO. To best support a strong, stable global economy, World Trade Organization (WTO) rules and commitments should be strengthened to address areas of growing relevance, such as services and e-commerce. Quickly resolving the impasse over the WTO's Appellate Body will help ensure that existing rules are applied and enforced. While agreements at the global level are especially important, well-designed and ambitious regional arrangements—such as the Comprehensive and Progressive Agreement for Trans-Pacific Partnership—can also help. The signing of the African Continental Free Trade Area, and of the new Economic Partnership Agreement between the euro area and Japan, and recent steps to reinvigorate negotiations of the EU–China Comprehensive Agreement on Investment are encouraging.

- *Global financial stability*: Cooperative global efforts on regulatory reform have been crucial in enhancing the safety of the financial system in the decade since the global financial crisis, as discussed in Chapter 2 of the October 2018 GFSR, and pressures to roll back portions of the reform should be resisted. Key areas for more action include completing the implementation of the reform agenda—such as fully implementing the leverage ratio and net stable funding ratio, devising effective resolution frameworks, and enhancing supervisory intensity for globally important financial institutions (especially across borders); bolstering tools and policymaking capabilities of macroprudential entities; and mitigating systemic risk from nonbank financial institutions via continued vigilance on the regulatory perimeter and filling data gaps. Continued close cooperation is also needed to confront emerging risks, such as those arising from the growing systemic importance of central counterparties and the potential for cyber-security breaches, as well as to combat cross-border money laundering and the financing of terrorism. As global banks withdraw from high-risk lending, correspondent banking relationships—through which global banks provide deposit-taking and remittance services to smaller banks in low-income countries—

are under pressure. These relationships play a crucial role because they ensure that these countries have access to vital international payments. To preserve them, domestic regulators will need to, among other things, address gaps in anti–money laundering and combating the financing of terrorism where needed. The rapid development of financial technology offers opportunities, including for enhanced financial inclusion, but risks should also be carefully monitored. In addition, an adequately financed global safety net remains critical so that countries have quick and predictable access to international financing in times of need.

- *Migration*: Immigration can relieve the strain of aging and contribute to productivity. However, although migrant skills typically complement those of the native population, immigration can provoke a political backlash. For source countries, emigration can weigh on long-term growth, including through lost human capital, though remittances and diaspora networks have mitigating effects. Cooperation between source and destination countries should facilitate prompt integration of migrants and support remittance flows. Recurrent surges in international migration, prompted by conflicts or climate-related events, cannot be avoided without cooperative action to improve international security, support low-income countries' efforts in achieving the Sustainable Development Goals, and resist and adapt to climate change.

- *Excess imbalances*: As discussed in the section titled "External Sector Outlook" and the 2018 *External Sector Report*, both deficit and surplus economies must implement measures that help rebalance the composition of global demand and prevent a further buildup of excess global imbalances.

- *Taxation*: Various features of the current international tax system are conducive to tax avoidance. The many possibilities that multinational enterprises have for shifting profits to jurisdictions with low tax rates reduce tax revenues and put downward pressure on corporate income tax rates. The complex treaty network can be exploited through "treaty shopping," which allows corporations to avoid or reduce any withholding taxes on dividends or interest. Further multilateral cooperation on taxation is therefore needed to continue efforts aimed at fighting profit shifting, such as through the Organisation for Economic Co-operation and Development–Group of Twenty Base Erosion and Profit Shifting initiative. In the longer term, conceptual and practical problems, which are intensifying as a result of globalization, may require more fundamental reforms.

- *Other issues*: A range of noneconomic factors imperils the sustainability and inclusiveness of global growth. Cross-border cooperation remains vital for mitigating greenhouse gas emissions and for containing the associated adverse consequences of rising global temperatures and devastating climate events. These developments disproportionately hurt low-income countries that have contributed the least to emissions and have low capacity to cope with their effects (see Chapter 3 of the October 2017 WEO). By adding to migrant flows, climate-related events compound an already-complex situation of refugees fleeing conflict areas, often to countries already under severe strain. Finally, a truly global effort is also needed to curb corruption, which is undermining faith in government and institutions in many countries.

Scenario Box 1. Global Trade Tensions

The Global Integrated Monetary and Fiscal Model (GIMF) is used to simulate the economic impact of the tariffs that have recently been imposed between the United States and several of its trading partners as well as some trade measures that have been announced or considered, but not yet imposed. The simulations capture several channels through which the rise in trade tensions can affect global economic activity. In addition to the direct impact of higher trade costs, the analysis includes estimates of how the trade tensions could affect confidence and thus firms' investment plans as well as how financial markets could react and the resulting implications for firms' cost of capital. The scenario, which builds on the one presented in the July 2018 Group of Twenty (G20) Surveillance Note, has been constructed with five distinct layers.

- The first layer corresponds to measures that have already been implemented and thus are included in the *World Economic Outlook* baseline projections. It estimates the impact of the United States imposing a 10 percent tariff on all aluminum imports, a 25 percent tariff on all steel imports, a 25 percent tariff on $50 billion of imports from China, and a 10 percent tariff on an additional $200 billion of imports from China that subsequently increases to 25 percent. All US trading partners are assumed to respond and levy tariffs on an equivalent amount of US exports, except in the case of the 10 percent tariff on $200 billion in Chinese imports. In this case, China is assumed to respond with an average tariff of 7 percent on $60 billion of US imports that rises to 17 percent when the US tariff increases to 25 percent. The steel and aluminum tariffs imposed by the United States are assumed to fall exclusively on intermediate goods, while the tariff responses by China and other US trading partners fall on a mix of final and intermediate goods. These tariffs are assumed to be permanent and take effect in the second half of 2018, except for the 10 percent tariff on $200 billion of Chinese imports and the associated retaliation, which is assumed to take place in the fourth quarter of 2018. The increase in the tariff from 10 to 25 percent on the $200 billion of imports from China and China's associated retaliation are assumed to occur in 2019.

- The second layer estimates the impact of the United States imposing a 25 percent tariff on a further $267 billion of imports from China and China responding by raising both the base that

tariffs apply to and the tariff rates such that all goods imports from the United States also face a 25 percent tariff (roughly $130 billion in imports from the United States). These tariffs fall on a mix of intermediate and final goods, are assumed to be permanent, and take effect in 2019.

- The third layer estimates the impact of the United States following through on the proposal to impose a 25 percent tariff on all imported cars and car parts (worth about $350 billion). Again, affected US trading partners are assumed to respond with similar tariffs on US exports of cars and car parts as well as other goods such that they are imposing tariffs on an equivalent amount of US exports. These tariffs are assumed to be permanent and take effect in 2019.

- The fourth layer estimates the potential impact that rising trade tensions could have on confidence and thus firms' investment plans. To calibrate how large this effect might be, it uses the Baker-Bloom-Davis overall Economic Policy Uncertainty measure and its estimated impact on investment in the United States.[1] A one standard deviation increase in the uncertainty measure (which is roughly one-sixth of the change that occurred during the global financial crisis) leads to an estimated 1 percent drop in the level of investment in the United States in one year. Half of this decline in US investment is assumed to occur in 2018, with the remainder coming in 2019. The impact of the decline in investment in other countries is then scaled by their trade openness relative to the United States—hence, countries more dependent on trade see a larger fall in investment than does the United States.

- The final layer estimates the impact of a potential tightening of financial conditions for corporates. The magnitude of this tightening is based on estimates by several financial market participants of the impact on US corporate earnings of a worst-case United States-versus-China trade war.[2] Based on historical relationships, this estimated 15 percent decline in earnings is then mapped into an increase in US corporate spreads. This rise in US spreads

---

[1] For details on the Economic Policy Uncertainty measure, see http://www.policyuncertainty.com.

[2] The worst-case scenario is the United States imposing tariffs of 25 percent on all Chinese imports and China responding in a reciprocal fashion.

Scenario Box 1 *(continued)*

is then mapped into corporate spreads in other countries, based on their credit rating relative to US corporates. This increase in spreads is assumed to occur in 2019, with half of the increase remaining in corporate spreads in 2020.

With regard to the room for a policy response to the macroeconomic implications of these trade measures, all layers assume that the euro area and Japan are unable to ease (conventional) monetary policy further in response to macroeconomic developments owing to the zero lower bound on nominal interest rates. Should additional unconventional monetary policy measures be implemented, the decline in GDP in Japan and the euro area would be about half as large in the short and medium terms than estimated here. In all other countries/regions, conventional monetary policy responds according to a Taylor-type reaction function. In addition, to better capture the potentially disruptive impact of tariffs on extended global value chains, the scenario assumes that, in the short term, firms have limited ability to substitute between imported intermediate inputs, whether from different countries or domestic sources. Over the long term, the substitutability between intermediate inputs is notably higher, on par with the substitutability between final goods.

Before turning to the results, it is important to note that these model simulations are illustrative of the disruptions that an escalation in trade restrictions could impose on the global economy, but are of course subject to limitations. Global macroeconomic models, such as GIMF, provide important insights into the cross-border transmission of shocks and the dynamic behavior of macroeconomic variables in response to policy changes, but cannot capture some of the sectoral distortions that the proposed trade restrictions are likely to generate. Given the structure of the model, the impact of higher tariffs on a specific sector of the economy—cars, for example—is derived by assuming a (much more modest) general increase in tariffs: for instance, if cars represent 20 percent of US imports, the impact of a 20 percent tariff on cars would be calculated as the impact of a 4 percent tariff on all US imports (and similarly for steel and aluminum). As a result, the sectoral distortions imposed by tariffs are not fully captured in the simulations. In addition, there is a high degree of uncertainty about the magnitude and persistence

of both the confidence effects on investment and the tightening of corporate spreads. These effects could turn out to be milder or more severe than assumed here and, in part, this motivates providing them as separate layers. Regarding the layer that contains the tightening of corporate spreads, one aspect that is not included in the analysis is the potential for safe-haven flows to mitigate the impact of the financial tightening in such countries as the United States, Germany, and Japan.

Turning to the simulated macroeconomic effects illustrated in Scenario Figure 1, the first point to note is that the impact of the tariffs that have been imposed to date (blue line) is small, but material, with the United States and China bearing the brunt of the costs. These costs would roughly double if the United States imposes a 25 percent tariff on an additional $267 billion of imports from China and if China responds with 25 percent tariffs on all US exports (red line). Some countries, however, do benefit in the short term, as households and firms in China and the United States substitute away from the higher-priced imports, now subject to tariffs, to imports from other countries. Over time, as Chinese and US households and firms are able to source domestically more of the goods that were previously imported, the benefits to other countries disappear. If the United States were to follow through with the imposition of tariffs on imported cars and car parts, and trading partners respond as assumed, the negative impact on the US economy is estimated to increase sharply (yellow line). This is due to the large volume of imports to which the tariffs apply and the fact that almost half are car parts (intermediate inputs that, it is assumed, are difficult, in the short term, to substitute away from). For similar reasons, other countries tightly linked to the US car market, such as its partners in the North American Free Trade Agreement (NAFTA) and Japan, would also see notable declines in output. As in the previous layer, some regions temporarily benefit (in this case China and the euro area), but once households and firms in the most affected countries have sufficient time to make the desired substitutions, the impact is negative everywhere. It is worth noting that these short-term benefits could be overstated. This arises because, as noted above, this car tariff layer is implemented as a much smaller but broad-based change in tariffs, which could result in overestimating

Scenario Box 1 *(continued)*

Scenario Figure 1. Real GDP in Trade Tensions Scenario
(Percent deviation from control)

— Tariffs in baseline
— Add China (25 percent on $267 billion) with retaliation
— Add cars, trucks, and parts with retaliation
— Add confidence effect
— Add market reaction

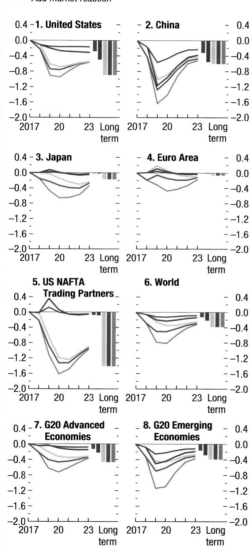

Source: IMF staff estimates.
Note: G20 = Group of Twenty; NAFTA = North American Free Trade Agreement.

the short-term substitutability between imports from China and the euro area and those now higher-priced tariffed goods.

Not surprisingly, if firms curtail investment, given their concerns about the impact of a deteriorating global trading environment, output suffers everywhere, with the impact more pronounced where there are constraints on conventional monetary policy (green line). Also, if financial markets respond to the deterioration in the global trading environment by tightening financial conditions for firms, the output declines would be even sharper, with emerging markets potentially suffering even more (gray line).

In the long term, once all adjustment has occurred (colored bars), output in the United States is almost 1 percent below a baseline with no tariffs, and output in China is just over ½ percent below baseline. The bulk of the negative impact outside of the United States and China is driven by the tariffs on cars and car parts. US NAFTA partners suffer the most, with output almost 1½ percent below baseline. In Japan, the long-term decline in GDP is just under 0.2 percent, and it is less than 0.1 percent in the euro area. Global GDP is down by roughly 0.4 percent in the long term, with advanced G20 economies bearing a slightly higher burden.

Box 1.1. Increasing Market Power

Concern over and the public policy debate about corporate market power are both growing. Concerns arise for at least two reasons. First, rising corporate market power may help account for several puzzling, and often worrisome, macroeconomic trends in advanced economies over the past two decades—low investment despite rising corporate profits, declining business dynamism, slow productivity growth, and falling labor income shares (Autor and others 2017; De Loecker and Eeckhout 2017; Gutiérrez and Philippon 2017). Second, the rise of tech giants has raised fresh questions about whether this trend might continue and, if so, whether some rethinking of policy is needed to maintain fair and strong competition in the digital age. However, corporate market power is hard to measure, and common indicators, such as the

Herfindahl index or market concentration ratios, can be misleading. Beyond the United States and select advanced economies, evidence of how corporate market power has evolved is also scarce.

This box presents new evidence, based on data from a large number of publicly traded firms, on trends in corporate market power across 74 advanced and emerging market and developing economies.[1] Market power, measured as firms' markups—the ratio of the price at which firms sell their output to the marginal cost of production—has generally increased, especially in advanced economies (Figure 1.1.1).

The authors of this box are Federico Díez, Daniel Leigh, and Suchanan Tambunlertchai.

[1] The evidence presented in the box draws on Díez, Leigh, and Tambunlertchai (2018), who calculate firm-level markups using the approach of De Loecker and Warzynski (2012) and De Loecker and Eeckhout (2017), and investigate the relationship between markups, investment, innovation, and the labor share of income at the firm level.

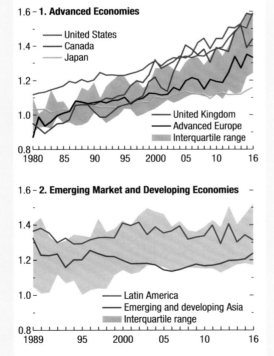

Figure 1.1.1. Market Power over Time
(Estimated markups)

Sources: Thomson Reuters Worldscope; and IMF staff calculations.
Note: Average markups of listed firms weighted by sales.

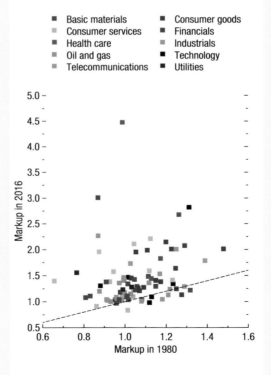

Figure 1.1.2. Markup Increase, by Subsector

Sources: Thomson Reuters Worldscope; and IMF staff calculations.
Note: Dashed line indicates 45-degree line along which markups are equal over time.

Box 1.1 *(continued)*

Figure 1.1.1 unveils two clear facts. First, markups among advanced economies have significantly increased since the 1980s, by 43 percent on average, and this trend has accelerated during the current decade. Second, emerging market and developing economies show less evidence of a rise in markups.[2]

The pattern of rising markups in advanced economies is found across all broad economic sectors. Figure 1.1.2 presents, for each narrowly defined economic subsector, the markup in 2016 compared with that in 1980, where the color refers to the corresponding 10 broad FTSE Russell Industry Classification Benchmark economic sectors. In the figure, a colored marker located above the 45-degree line indicates an increase in markups. Markups increased across almost all narrow sectors, but there is significant heterogeneity in the magnitudes of the increases. Markups more than doubled in the biotechnology, retail real estate investment trusts (retail REITs), consumer finance,

[2]This increase, documented by Díez, Leigh, and Tambunlertchai (2018), is also consistent with the findings by De Loecker and Eeckhout (2018). Furthermore, the increase in markups is accompanied by an increase in profits, strengthening the notion of increased corporate market power.

and software subsectors. In contrast, subsectors, such as auto parts, computer hardware, and electrical components and equipment, saw markups decline. So, while markups have generally increased since 1980, much cross-sector heterogeneity is observed.

Figure 1.1.4. Advanced Economies: Distribution of Markups of Firms, by Industry
(Kernel density)

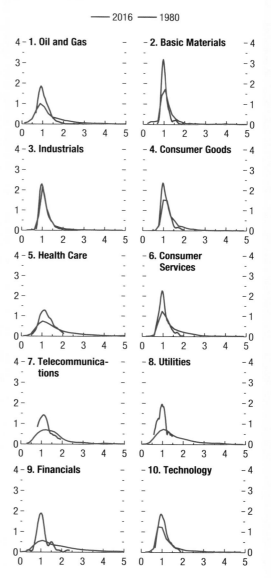

Sources: Thomson Reuters Worldscope; and IMF staff estimates.
Note: Results for 10 "industries" of the FTSE Russell Industrial Classification Benchmark from Thomson Reuters Worldscope. *X*-axis truncated at 5 for graphical clarity.

Figure 1.1.3. Advanced Economies: Distribution of Markups of All Firms
(Kernel density)

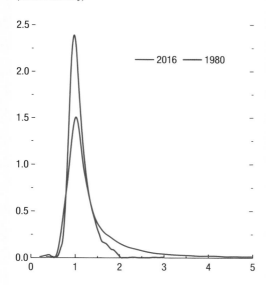

Sources: Thomson Reuters Worldscope; and IMF staff calculations.
Note: *X*-axis truncated at 5 for graphical clarity.

Box 1.1 *(continued)*

More in-depth analysis shows that the increase in market power in advanced economies is mostly driven by a fraction of "superstar" firms that have managed to extract especially large markups, while the market power of other firms has increased little since 1980. This fact implies that the rise in markups has been accompanied by an increasingly skewed distribution, not only at the aggregate level, but also within broad economic sectors (Figures 1.1.3 and 1.1.4).

This increase in corporate market power has important macroeconomic effects. Most strikingly, starting from low levels, higher markups are initially associated with increasing investment and innovation, but this relationship becomes negative when market power becomes too strong. The inverted U-shape relationship between competition on one hand and investment and innovation on the other is consistent with findings by Aghion and others (2005) and suggests that, at low levels of market power, firms invest to escape competition, whereas, at high levels of market power, firms have weaker incentives to invest because of the lack of competitive pressure. Furthermore, higher corporate market power also seems to be associated with lower labor shares: the fraction of firms' revenue going to workers decreases, while the share of revenue going to profits increases.

The ultimate policy implications will depend on the drivers of this increase in global market power, which are still being debated. The potential causes include, among others, the rise of intangible assets (for example, patents), network effects in the digital economy (see April 2018 *Fiscal Monitor*), and outdated or weaker enforcement of antitrust laws. More research is needed to disentangle the various factors at play.

Box 1.2. Growth Outlook: Advanced Economies

Advanced economies are projected to expand by 2.4 percent in 2018 (a marginally faster pace than in 2017) and 2.1 percent in 2019. Growth in advanced economies is expected to decline to 1.7 percent in 2020 as the US tax cuts are partially reversed, and to 1.5 percent in the medium term as working-age population growth continues to slow.

- Growth in the *United States* is expected to peak at 2.9 percent in 2018, supported by the procyclical fiscal stimulus after eight consecutive years of expansion and still-loose financial conditions (despite expected monetary tightening). Growth is expected to soften to 2.5 percent in 2019 (a downward revision of 0.2 percentage point relative to the April 2018 *World Economic Outlook* (WEO) due to the recently introduced trade measures) and to drop to 1.8 percent in 2020 as the fiscal stimulus begins to unwind. Strong domestic demand is projected to push the economy above full employment and increase imports and the current account deficit. Medium-term growth is forecast to temporarily decline below potential at 1.4 percent as the positive output gap is gradually closed.

- Growth is projected to remain strong in the *euro area*, but has been revised down by 0.4 percentage point to 2.0 percent for 2018, reflecting weaker-than-expected performance in the first half of the year. Growth is forecast to gradually slow further to 1.9 percent in 2019, 0.1 percentage point lower than the April forecast. Healthy consumer spending and job creation amid supportive monetary policy are expected to continue to provide strong aggregate demand, though at a moderating pace. Short-term profiles of country-specific growth rates vary. In *France*, growth is expected to moderate to 1.6 percent in 2018 and 2019, 0.5 (0.4) percentage point weaker than in the April 2018 WEO for 2018 (2019), reflecting softer external demand as well as lower outturns and high-frequency indicators in 2018. In *Germany*, growth was revised down to 1.9 percent in 2018 and 2019 (by 0.6 percentage point and 0.1 percentage point, respectively) because of a slowdown in exports and industrial production. *Italy*'s growth forecast is also lower than in the April 2018 WEO, estimated at 1.2 percent for 2018 and 1 percent

in 2019, because of the underlying deterioration in external and domestic demand and uncertainty about the new government's policy agenda. In *Spain*, growth is expected to be 2.7 percent in 2018 and 2.2 percent in 2019, which is a 0.1 percentage point decline relative to the April forecast for 2018, and no change for 2019. Medium-term growth in the *euro area,* projected at about 1.4 percent, is expected to be constrained by slow productivity growth and unfavorable demographics.

- In the *United Kingdom*, growth is projected to slow to 1.4 percent in 2018 and 1.5 percent in 2019 (from 1.7 percent in 2017). This forecast represents a downward revision of 0.2 percentage point for 2018 relative to the April 2018 WEO, driven by weak growth in the first quarter of the year, partly due to weather-related factors. The medium-term growth forecast remains at 1.6 percent, weighed down by the anticipated higher barriers to trade following Brexit. (Assumptions regarding the Brexit outcome remain broadly unchanged relative to the April 2018 and October 2017 WEOs. Tariffs on trade with the European Union are expected to remain at zero, and nontariff costs will likely increase moderately.)

- *Japan*'s growth is projected to moderate to 1.1 percent in 2018 (from a strong, above-trend outturn of 1.7 percent in 2017), before softening to 0.9 percent in 2019. The downward revision of 0.1 percentage point for 2018 relative to the April 2018 WEO is largely due to the contraction observed in the first quarter of 2018, and given the uptick in growth and domestic demand in the second quarter of 2018, this is likely to represent a temporary dip rather than the beginning of a turn in the cycle. Japan's medium-term prospects are impeded by unfavorable demographics and a trend decline in the labor force.

- Among other advanced economies, growth is projected to moderate in *Canada* to 2.1 percent in 2018 and 2.0 percent in 2019, and to exceed 3 percent in *Australia* in 2018, before declining to 2.8 percent in 2019. In *Korea*, growth is projected at 2.8 percent in 2018 and 2.6 percent in 2019. The downward revisions to the 2019 growth forecast for Australia and Korea relative to the April 2018 WEO partially reflect the negative effect of the recently introduced trade measures.

The author of this box is Natalija Novta.

Box 1.3. Growth Outlook: Emerging Market and Developing Economies

Growth in emerging market and developing economies is expected to remain steady at 4.7 percent in 2018–19, and to rise modestly over the medium term.

- In *China*, growth is projected to moderate from 6.9 percent in 2017 to 6.6 percent in 2018 and 6.2 percent in 2019, reflecting slowing external demand growth and necessary financial regulatory tightening. The 0.2 percentage point downgrade to the 2019 growth forecast is attributable to the negative effect of recent tariff actions, assumed to be partially offset by policy stimulus. Over the medium term, growth is expected to gradually slow to 5.6 percent as the economy continues to make the transition to a more sustainable growth path with continued financial de-risking and environmental controls.

- Growth is projected to remain strong elsewhere in emerging and developing Asia. *India*'s growth is expected to increase to 7.3 percent in 2018 and 7.4 percent in 2019 (slightly lower than in the April 2018 *World Economic Outlook* [WEO] for 2019, given the recent increase in oil prices and the tightening of global financial conditions), up from 6.7 percent in 2017. This acceleration reflects a rebound from transitory shocks (the currency exchange initiative and implementation of the national Goods and Services Tax), with strengthening investment and robust private consumption. India's medium-term growth prospects remain strong at 7¾ percent, benefiting from ongoing structural reform, but have been marked down by just under ½ percentage point relative to the April 2018 WEO. In the ASEAN-5 (*Indonesia, Malaysia, Philippines, Thailand, Vietnam*), growth is expected to be 5.3 percent in 2018, before softening to 5.2 percent in 2019. The 0.2 percentage point downward revision to the 2019 growth forecast reflects largely the economic costs of recent trade measures.

- Growth in *Latin America and the Caribbean* is projected to decrease from 1.3 percent in 2017 to 1.2 percent in 2018 and to rise to 2.2 percent in 2019, a more subdued recovery than envisaged in the April 2018 WEO.
  - *Mexico*'s growth is projected to increase from 2.0 percent in 2017 to 2.2 percent in 2018 and 2.5 percent in 2019, supported by higher US growth. The growth forecast is, however,

lower than expected in the April 2018 WEO, reflecting the impact on investment and domestic demand of prolonged uncertainty related to trade.
  - *Brazil*'s economy is expected to grow at 1.4 percent and 2.4 percent in 2018 and 2019, respectively, up from 1 percent growth in 2017, driven by a recovery of private demand as the output gap gradually closes. The growth forecast for 2018 is lower than in the April 2018 WEO by 0.9 percentage point on account of disruptions caused by the nationwide truck drivers' strike and tighter external financial conditions, which are a source of risk to the outlook. Growth is expected at 2.2 percent in the medium term.
  - After growing by 2.9 percent in 2017, *Argentina* is expected to contract by 2.6 percent in 2018, a large downward revision relative to the April 2018 WEO forecast, reflecting recent financial market disruptions, high real interest rates, and the faster fiscal consolidation under the exceptional access Stand-By Arrangement approved in June. The economy is expected to contract by a further 1.6 percent in 2019. Growth of 3.2 percent is expected over the medium term under the steady implementation of reforms and returning confidence.
  - *Venezuela*'s economy continues to decline for the fifth consecutive year, following a 14 percent drop in 2017. Real GDP is projected to shrink by 18 percent in 2018 and a further 5 percent in 2019, driven by plummeting oil production, and political and social instability.

- The outlook for the *Commonwealth of Independent States* is more favorable than in the April 2018 WEO, with growth for the region expected at 2.3 percent in 2018 and 2.4 percent in 2019 (up from 2.1 percent in 2017), moderating to 2.1 percent in the medium term. Growth in *Russia* is projected at 1.7 percent in 2018, up from 1.5 percent in 2017, supported by higher oil prices and recovering domestic demand. Medium-term growth is expected to remain muted at about 1.2 percent, absent structural reforms. Growth projections for *Kazakhstan* have been revised upward to 3.7 percent in 2018 and 3.1 percent in 2019, reflecting higher non-oil growth and increased oil production.

- Growth in *emerging and developing Europe* is projected to moderate from 6.0 percent in 2017

The authors of this box are Wenjie Chen and Zsóka Kóczán.

Box 1.3 *(continued)*

to 3.8 percent in 2018 and decline further to 2.0 percent in 2019 (well below the April 2018 WEO forecasts). *Poland* is in a strong cyclical upswing, with growth projected at 4.4 percent in 2018 (revised up by 0.3 percentage point since the April 2018 WEO, reflecting stronger-than-expected investment growth), though it is expected to moderate to 3.5 percent in 2019 and 2.8 percent in the medium term, held back by adverse demographics and structural bottlenecks. *Romania*'s economy grew at a robust 6.9 percent in 2017 on fiscal stimulus and strong external demand. Growth is expected to decline to 4 percent in 2018 and further to 3.4 percent in 2019 (1.1 and 0.1 percentage points lower than in the April 2018 WEO) as the stimulus moderates. Growth in *Turkey* was very strong in 2017 and early 2018, but is expected to slow sharply. Real GDP growth is projected at 3.5 percent in 2018 but to drop to 0.4 percent in 2019 (some 3.6 percentage points lower for 2019 than in the April 2018 WEO) as the weaker lira, higher borrowing costs, and elevated uncertainty weigh on investment and consumer demand. Turkey's economy remains highly vulnerable to sudden shifts in capital flows and geopolitical risks.

• Growth is on the mend for *sub-Saharan Africa*, with the region's average growth projected to rise to 3.1 percent in 2018 (from 2.7 percent in 2017) and 3.8 percent in 2019. The growth forecast for 2018 is 0.3 percentage point lower than the April 2018 WEO forecast. The acceleration relative to 2016–17 reflects a more supportive external environment, including stronger global growth, higher commodity prices, and improved capital market access, following efforts to improve fiscal balances in the aftermath of the commodity price slump. Growth performance varies, however, across countries. About half of the expected pickup in growth between 2017 and 2018 reflects the growth rebound in *Nigeria*. Nigeria's growth is projected to increase from 0.8 percent in 2017 to 1.9 percent in 2018 and 2.3 percent in 2019 (0.4 percentage point higher than in the April 2018 WEO for 2019), buoyed by the impact of recovering oil production and prices. In *Angola*, the region's second largest oil exporter, real GDP is expected to shrink by 0.1 percent in 2018, following a 2.5 percent contraction in 2017, but is projected to increase by 3.1 percent in 2019, with the recovery driven by a more efficient foreign currency allocation system and additional

availability of foreign currency due to higher oil prices. Meanwhile, in *South Africa*, prospects remain modest amid uncertainty in the run-up to the 2019 general elections, with growth projected to fall to 0.8 percent in 2018 from 1.3 percent in 2017, before recovering to 1.8 percent in the medium term. The pace of structural reform implementation and the level of policy credibility will determine the extent of economic recovery.

• In the *Middle East, North Africa, Afghanistan, and Pakistan* region, growth is projected to increase from 2.2 percent in 2017 to 2.4 percent in 2018 and to 2.7 percent in 2019, stabilizing at about 3 percent in the medium term—a sizable downward revision compared with the April 2018 WEO forecast. The downward revisions reflect to an important extent the worsening of growth prospects for *Iran*, following the reimposition of US sanctions. The economy is now forecast to contract in 2018 (–1.5 percent) and especially in 2019 (–3.6 percent) on account of reduced oil production, before returning to modest positive growth in 2020–23. Elsewhere, in *Saudi Arabia*, following a 0.9 percent contraction in 2017, output is projected to expand by 2.2 percent in 2018 and 2.4 percent in 2019 (0.5 percentage point higher for both years than in the April 2018 WEO), driven by a pickup in non-oil economic activity and a projected increase in crude oil production in line with the revised Organization of the Petroleum Exporting Countries Plus agreement. Growth in *Egypt* is projected to rise to 5.3 percent in 2018 and 5.5 percent in 2019, up from 4.2 percent in 2017, reflecting a recovery in tourism, rising natural gas production, and continued improvements in confidence due to implementation of an ambitious reform program supported by the IMF's Extended Fund Facility. Growth in *Pakistan* is expected to strengthen from 5.4 percent in 2017 to 5.8 percent in 2018 (0.2 percentage point higher than in the April 2018 WEO), underpinned by improved energy supply, investment related to the China-Pakistan Economic Corridor, and strong credit growth. However, macroeconomic stability gains have been eroding, putting the outlook at risk. Growth is expected to moderate to 4.0 percent in 2019, and slow to about 3.0 percent in the medium term. The medium-term growth revisions for Pakistan, together with those for *Iran* and a sizable markdown in prospects for *Sudan*, explain the lower projected growth for the region beyond 2019.

Box 1.4. Inflation Outlook: Regions and Countries

Inflation in advanced economies is projected at 2.0 percent in 2018, up from 1.7 percent in 2017. Inflation in emerging market and developing economies excluding Venezuela is expected to increase to 5.0 percent this year, up from 4.3 percent in 2017. These weighted averages mask significant heterogeneity across countries depending on their cyclical positions as well as the impact of currency depreciations and rising energy prices.

Advanced Economies

- In the *United States*, headline consumer price inflation is projected to increase to 2.4 percent in 2018 and 2.1 in 2019, from 2.1 percent in 2017. Core personal consumption expenditure price inflation, the Federal Reserve's preferred measure, is expected to be 2.1 percent in 2018 and 2.3 percent in 2019 compared with 1.6 percent in 2017, as output climbs above potential following the sizable fiscal expansion. This projection slightly exceeds current Federal Reserve projections and suggests earlier-than-anticipated overshooting of the Federal Reserve's target inflation rate. Toward the end of the projection horizon (2022–23), inflation is assumed to decline to the target, thanks to a monetary policy response that will keep expectations and actual inflation well anchored.

- Headline inflation in the *euro area* is expected to be 1.7 percent in 2018 and 2019. With the recovery boosting growth above potential for 2018–19, core inflation is expected to increase to 1.2 percent in 2018 and 1.6 percent in 2019, up from 1.1 percent in 2017. The core harmonized index of consumer prices is projected to increase slowly to 2 percent by 2022, given a strong backward-looking element in the euro area inflation process.

- In *Japan*, headline inflation is expected to increase to 1.2 percent in 2018, up from 0.5 percent in 2017, again mainly due to rising global energy prices. Inflation excluding fresh food and energy prices is expected to rise to 0.5 percent in 2018 and further to 0.8 percent in 2019, up from 0.1 percent in 2017. Inflation is still expected to remain below the Bank of Japan's target over the five-year forecast horizon, given tepid wage growth and stickiness in inflation expectations.

- In the *United Kingdom*, as the pass-through effects of the pound depreciation fade, core inflation is expected to decline to 2.1 percent in 2018, down from 2.4 percent in 2017, and is expected to stabilize at its medium-term level of 2.0 percent in early 2020. Headline inflation is expected to edge down to 2.5 percent

in 2018, from 2.7 percent in 2017, with a gradual convergence to 2 percent projected in 2020.

Emerging Market and Developing Economies

- Headline inflation in *China* is expected to pick up to 2.2 percent this year, up from 1.6 percent in 2017, and to about 3 percent over the medium term, driven by higher food and energy prices. Inflation in *India* is on the rise, estimated at 3.6 percent in fiscal year 2017/18 and projected at 4.7 percent in fiscal year 2018/19, compared with 4.5 percent in fiscal year 2016/17, amid accelerating demand and rising fuel prices.

- In *Mexico,* inflation is projected to continue to fall—to 4.8 percent in 2018—and to converge toward the central bank's 3 percent target in 2020, as monetary policy remains tight. In contrast, inflation is projected to accelerate in *Brazil* to 3.7 percent in 2018 and 4.2 percent in 2019, as monetary policy remains supportive and food price inflation rebounds after a notable drop caused by an exceptional harvest in 2017. In *Argentina,* inflation is expected to reach 31.8 percent in 2018, driven by the significant currency depreciation, and to remain at broadly the same level (31.7 percent) in 2019. *Venezuela*'s hyperinflation is expected to worsen rapidly, fueled by monetary financing of large fiscal deficits and loss of confidence in the currency.

- *Russia*'s inflation, expected to average 2.8 percent in 2018, is below the target of 4 percent, driven by moderately tight monetary policy. However, it is projected to rise to 5.1 percent in 2019, supported by an ongoing recovery in domestic demand, higher fuel prices, and pass-through from the recent depreciation. *Turkey*'s inflation is projected at 15 percent in 2018 and 16.7 percent in 2019, reflecting pass-through from the lira's depreciation, higher energy prices, high wage growth, and unanchored inflation expectations.

- Inflation pressures in *sub-Saharan Africa* have broadly softened, with annual inflation projected to drop to 8.6 percent in 2018 and 8.5 percent in 2019, from 11 percent in 2017. In *South Africa*, inflation has moderated to 4.8 percent in 2018 from 5.3 percent in 2017 with the easing of drought conditions, but is expected to edge back to 5.3 percent in 2019 as temporary disinflationary effects subside. In *Nigeria* and *Angola*, tighter monetary policy and moderation in food price increases contributed to tapering inflation. In *Nigeria*, inflation is projected to fall to 12.4 percent in 2018, from 16.5 percent in 2017, and to rise to 13.5 percent in 2019. In *Angola*, inflation is projected to fall to 20.5 percent in 2018 from 29.8 percent in 2017 and to decline further to 15.8 percent in 2019.

The authors of this box are Wenjie Chen, Zsóka Kóczán, and Natalija Novta.

Box 1.5. Sharp GDP Declines: Some Stylized Facts

A number of countries, including Greece, have suffered very large declines in GDP per capita in the aftermath of the global financial crisis. In some countries affected by conflict, such as Libya, South Sudan, Syria, and Yemen, ongoing declines in GDP per capita have been staggering.[1] In Venezuela, GDP per capita is estimated to have declined by more than 35 percent over 2013–17 and is projected to decline by close to 60 percent between 2013 and 2023. Are these episodes rare occurrences? To address this question, this box documents the frequency and characteristics of large declines in GDP per capita over the past 50 years. It shows that such episodes are unfortunately not rare. They tend to be protracted and originate from a variety of sources, and the post-trough recovery, in many cases, is insufficient to even restore the starting level of GDP per capita.

The chosen threshold (a decline in GDP per capita of at least 20 percent from peak to trough) is designed to isolate extreme episodes, typically occurring over several years, rather than more frequent cases of macroeconomic distress (caused, for example, by a financial or exchange rate crisis).

There is a vast literature on the macroeconomic implications of different types of crises (financial, external, currency, banking, fiscal). While these crises are typically associated with severe macroeconomic distress, such distress rarely causes a decline in the level of GDP exceeding 20 percent. The literature on large GDP declines is relatively small. An important study in this respect is by Becker and Mauro (2006), who examine output drops in a large panel of countries and systematically relate them to a variety of shocks (terms-of-trade declines, financial shocks, wars, and so on). A related literature looks at large declines in GDP and consumption ("disasters") with the objective of calibrating the impact of these rare events on financial market variables such as equity premiums (see, for instance, Barro and Ursua 2008; Barro and Jin 2011; Nakamura and others 2013). These studies typically rely on long time series data (stretching to the

early 19th century) for advanced economies and a few emerging markets.[2]

There are four main causes, often intertwined, of GDP declines in the sample under consideration. These include strife (war, civil war, armed rebellion), commodity shocks,[3] crises (including banking crises, external crises, and so on), and the transition from a centrally planned to a market economy. Misguided macroeconomic policies during the episodes play a role in a number of cases as well, often interacting with other factors. Prime examples are cases of hyperinflation, including the ongoing case of Venezuela. Declines attributable to other causes (for example, natural disasters) are much less frequent—the one example in the sample is the 2015 Ebola epidemic in Sierra Leone.

Stylized Facts on Sharp GDP Declines

The 133 episodes of large GDP per capita declines identified in the period 1960–2017 are listed in Table 1.5.1.[4]

They affect 92 countries (a number of them repeatedly).[5] Figure 1.5.1 depicts the number of ongoing episodes of sharp declines in GDP per capita by year, as well as the share of countries affected (in relation to the total number with available data). The figure indicates that the lion's share of episodes took place during the 1980s, following the global economic

---

The author of this box is Gian Maria Milesi-Ferretti.

[1] Data for Syria since the start of the conflict are not available, but estimates presented in Gobat and Kostial (2016) and WB (2017) point to a dramatic collapse in GDP exceeding 50 percent.

[2] Applying the same definition of output declines to the Barro and Ursua (2008) data set yields episodes concentrated around the two World Wars and the Great Depression.

[3] The "shock" can be a decline in a country's export prices (such as oil price declines affecting fuel exporters), or a decline in domestic production (for instance, declining oil production in Timor-Leste in recent years or dwindling phosphate deposits in Kiribati in the 1970s).

[4] It should be kept in mind that data availability is spotty for the earlier part of the sample and that data limitations are severe, particularly for low-income countries. These limitations can become even more severe during periods of distress, such as those studied in this box.

[5] The length of an episode is measured as the number of years between a peak in GDP per capita and its subsequent trough, as long as the peak-to-trough decline in GDP per capita is at least 20 percent. If GDP per capita falls substantially below a previous trough within a few years of that trough the episode is deemed a continuation of the preceding one. Otherwise, the episode is potentially considered a distinct one (as long as GDP per capita falls by at least 20 percent between the new peak and the new trough).

Box 1.5 *(continued)*

Table 1.5.1. Episodes of Declines in GDP per Capita Exceeding 20 Percent

	Peak	Trough	GDP per capita at peak	Percent change in GDP per capita		Peak	Trough	GDP per capita at peak	Percent change in GDP per capita
Albania	1989	1992	2,193	−41	Guinea-Bissau	1997	1999	732	−30
Algeria	1960	1962	2,466	−34	Guyana	1976	1984	2,156	−28
Andorra	1974	1994	44,648	−27	Haiti	1980	1994	1,106	−38
Andorra	2006	2012	49,708	−23	Iran	1976	1981	10,266	−57
Angola	1974	1982	3,029	−31	Iran	1983	1988	5,557	−34
Angola	1988	1994	2,248	−41	Iraq	1980	1985	3,346	−22
Antigua and Barbuda	2007	2011	15,467	−24	Iraq	1990	1991	4,079	−65
Argentina	1980	1990	8,053	−26	Iraq	1999	2003	4,379	−42
Argentina	1998	2002	8,729	−22	Jamaica	1972	1980	5,368	−32
Armenia	1990	1993	1,797	−51	Jordan	1986	1991	3,270	−28
Azerbaijan	1990	1995	3,119	−61	Kazakhstan	1990	1995	5,890	−37
The Bahamas	1969	1975	27,539	−39	Kiribati	1975	1981	4,521	−54
Bahrain	1978	1986	21,788	−24	Kiribati	1984	1995	2,225	−27
Bangladesh	1970	1972	406	−22	Kuwait	1971	1975	84,352	−26
Belarus	1990	1995	3,102	−35	Kuwait	1979	1982	64,424	−50
Bolivia	1977	1986	1,745	−26	Kuwait	1989	1991	32,605	−33
Brunei Darussalam	1979	1993	66,002	−44	Kuwait	1993	2001	49,737	−30
Burundi	1991	2005	338	−35	Kuwait	2007	2017	49,589	−32
Cameroon	1986	1994	1,834	−42	Kyrgyz Republic	1990	1995	1,096	−51
Central African Republic	1977	1983	625	−22	Lebanon	1973	1976	10,752	−71
					Lebanon	1981	1982	5,653	−37
Central African Republic	1986	1996	530	−24	Lebanon	1987	1989	8,287	−59
					Liberia	1979	1995	1,575	−93
Central African Republic	2012	2013	476	−37	Liberia	2002	2003	395	−31
					Libya	1979	1988	24,382	−61
Chad	1962	1973	715	−25	Libya	1991	2002	12,012	−30
Chad	1977	1981	593	−32	Libya	2010	2011	12,121	−62
Chile	1971	1975	5,001	−22	Libya	2012	2016	10,209	−43
China	1960	1962	192	−31	Macao SAR	2013	2016	72,184	−28
Comoros	1984	1999	938	−20	Madagascar	1971	2002	755	−50
Congo, Democratic Republic of the	1974	1983	1,134	−29	Malawi	1979	1994	417	−24
					Maldives	1972	1978	2,645	−26
Congo, Democratic Republic of the	1986	2002	832	−67	Marshall Islands	1995	1999	3,176	−22
					Mauritania	1970	1994	1,296	−25
Congo, Republic of	1984	1999	3,292	−31	Moldova	1992	1999	1,611	−41
Côte d'Ivoire	1978	1994	2,392	−47	Mongolia	1989	1993	1,856	−27
Cuba	1985	1993	4,480	−38	Mozambique	1981	1986	195	−33
Cyprus	1973	1975	11,321	−33	Myanmar	1985	1988	240	−20
Djibouti	1990	2001	1,932	−37	Nicaragua	1977	1979	2,565	−36
El Salvador	1978	1986	3,157	−35	Nicaragua	1981	1993	1,704	−38
Equatorial Guinea	1980	1991	646	−25	Niger	1965	1976	716	−37
Equatorial Guinea	2008	2017	20,334	−44	Niger	1979	1984	545	−31
Eritrea	1997	2008	622	−24	Niger	1988	2000	408	−21
Ethiopia	1987	1992	223	−27	Nigeria	1965	1968	1,459	−25
Gabon	1976	1982	19,493	−40	Nigeria	1977	1987	2,040	−44
Gabon	1984	1987	12,666	−26	Papua New Guinea	1973	1990	1,943	−23
Gabon	1998	2009	11,926	−29	Papua New Guinea	1994	2003	2,105	−23
Georgia	1990	1994	3,525	−73	Peru	1987	1992	3,791	−31
Ghana	1971	1976	1,121	−20	Qatar	1973	1991	115,147	−67
Ghana	1978	1983	960	−27	Russian Federation	1990	1998	9,534	−42
Greece	2007	2013	30,055	−26	Rwanda	1962	1964	340	−24

(continued)

Box 1.5 *(continued)*

Table 1.5.1. (continued)

	Peak	Trough	GDP per capita at peak	Percent change in GDP per capita		Peak	Trough	GDP per capita at peak	Percent change in GDP per capita
Rwanda	1992	1994	401	−49	Togo	1980	1983	683	−21
San Marino	2008	2015	84,794	−38	Togo	1989	1993	561	−27
São Tomé and Príncipe	1980	1993	1,352	−36	Trinidad and Tobago	1982	1989	9,856	−34
					Turkmenistan	1990	1997	3,713	−49
Saudi Arabia	1974	1987	39,125	−60	Uganda	1970	1980	407	−30
Senegal	1961	1994	1,083	−27	Ukraine	1990	1998	3,965	−57
Sierra Leone	1982	2001	502	−45	United Arab Emirates	1970	1978	126,104	−26
Sierra Leone	2014	2015	563	−22	United Arab Emirates	1980	1988	113,682	−50
Solomon Islands	1979	1986	1,643	−24	United Arab Emirates	1997	2010	64,176	−45
Solomon Islands	1995	2002	1,655	−36	Uruguay	1981	1984	7,420	−21
South Sudan	2011	2012	3,111	−54	Uzbekistan	1990	1996	997	−27
South Sudan	2013	2017	1,789	−26	Venezuela	1977	1985	15,557	−24
St. Vincent and the Grenadines	1972	1975	2,319	−28	Venezuela	1997	2003	12,787	−24
					Venezuela	2012	2017	14,474	−37
Sudan	1962	1973	900	−22	West Bank and Gaza	1999	2002	2,683	−23
Sudan	1977	1985	984	−28	Yemen	2010	2017	1,309	−70
Suriname	1978	1987	8,724	−38	Zambia	1972	1994	1,613	−44
Tajikistan	1990	1996	1,278	−71	Zimbabwe	1974	1978	1,347	−21
Timor-Leste	2012	2014	4,058	−37	Zimbabwe	1998	2008	1,348	−56

Source: IMF staff calculations based on data from the World Economic Outlook and World Bank World Development Indicators databases.
Note: Peak indicates the year before the decline in GDP per capita begins, and trough the year in which GDP per capita is at the lowest level in the episode. GDP per capita at peak indicates GDP per capita in constant 2010 US dollars the year before the decline starts (source: World Bank). "Percent change in GDP per capita" indicates the percent change in per capita GDP from peak to trough.

downturn and the 1982 debt crisis. The number of episodes declined in the late 1980s but rose again in the early 1990s because of the GDP declines associated with the transition to a market economy in countries of the former Soviet Union and in central and eastern Europe. The number of ongoing episodes has since declined sharply, despite some increase associated with the global financial crisis and its aftermath. Episodes associated with war are the most frequent, followed by commodity shocks, crises, and transition.

Table 1.5.2 provides some stylized facts on these downturn episodes. It shows mean and median declines in GDP per capita of more than one-third. These episodes are typically protracted, lasting over five years, and the growth rate in the five years after the end of the episode generally fails to return GDP per capita to its predecline level. Distinguishing among episodes according to their main driving factor suggests that for the median country in episodes involving wars, GDP and GDP per capita are lower, the median duration of the episode is shorter (4.5 years), and the

increase in GDP per capita after the crisis is larger (some 15 percent). Transition episodes feature the largest median decline in GDP per capita (45 percent), a relatively short duration (five years), and an increase in GDP per capita after the crisis of about 14 percent. The median crises and commodity shock episodes last longer and have weaker postdecline rebounds in GDP per capita.

The Aftermath of GDP Declines

The focus now turns to the speed at which GDP per capita rebounds after these sharp declines. For that purpose, the analysis considers both the growth rate in the five years following a trough as well as the length of time it takes for countries to return to their predecline levels of GDP, and explores whether these variables are correlated with basic characteristics of the episodes: the initial level of development, the size of the country, the extent of the GDP decline, and the duration of the episode. Constructing these postdecline variables reveals a striking stylized fact: out of the 92 countries experiencing a sharp decline in GDP

Box 1.5 *(continued)*

Figure 1.5.1. Ongoing Episodes of Large Declines in GDP per Capita (20 percent or more)

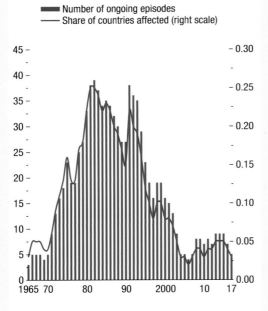

Source: IMF staff calculations.

per capita in the sample, 45 had GDP per capita in 2017 still below its predecline level.[6] These countries account for over 5 percent of global GDP at purchasing power parity in 2017, and about 7½ percent

---

[6]Using the data from the *World Economic Outlook* projection period changes results only slightly—three countries (Djibouti, Kyrgyz Republic, Sierra Leone) are projected to reach their precollapse levels of GDP per capita during 2018–23 but Sudan is projected to experience a more than 20 percent decline in GDP per capita during the projection period.

of world population. They are predominantly small. Exceptions include Iran, Ukraine, Venezuela, and some economies in the Gulf Cooperation Council with high GDP per capita that have experienced very rapid population growth, including because of immigration (Kuwait, Qatar, Saudi Arabia, United Arab Emirates). Excluding these four countries, those countries still below their past peak in GDP per capita account for about 3 percent of global GDP.

• Table 1.5.3 presents the results of simple regression analyses. In columns (1) and (2), the dependent variable is the growth rate in the five years after a trough; in columns (3) and (4), it is the number of years following the trough it takes for GDP per capita to return to its level immediately before the collapse. The purpose of these regressions is simply to identify correlations in the data—there are clearly many omitted factors that can play a role in explaining postcollapse economic performance, ranging from economic policies to the external environment (growth in trading partners, terms of trade, and so on). With those caveats in mind, a surprising result is that the postdecline growth rate is uncorrelated with the extent of the previous change in GDP per capita, holding constant the length of the episode. In other words, deeper downturns are not followed by sharper recoveries. However, the postdecline growth rate is strongly negatively correlated with the length of that decline. The regressions also suggest that, on average, recoveries tend to be weaker in smaller countries, consistent with the evidence on challenges to economic performance in small states. The sample size for the second set of regressions, in which the dependent variable is the number of years it takes to return to the predecline level of GDP per capita, is considerably smaller given that, as mentioned above, many countries have not yet reached that predecline level.

Table 1.5.2. Declines in GDP per Capita: Stylized Facts

	Mean	Median	Standard Deviation	Observations
GDP per Capita at Beginning of Episode (in constant 2010 US dollars)	11,933	2,466	23,639	133
Percent Change in GDP per Capita in the Five Years before the Peak	24	14	34	101
Percent Change in GDP per Capita Peak to Trough	−36	−32	14	133
Length of Episode of GDP Decline in Years	8	6	6	133
Percent Change in GDP per Capita in the Five Years after the Trough	14	11	18	121
Number of Years to Return to Predecline GDP per Capita	12	10	7	70

Source: IMF staff calculations based on data from the World Economic Outlook and World Bank World Development Indicators databases.

Box 1.5 *(continued)*

Table 1.5.3. Postcrisis Outcomes and Crisis Depth

	Cumulative Growth in the Five Years after the Trough		Number of Years to Return to Precrisis Peak	
	(1)	(2)	(3)	(4)
Log GDP per Capita at Peak	−0.70	0.01	−1.41**	−1.13*
	(−0.72)	(0.01)	(−2.28)	(−1.86)
Log GDP at Peak	1.75***	1.39**	−0.25	−0.15
	(2.77)	(2.08)	(−0.62)	(−0.40)
Change in GDP per Capita	0.02	−0.02	−0.11*	−0.12**
(peak to trough)	(0.33)	(−0.23)	(−1.68)	(−2.13)
Length of GDP Decline (years)	−0.61***	−0.79***	0.39**	0.47***
	(−2.84)	(−3.37)	(2.57)	(3.57)
Adjusted R^2	0.09	0.15	0.11	0.16
Number of Observations	120	102	69	64

Source: IMF staff calculations based on data from the World Economic Outlook and World Bank World Development Indicators databases.
Note: Robust errors in parenthesis. *** (**) indicate statistical significance at the 99 (95) percent confidence level. Columns (2) and (4) exclude episodes when the five years after the trough include the beginning of a new GDP decline episode.

For this more restricted sample, results suggest that, as expected, it takes longer to recover from deeper and longer-duration GDP declines. They also suggest that GDP per capita in poorer countries takes longer to recover from sharp declines. These results warrant a closer look at these episodes of large declines in GDP per capita and their driving factors in future research.

Box 1.6. Predicting Recessions and Slowdowns: A Daunting Task

Statistical models generally have limited success in accurately predicting recessions—a decline in the level of GDP.[1] *World Economic Outlook* (WEO) forecasts might be expected to do better, given that they also incorporate judgment about how policies, external factors, and recent economic news affect economies' growth trajectories. However, an analysis of WEO and private sector forecasts over 1991–2016 confirms the difficulties of forecasting recessions.[2]

The number of economies experiencing negative growth in any given year has been systematically underpredicted in the October WEO forecasts of the previous year, both for advanced economies and emerging market and developing economies (Figure 1.6.1). While the average country in the sample experienced 2.7 recessions during 1991–2016, out of the 313 recessions in a sample of 117 economies, only 47 have been anticipated.[3] Even for 2009, the year after global output shrank when Lehman Brothers collapsed, only six advanced economies (and no emerging market and developing economies) had been predicted in the October 2008 WEO to enter into a recession; subsequently, output was estimated to have contracted in 56 (almost half) of the economies in the sample.[4] The accuracy in predicting a switch from positive (or zero) to negative growth has been even lower: only nine out of 212 "new" recessions were accurately forecast between 1991 and 2016.

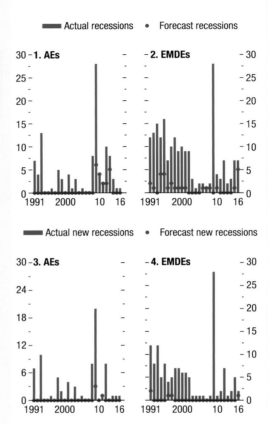

Figure 1.6.1. World Economic Outlook Data: Recessions, Actual and Forecast
(Number of countries)

Source: IMF staff calculations.
Note: AEs = advanced economies; EMDEs = emerging market and developing economies. In the top two panels, dots denote the number of recessions (output contractions) forecast in the October WEO of the previous year; bars denote the number of actual recessions (based on the October WEO estimates of the subsequent year). In the bottom two panels, dots denote the number of new recessions forecast in the October WEO of the previous year; bars denote the number of actual new recessions (based on the October WEO estimates of the subsequent year). New recessions are years in which growth turns from nonnegative to negative.

The author of this box is Francesco Grigoli. Jungjin Lee and Jillian Zirnhelt provided research support.

[1]See, for example, Estrella and Mishkin (1998); Berge and Jordà (2011); Levanon (2011); Liu and Moench (2014); Ng (2014); Bluedorn, Decressin, and Terrones (2016); and Ergungor (2016). Stock and Watson (2003) provide a review of the variables generally used to predict recessions.

[2]IMF forecasts represent the growth outcome seen as most likely by IMF staff; that is, the mode, rather than the mean, of the distribution of expected growth.

[3]The analysis is based on annual data, which are available for most of the member countries. Observations corresponding to years in which natural disasters caused damage of at least 1 percent of GDP, data for economies that had at least one conflict during 1991–2017, and data for economies with average populations smaller than 1 million people are excluded from the WEO data set.

[4]Forecasts are formulated based on the information set available in real time, hence ex post assessments of the forecasts' accuracy should rely on first estimates rather than the latest estimates of actual data. The use of revised data would unfairly underestimate the forecasts' accuracy, given that real GDP growth is generally revised downward over time.

The unsatisfactory record, however, is common across forecasters. Data from Consensus Economics, reflecting the average of private forecasters' expectations for 44 economies (as of October of the previous year), reveal a pattern that is strikingly comparable to that of the WEO forecasts (Figure 1.6.2). For

Box 1.6 *(continued)*

Figure 1.6.2. Consensus Economics Data: Recessions, Actual and Forecast
(Number of countries)

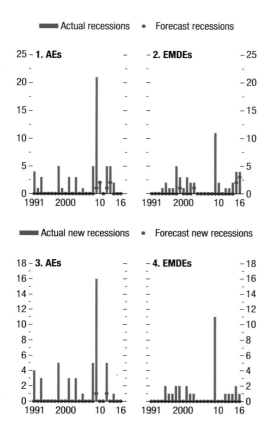

Source: IMF staff calculations.
Note: AEs = advanced economies; EMDEs = emerging market and developing economies. In the top two panels, dots denote the number of recessions (output contractions) forecast in the October Consensus Economics of the previous year; bars denote the actual number of recessions (based on the October Consensus Economics estimates of the subsequent year). In the bottom two panels, dots denote the number of new recessions forecasted in the October Consensus Economics of the previous year; bars denote the number of actual new recessions (based on the October Consensus Economics estimates of the subsequent year). New recessions are years in which growth turns from nonnegative to negative.

this restricted sample of 44 economies through 1991–2016, the WEO and Consensus Economics forecasts projected a similar number of recessions, 16 and 13, respectively, out of 107 cases of negative GDP growth. In 2009, only one advanced economy was projected to fall into recession, but by the end of the

year output had contracted in 32 economies. Going back to the full period under analysis, if one exclusively considers the instances in which the economies were not already in a recession in the previous year, Consensus Economics predicted only two out of 75 "new" recessions in its forecasts.

The poor track record of predicting recessions is symptomatic of the overall difficulty of forecasting slowdowns in growth. WEO forecasts do a somewhat better job of predicting slowdowns—defined as declines in the rate of real GDP growth—compared with recessions. Across all economies over 1991–2016, growth slowdowns occurred about half of the time, and about half of those were accurately forecast (in the sense that the WEO forecasts predicted a decline in growth for that year). The predictive performance was somewhat better in 2009, when three-fourths of the 96 slowdowns were correctly predicted. However, restricting the 1991–2016 sample to "new" slowdowns reveals that the direction of the change in growth is correctly anticipated only about half of the time.

The slowdown metric does not distinguish between *mild* slowdowns and *severe* ones. Focusing only on severe slowdowns—defined as episodes in which real GDP growth fell by more than the 75th percentile of growth declines in the sample period—is an alternative approach. To account for differences in growth volatility across advanced economies and emerging market and developing economies, thresholds are based on group-specific distributions, leading to the exclusion of growth declines smaller than 0.5 percentage point and 0.6 percentage point in the two groups, respectively.[5] Over 1991–2016, the average country faced 9.3 severe slowdowns, and the count of severe slowdowns in the sample reached 1,040 (Figure 1.6.3). In these episodes, declines in growth were anticipated in 54 percent of the cases, while severe slowdowns (slowdowns of 0.5–0.6 percentage point or more) were forecast only in 31 percent.[6]

---

[5]The standard deviation of real GDP growth during severe slowdowns ranges between 2.6 percentage points in Latin America and the Caribbean and 4.4 percentage points in the Commonwealth of Independent States. Despite this, the results are qualitatively unchanged if the 75th percentiles are calculated using country-specific distributions.

[6]A severe slowdown is defined as being "anticipated" if the forecast decline in growth is at least 0.5 percentage point for advanced economies and 0.6 percentage point for emerging market and developing economies.

Box 1.6 *(continued)*

Figure 1.6.3. Severe Slowdowns, Actual and Forecast
(Number of countries)

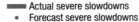

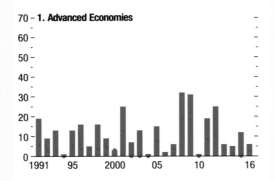

Source: IMF staff calculations.
Note: WEO = *World Economic Outlook*. Bars denote the number of severe slowdowns (growth declines larger than 0.5 percentage point and 0.6 percentage point for advanced economies and emerging market and developing economies, respectively) in the October WEO of the previous year; dots denote the number of forecasted severe slowdowns (based on the October WEO estimates of the subsequent year).

Figure 1.6.4. Forecast Errors during Severe Slowdowns
(Percentage points)

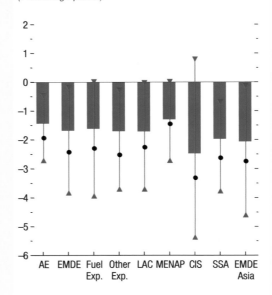

Source: IMF staff calculations.
Note: AE = advanced economies; CIS = Commonwealth of Independent States; EMDE = emerging market and developing economies; Fuel exp. = fuel exporters; LAC = Latin America and the Caribbean; MENAP = Middle East, North Africa, and Pakistan; Other exp. = other exporters; SSA = sub-Saharan Africa; WEO = *World Economic Outlook*. Bars denote the median of the real GDP growth forecast errors (calculated as the estimate for growth in year t as of the October WEO of year $t+1$ minus the forecast for growth in year t as of the October WEO of year $t-1$) during severe slowdowns. The vertical lines and the dots denote the interquartile ranges and the averages, respectively.

Errors in forecasting growth tend to be larger in years of severe slowdowns than in other years. The median forecast error (defined as actual minus predicted growth) during severe slowdowns is –1.6 percentage points, revealing a positive bias in the forecasts for those years (the median forecast error is –0.2 percentage point for nonsevere, or mild, slowdowns; –0.2 percentage point if all observations are considered; and 0.5 percentage point for nonslowdown years). Across groups, the median forecast error during severe slowdowns is –1.4 percentage points for

advanced economies and –1.7 percentage points for emerging market and developing economies (Figure 1.6.4). Across regions in the latter group, it ranges between –2.5 percentage points in the Commonwealth of Independent States and –1.3 percentage points in the Middle East, North Africa, Afghanistan, and Pakistan.[7]

In years of synchronized slowdowns, accurately predicting the growth rate of advanced economies helps improve the accuracy of growth predictions for other economies. Severe slowdowns appear more

[7]Means and medians of the forecast errors for all groups are different from zero at the 10 percent significance level, except the median for emerging and developing Asia.

Box 1.6 *(continued)*

Figure 1.6.5. Forecast Performance
(Percent)

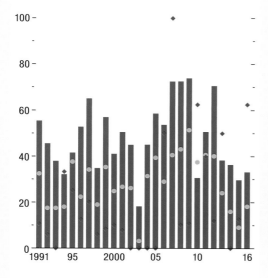

- ▬ Ratio of correctly forecast slowdowns
- ◆ Ratio of correctly forecast recessions
- ● Ratio of correctly forecast severe slowdowns

Source: IMF staff calculations.

synchronized in some years. For instance, in 2001, 2008, 2009, and 2012, more than 20 (40) advanced economies (emerging market and developing economies) experienced a significant decline in growth. The median decline in growth in these years was as large as 2.7 percentage points, almost 1 percentage point larger than for the severe slowdowns that occurred in other years, consistent with a larger drag from weaker external demand during synchronized slowdowns. Forecast errors were larger, at –2.4 percentage points, in these episodes, compared with –1.3 percentage points for other severe slowdowns. A simple regression of the probability of accurately predicting a severe slowdown in emerging market and developing economies on the share of the correctly predicted severe slowdowns in advanced economies suggests that, if severe slowdowns in advanced economies are missed, the chances of successfully predicting severe slowdowns elsewhere are significantly reduced.[8]

All in all, WEO forecasts perform somewhat better in predicting growth slowdowns than in predicting recessions, but the record leaves much room for improvement in both cases, and forecast errors during episodes of severe slowdowns are large (Figure 1.6.5).

[8]Probit regressions reveal that a 1 percentage point increase in the share of correctly predicted severe slowdowns in advanced economies is associated with a 29 percent higher probability of accurately predicting a severe slowdown in emerging market and developing economies.

Special Feature: Commodity Market Developments and Forecasts with a Focus on Recent Trends in Energy Demand

Energy prices have increased since the release of the April 2018 World Economic Outlook *(WEO), mostly driven by higher oil prices. Notwithstanding record-high US production, tight supply conditions and sustained economic activity in the first half of 2018 reduced Organisation for Economic Co-operation and Development (OECD) oil inventories rapidly, pushing up oil prices in May and June to their highest levels since November 2014. Since then, however, higher production in Saudi Arabia and Russia has rebalanced the oil market. A decline in metals demand from China and trade tensions have put downward pressure on metals prices. Agricultural market fundamentals, in contrast, remain solid and have partially offset the introduction of tariffs on some key agricultural products. This special feature includes an in-depth analysis of the long-term determinants of energy demand.*

The IMF's Primary Commodities Price Index rose 3.3 percent between February 2018 and August 2018, the reference periods for the April 2018 and current WEOs, respectively (Figure 1.SF.1, panel 1). Energy prices drove that increase, rising by 11.1 percent; food prices declined by 6.4 percent, while metals prices decreased by 11.7 percent because of trade tensions and weaker-than-expected metal demand from China. Oil prices increased to more than $76 a barrel in June, attaining their highest level since November 2014. Since July, however, oil prices have stabilized as Organization for the Petroleum Exporting Countries (OPEC) and non-OPEC oil exporters (including Russia) agreed to boost production. Coal prices increased strongly because of relatively tight supply conditions, while natural gas prices increased in part following higher oil and coal prices.

Oil Prices at the Highest Level since 2014

On June 22, 2018, OPEC agreed to increase its members' oil output by 0.7 million barrels a day (mbd) to offset declining output in Angola and especially in Venezuela, both OPEC members, and regain its origi-

The authors of this special feature are Christian Bogmans, Lama Kiyasseh, Akito Matsumoto (team co-leader), Andrea Pescatori (team leader), and Julia Xueliang Wang, with research assistance from Rachel Yuting Fan, Lama Kiyasseh and Julia Xueliang Wang.

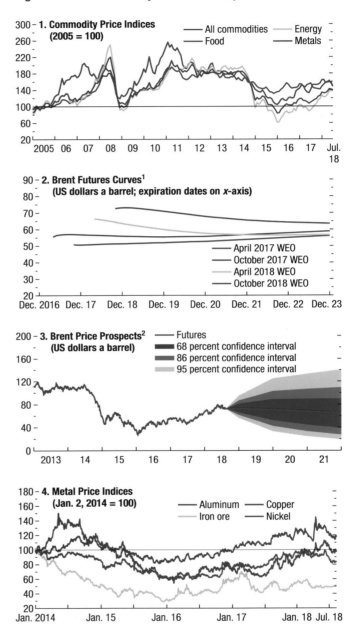

Figure 1.SF.1. Commodity Market Developments

1. Commodity Price Indices (2005 = 100) — All commodities, Energy, Food, Metals

2. Brent Futures Curves[1] (US dollars a barrel; expiration dates on *x*-axis) — April 2017 WEO, October 2017 WEO, April 2018 WEO, October 2018 WEO

3. Brent Price Prospects[2] (US dollars a barrel) — Futures, 68 percent confidence interval, 86 percent confidence interval, 95 percent confidence interval

4. Metal Price Indices (Jan. 2, 2014 = 100) — Aluminum, Copper, Iron ore, Nickel

Sources: Bloomberg Finance L.P.; Thomson Reuters Datastream; IMF, Primary Commodity Price System; and IMF staff estimates.
Note: WEO = *World Economic Outlook.*
[1]WEO futures prices are baseline assumptions for each WEO and are derived from futures prices. October 2018 WEO prices are based on August 13, 2018, closing.
[2]Derived from prices of futures options on August 13, 2018.

nal target level set in the November 2016 agreement.[1] Notwithstanding record-high US production, tight supply conditions and sustained economic activity in the first half of 2018 reduced OECD oil inventories from historically high levels to their five-year average, pushing oil prices to more than $76 a barrel in June—the highest level since November 2014. In July, however, oil prices retrenched from recent peaks and, as of August, stood at about $71 a barrel as higher Saudi and Russian production offset the effects of unplanned outages in Canada and Libya and a tougher US stance on the implementation of sanctions on Iran. Natural gas and coal prices have increased, supported by strong demand from China and India.

Oil futures contracts point to a decline of prices to about $60 a barrel in 2023 (Figure 1.SF.1, panel 2). Baseline assumptions for the IMF's average petroleum spot prices, based on futures prices, suggest average annual prices of $69.3 a barrel in 2018—an increase of 31 percent from the 2017 average—and $68.8 a barrel in 2019 (Figure 1.SF.1, panel 3). On one hand, global economic growth is expected to be relatively strong, albeit with regional differences, supporting underlying oil demand—the International Energy Agency expects oil demand to grow by 1.4 mbd and 1.5 mbd in 2018 and 2019, respectively. On the other hand, the US Energy Information Administration expects US crude production to reach 10.7 mbd in 2018 and 11.7 mbd in 2019, putting downward pressure on oil prices in the medium term. Canada's oil production is expected to grow steadily, too.

Although risks are balanced, uncertainty remains substantial around the baseline assumptions for oil prices because Saudi Arabia's spare capacity is shrinking and US sanctions against Iran will both weigh on Iran's oil production prospects in the medium term and reduce Iran's crude exports in the short term, requiring others with spare production capacity to step in. Upside risks to prices in the short term include a faster-than-expected deterioration of Venezuelan production and a larger-than-anticipated reduction in Iran's crude exports. Downside risks include higher OPEC output and stronger-than-expected Canadian and US production even though, in the short term, the United States faces bottlenecks caused by labor shortages and lack of pipeline infrastructure.

---

[1]The 0.7 mbd increase is the production increase necessary to bring OPEC output back to 100 percent compliance from current overcompliance (the calculations are based on International Energy Agency data).

In addition, trade tensions and other risks to global growth (highlighted in the section titled "Risks" in Chapter 1) can potentially affect global activity and its prospects, reducing, in turn, oil demand. Coal prices are expected to decline from current levels due to a rebound in supply and in line with declining oil and natural gas prices.

Metal Prices Decreasing

After peaking in February, metal prices declined by 11.7 percent between February 2018 and August 2018 because of weaker metal demand from China following stringent environmental regulations and tighter credit conditions. Global trade tensions have also added downward price pressures and substantially increased volatility in metal markets.

The price of iron ore, the key input in steelmaking, dropped by 12.4 percent between the reference periods because of US tariffs on steel, substitution with scrap by Chinese steelmakers, and China's production curbs across major steel mills. Copper prices declined after the fear of a strike at the world's largest copper mine in Chile faded, while aluminum prices went through a period of high volatility following US sanctions on the giant Russian aluminum and alumina producer (United Company Rusal), along with trade tensions. Nickel, the main input for stainless steel and batteries in electric vehicles, reached multiyear highs in early June 2018 and then declined to its February price on trade tensions. Zinc, mainly used to galvanize steel, dropped 28.9 percent between February and August 2018 following surging stockpiles and weak demand from China.

The IMF annual metals price index is projected to increase by 5.3 percent in 2018 (relative to its average in 2017) but to decline by 3.7 percent in 2019 from its 2018 average. Upside risks to the outlook for metal prices include sanctions against metals producers and easing environmental regulations in China. Downside risks are mounting because of trade tensions, higher-than-expected metals production in China, and a slowdown of the Chinese economy, which accounts for more than half of the world's metals consumption.

Food Prices Decreasing and Trade Risks Remain

Although agricultural market fundamentals remain solid, the IMF's agricultural price index decreased between February 2018 and August 2018

Figure 1.SF.2. Primary Energy Consumption and Supply

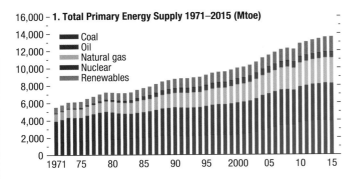

1. Total Primary Energy Supply 1971–2015 (Mtoe)

- Coal
- Oil
- Natural gas
- Nuclear
- Renewables

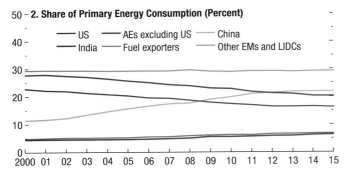

2. Share of Primary Energy Consumption (Percent)

- US
- India
- AEs excluding US
- Fuel exporters
- China
- Other EMs and LIDCs

Sources: International Energy Agency; and IMF staff calculations.
Note: AEs = advanced economies; EMs = emerging markets; LIDCs = low-income developing countries; Fuel exporters = Algeria, Angola, Azerbaijan, Bahrain, Bolivia, Brunei Darussalam, Ecuador, Gabon, Iraq, Kazakhstan, Kuwait, Libya, Nigeria, Oman, Qatar, Saudi Arabia, United Arab Emirates, Venezuela; Mtoe = million tons of oil equivalent.

by 6.4 percent on trade tensions and concerns over global growth.

Wheat prices increased by 22.6 percent between February 2018 and August 2018 following adverse weather conditions during spring and summer in Russia and western Europe, respectively. Soybean prices fell sharply, however, in June and July after China announced a 25 percent retaliatory tariff on US soybean imports and US production numbers for 2018 were revised upward. As a result, prices stood 14.7 percent lower in August 2018 than in February 2018.

Food prices are projected to increase in 2018 by 2.3 percent, and by a further 1.7 percent in 2019. Weather disruptions are an upside risk to the forecast. As of August 9, 2018, the National Oceanic and Atmospheric Administration puts the chances of El Niño during winter 2018–19 at 70 percent. A deepening of the trade conflict between the United States—the world's largest food exporter—and several of its key trading partners constitutes a major downside risk.

Global Energy Demand

The consumption of energy services and liquid fuels is pervasive and essential in the economic system and is the major driver of demand for primary energy sources, such as fossil fuels, nuclear, and renewables. Increased energy efficiency, however, has raised the possibility of reaching a saturation point in the global demand for energy (or some of its primary energy sources), which could leave producer countries with overcapacity and stranded assets. Moreover, the use of energy, especially in the form of fossil fuels, gives rise to a multitude of environmental externalities, the severity of which, in turn, depends on the energy mix used and the technologies adopted (Stern 2006; IPCC 2014).

This section analyzes the main drivers of energy demand and the evolution of the primary energy–source mix by looking at long-term trends in energy efficiency; exploring the role of power generation in energy demand; and investigating the presence of an S-shaped relationship between energy and income that would, ultimately, induce saturation in energy demand (Wolfram, Shelef, and Gertler 2012).

Basic Facts

The demand for energy services and liquid fuels induces a direct and indirect (through power generation) demand for primary energy sources. Electricity has been a key force in the past decades: energy demand from power generation increased by nearly 300 percent between 1971 and 2015—almost twice the rate of total energy. This phenomenon, dubbed *electrification*, has sustained the demand for coal and has led to a major decline of oil as a share of total energy and to increases in natural gas usage, and, more recently, in renewables (Figure 1.SF.2, panel 1). Indeed, power generation today accounts for more than 40 percent of the demand for primary energy, and for about 55 percent if oil is excluded, which instead is mostly used in the transport sector.

Although power generation has contributed significantly to global energy demand growth, it is worth looking at contributions by country. Emerging markets, especially China and, more recently, India, have driven most of the energy demand growth of the past 15 years (Figure 1.SF.2, panel 2), while the contribution of advanced economies has been minimal, leading to a decline in their world consumption shares and raising the prospects of saturation in energy

Table 1.SF.1. Total Demand Determinants for Baseline Specification

	(1)	(2)	(3)	(4)
Population	1.079***	0.965***	0.959***	1.161***
GDP per Capita	−7.103*	−8.676**	−5.068*	−6.889***
(GDP per Capita)^2	0.843*	1.044**	0.639*	0.865***
(GDP per Capita)^3	−0.0293	−0.0378**	−0.0231	−0.0330***
Area		0.0798	0.0953*	
Oil Exporter		−0.0173	0.00523	
Gas Exporter		0.0483	−0.0478	
Coal Exporter		0.378**	0.315**	
Coal Producer		0.251*	0.132	
Latitude			0.0138***	
Static Saturation Point	401,087	179,389	323,516	82,921
Dynamic Saturation Point (1% eff. gain)	127,286	63,590	74,050	17,831
Dynamic Saturation Point (spec. eff. gain)	33,576	38,410	41,298	25,281
Inflection Point	14,447	10,039	10,184	6,204
Max Elasticity	0.9723	0.9416	0.8280	0.6660
Average Elasticity	0.9721	0.9233	0.8177	0.5888
R^2	0.95	0.96	0.97	1.00
Model	WLS	WLS	WLS	WLS − FE

Sources: International Energy Agency; World Bank, World Development Indicators database; and IMF staff calculations.
Note: Energy exporters and producers are derived from the International Energy Agency. Average elasticity is calculated at $15,000 2011 international US dollars. "eff. gain" is efficiency gain. "spec. eff. gain" is specific efficiency gain calculated using each specification's average growth of time dummies. FE = fixed effects; WLS = weighted least squares. Latitude is the absolute value of latitude in degrees for national capitals.
*$p < 0.05$, **$p < 0.01$, ***$p < 0.001$.

demand for advanced economies (Wolfram, Shelef, and Gertler 2012). This dissimilarity suggests a relationship between stages of development and the elasticity of energy demand to income. Farrell (1954) and, more recently, Gertler and others (2016) postulate an S-shaped relationship between electricity demand and household purchases of durable goods (such as domestic appliances and automobiles). Dargay and Gately (1999) and Dargay, Gately, and Sommer (2007) find such an S-shaped relationship for car ownership. The next section tests whether such a relationship holds more generally for energy demand and income.

Energy and Income: An S-Shaped Relationship

Using an unbalanced panel of 136 countries, this analysis tests for the presence of an S-shaped relationship between energy demand and per capita income, controlling for the size of the country (that is, population and land area) and fossil fuel abundance. Time fixed effects are used to capture worldwide gains in energy efficiency and fluctuations in global economic activity and energy prices. The sample is annual and spans 1971–2015, covering two major energy price cycles. Specifically, the exercise estimates the following specification relating (log) total energy demand E to (log) population, *pop*; a third-order polynomial in

(log) income per capita, *gdp*; and a vector of control variables, X:[2]

$$E_{it} = \beta_0 + \beta_1 pop_{it} + \beta_2 gdp_{it} + \beta_3 (gdp_{it})^2$$
$$+ \beta_4 (gdp_{it})^3 + \beta_5 \times X_{it} + \lambda_t + \varepsilon_{it} \qquad (1.1)$$

in which λ_t are year fixed effects, while X_{it} includes a time-varying energy-export and coal producer dummy, distance from the equator, and the log of land area; the indices i and t refer to countries and years, respectively.[3]

Results for the baseline specification, column (2), and robustness checks are reported in Table 1.SF.1 and in Online Annex 1.SF.1.[4] Not surprisingly, the analysis finds that energy demand moves in lockstep with population. Point estimates suggest that having a sizable land

---

[2]Energy demand (in million tons of oil equivalent) is the sum of electricity and primary energy supply (that is, coal, oil, natural gas, hydropower, nuclear energy, and renewables). Energy data are from the International Energy Agency; data on population, GDP per capita (in 2011 US dollars), and country area size (in square kilometers) are from the World Bank's World Development Indicators database. Latitude is from the GeoDist database by Centre d'Etudes Prospectives et d'Informations Internationales.

[3]An oil exporter is defined as having oil production exceeding consumption. A similar definition is used for natural gas and coal exporters. A coal producer is defined as having production able to satisfy between 60 percent and 100 percent of the country's coal consumption. Distance from equator is the absolute value of latitude.

[4]The annex is available online at www.imf/en/Publications/WEO.

Figure 1.SF.3. Energy Efficiency

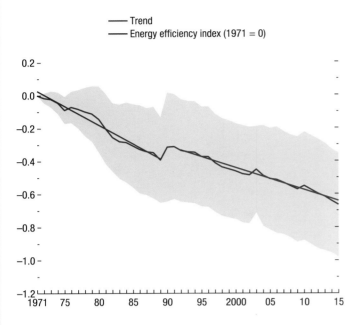

Sources: International Energy Agency; World Bank, World Development Indicators database; and IMF staff calculations.
Note: The red line represents the time fixed effects estimated in Table 1.SF.1 column (2) with 95 percent confidence intervals (shaded area). The blue line is a linear trend estimated for the period 1971–89 (1992–2015) with a slope of 0.23 (0.13).

area, coupled with being a coal exporter (producer), increases energy demand by about 45 (33) percent.

Turning to income, the data strongly support the presence of an S-shaped relationship between per capita energy consumption and per capita income. The inflection point in the energy-income relationship (that is, the maximum income elasticity) is about $10,000 (in 2011 US dollars), which is below the global per capita income in 2015, which stood at $15,000 (2011 US dollars). Indeed, this inflection point has already been reached by many emerging markets. At that income level, the energy income elasticity is close to one.

At higher income levels, the elasticity starts to decline. Ultimately, as income keeps growing, the economy would reach a saturation point for energy demand; however, at an estimated $180,000 per capita (in 2011 US dollars) the saturation point looks, at current technology, to still be very far into the future.[5]

Energy-saving technologies, however, can lead to faster actual saturation by shifting the energy-income

curve downward because the same economic activities (such as heating, cooling, and transport) require less energy. In the regression, improvements in energy efficiency globally are captured by the time dummies, which show a remarkably steady decline (Figure 1.SF.3).

Indeed, except for during 1990–92 (mostly affected by the inclusion in the sample of former Soviet Union countries, whose energy efficiency was lower), the improvement in energy efficiency has been very steady, averaging about 1 percent a year over the entire sample. If it is conservatively assumed that energy efficiency globally keeps increasing at its historical rate of 1 percent a year, the saturation point previously estimated drops to about $64,000 per capita.[6]

The estimated S-shaped energy-income relationship (Figure 1.SF.4) not only predicts energy demand growth to be highest in emerging markets but also captures the behavior of energy demand at low-income levels. Typically, in most low-income countries, energy consumption initially declines in response to income growth probably as the result of graduation from biomass (solid biofuels excluding charcoal)—an inefficient source of energy. Biomass, in fact, is an inferior good, implying that households reduce its use as income grows. The share of biomass in total primary energy supply of the country tends to decline as income grows (Figure 1.SF.5).

In conclusion, the evidence suggests that the relationship between energy demand and income follows an S-shaped curve, with an initial decline of energy demand at low levels of income followed by stages of acceleration and then saturation at middle- and high-income levels, respectively. Thus, the main driver of future energy demand hinges on the dynamics of middle-income countries. In fact, even though some advanced economies may have already reached saturation in energy demand, estimates suggest that global saturation is still far into the future. However, total energy is not all that matters. The same level of energy consumption can be the result of varying mixes of primary energy sources, which is the topic of the next section.

The Primary Energy Mix

The optimal energy mix in each country is the result of relative resource abundance, technology, and social

[5]An economy with a $50,000 per capita income today (for example, Germany) growing at 2 percent a year would take 65 years to reach a per capita income of $180,000.

[6]An economy with a $50,000 per capita income today (for example, Germany) growing at 2 percent a year would take 13 years to reach a per capital income of $64,000.

Figure 1.SF.4. Energy Demand and GDP per Capita

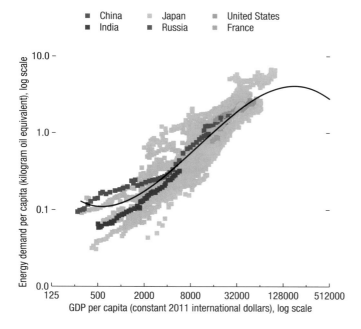

Sources: International Energy Agency; World Bank, World Development Indicators database; and IMF staff calculations.
Note: Adjusted fitted values show the S-shaped energy-income relation (constructed using the cubic polynomial) while energy demand per capita is adjusted for estimated time fixed effects. Estimates are from the baseline specification.

Figure 1.SF.5. Biomass

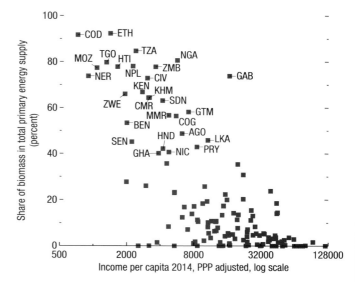

Sources: International Energy Agency, IEA Renewables Information Statistics; World Bank, World Development Indicators database; and IMF staff calculations.
Note: Data labels for countries with biomass shares greater than 40 percent are displayed in the figure. Data labels in the figure use International Organization for Standardization (ISO) country codes. PPP = purchasing power parity.

preferences. The local relative abundance or availability of an energy source determines its local costs, while the efficiency of use in production determines its desirability (that is, its marginal benefit).[7] These two factors combined help determine the relative price of an energy source. Technical substitutability across resources then determines the impact of changes in efficiency of use or relative prices on the energy mix. For example, the relative importance of oil as a primary energy source has substantially declined over time as other energy sources became cheaper (such as coal and nuclear in the early part of the sample) or more desirable to use (such as natural gas and, more recently, renewables). The link between high and volatile crude oil prices and the decline in the oil share is indeed noticeable (Figure 1.SF.6).[8] Over the long

term, however, efficiency is also determined by capital investment, which allows the potential of an energy source (for example, investment in solar power or natural gas infrastructure) to be better exploited. This generates a relationship between the energy mix and the stage of development (see Online Annex 1.SF.1 for further details).

At medium- and low-income levels, the semi-elasticity of the oil share to income is positive as the transport sector expands (for example, car and truck ownership increases), but it turns negative at higher income levels when the stock of motor vehicles plateaus, fuel efficiency reduces gasoline consumption, and cleaner natural gas is preferred in heating and power generation. Regressions, indeed, suggest that peak oil demand may have already been reached for some advanced economies, given that their oil share declines while energy demand is close to saturation (see Online Annex 1.SF.1). In contrast, the share of natural gas seems mostly independent of income.

The relationship between income and the share of coal is weak because higher incomes are associated with cleaner energy sources but also with higher electrification rates (the main driver of coal consumption). At medium incomes, however, coal has proved

---

[7]It is up to policy to align private and social marginal benefits.

[8]In most advanced economies, the two oil shocks of the 1970s that generated high oil prices called into question the energy security of oil and led to a switch in the power sector, with oil being replaced by alternative sources of power generation, such as coal, natural gas, and nuclear power.

Figure 1.SF.6. Primary Energy Source Shares
(Percent)

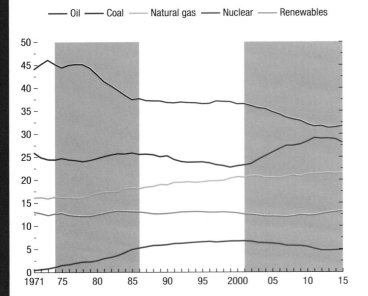

Sources: International Energy Agency; and IMF staff calculations.
Note: Sample is International Energy Agency world aggregate; grey shaded area = high and volatile oil prices; nonshaded area = low and stable oil prices.

Figure 1.SF.7. Decomposition of Change in World Coal Intensity
(Percent)

Sources: International Energy Agency; World Bank, World Development Indicators database; and IMF staff calculations.

to be a cheap and abundant energy source able to satisfy a quickly growing demand for electricity, especially in some large, coal-abundant emerging markets, such as China and India (being a coal producer or exporter increases a country's coal share by 10 percentage points or 18 percentage points, respectively). Hence, notwithstanding a reduction of coal intensity at the country level, the legacy of high coal usage in large and fast-growing economies led to a surprise increase in global coal intensity in the mid-2000s (Figure 1.SF.7). As China and other major emerging markets develop, however, demand for cleaner fuels is expected to increase, leading to a decline in the coal share.

Although it is too early to assess the evolution of renewables, the analysis clearly points to an increase in the use of renewables in high-income countries, especially for power generation. Advanced economies, in fact, are typically highly electrified while emerging markets, as they become more urbanized and expand the electricity grid, are expected to substantially increase their electrification rate in the medium term. The projected rise of the electric car and growth in the services sector, moreover, are expected to increase the electrification rate in advanced economies, too.

The implication of higher electrification rates is important for primary energy demand. In fact, while oil saturation will probably be reached sooner than total energy saturation (as oil's share in the mix declines), saturation for natural gas and renewables will come later. Recent sharp declines in the price of solar photovoltaic cells and government support for the development of renewables are paving the way for the rapid growth of renewables (see Box 1.SF.1). Although coal may remain attractive for some countries, local air pollution has compelled China and India, to some extent, to shift toward renewables. Thus, cost changes and environmental concerns will play a key role for the increased penetration of renewables and the saturation point for coal.

Conclusion

Most of the increase in energy consumption is expected to come from emerging markets whose energy demand is approximately at its peak income elasticity, which is about one. In contrast, that elasticity is close to zero for advanced economies, suggesting that their contribution to energy demand growth will be more modest or possibly absent. Nonetheless, emerging markets' saturation point for energy demand is still far in the future—even assuming steady gains in energy efficiency. Saturation, however, is probably much closer for some energy sources, such as coal and oil, raising the risk of stranded assets for high-cost projects, while other sources, such as natural gas and renewables, are expected to become more important in the energy mix as electrification rates increase. Even though dynamics in energy

transitions and technological innovations are hard to predict, substantial long-term investment is required to change the energy infrastructure of an economic system (for example, the life of power plants and airplanes is about 40 years). Nonetheless, climate concerns, energy policies, and market forces will be key in forging future energy markets as energy regulation and prices interact to stimulate or constrain technological innovation. It is the role of policymakers to exploit these interactions to develop ecologically sustainable economies.

Box 1.SF.1. The Demand and Supply of Renewable Energy

The rapid growth of renewable energy since the beginning of the 21st century (see Online Annex 1.SF.1) can be attributed to several demand- and supply-side factors. First, governments have implemented a variety of energy policies over the years that have helped countries lower their greenhouse gas emissions. Second, aided by regulatory pressure, technological innovation has reduced the cost of wind and solar energy substantially in recent years (Goldman Sachs 2015; IRENA 2017).[1]

Using a model that relates renewable energy capacity to GDP per capita, population, a set of control variables, and a trend, this box analyzes the outlook for renewable energy capacity (see Online Annex 1.SF.1). Results depend on whether the relationship is estimated over the full sample (1990–2015) or only over the most recent sample (2000–15), as the trend coefficient increases from 1.7 percent a year to 3.9 percent in the most recent sample. The rising trend reflects performance improvements and price reductions in several major renewable energy technologies, most notably solar panels and wind turbines.

An out-of-sample prediction, focusing on 45 countries for which long-term forecasts for GDP per capita and population size are available (OECD 2014), shows that, under the conservative forecast, the world will have accumulated more than 4,600 gigawatt of renewable energy-generating assets by 2040. This number increases to more than 8,400 gigawatt in the baseline scenario—a fourfold increase from 2015.

The increase in renewable energy capacity under the conservative and baseline scenarios will, respectively, deliver 732 million tons and 1,733 million tons of oil equivalent of energy to the electricity grid, equal to 50 percent and 117 percent, respectively, of all electricity generated by fossil fuels in 2015. Indeed, if the new renewable energy capacity were to dis-

The authors of this box are Christian Bogmans and Lama Kiyasseh.

[1]Other factors of importance are the rate of interest; cross-country differences in endowments of human capital and raw potential for wind, solar, and hydro energy (Collier and Venables 2012); and government support for renewable industries (see Zhang and others 2013).

Figure 1.SF.1.1. Renewables Capacity
(Gigawatts)

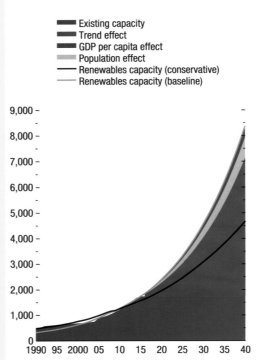

Sources: Organisation for Economic Co-operation and Development; US Energy Information Administration; World Bank, World Development Indicators database; and IMF staff calculations.

place fossil-fuel-based electricity generation, it would constitute a sizable step in reducing global greenhouse gas emissions.

Figure 1.SF.1.1. decomposes future renewable energy growth under the baseline scenario into income, population, and the trend effect. This shows that renewable energy investment is driven mostly by supply (technology) rather than demand (income and population), which is in line with the popular rationale of an energy transition led by innovations in wind, solar, and other technologies. The same dependence on a persistence in the trend factor, however, makes the outlook for renewable energy uncertain.

Annex Table 1.1.1. European Economies: Real GDP, Consumer Prices, Current Account Balance, and Unemployment
(Annual percent change, unless noted otherwise)

	Real GDP			Consumer Prices[1]			Current Account Balance[2]			Unemployment[3]		
		Projections			Projections			Projections			Projections	
	2017	2018	2019	2017	2018	2019	2017	2018	2019	2017	2018	2019
Europe	**3.1**	**2.3**	**1.9**	**2.6**	**3.1**	**3.2**	**2.4**	**2.4**	**2.4**	**. . .**	**. . .**	**. . .**
Advanced Europe	**2.4**	**2.0**	**1.9**	**1.7**	**1.8**	**1.8**	**3.0**	**2.9**	**2.8**	**7.9**	**7.2**	**7.0**
Euro Area[4],[5]	2.4	2.0	1.9	1.5	1.7	1.7	3.5	3.0	2.9	9.1	8.3	8.0
Germany	2.5	1.9	1.9	1.7	1.8	1.8	7.9	8.1	7.9	3.8	3.5	3.4
France	2.3	1.6	1.6	1.2	1.9	1.8	−0.6	−0.9	−0.7	9.4	8.8	8.5
Italy	1.5	1.2	1.0	1.3	1.3	1.4	2.8	2.0	1.6	11.3	10.8	10.5
Spain	3.0	2.7	2.2	2.0	1.8	1.8	1.9	1.2	1.2	17.2	15.6	14.7
Netherlands	2.9	2.8	2.6	1.3	1.4	1.6	10.5	9.9	9.7	4.9	3.9	3.8
Belgium	1.7	1.5	1.5	2.2	2.2	1.8	−0.2	0.1	−0.1	7.1	6.4	6.6
Austria	3.0	2.8	2.2	2.2	2.0	2.1	1.9	2.2	1.8	5.5	5.2	5.1
Greece	1.4	2.0	2.4	1.1	0.7	1.2	−0.8	−0.8	−0.4	21.5	19.9	18.1
Portugal	2.7	2.3	1.8	1.6	1.7	1.6	0.5	0.0	−0.3	8.9	7.0	6.7
Ireland	7.2	4.7	4.0	0.3	0.7	1.2	8.5	7.4	6.7	6.7	5.3	5.1
Finland	2.8	2.6	1.8	0.8	1.2	1.7	0.7	0.9	0.9	8.5	7.7	7.4
Slovak Republic	3.4	3.9	4.1	1.3	2.6	2.2	−2.1	−1.8	−0.9	8.1	7.5	6.9
Lithuania	3.9	3.5	2.9	3.7	2.5	2.2	0.8	0.3	0.0	7.1	6.5	6.3
Slovenia	5.0	4.5	3.4	1.4	2.1	2.0	7.1	6.3	5.5	6.6	5.8	5.4
Luxembourg	2.3	4.0	3.5	2.1	1.5	1.8	5.0	4.9	4.8	5.8	5.4	5.2
Latvia	4.5	3.7	3.3	2.9	2.7	2.4	−0.8	−2.0	−2.6	8.7	7.9	7.8
Estonia	4.9	3.7	3.2	3.7	3.0	2.5	3.1	2.2	1.1	5.8	6.7	6.9
Cyprus	3.9	4.0	4.2	0.7	0.8	1.8	−6.7	−3.1	−5.2	11.1	9.5	8.0
Malta	6.7	5.7	4.6	1.3	1.8	2.1	13.6	11.6	11.1	4.6	4.1	4.1
United Kingdom	1.7	1.4	1.5	2.7	2.5	2.2	−3.8	−3.5	−3.2	4.4	4.1	4.2
Switzerland	1.7	3.0	1.8	0.5	1.1	1.4	9.8	10.2	9.8	3.2	2.8	2.8
Sweden	2.1	2.4	2.2	1.9	1.9	1.7	3.3	2.6	2.8	6.7	6.2	6.2
Norway	1.9	2.1	2.1	1.9	1.9	2.0	5.5	7.8	7.8	4.2	3.8	3.7
Czech Republic	4.3	3.1	3.0	2.4	2.3	2.3	1.1	−0.4	−0.9	2.9	2.5	3.0
Denmark	2.3	2.0	1.9	1.1	1.4	1.7	7.6	7.7	7.5	5.7	5.4	5.3
Iceland	4.0	3.7	2.9	1.8	2.5	2.6	3.5	2.4	2.0	2.8	3.2	3.3
San Marino	1.9	1.4	1.0	1.0	1.5	1.6	. . .	. . .	. . .	8.1	8.2	8.3
Emerging and Developing Europe[6]	**6.0**	**3.8**	**2.0**	**6.2**	**8.3**	**9.0**	**−2.6**	**−2.8**	**−1.4**	**. . .**	**. . .**	**. . .**
Turkey	7.4	3.5	0.4	11.1	15.0	16.7	−5.6	−5.7	−1.4	10.9	11.0	12.3
Poland	4.6	4.4	3.5	2.0	2.0	2.8	0.3	−0.8	−1.3	4.9	4.1	4.0
Romania	6.9	4.0	3.4	1.3	4.7	2.7	−3.4	−3.5	−3.4	4.9	4.7	4.8
Hungary	4.0	4.0	3.3	2.4	2.8	3.3	3.2	2.3	2.1	4.2	3.9	3.5
Bulgaria[5]	3.6	3.6	3.1	1.2	2.6	2.3	4.5	2.4	1.6	6.2	5.6	5.5
Serbia	1.9	4.0	3.5	3.1	2.1	2.3	−5.7	−5.7	−5.6	14.1	13.8	13.5
Croatia	2.8	2.8	2.6	1.1	1.6	1.5	3.9	2.7	2.3	12.4	12.0	11.2

Note: Data for some countries are based on fiscal years. Please refer to Table F in the Statistical Appendix for a list of economies with exceptional reporting periods.
[1]Movements in consumer prices are shown as annual averages. Year-end to year-end changes can be found in Tables A6 and A7 in the Statistical Appendix.
[2]Percent of GDP.
[3]Percent. National definitions of unemployment may differ.
[4]Current account position corrected for reporting discrepancies in intra-area transactions.
[5]Based on Eurostat's harmonized index of consumer prices except for Slovenia.
[6]Includes Albania, Bosnia and Herzegovina, Kosovo, FYR Macedonia, and Montenegro.

Annex Table 1.1.2. Asian and Pacific Economies: Real GDP, Consumer Prices, Current Account Balance, and Unemployment
(Annual percent change, unless noted otherwise)

	Real GDP			Consumer Prices[1]			Current Account Balance[2]			Unemployment[3]		
		Projections			Projections			Projections			Projections	
	2017	2018	2019	2017	2018	2019	2017	2018	2019	2017	2018	2019
Asia	**5.7**	**5.6**	**5.4**	**2.1**	**2.7**	**2.9**	**2.1**	**1.5**	**1.4**	...	...	...
Advanced Asia	**2.4**	**2.1**	**1.8**	**1.0**	**1.4**	**1.6**	**4.4**	**4.1**	**4.1**	**3.4**	**3.4**	**3.3**
Japan	1.7	1.1	0.9	0.5	1.2	1.3	4.0	3.6	3.8	2.9	2.9	2.9
Korea	3.1	2.8	2.6	1.9	1.5	1.8	5.1	5.0	4.7	3.7	3.7	3.7
Australia	2.2	3.2	2.8	2.0	2.2	2.3	−2.6	−2.8	−3.1	5.6	5.3	5.0
Taiwan Province of China	2.9	2.7	2.4	1.1	1.5	1.3	14.5	13.8	13.6	3.8	3.8	3.7
Singapore	3.6	2.9	2.5	0.6	1.0	1.4	18.8	18.5	18.3	2.2	2.0	1.9
Hong Kong SAR	3.8	3.8	2.9	1.5	2.3	2.1	4.3	3.4	3.1	3.1	2.6	2.6
New Zealand	3.0	3.1	3.0	1.9	1.4	1.7	−2.7	−3.6	−3.8	4.7	4.5	4.4
Macao SAR	9.1	6.3	6.3	1.2	2.2	2.4	33.3	35.9	38.1	2.0	2.0	2.0
Emerging and Developing Asia	**6.5**	**6.5**	**6.3**	**2.4**	**3.0**	**3.2**	**0.9**	**0.1**	**0.2**	...	...	...
China	6.9	6.6	6.2	1.6	2.2	2.4	1.4	0.7	0.7	3.9	4.0	4.0
India[4]	6.7	7.3	7.4	3.6	4.7	4.9	−1.9	−3.0	−2.5	...	...	...
ASEAN-5	**5.3**	**5.3**	**5.2**	**3.1**	**2.9**	**3.2**	**2.0**	**1.3**	**1.0**	...	...	...
Indonesia	5.1	5.1	5.1	3.8	3.4	3.8	−1.7	−2.4	−2.4	5.4	5.2	5.0
Thailand	3.9	4.6	3.9	0.7	0.9	0.9	11.2	9.1	8.1	0.7	0.7	0.7
Malaysia	5.9	4.7	4.6	3.8	1.0	2.3	3.0	2.9	2.3	3.4	3.2	3.0
Philippines	6.7	6.5	6.6	2.9	4.9	4.0	−0.8	−1.5	−1.5	5.7	5.5	5.5
Vietnam	6.8	6.6	6.5	3.5	3.8	4.0	2.5	2.2	2.0	2.2	2.2	2.2
Other Emerging and Developing Asia[5]	**6.2**	**6.1**	**6.3**	**4.9**	**5.3**	**5.5**	**−2.0**	**−3.4**	**−2.8**	...	...	...
Memorandum												
Emerging Asia[6]	6.5	6.5	6.3	2.3	2.9	3.1	1.0	0.3	0.3	...	...	...

Note: Data for some countries are based on fiscal years. Please refer to Table F in the Statistical Appendix for a list of economies with exceptional reporting periods.
[1]Movements in consumer prices are shown as annual averages. Year-end to year-end changes can be found in Tables A6 and A7 in the Statistical Appendix.
[2]Percent of GDP.
[3]Percent. National definitions of unemployment may differ.
[4]See country-specific note for India in the "Country Notes" section of the Statistical Appendix.
[5]Other Emerging and Developing Asia comprises Bangladesh, Bhutan, Brunei Darussalam, Cambodia, Fiji, Kiribati, Lao P.D.R., Maldives, Marshall Islands, Micronesia, Mongolia, Myanmar, Nauru, Nepal, Palau, Papua New Guinea, Samoa, Solomon Islands, Sri Lanka, Timor-Leste, Tonga, Tuvalu, and Vanuatu.
[6]Emerging Asia comprises the ASEAN-5 (Indonesia, Malaysia, Philippines, Thailand, Vietnam) economies, China, and India.

Annex Table 1.1.3. Western Hemisphere Economies: Real GDP, Consumer Prices, Current Account Balance, and Unemployment
(Annual percent change, unless noted otherwise)

	Real GDP			Consumer Prices[1]			Current Account Balance[2]			Unemployment[3]		
		Projections			Projections			Projections			Projections	
	2017	2018	2019	2017	2018	2019	2017	2018	2019	2017	2018	2019
North America	**2.2**	**2.7**	**2.5**	**2.5**	**2.7**	**2.3**	**−2.3**	**−2.5**	**−2.9**	. . .	. . .	. . .
United States	2.2	2.9	2.5	2.1	2.4	2.1	−2.3	−2.5	−3.0	4.4	3.8	3.5
Canada	3.0	2.1	2.0	1.6	2.6	2.2	−2.9	−3.0	−2.5	6.3	6.1	6.2
Mexico	2.0	2.2	2.5	6.0	4.8	3.6	−1.7	−1.3	−1.3	3.4	3.5	3.5
Puerto Rico[4]	−2.4	−2.3	−1.1	1.8	2.7	1.2	. . .	. . .	. . .	10.8	11.0	11.0
South America[5]	**0.7**	**0.6**	**1.9**	**6.4**	**6.9**	**7.1**	**−1.4**	**−1.6**	**−1.8**	. . .	. . .	. . .
Brazil	1.0	1.4	2.4	3.4	3.7	4.2	−0.5	−1.3	−1.6	12.8	11.8	10.7
Argentina	2.9	−2.6	−1.6	25.7	31.8	31.7	−4.9	−3.7	−3.2	8.4	8.9	9.4
Colombia	1.8	2.8	3.6	4.3	3.2	3.4	−3.3	−2.4	−2.4	9.3	9.2	9.1
Venezuela	−14.0	−18.0	−5.0	1,087.5	1,370,000.0	10,000,000.0	2.0	6.1	4.0	27.1	34.3	38.0
Chile	1.5	4.0	3.4	2.2	2.4	3.0	−1.5	−2.5	−2.7	6.7	6.9	6.5
Peru	2.5	4.1	4.1	2.8	1.4	2.0	−1.1	−1.8	−2.2	6.9	6.9	6.8
Ecuador	2.4	1.1	0.7	0.4	−0.2	0.5	−0.3	−0.5	0.7	4.6	4.8	5.2
Bolivia	4.2	4.3	4.2	2.8	3.2	4.2	−6.3	−5.2	−5.1	4.0	4.0	4.0
Uruguay	2.7	2.0	3.2	6.2	7.6	6.7	1.5	0.9	0.2	7.6	7.9	7.6
Paraguay	4.8	4.4	4.2	3.6	4.2	4.0	−0.8	−1.3	−0.9	5.7	5.7	5.7
Central America[6]	**3.7**	**2.8**	**3.8**	**2.6**	**3.0**	**3.4**	**−2.0**	**−3.2**	**−3.2**	. . .	. . .	. . .
Caribbean[7]	**2.6**	**4.4**	**3.7**	**3.7**	**4.3**	**4.3**	**−0.9**	**−1.6**	**−1.7**	. . .	. . .	. . .
Memorandum												
Latin America and the Caribbean[8]	1.3	1.2	2.2	6.0	6.1	5.9	−1.5	−1.6	−1.8	. . .	. . .	. . .
East Caribbean Currency Union[9]	1.8	2.0	3.8	1.1	1.7	1.8	−8.0	−11.6	−10.2	. . .	. . .	. . .

Note: Data for some countries are based on fiscal years. Please refer to Table F in the Statistical Appendix for a list of economies with exceptional reporting periods.
[1]Movements in consumer prices are shown as annual averages. Aggregates exclude Venezuela, but include Argentina starting from 2017 onward. Year-end to year-end changes can be found in Tables A6 and A7 in the Statistical Appendix.
[2]Percent of GDP.
[3]Percent. National definitions of unemployment may differ.
[4]Puerto Rico is a territory of the United States but its statistical data are maintained on a separate and independent basis.
[5]Includes Guyana and Suriname. See country-specific notes for Argentina and Venezuela in the "Country Notes" section of the Statistical Appendix.
[6]Central America comprises Belize, Costa Rica, El Salvador, Guatemala, Honduras, Nicaragua, and Panama.
[7]The Caribbean comprises Antigua and Barbuda, Aruba, The Bahamas, Barbados, Dominica, Dominican Republic, Grenada, Haiti, Jamaica, St. Kitts and Nevis, St. Lucia, St. Vincent and the Grenadines, and Trinidad and Tobago.
[8]Latin America and the Caribbean comprises Mexico and economies from the Caribbean, Central America, and South America. See country-specific notes for Argentina and Venezuela in the "Country Notes" section of the Statistical Appendix.
[9]Eastern Caribbean Currency Union comprises Antigua and Barbuda, Dominica, Grenada, St. Kitts and Nevis, St. Lucia, and St. Vincent and the Grenadines as well as Anguilla and Montserrat, which are not IMF members.

Annex Table 1.1.4. Commonwealth of Independent States Economies: Real GDP, Consumer Prices, Current Account Balance, and Unemployment

(Annual percent change, unless noted otherwise)

	Real GDP			Consumer Prices[1]			Current Account Balance[2]			Unemployment[3]		
		Projections			Projections			Projections			Projections	
	2017	2018	2019	2017	2018	2019	2017	2018	2019	2017	2018	2019
Commonwealth of Independent States[4]	2.1	2.3	2.4	5.5	4.5	5.7	1.1	4.1	3.3	...	...	...
Net Energy Exporters	2.0	2.1	2.2	4.8	4.0	5.6	1.6	5.1	4.3	...	...	...
Russia	1.5	1.7	1.8	3.7	2.8	5.1	2.2	6.2	5.2	5.2	5.5	5.3
Kazakhstan	4.0	3.7	3.1	7.4	6.4	5.6	−3.4	−0.2	0.2	5.0	5.0	5.0
Uzbekistan	5.3	5.0	5.0	12.5	19.2	14.9	3.5	−0.5	−1.5	...	...	...
Azerbaijan	0.1	1.3	3.6	13.0	3.5	3.3	4.1	6.6	8.1	5.0	5.0	5.0
Turkmenistan	6.5	6.2	5.6	8.0	9.4	8.2	−11.5	−8.2	−6.4	...	...	...
Net Energy Importers	3.2	3.9	3.2	10.2	7.9	6.2	−2.6	−4.1	−4.8	...	...	...
Ukraine	2.5	3.5	2.7	14.4	10.9	7.3	−1.9	−3.1	−3.9	9.2	9.4	9.2
Belarus	2.4	4.0	3.1	6.0	5.5	5.5	−1.7	−2.5	−4.2	0.8	0.8	0.8
Georgia	5.0	5.5	4.8	6.0	2.8	2.7	−8.9	−10.5	−10.2	...	...	...
Armenia	7.5	6.0	4.8	0.9	3.0	4.4	−2.8	−3.8	−3.8	18.9	18.9	18.6
Tajikistan	7.1	5.0	5.0	7.3	5.8	5.5	−0.5	−4.7	−4.3	...	...	...
Kyrgyz Republic	4.6	2.8	4.5	3.2	2.9	4.6	−4.0	−12.3	−11.8	7.1	7.0	7.0
Moldova	4.5	3.8	3.8	6.6	3.6	4.9	−6.3	−7.4	−6.3	4.1	4.1	4.0
Memorandum												
Caucasus and Central Asia[5]	4.1	4.0	4.0	9.0	8.4	7.2	−2.5	−1.3	−0.8	...	...	...
Low-Income CIS Countries[6]	5.5	4.9	4.9	9.5	12.8	10.7	−0.9	−4.6	−4.7	...	...	...
Net Energy Exporters Excluding Russia	3.9	3.8	3.9	9.6	9.2	7.7	−2.2	−0.3	0.1	...	...	...

Note: Data for some countries are based on fiscal years. Please refer to Table F in the Statistical Appendix for a list of economies with exceptional reporting periods.
[1]Movements in consumer prices are shown as annual averages. Year-end to year-end changes can be found in Table A7 in the Statistical Appendix.
[2]Percent of GDP.
[3]Percent. National definitions of unemployment may differ.
[4]Georgia, Turkmenistan, and Ukraine, which are not members of the Commonwealth of Independent States (CIS), are included in this group for reasons of geography and similarity in economic structure.
[5]Caucasus and Central Asia comprises Armenia, Azerbaijan, Georgia, Kazakhstan, the Kyrgyz Republic, Tajikistan, Turkmenistan, and Uzbekistan.
[6]Low-Income CIS countries comprise Armenia, Georgia, the Kyrgyz Republic, Moldova, Tajikistan, and Uzbekistan.

Annex Table 1.1.5. Middle East, North African Economies, Afghanistan, and Pakistan: Real GDP, Consumer Prices, Current Account Balance, and Unemployment

(Annual percent change, unless noted otherwise)

	Real GDP			Consumer Prices[1]			Current Account Balance[2]			Unemployment[3]		
		Projections			Projections			Projections			Projections	
	2017	2018	2019	2017	2018	2019	2017	2018	2019	2017	2018	2019
Middle East, North Africa, Afghanistan,												
and Pakistan	**2.2**	**2.4**	**2.7**	**6.4**	**10.8**	**10.2**	**−0.7**	**1.8**	**1.9**	...	...	...
Oil Exporters[4]	**1.2**	**1.4**	**2.0**	**3.6**	**9.8**	**9.9**	**1.6**	**4.7**	**4.8**	...	...	...
Saudi Arabia	−0.9	2.2	2.4	−0.9	2.6	2.0	2.2	8.4	8.8	6.0	...	...
Iran	3.7	−1.5	−3.6	9.6	29.6	34.1	2.2	1.3	0.3	11.8	12.8	14.3
United Arab Emirates	0.8	2.9	3.7	2.0	3.5	1.9	6.9	7.2	7.5	...	...	...
Algeria	1.4	2.5	2.7	5.6	6.5	6.7	−13.2	−9.0	−7.9	11.7	11.6	12.3
Iraq	−2.1	1.5	6.5	0.1	2.0	2.0	2.3	6.9	3.1	...	...	...
Qatar	1.6	2.7	2.8	0.4	3.7	3.5	3.8	4.8	6.6	...	...	...
Kuwait	−3.3	2.3	4.1	1.5	0.8	3.0	5.9	11.3	11.0	1.1	1.1	1.1
Oil Importers[5]	**4.1**	**4.5**	**4.0**	**12.4**	**12.9**	**10.8**	**−6.6**	**−6.5**	**−6.1**	...	...	...
Egypt	4.2	5.3	5.5	23.5	20.9	14.0	−6.3	−2.6	−2.4	12.2	10.9	9.9
Pakistan	5.4	5.8	4.0	4.1	3.9	7.5	−4.1	−5.9	−5.3	6.0	6.1	6.1
Morocco	4.1	3.2	3.2	0.8	2.4	1.4	−3.6	−4.3	−4.5	10.2	9.5	9.2
Sudan	1.4	−2.3	−1.9	32.4	61.8	49.2	−10.5	−14.2	−13.1	19.6	19.5	19.6
Tunisia	2.0	2.4	2.9	5.3	8.1	7.5	−10.5	−9.6	−8.5	15.5	15.2	15.0
Lebanon	1.5	1.0	1.4	4.5	6.5	3.5	−22.8	−25.6	−25.5	...	...	...
Jordan	2.0	2.3	2.5	3.3	4.5	2.3	−10.6	−9.6	−8.6	18.3	...	...
Memorandum												
Middle East and North Africa	1.8	2.0	2.5	6.7	11.8	10.6	−0.3	2.6	2.6	...	...	...
Israel[6]	3.3	3.6	3.5	0.2	0.9	1.3	2.9	2.3	2.3	4.2	3.9	3.9
Maghreb[7]	5.6	3.2	3.4	5.3	6.7	6.0	−8.0	−6.6	−5.8	...	...	...
Mashreq[8]	3.9	4.8	5.0	20.8	18.8	12.6	−9.5	−7.2	−6.6	...	...	...

Note: Data for some countries are based on fiscal years. Please refer to Table F in the Statistical Appendix for a list of economies with exceptional reporting periods.
[1]Movements in consumer prices are shown as annual averages. Year-end to year-end changes can be found in Tables A6 and A7 in the Statistical Appendix.
[2]Percent of GDP.
[3]Percent. National definitions of unemployment may differ.
[4]Includes Bahrain, Libya, Oman, and Yemen.
[5]Includes Afghanistan, Djibouti, Mauritania, and Somalia. Excludes Syria because of the uncertain political situation.
[6]Israel, which is not a member of the economic region, is included for reasons of geography but is not included in the regional aggregates.
[7]The Maghreb comprises Algeria, Libya, Mauritania, Morocco, and Tunisia.
[8]The Mashreq comprises Egypt, Jordan, and Lebanon. Syria is excluded because of the uncertain political situation.

Annex Table 1.1.6. Sub-Saharan African Economies: Real GDP, Consumer Prices, Current Account Balance, and Unemployment
(Annual percent change, unless noted otherwise)

	Real GDP			Consumer Prices[1]			Current Account Balance[2]			Unemployment[3]		
		Projections			Projections			Projections			Projections	
	2017	2018	2019	2017	2018	2019	2017	2018	2019	2017	2018	2019
Sub-Saharan Africa	**2.7**	**3.1**	**3.8**	**11.0**	**8.6**	**8.5**	**−2.3**	**−2.8**	**−3.4**	...	...	...
Oil Exporters[4]	**0.0**	**1.4**	**2.3**	**18.2**	**13.4**	**13.5**	**1.1**	**0.9**	**0.5**	...	...	...
Nigeria	0.8	1.9	2.3	16.5	12.4	13.5	2.8	2.0	1.0	16.5	...	...
Angola	−2.5	−0.1	3.1	29.8	20.5	15.8	−1.0	−2.1	−1.9	...	...	...
Gabon	0.5	2.0	3.4	2.7	2.8	2.5	−4.9	−1.6	−0.5	...	...	...
Chad	−3.1	3.5	3.6	−0.9	2.1	2.6	−5.7	−4.2	−5.5	...	...	...
Republic of Congo	−3.1	2.0	3.7	0.5	1.2	2.0	−12.9	9.1	12.4	...	...	...
Middle-Income Countries[5]	**3.1**	**2.7**	**3.3**	**5.1**	**4.7**	**4.9**	**−2.6**	**−3.4**	**−3.6**	...	...	...
South Africa	1.3	0.8	1.4	5.3	4.8	5.3	−2.5	−3.2	−3.5	27.5	27.9	28.3
Ghana	8.4	6.3	7.6	12.4	9.5	8.0	−4.5	−4.1	−4.0	...	...	...
Côte d'Ivoire	7.8	7.4	7.0	0.8	1.7	2.0	−4.6	−4.6	−4.2	...	...	...
Cameroon	3.5	3.8	4.4	0.6	1.0	1.1	−2.7	−3.2	−3.0	...	...	...
Zambia	3.4	3.8	4.5	6.6	8.5	8.2	−3.9	−4.0	−3.4	...	...	...
Senegal	7.2	7.0	6.7	1.3	0.4	0.9	−7.3	−7.7	−7.1	...	...	...
Low-Income Countries[6]	**6.1**	**5.7**	**6.2**	**8.9**	**7.3**	**6.6**	**−6.3**	**−6.7**	**−7.8**	...	...	...
Ethiopia	10.9	7.5	8.5	9.9	12.7	9.5	−8.1	−6.2	−6.2	...	...	...
Kenya	4.9	6.0	6.1	8.0	5.0	5.6	−6.3	−5.6	−5.3	...	...	...
Tanzania	6.0	5.8	6.6	5.3	3.8	4.7	−2.8	−4.3	−5.5	...	...	...
Uganda	4.8	5.9	6.1	5.6	3.8	4.2	−4.6	−6.9	−8.9	...	...	...
Madagascar	4.2	5.0	5.4	8.3	7.8	7.2	−0.3	−2.2	−3.4	...	...	...
Democratic Republic of the Congo	3.4	3.8	4.1	41.5	23.0	13.5	−0.5	0.0	−1.8	...	...	...
Memorandum												
Sub-Saharan Africa Excluding												
South Sudan	2.8	3.1	3.8	10.4	8.3	8.2	−2.3	−2.8	−3.4	...	...	...

Note: Data for some countries are based on fiscal years. Please refer to Table F in the Statistical Appendix for a list of economies with exceptional reporting periods.
[1]Movements in consumer prices are shown as annual averages. Year-end to year-end changes can be found in Table A7 in the Statistical Appendix.
[2]Percent of GDP.
[3]Percent. National definitions of unemployment may differ.
[4]Includes Equatorial Guinea and South Sudan.
[5]Includes Botswana, Cabo Verde, Eswatini, Lesotho, Mauritius, Namibia, and Seychelles.
[6]Includes Benin, Burkina Faso, Burundi, the Central African Republic, Comoros, Eritrea, The Gambia, Guinea, Guinea-Bissau, Liberia, Malawi, Mali, Mozambique, Niger, Rwanda, São Tomé and Príncipe, Sierra Leone, Togo, and Zimbabwe.

Annex Table 1.1.7. Summary of World Real per Capita Output

(Annual percent change; in international currency at purchasing power parity)

	Average 2000–09	2010	2011	2012	2013	2014	2015	2016	2017	Projections 2018	Projections 2019	Projections 2023
World	2.4	4.0	3.0	2.0	2.2	2.3	2.1	2.0	2.4	2.5	2.5	2.4
Advanced Economies	1.1	2.5	1.1	0.7	0.9	1.6	1.7	1.2	1.9	1.9	1.7	1.1
United States	0.9	1.8	0.8	1.5	1.1	1.7	2.1	0.8	1.5	2.2	1.9	0.7
Euro Area[1]	1.0	1.8	1.3	−1.1	−0.5	1.2	1.7	1.6	2.3	1.8	1.8	1.3
Germany	0.9	4.2	3.7	0.5	0.3	1.8	0.6	1.3	2.1	1.8	1.8	1.2
France	0.8	1.5	1.7	−0.2	0.1	0.5	0.6	0.7	2.0	1.1	1.2	1.2
Italy	0.1	1.2	0.2	−3.2	−2.3	−0.3	0.9	1.1	1.6	0.9	1.1	0.7
Spain	1.3	−0.4	−1.4	−3.0	−1.3	1.7	3.7	3.2	3.1	2.8	2.3	1.8
Japan	0.4	4.2	−0.3	1.7	2.2	0.5	1.5	1.0	1.9	1.4	1.3	0.9
United Kingdom	1.2	0.9	0.8	0.8	1.4	2.2	1.5	1.0	1.1	0.7	0.9	1.2
Canada	1.0	1.9	2.1	0.6	1.3	1.7	0.1	0.3	1.8	0.9	1.1	0.7
Other Advanced Economies[2]	2.6	5.0	2.5	1.3	1.6	2.1	1.3	1.5	2.1	2.0	1.7	1.6
Emerging Market and Developing Economies	4.4	5.9	4.9	3.6	3.6	3.2	2.8	2.9	3.2	3.3	3.3	3.6
Commonwealth of Independent States	5.9	4.3	4.7	3.2	2.0	1.4	−2.5	0.0	1.7	1.8	2.1	1.9
Russia	5.7	4.5	5.0	3.6	1.7	0.6	−2.6	−0.3	1.5	1.7	1.8	1.4
CIS Excluding Russia	7.0	4.3	4.7	2.7	3.4	2.6	−1.7	1.0	2.7	2.7	3.1	3.5
Emerging and Developing Asia	6.9	8.5	6.7	5.9	5.9	5.8	5.8	5.4	5.5	5.5	5.3	5.2
China	9.6	10.1	9.0	7.4	7.3	6.7	6.4	6.1	6.3	6.1	5.7	5.5
India[3]	5.2	8.7	5.2	4.1	5.0	6.0	6.8	5.7	5.3	5.9	6.0	6.3
ASEAN-5[4]	3.6	5.5	3.2	4.7	3.7	3.3	3.6	3.7	4.1	4.0	3.9	4.1
Emerging and Developing Europe	3.5	3.7	6.2	2.0	4.3	3.5	4.3	2.8	5.5	3.2	1.5	2.3
Latin America and the Caribbean	1.6	4.8	3.4	1.7	1.7	0.2	−0.9	−1.8	0.2	0.3	1.4	2.0
Brazil	2.1	6.5	3.0	1.0	2.1	−0.4	−4.3	−4.2	0.2	0.7	1.7	1.6
Mexico	0.2	3.8	2.4	2.4	0.2	1.7	2.2	1.8	1.0	1.2	1.6	2.1
Middle East, North Africa, Afghanistan, and Pakistan	1.9	2.3	3.9	0.6	0.0	−0.1	0.3	2.9	−0.5	0.4	0.7	1.1
Saudi Arabia	0.5	1.6	6.8	2.5	−0.1	1.1	3.3	−0.7	−3.3	0.2	0.4	0.3
Sub-Saharan Africa	2.7	4.3	2.4	1.5	2.5	2.5	0.6	−1.3	0.0	0.5	1.1	1.5
Nigeria	5.4	8.3	2.1	1.5	2.6	3.5	−0.1	−4.2	−1.9	−0.8	−0.5	−0.3
South Africa	2.3	1.6	1.8	0.7	1.0	0.3	−0.3	−1.0	−0.3	−0.8	−0.2	0.2
Memorandum												
European Union	1.4	1.8	1.5	−0.6	0.1	1.6	2.0	1.7	2.4	1.9	1.9	1.5
Low-Income Developing Countries	3.7	5.0	3.5	1.6	3.7	3.8	2.3	1.2	2.4	2.4	3.0	3.2

Note: Data for some countries are based on fiscal years. Please refer to Table F in the Statistical Appendix for a list of economies with exceptional reporting periods.
[1]Data calculated as the sum of individual euro area countries.
[2]Excludes the G7 (Canada, France, Germany, Italy, Japan, United Kingdom, United States) and euro area countries.
[3]See country-specific note for India in the "Country Notes" section of the Statistical Appendix.
[4]Indonesia, Malaysia, Philippines, Thailand, Vietnam.

References

Aghion, Philippe, Nick Bloom, Richard Blundell, Rachel Griffith, and Peter Howitt. 2005. "Competition and Innovation: An Inverted-U Relationship." *Quarterly Journal of Economics* 120 (2): 701–28.

Autor, David, David Dorn, Lawrence F. Katz, Christina Patterson, and John van Reenen. 2017. "The Fall of the Labor Share and the Rise of Superstar Firms." NBER Working Paper 23396, National Bureau of Economic Research, Cambridge, MA.

Baker, Scott, Nicholas Bloom, and Steven Davis. 2016. "Measuring Economic Policy Uncertainty." *Quarterly Journal of Economics* 131 (4): 1593–636.

Barro, Robert J., and Tao Jin. 2011. "On the Size Distribution of Macroeconomic Disasters." *Econometrica* 79 (5): 1567–89.

Barro, Robert J., and Jose F. Ursua. 2008. "Macroeconomic Crises since 1870." *Brookings Papers on Economic Activity* 39 (1): 255–350.

Baumeister, Christiane, and James D. Hamilton. 2015. "Sign Restrictions, Structural Vector Autoregressions, and Useful Prior Information." *Econometrica* 83 (5): 1963–99.

Becker, Torbjörn, and Paolo Mauro. 2006. "Output Drops and the Shocks That Matter." IMF Working Paper 06/172, International Monetary Fund, Washington, DC.

Berge, Travis J., and Òscar Jordà. 2011. "Future Recession Risks: An Update." Federal Reserve Bank of San Francisco Economic Letter 35.

Bluedorn, John C., Jörg Decressin, and Marco E. Terrones. 2016. "Do Asset Price Drops Foreshadow Recessions?" *International Journal of Forecasting* 32 (2): 518–26.

Caldara, Dario, and Matteo Iacoviello. 2018. "Measuring Geopolitical Risk." Working Paper, Board of Governors of the Federal Reserve Board, January.

Collier, Paul, and Anthony J. Venables. 2012. "Greening Africa? Technologies, Endowments and the Latecomer Effect." *Energy Economics* 34: S75–S84.

Dargay, Joyce, and Dermot Gately. 1999. "Income's Effect on Car and Vehicle Ownership, Worldwide: 1960–2015." *Transportation Research Part A: Policy and Practice* 33 (2): 101–38.

Dargay, Joyce, Dermot Gately, and Martin Sommer. 2007. "Vehicle Ownership and Income Growth, Worldwide: 1960–2030." *Energy Journal* 28 (4): 143–170.

De Loecker, Jan, and Jan Eeckhout. 2017. "The Rise of Market Power and the Macroeconomic Implications." NBER Working Paper 23687, National Bureau of Economic Research, Cambridge, MA.

———. 2018. "Global Market Power." NBER Working Paper 24768, National Bureau of Economic Research, Cambridge, MA.

De Loecker, Jan, and Frederic Warzynski. 2012. "Markups and Firm-Level Export Status." *American Economic Review* 102 (6): 2437–71.

Díez, Federico, Daniel Leigh, and Suchanan Tambunlertchai. 2018. "Global Market Power and Its Macroeconomic Implications." IMF Working Paper 18/137, International Monetary Fund, Washington, DC.

Energy Information Administration (EIA). 2018. "Petroleum, Natural Gas, and Coal Still Dominate US Energy Consumption." EIA, Washington, DC. Accessed August 23.

Ergungor, O. Emre. 2016. "Recession Probabilities." *Economic Commentary* 2016–09.

Estrella, Arturo, and Frederic S. Mishkin. 1998. "Predicting US Recessions: Financial Variables as Leading Indicators." *Review of Economics and Statistics* 80 (1): 45–61.

Farrell, M. J. 1954. "The Demand for Motor-Cars in the United States." *Journal of the Royal Statistical Society* 117 (2): 171–201.

Fell, Michael James. 2017. "Energy Services: A Conceptual Review." *Energy Research and Social Science* 27 (May): 129–40.

Gertler, Paul J., Orie Shelef, Catherine D. Wolfram, and Alan Fuchs. 2016. "The Demand for Energy-Using Assets among the World's Rising Middle Classes." *American Economic Review* 106 (6): 1366–401.

Gobat, Jeanne, and Kristina Kostial. 2016. "Syria's Conflict Economy." IMF Working Paper 16/123, International Monetary Fund, Washington, DC.

Goldman Sachs. 2015. "The Low Carbon Economy." Goldman Sachs Equity Research. https://www.goldmansachs.com/ insights/pages/new-energy-landscape-folder/report-the-low -carbon-economy/report.pdf. Accessed December 10, 2017.

Greening, Lorna A., David L. Greene, and Carmen Difiglio. 2000. "Energy Efficiency and Consumption—The Rebound Effect—A Survey." *Energy Policy* 28 (6–7): 389–401.

Gruss, Bertrand. 2014. "After the Boom—Commodity Prices and Economic Growth in Latin America and the Caribbean." IMF Working Paper 14/154, International Monetary Fund, Washington, DC.

Gutiérrez, Germán, and Thomas Philippon. 2017. "Declining Competition and Investment in the US." NBER Working Paper 23583, National Bureau of Economic Research, Cambridge, MA.

Hall, Robert E., and Charles I. Jones. 1999. "Why Do Some Countries Produce So Much More Output per Worker Than Others?" *Quarterly Journal of Economics* 114 (1): 83–116.

Hamilton, James D. 2009. "Understanding Crude Oil Prices." *Energy Journal* 30 (2): 179–206.

Intergovernmental Panel on Climate Change (IPCC). 2014. "Climate Change 2014: Synthesis Report." *Contribution of Working Groups I, II, and III to the Fifth Assessment Report of the Intergovernmental Panel on Climate Change.* Geneva: IPCC.

International Renewable Energy Agency (IRENA). 2017. *Electricity Storage and Renewables: Costs and Markets to 2030.* Abu Dhabi: IRENA. http://www.irena.org/publications/2017/ Oct/Electricity-storage-and-renewables-costs-and-markets. Accessed December 10.

Jevons, William Stanley. 1865. *The Coal Question: An Inquiry Concerning the Progress of the Nation, and the Probable Exhaustion of the Coal-Mines.* London and New York: Macmillan.

Levanon, Gad. 2011. "Forecasting Recession and Slow-Down Probabilities with Markov Switching Probabilities as Right-Hand-Side Variables." *Business Economics* 46 (2): 99–110.

Liu, Weiling, and Emanuel Moench. 2014. "What Predicts US Recessions?" Federal Reserve Bank of New York, Staff Report 691, September.

Medlock, Kenneth B., and Ronald Soligo. 2001. "Economic Development and End-Use Energy Demand." *Energy Journal* 22 (2): 77–105.

Nakamura, Emi, Jón Steinsson, Robert J. Barro, and José Ursua. 2013. "Crises and Recoveries in an Empirical Model of Consumption Disasters." *American Economic Journal: Macroeconomics* 5 (3): 35–74.

Ng, Serena. 2014. "Boosting Recessions. *Canadian Journal of Economics/Revue canadienne d'économique* 47 (1): 1–34.

Organisation for Economic Co-operation and Development (OECD). 2014. "Long-Term Baseline Projections." 95 (Edition 2014). OECD Economic Outlook: Statistics and Projections (database). https://doi.org/10.1787/eo-data-en.

Silva, J. M. C. Santos, and Silvana Tenreyro. 2006. "The Log of Gravity." *Review of Economics and Statistics* 88 (4): 641–58.

Sorrell, Steve. 2009. "Jevons' Paradox Revisited: The Evidence for Backfire from Improved Energy Efficiency." *Energy Policy* 37 (4): 1456–69.

Stern, Nicholas. 2006. *The Economics of Climate Change: The Stern Review.* London: HM Treasury.

Stock, James H., and Mark W. Watson. 2003. "Forecasting Output and Inflation: The Role of Asset Prices." *Journal of Economic Literature* 41 (3): 788–829.

United Nations (UN). 2017. "World Population Prospects: The 2017 Revision." DVD edition. United Nations, Department of Economic and Social Affairs, Population Division, New York.

van Benthem, Arthur A. 2015. "Energy Leapfrogging." *Journal of the Association of Environmental and Resource Economists* 2 (1): 93–132.

Wolfram, Catherine, Orie Shelef, and Paul J. Gertler. 2012. "How Will Energy Demand Develop in the Developing World?" *Journal of Economic Perspectives* 26 (1): 119–38.

World Bank (WB). 2017. *The Toll of War: The Economic and Social Consequences of the Conflict in Syria.* Washington, DC: World Bank.

Zhang, Sufang, Philip Andrews-Speed, Xiaoli Zhao, and Yongxiu He. 2013. "Interactions between Renewable Energy Policy and Renewable Energy Industrial Policy: A Critical Analysis of China's Policy Approach to Renewable Energies." *Energy Policy* 62 (November): 342–53.

This chapter takes stock of the global economic recovery a decade after the 2008 financial crisis. Output losses after the crisis appear to be persistent, irrespective of whether a country suffered a banking crisis in 2007–08. Sluggish investment was a key channel through which these losses registered, accompanied by long-lasting capital and total factor productivity shortfalls relative to precrisis trends. Policy choices preceding the crisis and in its immediate aftermath influenced postcrisis variation in output. Underscoring the importance of macroprudential policies and effective supervision, countries with greater financial vulnerabilities in the precrisis years suffered larger output losses after the crisis. Countries with stronger precrisis fiscal positions and those with more flexible exchange rate regimes experienced smaller losses. Unprecedented and exceptional policy actions taken after the crisis helped mitigate countries' postcrisis output losses.

Introduction

Over the weekend of September 13–14, 2008, two large US financial institutions teetered close to failure while a third urgently sought a buyer to avoid that same fate. By Sunday night that weekend, Merrill Lynch was acquired by Bank of America. Insurance giant AIG still desperately pursued credit lines, just days away from a ratings downgrade that looked likely to push it over the edge. And in the early hours of Monday, September 15, 2008, the investment bank Lehman Brothers filed for bankruptcy, brought down largely by its exposure to a US housing market in deep decline.

The post-Lehman scramble for liquidity in global markets heralded the most acute phase of the financial turmoil that, by then, had been brewing in the United States and Europe close to 18 months.[1] The ensu-

ing panic—marked by distressed asset sales, deposit withdrawals from banks and money market funds, and the freezing of credit—triggered a collapse in cross-border trade and led to the worst global recession in seven decades.

Ten years later, the sequence of aftershocks and policy responses that followed the Lehman bankruptcy has led to a world economy in which the median general government debt-GDP ratio stands at 52 percent, up from 36 percent before the crisis; central bank balance sheets, particularly in advanced economies, are several multiples of the size they were before the crisis; and emerging market and developing economies now account for 60 percent of global GDP in purchasing-power-parity terms (compared with 44 percent in the decade before the crisis), reflecting, in part, a weak recovery in advanced economies.

Against this backdrop, this chapter takes stock of the global economic recovery 10 years after the financial meltdown of 2008 and the policy lessons that can help prepare for the next downturn. Specifically, the chapter addresses the following questions:

- Compared with precrisis trends, how did output evolve across countries in the aftermath of the crisis?
- How did the associated components—capital, labor inputs, total factor productivity (TFP)—advance after the crisis? What does this decomposition show about why it took a long time for output in many economies to return to its precrisis level?
- Even as the world economy experienced its worst slump in seven decades, postcrisis macroeconomic performance varied across countries. What accounts for this variation? Which policies and structural attributes helped limit the damage and facilitate recovery?

The chapter uses a sample of 180 countries—covering advanced, emerging market, and low-income

The authors of this chapter are Wenjie Chen, Mico Mrkaic, and Malhar Nabar (lead), with contributions from Deniz Igan, Christopher Johns, and Yuan Zeng, and supported by Luisa Calixto, Meron Haile, and Benjamin Hilgenstock.

[1]Identifying a precise starting point for the timeline—the "patient zero" of the epidemic—is difficult. This chapter takes the April 2007 collapse of subprime mortgage lender New Century Financial as the first major distress sign following the mid-2006 turn in the US housing market. Key markers of financial stress over the subsequent 18 months include the suspension of redemptions from

mortgage-related hedge funds associated with Bear Stearns (June 2007) and BNP Paribas (August 2007); the United Kingdom's first bank run since the 19th century, on Northern Rock (September 2007); the failure of mortgage lender Countrywide Financial (January 2008); JPMorgan's acquisition of Bear Stearns with US Federal Reserve support (March 2008); and the US government's takeover of mortgage giants Fannie Mae and Freddie Mac (September 2008).

developing economies—to quantify output losses, explore the precrisis correlates of postcrisis variation in output performance, and examine whether actions taken in the immediate aftermath of the crisis are associated with limiting output losses over the medium term (2015–17). Previous *World Economic Outlook* (WEO) analysis (October 2009) examines output performance after an earlier set of financial crises during 1970–2002. The current chapter builds on that by zeroing in on the aftermath of the 2008 crisis.

An important consideration when comparing pre- and postcrisis output patterns is the extent to which precrisis growth was fueled by excessive credit growth and unsustainable investment that had to be worked off. A related issue is whether structural change unrelated to the crisis may have affected trend growth over time in some countries (specifically, whether some countries experienced temporarily elevated potential growth rates before the crisis that subsequently reverted to the long-term average). As discussed in the next section, the analysis attempts to adjust precrisis trends for the influence of factors, such as credit growth, that may affect the path of output beyond the influence of typical demand fluctuations. Even with this correction, for some countries, the output deviations from precrisis trends may still capture the effect of slow-moving structural changes in trend growth rates over time. Nonetheless, the chapter's cross-country analysis—comparing countries that experienced banking crises in 2007–08 with those that did not, as well as across income levels—can help identify precrisis drivers of postcrisis output deviations.

Among the main findings of the analysis are that output losses appear to be persistent and not restricted to countries that suffered a banking crisis in 2007–08. Sluggish investment appears to be a key channel through which these losses registered, with associated long-lasting capital and TFP shortfalls relative to their precrisis trends. Consistent with these TFP shortfalls, research and development expenditure and technology adoption appear to have increased more slowly in countries that suffered larger output losses. The findings are similar to those of recent papers showing that output tends to stay below previous trends after crises and recessions (for example Cerra and Saxena 2008, 2017; Blanchard, Cerutti, and Summers 2015; and Aslam and others, forthcoming).

The analysis finds that policy choices leading up to the crisis and in its immediate aftermath influenced postcrisis variations in output performance. These can be grouped into three categories.

- *Financial:* Underscoring the importance of macroprudential policies and effective supervision, the analysis finds that countries in which financial vulnerabilities had accumulated to a larger degree in the precrisis years suffered greater output losses after the crisis. In the years running up to the crisis, countries with larger excess current account deficits and those with more rapid credit growth found that constraints bound relatively more strongly when financial conditions tightened after the crisis. Stricter banking regulation (proxied by an index of restrictions on certain aspects of bank activity) in the precrisis years is associated with a lower probability of a banking crisis in 2007–08.
- *Policy constraints and frameworks:* The evidence suggests that countries with stronger precrisis fiscal positions experienced smaller output losses in the aftermath. The analysis also finds that flexible exchange rate regimes helped lessen GDP damages.
- *Postcrisis actions:* Several countries took unprecedented and exceptional policy actions to support their economies after the 2008 financial meltdown. The chapter finds that these actions (specifically, quasi-fiscal measures to support the financial sector, including guarantees and capital injections) helped temper postcrisis output losses.

Some of these factors appear to be particularly relevant for the euro area. The 2008 financial crisis exposed thin buffers in some member economies and gaps in the architecture of the currency union. The interaction of domestic and area-level factors exacerbated adjustment difficulties in the euro area following the 2008 shock and gave rise to an intensifying sovereign debt crisis during 2010–12, which spurred efforts to strengthen the architecture of the currency union (IMF 2012, 2013a; Allard and others 2013; Goyal and others 2013; Berger, Dell'Ariccia, and Obstfeld 2018). In contrast to the 2009 shock, euro area countries hit by the sovereign crisis were not in a position to use expansionary fiscal policy to counter the "sudden stop." Rather, they needed to reduce their fiscal deficits to regain creditors' confidence and contain sovereign borrowing costs. In the event, the contractionary effect of this fiscal tightening was larger than anticipated at the time (Blanchard and Leigh 2013; IMF 2013b, 2015).

The next section quantifies the losses in output and discusses the channels through which they occurred. The subsequent section examines the policy and structural attributes that, in part, account for variation in postcrisis output. The main takeaways are summarized in the conclusion.

Persistent Post–Global Financial Crisis Deviations in Output

Following the global financial meltdown in late 2008, 91 economies, representing two-thirds of global GDP in purchasing-power-parity terms, experienced a decline in output in 2009. By way of comparison, during the 1982 global recession, 48 economies, accounting for 46 percent of world GDP, registered output declines compared with the previous year.

To get a sense of the long-lasting changes in output after the 2008 crisis, this chapter measures postcrisis deviations of output from the level that would have prevailed had output followed its pre-2009 trend growth rate (Ball 2014). Considering that generally accommodative financial conditions likely contributed to unsustainable growth in many countries prior to 2008, it is important to adjust for these influences when estimating an underlying trend path for output as the benchmark for comparison (Online Annex 2.2.B).[2,3] Nevertheless, despite this adjustment, in some cases, the measured output deviations may include country-specific changes in trend growth rates that are unrelated to the crisis. Consider the world's two largest economies, for example. In the United States, a slowdown in total productivity growth that predates the 2008 crisis has contributed to lower potential growth over time (Fernald 2015; Adler and others 2017). China's economy has experienced major structural shifts that span the 2008 crisis and an associated transition to slower, albeit still-robust, growth—an example of a more general phenomenon of changes in trend growth rates documented by Pritchett and Summers (2013). Given these developments (and possibly similar underlying shifts over this period in trend growth rates in other countries), comparisons of current GDP with precrisis outcomes must be careful to avoid attributing all of the observed changes to the 2008 crisis.[4]

Figure 2.1. Correlation of GDP Deviations between Periods
(Percent)

Postcrisis performance is persistent, with a correlation coefficient between GDP deviations for 2011–13 and 2015–17 of about 0.90.

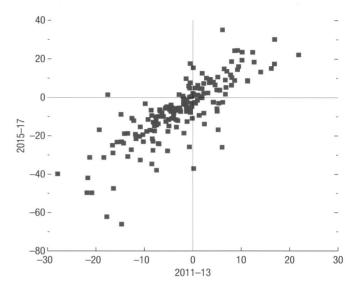

Source: IMF staff calculations.
Note: GDP deviations are average percent deviations from precrisis trend.

The post-2008 output deviations exhibit strong persistence over time (Figure 2.1).[5] A second noteworthy aspect is that economies with larger output and employment losses in the initial aftermath of the crisis registered greater increases in income inequality compared with their precrisis average (Figure 2.2).[6] These developments help shed light on the lingering sense of subpar economic performance in many economies and concerns about a "new mediocre" (Lagarde 2014, 2016). They may also hold clues to the disenchantment with existing institutions and establishment political parties, and the growing appeal of protectionism (Lipton 2018).

---

[2]All annexes are available online at www.imf.org/en/Publications/WEO.

[3]Online Annex 2.2.B discusses the differences between the chapter's approach and the standard filtering approach used for separating output into trend and business cycle components.

[4]For the United States, for example, there is a range of estimates regarding the postcrisis output loss due to the 2008 financial crisis versus those related to changes in potential output growth already underway prior to the crisis (see CBO 2014; Hall 2014; and Barnichon, Matthes, and Ziegenbein 2018).

[5]The correlation coefficient between GDP deviations for 2011–13 and 2015–17 is about 0.90. As shown in Online Annex Figure 2.2.4, the output deviations close to a decade after the 2008 crisis are more skewed toward losses than those registered at a similar interval after the 1982 global recession.

[6]Employment losses are measured as the gap between the number of employed workers and the number consistent with employment growing at the same rate during the postcrisis period as the economically active cohort between the ages of 15 and 65 (Schanzenbach and others 2017; see Online Annex 2.2.B).

Figure 2.2. Postcrisis Change in Inequality

Economies with larger output and employment losses in the initial aftermath of the crisis registered greater increases in income inequality compared with the precrisis average.

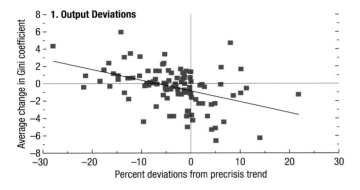

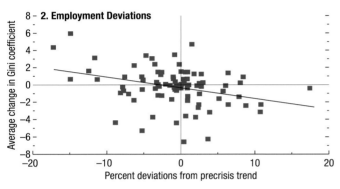

Sources: Standardized World Income Inequality Database (Solt 2016); and IMF staff calculations.
Note: The Gini coefficient is based on income before taxes and transfers and ranges from 0 to 100. The change in Gini coefficient is calculated as the difference between the averages during 2005–08 and 2014–15. Movement from left to right on the x-axis indicates less negative/more positive average deviations from precrisis trend in 2011–13.

Output Remains below Precrisis Trend in More than 60 Percent of Economies

The deviations from pre-2009 trends are estimated for two broad samples of economies: those that experienced banking crises in 2007–08 (as defined in Laeven and Valencia 2013) and all other economies.[7] According to the Laeven-Valencia definition, there were banking crises in 24 countries during 2007–08, 18 of which were in advanced economies (see Online Annex 2.2.A

[7]The Laeven-Valencia (2013) definition of a banking crisis is based on two criteria: significant financial distress (including bank runs and liquidations) and significant government intervention in the banking system (including recapitalization, liability guarantees, and nationalization).

Figure 2.3. Postcrisis Output Deviations from Precrisis Trend, 2015–17

(Kernel density)

Output losses are persistent for a variety of economies, not just those that suffered a systemic banking crisis in 2007–08.

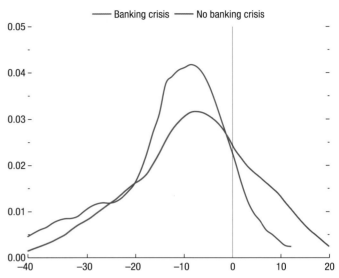

Sources: Laeven and Valencia (2013); and IMF staff calculations.
Note: Distribution of average percent deviations from precrisis trend, 2015–17. See Online Annex Table 2.2.1 for banking crises country list.

for the list). Figure 2.3 summarizes the distribution of postcrisis output deviations from precrisis trends when deviations are averaged over 2015–17.

Among the 24 economies in the banking crisis group, about 85 percent still show negative deviations from the pre-2009 trend a decade after the 2008 meltdown. In light of earlier evidence (see, for example, Abiad and others 2009; Chapter 4 of the April 2009 WEO; and Blanchard, Cerutti, and Summers 2015), it is not surprising that economies in the banking crisis group suffered persistent losses thereafter. As Blanchard, Cerutti, and Summers (2015) show, recessions associated with financial crises are more likely to lead to persistent shortfalls in output relative to precrisis trends. Less credit intermediation—from a combination of supply and demand factors—is a significant channel (Bernanke 2018). On the supply side, impaired financial systems cannot intermediate credit to the same extent as before the crash, and postcrisis regulatory tightening can also affect loan origination. In parallel with the supply disruptions, several factors may have held back credit demand. These include weak growth expectations, impaired corporate and household balance sheets weighing on collateral quality, and an imperative to rebuild net worth.

However, Figure 2.3 shows the persistence of output losses relative to precrisis trends for several economies, not just those that suffered a banking crisis in 2007–08 (consistent with Cerra and Saxena 2017 and Aslam and others, forthcoming, who find persistent losses associated with most recessions, not just those associated with financial crises). In the group without a banking crisis in 2007–08, output remains below precrisis trends in about 60 percent of economies. A possible channel—discussed later in the chapter—that affected this group is weaker external demand from trading partners that suffered banking crises, which contributed to lower investment and associated capital shortfalls (also see Candelon and others 2018).

Grouping the sample by advanced economies, emerging markets, and low-income developing countries shows that output deviations tend to be large across all groups (Figure 2.4). Output deviations are relatively more balanced across gains and losses for noncommodity-exporting (diversified) low-income developing countries and emerging market economies than for the other two groups. More generally, the greater variability in output deviations across emerging markets and low-income developing countries compared with advanced economies may reflect the variety of forces acting on their growth processes, including commodity price developments, export links to China, and receipt of outward investment from China (see also Aslam and others, forthcoming).

Proximate Causes: Sluggish Investment, Capital, and Total Factor Productivity Shortfalls

The persistence of output deviations suggests supply-side shifts in the factors of production. As shown in Online Annex Figure 2.2.3, deviations in output per worker trace similar patterns to deviations in aggregate output, indicating that changes in labor input cannot account for the bulk of the observed output deviations.[8] This similarity suggests shifts in other factors of production associated, for instance,

Figure 2.4. Postcrisis Output Deviations from Precrisis Trend by Country Group, 2015–17
(Kernel density)

Postcrisis output deviations tend to be large across advanced economies, emerging markets, and low-income developing countries, with relatively more balanced gains and losses for noncommodity-exporting low-income developing countries and emerging markets than for the other two groups.

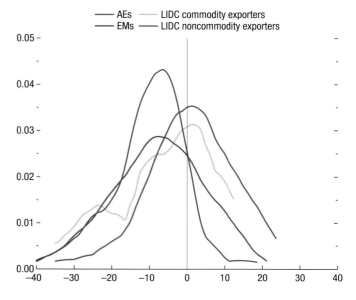

Source: IMF staff calculations.
Note: Distribution of average percent deviations from precrisis trend, 2015–17. AEs = advanced economies; EMs = emerging markets; LIDC = low-income developing country. See Online Annex 2.1 for country groupings.

with weaker aggregate investment, as documented in Chapter 4 of the April 2015 WEO.[9]

Investment shortfalls may have resulted from a lack of access to credit after the crisis, or from weak expectations of future growth and profitability (the latter view reprises the 1930s notion of secular stagnation—see Summers 2016 for a discussion; see also Kozlowski, Veldkamp, and Venkateswaran 2017). A similar calculation for output, as described earlier in this chapter, suggests shortfalls in investment relative to precrisis trends. Figure 2.5 shows the average across all economies of deviations relative to precrisis trends. By 2017, on average, investment was about 25 percent below precrisis trend.

---

[8]Nevertheless, as noted in Box 2.1, postcrisis economic performance appears to have had an impact on migration and fertility decisions, with attendant implications for future labor input.

[9]An important exception is China, where the investment share of GDP rose from below 40 percent in precrisis years to almost 50 percent after the crisis, driven by credit-fueled expansion of infrastructure, residential and commercial real estate, and corporate capital expenditure.

Figure 2.5. Postcrisis Investment Deviations from Precrisis Trend: Mean Trajectory
(Percent)

Investment dropped below precrisis trend during the crisis and deviated further in 2012. By 2017, on average, investment was about 25 percent below precrisis trend.

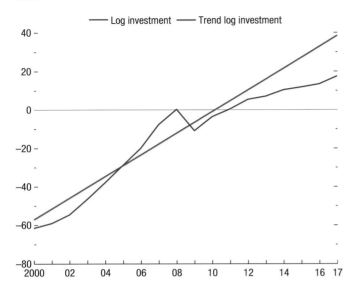

Source: IMF staff calculations.
Note: 2008 log investment normalized to zero.

Figure 2.6. Postcrisis Capital Stock Deviations from Precrisis Trend, 2015–17
(Kernel density)

Close to 80 percent of economies that suffered a banking crisis in 2007–08 experienced shortfalls in capital relative to precrisis trend. Among economies that did not suffer a banking crisis in 2007–08, about 65 percent appear to be operating with capital stocks below precrisis trend.

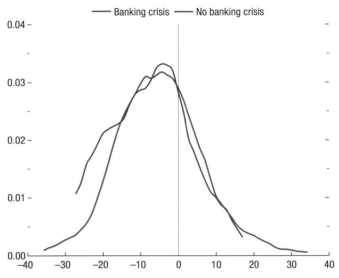

Sources: Laeven and Valencia (2013); and IMF staff calculations.
Note: Distribution of average percent deviations from precrisis trend, 2015–17. See Online Annex Table 2.2.1 for banking crises country list.

Two important consequences of sluggish investment that may hold clues to why the recovery appears to have been so slow, are shortfalls in the capital stock and, to the extent technology is embedded in machinery, slower technology adoption. A useful way to see this is to decompose the deviations in output per worker from precrisis trends into deviations in capital stock per worker and residual TFP deviations. A caveat here is that, even though TFP, in principle, reflects both technology and the efficiency of combining inputs, in practice it also reflects measurement error in the factors of production and changes in capacity utilization. Evidence from standard growth accounting techniques (described in Online Annex 2.2.B and summarized in Figure 2.6) suggests that there are large capital shortfalls relative to precrisis trends. Close to 80 percent of economies that suffered a banking crisis in 2007–08 experienced shortfalls in capital relative to precrisis trends. Among economies without a banking crisis in 2007–08, capital stocks of about 65 percent appear to be lower than they would be if capital accumulation had followed the extrapolated precrisis trend

path.[10] At the sectoral level, these capital shortfalls are widespread, extending beyond the construction sector, which underwent a needed correction after the precrisis boom (Online Annex Figure 2.2.5).

A second possible consequence of sluggish investment is slow technology adoption—to the extent that new technologies are embodied in equipment. The growth accounting approach attributes a significant role to the residual (TFP) component of deviations from precrisis trend in output per worker once the influence of deviations in capital per worker is taken into account (Figure 2.7). These estimated deviations in TFP from precrisis trends are consistent with evidence of widespread postcrisis deceleration in TFP growth discussed in Adler and others (2017). As reported in Table 2.1, the median share of output per worker deviation accounted for by TFP deviation is close to 80 percent for both groups of economies. While the evidence points to the

[10]Online Annex 2.2.B shows that the distributions of capital stock deviations are not distinguishable across the two groups in a statistical sense, while those of output and TFP are.

Figure 2.7. Postcrisis Total Factor Productivity Deviations from Precrisis Trend, 2015–17
(Kernel density)

Estimated deviations in TFP from precrisis trend are consistent with the evidence of a widespread postcrisis deceleration in TFP growth. These TFP deviations account for close to 80 percent of output per worker deviations for both groups of economies, that is, those that suffered banking crises in 2007–08 and those that did not.

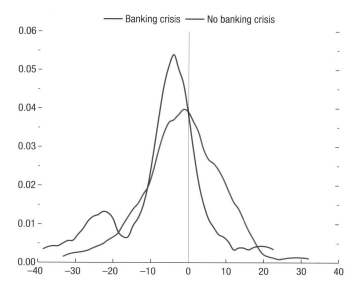

Sources: Laeven and Valencia (2013); and IMF staff calculations.
Note: Distribution of average percent deviations from precrisis trend, 2015–17. TFP = total factor productivity. See Online Annex Table 2.2.1 for banking crises country list.

importance of TFP deviations in accounting for output per worker deviations, the cross-country data do not permit a further separation of TFP deviations into those due to sluggish investment from those related to worsening efficiency or other factors unrelated to investment.

Slower Technology Adoption

The estimates of TFP deviation suggest that the pace of technology adoption (and associated pace of upgrading of capital stock with embodied technology) may have slowed following the crisis. However, as noted above, TFP is an imperfect proxy for the pace of technology adoption. A clearer picture emerges from examining variables directly associated with innovation and technology adoption. Cross-country evidence on a key innovation input—research and development spending—suggests that countries with above-median output losses registered slower increases in research and development shares of GDP. This is especially evident among advanced economies (Figure 2.8).

Table 2.1. Total Factor Productivity Deviations Account for a Large Share of GDP per Worker Deviations
(Percent)

Median Share of GDP Deviation Accounted for by Deviation in GDP per Worker, 2015–17	
Countries without banking crisis in 2007–08	70.4
2007–08 banking crisis countries	80.5
Median Share of GDP per Worker Deviation Accounted for by Total Factor Productivity, 2015–17	
Countries without banking crisis in 2007–08	79.3
2007–08 banking crisis countries	78.2

Source: IMF staff calculations.
Note: See Online Annex Table 2.2.1 for banking crises country list.

Further confirmation of slower innovation and technology adoption among countries hit harder by the crisis is seen through the example of industrial robots—an observable and much-discussed class of automation technology expected to replace human labor in an increasing range of tasks. (Box 2.2 examines the postcrisis employment impact of industrial robots.)[11]

An inspection of the industrial robot data (Figure 2.9) indicates that the average change in density—measured as robot shipments per thousand hours worked—during the postcrisis period was higher in countries that had smaller postcrisis losses in output.

As with the general measure of innovation (research and development expenditure), the gap in changes in robot density between high- and low-output-loss countries is higher among advanced economies than among emerging markets. As part of the generalized slower investment in the postcrisis period, robot adoption may have been affected more negatively in countries hit harder by the crisis.[12] This "suppressed-investment"

[11]As described in Online Annex 2.3.A, data from the International Federation of Robotics, which compiles information on worldwide shipment of robots, are used to examine the postcrisis diffusion of automation technology. The data are reported at the level of industries for 75 countries extending back to 2004 (for some countries, data are available going back to 1993).

[12]While there is possibly an element of reverse causality in these correlations (lower robot investment contributed to higher output loss), empirically, the magnitude of robot investment compared with manufacturing output in the United States, for example, suggests that the effect of robot investment on manufacturing—as well as aggregate—output is small. Based on US Bureau of Economic Analysis data, the International Federation of Robotics (the data source for robots used in the analysis) reports that the value of industrial robot shipments to the United States as a share of US gross manufacturing output ranged between 0.016 percent in 2002 and 0.027 percent in 2016.

Figure 2.8. Changes in Research and Development Expenditure, by Output Losses and Country Groups
(Percent of GDP)

Countries with above-median output losses registered slower increases in research and development expenditure shares of GDP. This was especially evident among advanced economies.

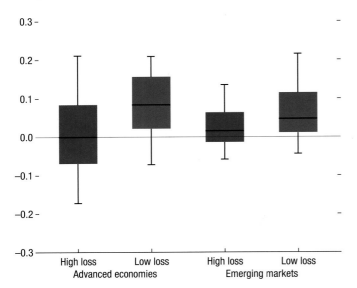

Sources: World Bank, World Development Indicators database; and IMF staff calculations.
Note: The bars depict the difference in averages between 2014–16 and 2011–13. The bar chart shows the interquartile range, and lines display lesser of the maximum (minimum) and +/– 1.5 times the upper (lower) quartile range. High (low) loss indicates above (below) median losses in output relative to precrisis trend as calculated in Online Annex 2.2.B.

Figure 2.9. Average Change in Robot Density, by Output Losses and Country Groups, 2010–14
(Robot shipment per 1,000 hours worked)

The gap in changes in robot density between high and low loss countries is higher among advanced economies than among emerging markets.

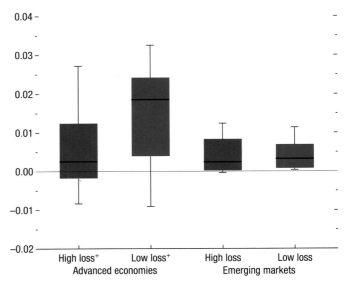

Sources: International Federation of Robotics; World Input-Output Database; and IMF staff calculations.
Note: Robot density is defined as robot shipment/1,000 hours worked. The bar chart shows the interquartile range, and lines display lesser of the maximum (minimum) and +/– 1.5 times the upper (lower) quartile range. High (low) loss indicates above (below) median losses in output relative to precrisis trend as calculated in Online Annex 2.2.B.
+denotes differences in medians between high- and low-output loss samples among advanced economies statistically significant at 10 percent. See Online Annex 2.3 and Online Annex Table 2.3.2 for further details on data and estimation.

effect likely more than offset any tendency to automate rather than rehire unemployed workers.[13]

Policy Frameworks, Measures, and Postcrisis Output Performance

A large number of economies registered output losses relative to precrisis trends, but the postcrisis experience varied by individual country. In part, this variation may reflect differences in the nature of the shock at the level of individual countries. Some suffered severe banking crises as part of the global financial panic, while others were affected mostly through their trade and financial links to the first set of countries. But initial conditions

[13]Analysis at the industry-country level (Online Annex 2.3.B) corroborates this finding. Industries in advanced economies that suffered relatively bigger investment and TFP losses during the crisis experienced slower robot diffusion.

in the buildup to the meltdown of 2008, policy choices in the immediate aftermath of the crisis, and structural aspects may have also helped shape postcrisis variation in output performance—in the first instance, by influencing countries' vulnerability to the disruptive forces the financial meltdown of 2008 unleashed, and subsequently, by affecting the damage they experienced and their ability to recover.

Identifying why economies' responses differed can provide important lessons for the most effective policy responses. The exercise can also help shed light on actions that may help limit damage and facilitate recovery in future downturns.

Empirical Approach

The previous section noted the persistence of output losses, with a strong correlation between GDP deviations for 2011–13 and 2015–17. Understanding the sources of variation in output performance during 2011–13 can therefore provide insight into output patterns observed during 2015–17.

As explained in Online Annex 2.2.C, the empirical approach estimates cross-sectional regressions similar to those of other studies that have examined various aspects of cross-country variation in the impact of the global financial crisis (Blanchard, Faruqee, and Das 2010; Claessens and others 2010; Lane and Milesi-Ferretti 2010, 2014; Giannone, Lenza, and Reichlin 2011; Berkmen and others 2012; Tsangarides 2012; Cerra, Panizza, and Saxena 2013). The approach builds on Chapter 4 of the October 2009 WEO, which studies the determinants of medium-term output losses following financial crises in advanced, emerging market, and developing economies during 1970–2002 (see also Abiad and others 2009).

The Nature of the Shock Matters

Although the 2008 financial crisis originated in the United States and Europe, it had a global macroeconomic impact. The origins of the crisis are by now well documented.[14] Four aspects are common to most accounts. First, abundant global liquidity enabled a lending boom in the United States, United Kingdom, euro area, and central and eastern Europe before 2008. As discussed in Chapter 2 of the October 2018 *Global Financial Stability Report* (GFSR), the credit expansion was intermediated through complex links between traditional banks and nonbank financial institutions beyond the regulatory perimeter. Second, as a wave of US adjustable rate mortgages began to reset in 2006–07 and subprime borrowers found it difficult to stay current on their loans or refinance them, the US housing market began to turn in an unprecedented, synchronized manner across many states. Third, unlike the late-1990s US subprime mortgage collapse, which affected mostly loan originators, the financial losses were amplified in 2007–08 by the poorly monitored practice of securitizing subprime loans into complex financial products that became impossible to price in a declining market. Fourth, tightening global financial conditions during 2007–08 hastened the end of the lending boom in the euro area, United Kingdom,

and central and eastern Europe, triggering a wave of defaults by overextended property developers and households unable to roll over their loans, which further strained the balance sheets of European banks already caught in the web of losses on US subprime mortgage exposures. In the euro area, a debilitating nexus soon emerged between banks and sovereigns: taxpayer bailouts and guarantees of distressed banks severely undermined public debt sustainability in some countries; in others, weak fiscal positions and widening government spreads critically compromised banks with large holdings of sovereign securities.

For economies that experienced banking crises in 2007–08, the loss of intermediation services and diminished credit volumes, not surprisingly, had a far-reaching impact on activity. The associated corporate failures and employment losses undermined the ability of borrowers to service their loans, spiraled back to sap bank balance sheets, forced banks to retrench credit further, and amplified the output decline.[15] The analysis suggests that, on average, countries that experienced banking crises suffered a 4 percentage point higher output loss during 2011–13 relative to the precrisis trend than those that did not experience banking crises in 2007–08. (Online Annex Table 2.2.5; Table 2.2 summarizes the direction of impacts for the various drivers.)

Macroeconomic Imbalances and Financial Factors

Regardless of whether a country suffered a banking crisis in 2007–08, tighter financial conditions after the crisis brought out the central role of precrisis financial vulnerabilities in influencing postcrisis output performance. This influence is reflected, at a general level, in the variation of output performance as a function of initial macroeconomic and financial imbalances. It is also seen in the role played by specific factors, such as the pace of precrisis credit growth.

A useful summary statistic of macroeconomic imbalances is the gap between the actual current account balance and its level consistent with medium-term fundamentals. This gap can be thought of as a real-time estimate of imbalances resulting from private

---

[14]See, for example, Obstfeld and Rogoff 2009; Sorkin 2009; Lewis 2010; Lowenstein 2010; Rajan 2010; Blinder 2013; Paulson 2013; Geithner 2014; Bernanke 2015; Bayoumi 2017; and Toloui 2018.

[15]Gertler and Gilchrist (2018) examine the relative contributions of banking disruption and household balance sheets to the contraction of US employment during the Great Recession. They find that banking disruption is key to the aggregate decline in US employment, while household balance sheet strength is relatively more important for explaining regional variation.

Table 2.2. Impact of Precrisis Conditions on 2011–13 GDP Deviations from Precrisis Trend

	(1)	(2)	(3)	(4)	(5)	(6)
	All Countries		AEs		EMs	
Domestic Credit Growth	_**	_***	_***	_***	_***	_**
Demand Exposure to Advanced Economies	_***	_	+	+	_	_
Demand Exposure to China	+	+	+	+*	+**	+
Financial Openness	_*	_	_	_	_	_
CA Balance	+		+***		_	
CA Gap		+***		+***		+
Share of Manufacturing in GDP	+		+		+	
Difficulty of Dismissal	_**		_*		_**	
Precrisis GG Debt Change	_***		_***		_***	
De Facto Peg Dummy	_**		_***		_	
Banking Crisis	_**	_				

Source: IMF staff calculations.

Note: + denotes positive impact, – denotes negative impact. Precrisis conditions are averaged over 2005–08. Results in columns (1) and (2) are reported in Online Annex Table 2.2.5. Results in columns (3) through (6) are reported in Online Annex Table 2.2.7. AEs = advanced economies; CA = current account; CA Gap = excess external balance, Lee and others (2008); EMs = emerging markets; GG = general government.
*** $p < 0.01$, ** $p < 0.05$, * $p < 0.1$.

and public saving-investment disparities (see Lee and others 2008; and Lane and Milesi-Ferretti 2010). The results suggest that countries with current account balances weaker than the level consistent with fundamentals entering the crisis suffered bigger output losses relative to precrisis trends (Online Annex Table 2.2.5; Table 2.2). This may, in part, reflect the more severe adjustment forced on countries with higher precrisis excess deficits.

In addition, countries more dependent on credit (those with faster credit growth in the buildup to the crisis) suffered larger losses in an environment of tighter financial conditions.

Labor Market Structure

Some economies are more flexible than others when it comes to relocating workers in the face of shocks. The strength of employment protection legislation—the balance it provides between security for workers and flexibility for firms—is a key influence on firms' decisions to hire new workers. The evidence suggests that economies in which it was more difficult for firms to terminate labor contracts (proxied by an index of ease of dismissal compiled by the Centre for Business Research [CBR] at Cambridge University) suffered larger postcrisis losses in output relative to precrisis trends (Table 2.2).[16] This

may indicate reluctance on the part of firms during the postcrisis recovery phase to expand operations and lock themselves into costly contracts in economies where subsequent exit would be more difficult.

Spillovers

The results in Table 2.2 are also consistent with spillover effects through trade. Controlling for the effect of banking crises, economies relatively more exposed to demand from advanced economies suffered larger output losses in the aftermath.

The size of gross external financial exposure acted as another key channel through which financial distress from the crippled core of advanced economies transmitted to the rest of the global economy. Countries more integrated into global financial markets (represented by larger fractions of external assets and liabilities relative to GDP) experienced bigger deviations from the precrisis trend.[17] This may reflect, in part, retrenchment in global banking after the crisis.

---

[16]The Cambridge University CBR index (Adams, Bishop, and Deakin 2016) is based on an average of nine detailed indicators of dismissal procedures constructed using leximetric coding methodology on country-level labor legislation. The index is used here because it has broader country coverage than the Organisation for Economic

Co-operation and Development's (OECD's) strength of employment protection indices. The index correlates well with the OECD measures for countries covered by the OECD's indices, as well as with a typical measure of labor market churn and dynamism (the probability of entering and exiting employment), which can be constructed for a limited set of countries along the lines of Elsby, Hobijn, and Sahin (2013), as described in Online Annex 2.2.C.

[17]This is consistent with Perri and Quadrini (2018), who develop a model of global, synchronized recessions that follow from cross-border transmission of liquidity shortages in highly integrated capital markets. The extensive cross-border financial links—particularly among advanced economies—on the eve of the crisis was unprecedented and may have compounded countries' vulnerabilities. See also Chapter 4 of

There is a similar pattern for postcrisis investment deviations among countries that did not experience a banking crisis in 2007–08 (Online Annex Table 2.2.6). In particular, countries with stronger trade ties to advanced economies going into the crisis experienced larger deviations in investment during 2011–13 relative to precrisis trends. This finding is consistent with the earlier observation (Figure 2.6) that persistent capital shortfalls were observed also in countries that did not experience a banking crisis in 2007–08.

An important offsetting influence on weak demand from advanced economies during this period was demand from China. China's 4 trillion yuan stimulus during 2008–11 (close to 10 percent of 2008 GDP) supported a large nationwide infrastructure expansion and construction of social housing, with associated favorable impacts on exporters of commodities and heavy equipment (Ahuja and Nabar 2012). The results in Online Annex Table 2.2.7 (summarized in Table 2.2), grouped according to advanced and emerging market economies, indicate that economies whose export baskets were more exposed to China before the crisis benefited disproportionately in the aftermath from higher exposure to China's domestic demand (measured as the share of trading partner demand accounted for by China), especially among emerging market economies.

Precrisis Policies and Policy Frameworks

The incidence of bank crises in 2007–08 was a key driver of subsequent losses. Regulatory and supervisory structures may thus have played a preemptive role in influencing subsequent damage. The bank regulation index constructed by Barth, Caprio, and Levine (2013) illustrates this link. Specifically, stronger restrictions in 2006 on banks' ability to underwrite, broker, and deal in securities; offer mutual fund products; and engage in insurance underwriting, real estate investment, development, and management are associated with a lower probability of a banking crisis during 2007–08 (Figure 2.10).[18] However, the index measures the strength of restrictions only on specific aspects of bank activity. Other dimensions (for instance, strength of capital, funding, and liquidity requirements; the accompanying supervisory approach to stress-testing balance sheets;

the April 2009 WEO, which documents the role of international links in transmitting financial stress across borders.

[18] The association shown here is robust to controlling for some other influences on the likelihood of a bank crisis (Online Annex Table 2.2.4).

Figure 2.10. Probability of Banking Crisis
(Probability)

Stronger restrictions in 2006 on banks' ability to underwrite, broker, and deal in securities; offer mutual fund products; and engage in insurance underwriting, real estate investment, development, and management are associated with a lower probability of banking crisis in 2007–08.

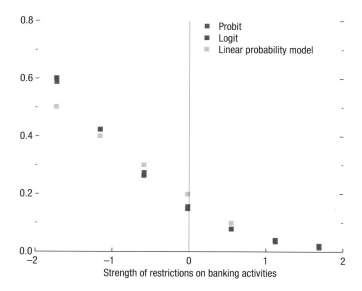

Sources: Barth, Caprio, and Levine (2013); and IMF staff calculations.
Note: Movement from left to right on the *x*-axis indicates stronger restrictions on banking activities. Figure is based on Online Annex Table 2.2.3.

overall intensity of financial sector monitoring activity; the porosity of the regulatory perimeter and opportunities for regulatory arbitrage) likely also played a role.

In general, the initial policy space available prior to a crisis can affect the extent of activity decline afterward (Blanchard, Dell'Ariccia, and Mauro 2010; Jordà, Schularick, and Taylor 2016; Romer and Romer 2018). For the 2008 episode specifically, countries with smaller increases in general government debt over 2005–08 experienced smaller losses relative to trends (Table 2.2). Countries with lower public sector borrowing requirements going into the crisis appear to have had more room to deploy fiscal policy for demand support in the immediate aftermath.

Policy frameworks also appear to matter for postcrisis output outcomes. Exchange rate flexibility is associated with less damage, pointing to a buffering role of nominal exchange rates (Table 2.2). This finding may, in part, reflect the difficulties experienced by some euro area economies. In these countries, the absence of an independent nominal exchange rate, together with fiscal stress and the lack of a common area-wide

Figure 2.11. Postcrisis Deviations of Euro Area and Other Advanced Economies
(Percent)

The median and PPP GDP-weighted mean of output loss for euro area economies are higher than for other advanced economies.

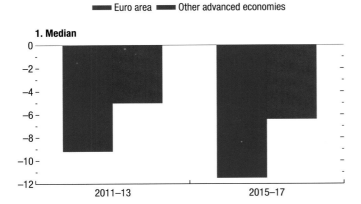

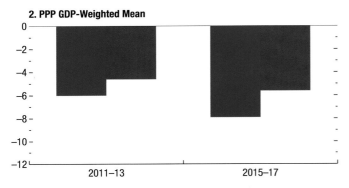

Source: IMF staff calculations.
Note: Other advanced economies are advanced economies that are not in the euro area. PPP = purchasing power parity.

banking union and fiscal backstop, meant the burden of adjustment after the crisis fell entirely on domestic prices and output.

The median output loss for euro area economies is notably higher than for other advanced economies in 2011–13 (Figure 2.11), covering an intense phase of the sovereign debt crisis, deposit flight from stressed euro area economies, and financial fragmentation within the euro area (see IMF 2012, 2013a). The difference in losses widened through 2015–17, pointing to a weaker recovery compared with other advanced economies. The divergence may, in part, reflect the limited policy levers available within a currency union for adjustment to asymmetric shocks, differences in the speed of financial sector repair (as discussed in

Box 2.3), and—despite substantial progress toward a banking union and the creation of the European Stability Mechanism for crisis management—remaining gaps in the euro area architecture.[19]

Extraordinary Actions Taken in the Aftermath of the Crisis

Several countries took exceptional and unprecedented policy measures to support their economies after the 2008 financial crisis. In many cases, notably among the advanced economies most severely affected by the crisis, the measures comprised (1) central bank monetary policy actions—unconventional monetary policy support through asset purchases as policy rates approached their effective lower bounds, and liquidity support to specific segments of credit markets through targeted central bank facilities; (2) discretionary fiscal stimulus; and (3) financial sector operations—bank balance sheet stress tests, government guarantees of banking sector liabilities, purchases of toxic assets from banks, and capital injections. Central banks also established ad hoc bilateral swap lines to support foreign exchange liquidity in jurisdictions beyond home markets.

Advanced economy monetary policy actions, in particular, represented a significant change in the approach to providing monetary accommodation—necessitated in some cases by central banks rapidly reducing policy rates to their effective lower bounds during the crisis (Bernanke 2017). The particular mix of tools varied across individual cases, but generally included a combination of quantitative easing (massive balance sheet expansion with purchases mainly of government bonds, mortgage-backed securities, and corporate bonds); state-dependent forward guidance (specifying particular levels of unemployment and inflation as conditions for rate hikes); negative interest rates (charging commercial banks a penalty on excess reserves held at the central bank); and yield-curve control (targeting the yields of longer-maturity government bonds through central bank purchases).

Estimates of the impact of advanced economy central banks' quantitative easing on interest rates and financial conditions vary (Gagnon 2016). In general, the positive effect of the actions on domestic output in

[19]Thomsen (2017); Arnold and others (2018); and Berger, Dell'Ariccia, and Obstfeld (2018) discuss the reforms implemented to strengthen the euro area architecture and the remaining steps to complete the banking and fiscal union.

Table 2.3. Financial Sector Support and Discretionary Fiscal Stimulus in Group of Twenty Economies
(Percent of GDP)

1. Headline Support for the Financial Sector (as of February 2009)

	Capital Injection	Purchase of Assets, Lending by Treasury	Central Bank Support with Treasury Backing	Central Bank Liquidity Support	Guarantees	Total
	(A)	(B)	(C)	(D)	(E)	(A+B+C+D+E)
G20 Average (PPP GDP-weighted)	2.0	3.3	1.0	9.2	14.3	29.8
Advanced Economies	2.9	5.0	1.2	12.9	21.3	43.3
Advanced Europe	2.4	3.6	2.1	1.0	19.5	28.6
Emerging Markets	0.3	0.1	0.3	1.8	0.2	2.7

2. Crisis-Related Discretionary Fiscal Stimulus in G20 Economies (as of October 2010)

	2009	2010	2011
G20 Average	2.1	2.1	1.1
Advanced Economies	1.9	2.1	1.2
Emerging Markets	2.4	2.0	0.9

Sources: IMF (2009); IMF Fiscal Affairs and Monetary and Capital Markets departments database on public interventions; Chapter 1 of the November 2010 *Fiscal Monitor.*

Note: Panel 1 is calculated based on country statistics originally published in IMF (2009). The data on guarantees for Australia are based on Schwartz and Tan (2016). In panel 1, G20 calculations do not include Mexico and South Africa. G20 = Group of Twenty.

advanced economies and imports from trading partners is believed to have outweighed negative effects as a result of elevated capital inflows and currency appreciation pressure elsewhere (IMF 2014). More broadly, quantitative easing may have also helped stabilize activity by reducing the tail risk of debilitating asset price declines. Nevertheless, the actions were the subject of controversy, with policymakers in emerging market and developing economies, at times, raising concern about adverse spillovers from advanced economy central banks' unconventional monetary policy approaches (Mantega 2010; Zhou 2010; Rajan 2014).

The analysis in this chapter focuses on the impact of fiscal and quasi-fiscal measures in support of the financial sector undertaken by some economies in the aftermath of the crisis (Table 2.3). The Group of Twenty (G20) economies, for example, on average, injected discretionary fiscal stimulus of just over 2 percent of GDP in 2009 and 2010. (The IMF was among the early advocates of the effort in the days leading up to the November 2008 G20 Summit.)[20] The number of such actions is larger than the

[20]During 2008 and 2009, the G20 forum (Argentina, Australia, Brazil, Canada, China, France, Germany, India, Indonesia, Italy, Japan, Mexico, Russia, Saudi Arabia, South Africa, South Korea, Turkey, United Kingdom, United States, European Union) was pivotal in forging international consensus on fiscal expansion, augmenting the lending resources of the IMF and multilateral development banks, and the need to strengthen financial regulation (see https://www.g20.org/en/g20/timeline). For the IMF's November 2008 call for fiscal stimulus by the G20 economies, see http://www.imf.org/en/News/Articles/2015/09/14/01/49/pr08278.

instances of asset purchase programs by advanced economy central banks and therefore more easily studied in a regression framework to assess their impact on output deviations.

Estimating the immediate effect of the actions is difficult. In the case of discretionary fiscal stimulus, for example, causality runs in both directions, with larger output collapses likely to prompt larger policy responses, all else equal. It is nonetheless possible to detect lagged effects of the measures on output deviations from precrisis trends averaged over 2015–17.

As shown in Figure 2.12, conditional on the size of initial losses during 2011–13, quasi-fiscal actions taken to stabilize the financial sector helped limit damage during 2015–17. Overall headline support for the financial sector has a statistically significant positive correlation with subsequent output deviations from trend; among the specific actions, capital injections and guarantees appear to have helped limit subsequent output losses. These interventions may have helped thaw credit markets, and resumption of credit services subsequently contributed to raising output.

Beyond action at the national level, as discussed in Chapter 2 of the October 2018 GFSR, there were extensive multilateral efforts to strengthen financial regulatory standards (aimed at expanding the regulatory perimeter, containing the buildup of systemic risk, strengthening resilience to shocks, and developing resolution frameworks). Multilateral cooperation also helped craft an important component of the monetary response to the crisis, with the IMF pro-

Figure 2.12. Impact on 2015–17 GDP Deviations from One Standard Deviation Increase in Drivers
(Percent)

Actions taken to stabilize the financial sector helped limit damages during 2015–17. Overall headline support for the financial sector has a statistically significant positive correlation with subsequent output deviations from precrisis trend. Among specific actions, capital injections and guarantees have helped limit subsequent output losses.

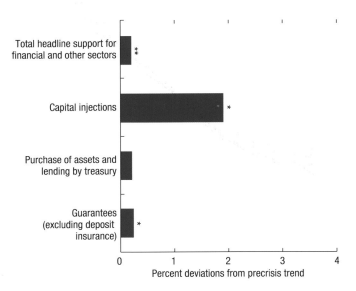

Source: IMF staff calculations.
Note: Movement from left to right on the *x*-axis indicates less negative/more positive deviations from precrisis trend. Extraordinary measures were taken during 2008–09. Coefficient bars correspond to estimates in Online Annex Table 2.2.8. *** $p < 0.01$, ** $p < 0.05$, * $p < 0.1$.

viding unconditional financial resources to its members through a general allocation of SDR 204 billion ($316 billion) during August–September 2009.[21] In addition, several economies relied on the global financial safety net to ease their adjustment to the funding shock after the crisis. The IMF, for example, approved SDR 420 billion in support to its members during 2008–13, of which SDR 119 billion was drawn during that interval.[22]

---

[21]The IMF's special drawing right (SDR), an international reserve asset based on a basket comprising the US dollar, Chinese renminbi, Japanese yen, euro, and British pound, is a claim on freely usable currencies of IMF members. The 2009 general SDR allocation augmented IMF members' international reserves, with the aim of easing postcrisis liquidity constraints (https://www.imf.org/en/News/Articles/2015/09/14/01/49/pr09283).

[22]The gross figure includes precautionary arrangements. See IMF (2015) for details.

Summary

The 2008 financial crisis had its roots in the US housing boom of the preceding half-decade. Its impact was seen worldwide from shuttered maquiladora factories in Mexico to the restructuring of regional savings and loan *cajas* in Spain and extended joblessness for migrant workers in China's Pearl River Delta. Output losses following the 2008 financial meltdown were persistent and experienced by a broad set of countries, not just the group afflicted by banking crises at the time. Protracted weak investment after the crisis was a major contributing factor, associated with persistent shortfalls in capital and total factor productivity, relative to precrisis trends, and slower technology adoption among countries hit harder by the crisis.

The crisis prompted a still-ongoing rethink of the nature of economic fluctuations, as well as of the role of policy frameworks and measures to combat downturns. The policy lessons of the crisis discussed in this chapter follow from the lens adopted to view its aftermath and to understand why the recovery appeared so slow in many countries. Other important developments covered in previous WEO reports, such as the declining share of labor income (Chapter 3 of the April 2017 WEO), subdued wage growth, and the rise of part-time work (Chapter 2 of the October 2017 WEO), pose additional policy challenges for ensuring the income security and welfare of those who rely mostly on their labor income.

The evidence documented in this chapter suggests that policy choices in the run-up to the crisis and in its immediate aftermath influenced postcrisis output performance in multiple ways. Stronger banking regulation—proxied by restrictions on certain aspects of bank activity—appears to have played a preventive role by lowering the probability of a banking crisis in 2007–08. The finding is relevant for ongoing debates on rolling back the regulatory standards adopted following the crisis.

Countries with stronger fiscal positions entering the crisis suffered smaller losses, suggesting that greater room for policy maneuver may have helped defend against harm. Extraordinary fiscal and quasi-fiscal actions to support the financial sector after the crisis appear to have helped lessen output losses over the medium term. Economies that moved quickly to assess the health of their banking systems and recapitalize banks appeared to have suffered smaller output losses subsequently. As IMF (2013c), Auerbach (2017),

Blanchard and Summers (2017), and Furman (2018) note, there is renewed recognition of discretionary fiscal policy as a countercyclical demand management tool. Moreover, as the analysis shows, China's large fiscal stimulus during 2008–11 appears to have had favorable spillovers on trading partners. Altogether, the evidence presented here suggests some confirmation of the efficacy of fiscal measures in limiting persistent losses after a recession. And as noted in earlier IMF research (IMF 2014), unconventional monetary policy actions by advanced economy central banks helped limit output declines and employment losses at home while supporting imports from abroad.

The policy efforts of the past decade helped forestall an even worse outcome with deeper output and employment losses. After faltering at times over the past 10 years, the global economic recovery experienced a long-awaited synchronized growth upswing in 2017–18. Nevertheless, large challenges loom for the global economy. The extraordinary policy actions to prevent a second Great Depression have had important side effects. The extended period of ultralow interest rates in advanced economies has contributed to the buildup of financial vulnerabilities, as discussed in the April and October 2018 GFSRs. The large accumulation of public debt and the erosion of fiscal buffers in many economies following the crisis point to the urgency of rebuilding those defenses to prepare for the next downturn. Moreover, some of the crisis management tools deployed in 2008–09 are no longer available (the Federal Reserve's bailouts of individual institutions, for example), suggesting financial rescues in the future may not be able to follow the same playbook.

Beyond these aspects, more fundamental challenges relate to long-lasting legacies of the crisis. There are already signs of possible long-term consequences of the crisis on potential growth through its impacts on migration, fertility, and future labor input (Box 2.1). And societal support for openness and global economic integration appears to have weakened in many countries after the crisis. The corollary of these developments is the rising appeal of protectionist nostrums and populism. A fuller reckoning of such long-lasting legacies of the 2008 financial crisis must necessarily await the broader perspective that will emerge with further passage of time.

Box 2.1. The Global Financial Crisis, Migration, and Fertility

Empirical and anecdotal evidence suggest that changes in economic performance affect migration flows and fertility rates. This box explores the relationships between postcrisis economic performance, policies, migration, and fertility. The main finding of the box is that postcrisis economic performance had a significant impact on both migration and fertility. Through these channels, the crisis has likely left long-lasting scars on future growth. The box also identifies several policies associated with significant impacts on migration and fertility.

The Great Recession and Migration

The decades leading up to the global financial crisis saw large increases in net migration (immigration-emigration) rates between advanced economies.[1] This trend, however, reversed after the crisis. Meanwhile, net migration has been consistently neutral in emerging markets through both periods, while low-income developing countries have increased net migration rates in the postcrisis years, even as they are generally more prone to volatile net migration rates (Figure 2.1.1, panel 1). Motivated by this heterogeneity of net migration among country groups, the analysis examines the relationship between the changes in trends before and after the crisis, looking at per capita GDP and migration flows by using data on migration inflows from 143 source countries to 20 destination advanced economies.[2]

Immigrants are typically more vulnerable to economic shocks than natives. They are often overrepresented in sectors most sensitive to the business cycle (OECD 2009) and may face discrimination in a tight labor market (Arai and Vilhelmsson 2004). Immigrants have also responded to changes in labor demand more strongly than natives (Kahanec and Guzi 2017). Simple correlations confirm the conjec-

The authors of this box are Christopher Johns, Mico Mrkaic, and Yuan Zeng.

[1]Net migration rate is defined as the number of immigrants minus the number of emigrants over a period, divided by the person-years lived by the population of the destination country over that period. It is expressed as net number of migrants per 1,000 population.

[2]The analysis uses migration inflows, given that inflows are tracked more precisely and more frequently than bilateral migration outflows and migrant stocks. Data on bilateral migration inflows facilitates accurate analysis of the push and pull factors influencing international migration.

Figure 2.1.1. International Migration and the Global Financial Crisis

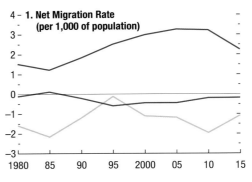

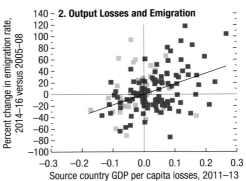

Sources: Organisation for Economic Co-operation and Development; United Nations Department of Economic and Social Affairs, *World Population Prospects: The 2017 Revision*; and IMF staff calculations.
Note: AEs = advanced economies; EMs = emerging market economies; LIDCs = low-income developing countries. Net migration rate by country group is population-weighted average. Losses are based on calculations in Online Annex 2.2.B.

ture that migrants respond to economic performance (Figure 2.1.1, panel 2), measured by the deviations of GDP per capita from precrisis trend (calculated as described in Online Annex 2.2.B).

Beyond the correlations, the analysis explores the links between economic performance and migration in a multivariate setting, controlling for the additional main drivers mentioned in the October 2016 *World Economic Outlook*—structural factors and immigration policies. While the box's discussion centers on the role of economic factors in migration decisions, it should be mentioned that some

Box 2.1 *(continued)*

migration decisions are driven entirely by such factors as political instability and war in the source country or region. To avoid biasing results, migration flows data exclude flows of refugees and asylum seekers.[3] Figure 2.1.2, panel 1 shows the impact of losses in GDP per capita on differences between emigration rates in 2011–13 and 2014–16 compared with years before the crisis (2005–08).[4] Losses in GDP per capita significantly impact migration flows in the short and medium terms. In addition to economic performance, migration flows are affected by the strength of poverty constraints in source countries[5] and the GDP per capita in the destination relative to the source country, education in destination and source countries, and the distance between destination country and source country.[6,7]

Policies imposed in the wake of the crisis to limit migration and reduce competition in labor markets also affect migration (Figure 2.1.2, panel 2). The analysis examines restrictions on legal entry, stay, and quotas (an increase in each variable denotes greater restrictiveness). Increased postcrisis restrictions significantly reduced migration flows, mostly in the medium term, over and above the impact of economic losses.

The Great Recession and Fertility

During a recession, relatively elevated unemployment rates may lead to deferred decisions on marriage, having children, or both. In nearly all recent recessions in advanced economies, the impact on fertility has been mainly to postpone births, which contributes to a short-run reduction in the number of births in the aftermath (long-run effects tend to be

Figure 2.1.2. Impact on Emigration Rate from One Standard Deviation Increase in Drivers at Different Horizons
(Percentage points)

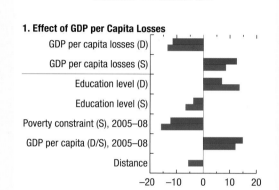

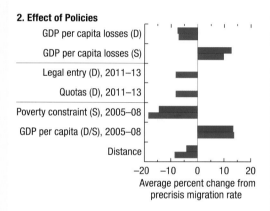

Sources: International Migration Institute; Organisation for Economic Co-operation and Development; Standardized World Income Inequality Database (Solt 2016); World Bank, World Development Indicators database; and IMF staff calculations.
Note: Explanatory variables are contemporaneous with dependent variable unless noted otherwise. All postcrisis variables except GDP per capita losses are average changes from precrisis (2005–08) levels. Losses are based on calculations in Online Annex 2.2.B. All coefficients are statistically significant at 5 percent. Increases in policy variables correspond to increases in restrictiveness. S = source country; D = destination country. Short term = 2011–13 average; Medium term = 2014–16 average.

---

[3]Inflows of foreign population data are from the Organisation for Economic Co-Operation and Development (OECD). Refugees and asylum seekers are excluded from the data for all countries except: Germany, Netherlands, and Norway—included if living in private households (as opposed to reception centers or hostels for immigrants); and United Kingdom—included if stayed in country longer than one year.

[4]Emigration rate is defined as inflows to destination country from source country over a period, divided by 1,000 population in source country.

[5]Defined as the disposable income Gini coefficient divided by the square of PPP GDP per capita.

[6]Distance is defined as great-circle distance between most populated cities in destination country and source country.

[7]Controls based on measures used in Borjas (1987); Hatton and Williamson (2002); and Clark, Hatton, and Williamson (2007).

less pronounced).[8] Although immigration may be a partial solution for low fertility and an aging population in the short term, in the long term, immigrants'

[8]Neels (2010); Cherlin, Cumberworth, and Morgan (2013).

Box 2.1 *(continued)*

Figure 2.1.3. Total Fertility Rate
(Number of births per woman)

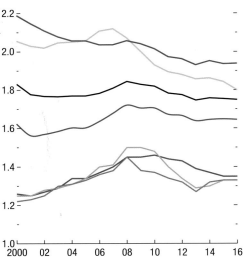

Sources: Organisation for Economic Co-operation and Development (OECD); World Bank, World Development Indicators database; and IMF staff calculations.
Note: OECD is the average fertility rate for OECD and partner countries. AEs = OECD and partner advanced economies; EMs = OECD and partner emerging market economies. See Online Annex 2.1 for country list.

Figure 2.1.4. Impact of Crisis Exposure on Fertility Rate at Different Horizons
(Average change in fertility rate on x-axis; postcrisis minus precrisis)

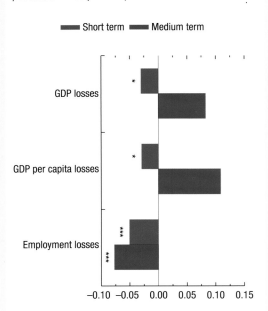

Sources: Organisation for Economic Co-operation and Development; and IMF staff calculations.
Note: Explanatory variables are contemporaneous with dependent variable. Average changes in fertility rate are the difference between postcrisis term and precrisis (2005–08) level. Losses are based on calculations in Online Annex 2.2.B. Short term = 2011–13 average; Medium term = 2015–16 average.
* $p < .10$; ** $p < .05$; *** $p < .01$.

fertility rates generally converge to that of natives (Espenshade 1994).

In the decade before the crisis, the total fertility rate rose in several advanced economies, only to decline afterward (Figure 2.1.3).[9] In the United States, the rate fell from a peak of 2.12 in 2007 to 1.8 in 2016. Similarly, the birth rate of foreign-born women (ages 15–50) in the United States declined by 16 births per thousand women from its peak of 76 in 2008 to its 2016 level. For European countries, such as Greece and Spain that suffered a double-dip recession, the fertility rate decreased from 1.5 to about 1.3 over the

[9]Total fertility rate in a specific year is defined as the total number of children that would be born to each woman if she were to live to the end of her child-bearing years and give birth to children in alignment with the prevailing age-specific fertility rates. It is calculated by aggregating age-specific fertility rates as defined over five-year intervals.

same time span. These persistently low fertility rates over the past decade may weigh on future labor input and thus weaken potential growth in the long run.

Evidence from OECD and partner countries shows that average changes in the fertility rate for the post-crisis period relative to the precrisis period (2005–08) have been negatively impacted by the crisis through several channels, of which employment losses were the most significant (Figure 2.1.4). Further evidence in the literature (Sobotka, Skirbekk, and Philipov 2011) shows that other complex social changes (higher female labor participation rate, smaller desired family size, and so on) and burdened welfare systems could affect women's reproductive decisions.

The fertility rate can be affected by labor market policies as well. Figure 2.1.5 shows how policies

Box 2.1 *(continued)*

affected fertility after the crisis. On one hand, the result in panel 1 demonstrates that a higher precrisis tax wedge on couples reduces fertility in the short term. On the other hand, panel 2 suggests that postcrisis increases in family allowances and improvements in job protection during maternity are associated with higher fertility rates. These findings are in line with evidence and case studies from European Union countries.[10]

Figure 2.1.5. Impact on Fertility from One Standard Deviation Increase in Drivers at Different Horizons

(Average change in fertility rate on x-axis; postcrisis minus precrisis)

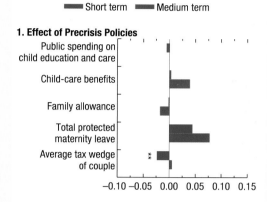

1. Effect of Precrisis Policies

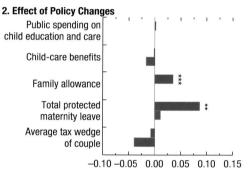

2. Effect of Policy Changes

Sources: Organisation for Economic Co-operation and Development; and IMF staff calculations.
Note: Explanatory variables are contemporaneous with dependent variable. Precrisis policy variables are average of period 2005–08. Policy changes are average postcrisis changes from precrisis (2005–08) levels. Average changes in fertility rate are of difference between postcrisis term and precrisis (2005–08) level. Short term = 2011–13 average; Medium term = 2015–16 average.
* $p < .10$; ** $p < .05$; *** $p < .01$.

[10]See, for example, Hoem (2008), Kalwij (2010), and Thévenon (2011).

Box 2.2. The Employment Impact of Automation Following the Global Financial Crisis: The Case of Industrial Robots

As discussed in the chapter, an important change in the production process after the global financial crisis appears to be the pace of technology adoption. This box addresses the following questions related to technology adoption, using the example of industrial robots: How did the diffusion of robots affect employment in the aftermath of the crisis? What type of workers were particularly affected? Did certain labor market policies alter the impact of robot adoption on employment?

Forces of automation were at work prior to the crisis (Autor, Levy, and Murnane 2003; Goos and Manning 2007; Acemoglu and Autor 2011; Autor and Dorn 2013), and one much-discussed aspect of the transformation of the workplace is the diffusion of industrial robots. Yet, existing work has mostly focused on exploring precrisis diffusion of automation in the United States (Autor, Levy, and Murnane 2003; Acemoglu and Autor 2011; Autor and Dorn 2013; Acemoglu and Restrepo 2017), and in a few European countries (Graetz and Michaels forthcoming; Chiacchio, Petropoulos, and Pichler 2018). Thus, less is known about postcrisis robot diffusion in and beyond these countries. Exploring these recent developments may provide some perspective on possible future workplace dynamics and labor market outcomes, where artificial-intelligence-powered equipment is expected to replace human input in an expanding range of nonroutine tasks (Berg, Buffie, and Zanna 2017; Frey and Osborne 2017; Acemoglu and Restrepo, 2018 and forthcoming).

Effect of Robot Diffusion on Employment

As noted in Acemoglu and Restrepo (2017), robot diffusion can affect employment in different ways. Greater diffusion of robots can affect employment negatively through displacement (by directly replacing workers performing certain tasks), but also positively, through productivity gains, as robots can free up human labor for other tasks, incentivize investment, and create employment.

Estimation results show that increased robot diffusion in industries located in countries with more negative output losses during the crisis is associated with lower employment growth (Figure 2.2.1) in the

The authors of this box are Wenjie Chen and Malhar Nabar.

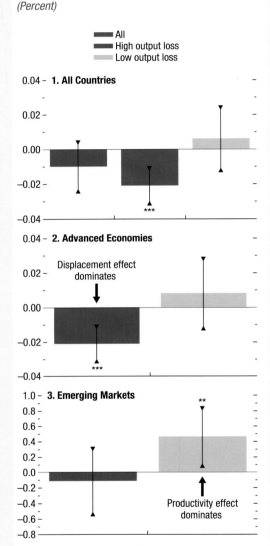

Figure 2.2.1. Effect of Robot Diffusion on Employment Growth
(Percent)

- All
- High output loss
- Low output loss

1. All Countries

2. Advanced Economies
Displacement effect dominates

3. Emerging Markets
Productivity effect dominates

Sources: IFR (2017); World Input-Output Database; and IMF staff calculations.
Note: Robot diffusion is defined as average change in robot shipments/1,000 hours worked 2010–14. Error bars around coefficient estimate are two standard errors. Losses are based on calculations in Online Annex 2.2.B. Figure is based on coefficients in Online Annex Table 2.3.4.
* p < .10; ** p < .05; *** p < .01.

Box 2.2 *(continued)*

aftermath of the crisis. This is particularly driven by industries in advanced economies with relatively bigger output deviations relative to precrisis trend. In emerging markets with relatively lower output deviations relative to precrisis trend, increased robot diffusion is associated with higher employment growth.

Hollowing Out of the Employment-Skills Distribution

The negative association between labor and robot diffusion appears to be more pronounced in industries initially more reliant on medium-skilled workers. The effect is largely seen in advanced economies (Figure 2.2.2). This finding is consistent with the hollowing-out effects documented by Autor, Levy, and Murnane (2003), and Goos, Manning, and Salomons (2014).

Labor Market Policies

To explore whether labor market policies can mitigate the impact of robot diffusion on employment, regression analysis is conducted on samples divided by the severity of crisis exposure.[1]

A consistent picture emerges (Figure 2.2.3): the postcrisis displacement effect of robots on employment was more pronounced in countries with more rigid labor market policies and less labor market dynamism (churn) prior to the crisis.[2] More specifically, lower active labor market spending as a share of GDP, stricter dismissal policies, less churn in the labor market, and more stringent employment protection legislation are associated with higher displacement effects of robot diffusion in countries that experienced relatively high output losses.

[1]Four specific measures of labor market policy are under consideration: (1) active labor market policy (ALMP) spending as share of GDP, (2) ease of dismissal index by Cambridge University's Center for Business Research, (3) labor churn as calculated in Online Annex 2.2.B, and (4) employment protection legislation index compiled by the Organisation for Economic Co-operation and Development. All measures are calculated as precrisis averages to capture the initial extent of labor market rigidities.

[2]Labor market dynamism, also referred to as job churn, is measured as described in Online Annex 2.2.B, following Elsby, Hobijn, and Sahin (2013).

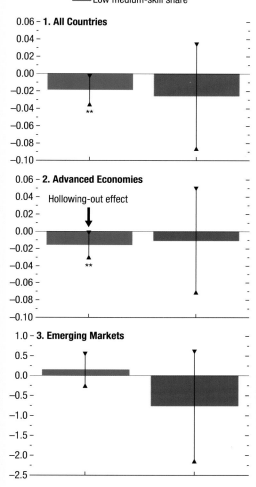

Figure 2.2.2. Hollowing-Out Effect of Robot Diffusion on Employment Growth
(Percent)

Sources: IFR (2017); World Input-Output Database (WIOD); and IMF staff calculations.
Note: Robot diffusion is defined as robot shipment/1,000 hours worked. Level of worker skills is based on education attainment from WIOD. Medium-skilled workers have attained secondary and/or postsecondary nontertiary education in 2009. Error bars around coefficient estimate are two standard errors. Figure is based on coefficients in Online Annex Table 2.3.5.
* p < .10; ** p < .05; *** p < .01.

Box 2.2 *(continued)*

Figure 2.2.3. Labor Market Policies and Effect of Robot Diffusion on Employment Growth

(Average change in employment growth, 2010–14)

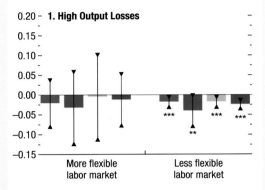

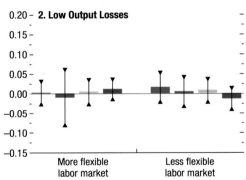

Sources: Cambridge University Center for Business Research (CBR); IFR (2017); Organisation for Economic Co-operation and Development; World Input-Output Database; and IMF staff calculations.
Note: More flexible labor market comprises countries that have above-median ALMP spending (percent of GDP), above-median job churn rates, below-median dismissal regulations as measured by CBR, and below-median EPL. Error bars around coefficient estimate are two standard errors. Losses are based on calculations in Online Annex 2.2.B. Figure is based on coefficients in Online Annex Table 2.3.6. ALMP = active labor market policy; EPL = employment protection legislation.
* $p < .10$; ** $p < .05$; *** $p < .01$.

In sum, industries in advanced economies with relatively bigger output losses experienced displacement effects from robot diffusion in the aftermath of the crisis. This negative effect on employment growth was particularly severe in industries in advanced economies with relatively large shares of medium-skilled workers. At the same time, in countries with more rigid labor market policies and less churn, the labor displacement effect of robot diffusion was more pronounced, suggesting that policies supportive of creating more flexible labor markets can help absorb employment displacement associated with automation.

Box 2.3. The Role of Financial Sector Repair in the Speed of the Recovery

As the financial crisis started rattling markets, policymakers broadly followed the crisis management rulebook: step one—stop panic from spreading (containment phase), step two—repair the damage (resolution phase). The principal forms of intervention were (1) liquidity provision through collateralized lending and other arrangements; (2) support for short-term wholesale funding markets; (3) (more extensive) guarantees of retail deposits and other liabilities; (4) purchases or exchanges of nonperforming or illiquid assets; and (5) capital injections to banks. Interventions often started with liquidity support to relieve the immediate pressure and then moved on to identifying and meeting recapitalization needs.

Yet the timing and strength of the response varied across countries, especially when it came to the challenge of repairing the damage (Figure 2.3.1). Part of the variation certainly reflected when and how severely a country was affected, plus how large the banking sector was relative to GDP, but there are differences even after controlling for crisis severity. Specific forms of intervention also differed. Some governments acquired minority stakes in distressed banks while others chose to close or nationalize them. Stress tests were introduced to restore confidence, with different approaches in design and governance. Sometimes, but not always, measures aiming to reduce debt overhang in the nonfinancial sector accompanied the interventions targeted at the financial institutions. Last but not least, cross-country differences in structural features, such as resolution frameworks, bankruptcy regimes, and the degree to which the system depended on bank- versus market-based financing, came into focus.

Drawing on this variation, several insights can be gained from comparing crisis management in the United States and in Europe:

- The containment phases were fairly similar. The major central banks were quick to offer liquidity support through traditional facilities and established unconventional facilities to ensure that pressure in funding markets subsided. They also established swap lines as early as December 2007 and extended these to other central banks as the crisis spread. In many respects, the response in the containment phase was better coordinated internationally during the recent crisis than in past crises (Laeven and Valencia 2013).

The author of this box is Deniz Igan.

Figure 2.3.1. Containment and Resolution

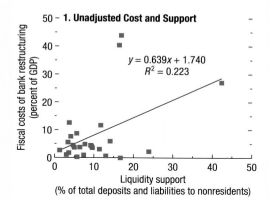

1. Unadjusted Cost and Support

$y = 0.639x + 1.740$
$R^2 = 0.223$

Fiscal costs of bank restructuring (percent of GDP)

Liquidity support (% of total deposits and liabilities to nonresidents)

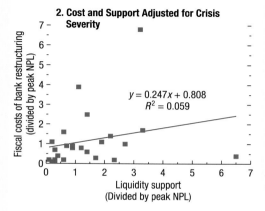

2. Cost and Support Adjusted for Crisis Severity

$y = 0.247x + 0.808$
$R^2 = 0.059$

Fiscal costs of bank restructuring (divided by peak NPL)

Liquidity support (Divided by peak NPL)

Sources: Laeven and Valencia (2013); and IMF staff calculations.
Note: To adjust for crisis severity, fiscal costs of bank restructuring and liquidity support are divided by the peak NPL. NPL = nonperforming loan ratio.

- The resolution phases diverged more, laying bare stark differences in regulatory and supervisory architecture across the two regions.
- The United States mobilized recapitalization plans faster than did countries in the European Union (EU) (Figure 2.3.2).
- In addition to speed, the actions taken in the United States were more decisive. Banks replenished their eroded capital base by issuing new equity early in the crisis, whereas, in the EU, there was no matching effort (Figure 2.3.3). At least in part, this was driven by the supervisory approach: US banks were compelled to raise fresh capital (and were able to do so because of support from the

Box 2.3 *(continued)*

Figure 2.3.2. Timing of Recapitalization
(Months)

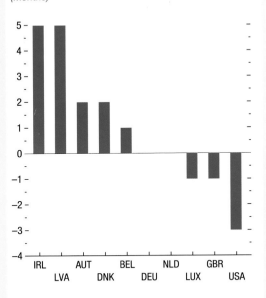

Sources: Laeven and Valencia (2013); and IMF staff calculations.
Note: Timing is measured by the months between moments when liquidity support became extensive and implementation of recapitalization. Data labels use International Organization for Standardization (ISO) country codes.

Figure 2.3.3. New Share Issuance by Banks
(Percent)

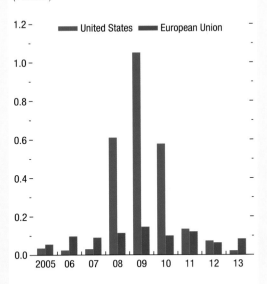

Sources: Homar and van Wijnbergen (2015); and IMF staff calculations.
Note: New share issuance by banks is measured by the volume in percent of the consolidated balance sheet.

Federal Reserve and other agencies); EU banks were instructed to improve their risk-weighted capital ratios, but options were left open on how to do that. Faced with tight funding conditions and broader uncertainty, banks chose to cut lending and increase their sovereign debt holdings—which carry a zero risk weight under Basel III.

- Further, while stress tests were conducted on both sides of the Atlantic, market perceptions of what they accomplished differed. In the United States, the Supervisory Capital Assessment Program aimed to address uncertainty about the solvency of systemic institutions (Bernanke 2009). Moreover, the Treasury Department committed to making capital available to eligible banks. Test results were publicly available on a bank-by-bank basis, providing the needed information to nervous markets (Fernandes, Igan, and Pinheiro 2015). In the European Union, the Committee of European Banking Supervisors conducted two rounds of tests. Individual results were kept confidential in the 2009 round, though

released in the 2010 exercise. The scenarios were criticized for being too benign and not capturing the risk of sovereign default—a major concern at the time (Abramovich 2011).[1] Moreover, the newly created European Financial Stability Facility (EFSF)—tasked with potential capital assistance— could offer funding to member states by selling bonds rather than investing directly in banks.[2] Finally, despite the seal of approval gained by passing the stress tests, many banks continued to struggle. Taken together, these led markets to label the exercise a "nonevent" with no useful information content (Shah 2010).[3] The EU experience under-

[1]Regulators reportedly chose not to include a default scenario "partly because they said that a sovereign default was unlikely and partly due to worries that it would send the wrong political message" (Enrich 2010).

[2]The EFSF was succeeded by the European Stability Mechanism, which, under some conditions, can provide funding directly to recapitalize banks.

[3]Regulators will prefer to fully reveal banks' capital shortfall at times of crisis if they are able to recapitalize them, but will hold onto some information if they cannot recapitalize (Spargoli 2012).

Box 2.3 *(continued)*

scored the importance of credibility—established through independent governance, the requisite technical expertise, and clearly communicated plans for any backstop needs (Ong and Pazarbasioglu 2013).

- Because the epicenter of the crisis in many countries was housing markets, mortgage defaults became endemic. In the United States, the Making Home Affordable (MHA) program was introduced in 2009 to help struggling homeowners (Chapter 3 of the April 2012 *World Economic Outlook*). The refinancing program under the MHA program, in particular, provided substantial welfare gains to highly indebted households (Mitman 2016) and boosted consumption (Agarwal and others 2015). In European countries caught up in their own credit-fueled housing boom-bust, there were no corresponding widespread programs at the outset of the crisis. Nonperforming loan ratios increased more than in the United States and remain high (Figure 2.3.4).[4]

- More generally, many European countries continue to grapple with large stocks of impaired assets a decade after the onset of the crisis. A large confluence of factors—the global financial crisis hit many hard and particularly hurt those with their own homegrown bubbles (Claessens and others 2010)—exposed the monetary union's incomplete architecture and triggered a sovereign debt crisis, subjecting banks to a second round of shocks. The deep and prolonged economic downturn that followed further weakened borrowers' debt service capacity, leading to an increase in loan defaults and large corporate and household debt overhangs. The nonperforming loans are concentrated most notably in small and medium-sized enterprises, which contribute almost two-thirds of Europe's output and employment and tend to rely more on bank financing than large firms. In addition, many European countries have bank-based financial systems.[5] Together with

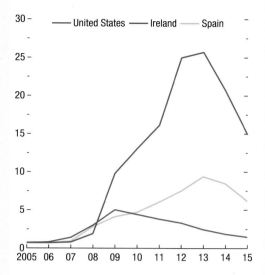

Figure 2.3.4. Nonperforming Loan Ratio
(Percent)

Source: World Bank, Global Financial Development Database.

the concentration of debt overhang in small and medium-sized enterprises, this further amplified the impact of the banks' problems and debt overhang on investment and consumption. Inadequate capital buffers, prudential problems with collateral valuation and treatment of nonperforming loans, legal obstacles to debt enforcement, loan restructuring and foreclosure, and a lack of distressed debt markets have been identified as primary obstacles to nonperforming loan resolution (Aiyar and others 2015).

- A related point of comparison between the US and EU experiences involves the resolution framework for banks themselves. In the former, having an established resolution authority that can act independently on the best option to resolve distressed banks (across state borders)—the Federal Deposit Insurance Corporation—helped ensure swift resolution of failing banks (although dealing with systemic financial institutions required further action). In the latter, the troubles of the banking system started a search for new mechanisms that culminated in the creation of a single supervisor and a unified resolution framework (Goyal and others 2013).

The postcrisis paths for credit, investment, consumption, and growth differed accordingly (Figure 2.3.5). The United States recovered faster and more strongly.

---

[4]Ireland and Spain were chosen for illustrative purposes as they both had housing booms and busts and significant banking distress. Other EU countries that could be used for direct comparison (for example, Greece, Italy, Portugal) either did not have a similar precrisis boom-bust pattern in housing markets, or their experience was dominated by the sovereign debt crisis that followed the global financial crisis.

[5]Market-based economies experience significantly and durably stronger rebounds than those that are bank-based; in particular, the more bank-based economies of continental Europe (Allard and Blavy 2011).

Box 2.3 *(continued)*

Figure 2.3.5. Postcrisis Paths
(Percent; 2007 = 100)

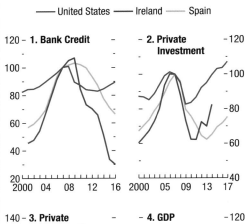

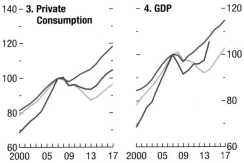

Sources: Organisation for Economic Co-operation and Development; World Bank, World Development Indicators database; and IMF staff calculations.

The deleveraging phase, notably, has been shorter and more shallow—consistent with the importance of repairing bank balance sheets in restoring growth.[6]

Summing up, comparison of the US and European experiences and cross-country studies highlights the following:

- *Swift and decisive action:* Recapitalizing or resolving banks shortly after the containment phase is key. The alternative leads to zombification, with significant macroeconomic costs. From a structural point of view, resolution frameworks should aim to ensure that such swift and decisive action is possible.

- *Appropriate backstops:* In extreme circumstances, establishing credibility and preventing panic and contagion may require use of public funds. In this context, having enough fiscal room and mitigating the sovereign-bank nexus become crucial. Any actual use of these backstops, however, should be a last-resort measure accompanied by appropriate burden sharing and clear exit strategies to minimize moral hazard, as well as the potential costs associated with direct government involvement in financial markets (for example, efficiency concerns).

---

[6]Other evidence corroborates this insight: early and decisive recapitalization of distressed banks helps corporate investment recover (Sun and Tong 2015) and can take several years off the duration of a recession (Homar and van Wijnbergen 2015).

References

Abiad, Abdul, Ravi Balakrishnan, Petya Koeva Brooks, Daniel Leigh, and Irina Tytell. 2009. "What's the Damage? Medium-Term Output Dynamics after Banking Crises." IMF Working Paper 09/245, International Monetary Fund, Washington, DC.

Abramovich, Alexander. 2011. "Comparative Analysis of Stress Testing in the United States and Europe." North Carolina Banking Institute 15 (1), Article 16, University of North Carolina School of Law, Chapel Hill, NC.

Acemoglu, Daron, and Autor, David. 2011. "Skills, Tasks and Technologies: Implications for Employment and Earnings." *Handbook of Labor Economics,* Elsevier.

Acemoglu, Daron, and David Autor. 2011. "Skills, Tasks, and Technologies: Implications for Employment and Earnings." In *Handbook of Labor Economics* (4), edited by Orley Ashenfelter and David E. Card. Amsterdam: Elsevier.

Acemoglu, Daron, and Pascual Restrepo. 2017. "Robots and Jobs: Evidence from US Labor Markets." NBER Working Paper 23285, National Bureau of Economic Research, Cambridge, MA.

———. 2018. "Artificial Intelligence, Automation, and Work." NBER Working Paper 24196, National Bureau of Economic Research, Cambridge, MA.

———. Forthcoming. "The Race between Man and Machine: Implications of Technology for Growth, Factor Shares, and Employment." *American Economic Review.*

Adams, Zoe, Louise Bishop, and Simon Deakin. 2016. *CBR Labour Regulation Index.* Cambridge: Centre for Business Research.

Adler, Gustavo, Romain Duval, Davide Furceri, Sinem Kiliç Çelik, Ksenia Koloskova, and Marcos Poplawski-Ribeiro. 2017. "Gone with the Headwinds: Global Productivity." IMF Staff Discussion Note 17/04, International Monetary Fund, Washington, DC.

Agarwal, Sumit, Gene Amromin, Souphala Chomsisengphet, Tomasz Piskorski, Amit Seru, and Vincent Yao. 2015. "Mortgage Refinancing, Consumer Spending, and Competition: Evidence from the Home Affordable Refinancing Program." NBER Working Paper 21512, National Bureau of Economic Research, Cambridge, MA.

Ahuja, Ashvin, and Malhar S. Nabar. 2012. "Investment-Led Growth in China: Global Spillovers." IMF Working Paper 12/267, International Monetary Fund, Washington, DC.

Aiyar, Shekhar, Wolfgang Bergthaler, Jose M. Garrido, Anna Ilyina, Andreas Jobst, Kenneth Kang, Dmitriy Kovtun, Yan Liu, Dermot Monaghan, and Marina Moretti. 2015. "A Strategy for Resolving Europe's Problem Loans." IMF Staff Discussion Note 15/19, International Monetary Fund, Washington, DC.

Allard, Céline, Petya Koeva Brooks, John C. Bluedorn, Fabian Bornhorst, Katharine Christopherson, Franziska Ohnsorge, Tigran Poghosyan, and an IMF Staff Team. 2013. "Toward a Fiscal Union for the Euro Area." IMF Staff Discussion Note 13/09, International Monetary Fund, Washington, DC.

Allard, Julien, and Rodolphe Blavy. 2011. "Market Phoenixes and Banking Ducks: Are Recoveries Faster in Market-Based Economies?" IMF Working Paper 11/213, International Monetary Fund, Washington, DC.

Arai, Mahmood, and Roger Vilhelmsson. 2004. "Unemployment-Risk Differentials between Immigrant and Native Workers in Sweden." *Industrial Relations* 43: 690–98.

Arnold, Nathaniel, Bergljot Barkbu, Elif Ture, Hou Wang, and Jiaxiong Yao. 2018. "A Central Fiscal Stabilization Capacity for the Euro Area." IMF Staff Discussion Note 18/03, International Monetary Fund, Washington, DC.

Aslam, Aqib, Patrick Blagrave, Eugenio Cerutti, Sung Eun Jung, and Carolina Osorio-Buitron. Forthcoming. "Recessions and Recoveries: Are EMs Different from AEs?" IMF Working Paper, International Monetary Fund, Washington, DC.

Auerbach, Alan. 2017. "Fiscal Policy." Peterson Institute for International Economics, Washington, DC.

Autor, David, and David Dorn. 2013. "The Growth of Low-Skill Service Jobs and the Polarization of the U.S. Labor Market." *American Economic Review* 103 (5): 1553–1597.

Autor, David, Frank Levy, and Richard Murnane. 2003. "The Skill Content of Recent Technological Change: An Empirical Exploration." *Quarterly Journal of Economics* 118 (4): 1279–333.

Ball, Laurence. 2014. "Long-Term Damage from the Great Recession in OECD Countries." NBER Working Paper 20185, National Bureau of Economic Research, Cambridge, MA.

Barnichon, Regis, Christian Matthes, and Alexander Ziegenbein. 2018. "The Financial Crisis at 10: Will We Ever Recover?" Federal Reserve Bank of San Francisco Economic Letter 2018–19, August.

Barth, James R., Gerard Caprio, Jr., and Ross Levine. 2013. "Bank Regulation and Supervision in 180 Countries from 1999 to 2011." NBER Working Paper 18733, National Bureau of Economic Research, Cambridge, MA.

Bayoumi, Tamim. 2017. *Unfinished Business: The Unexplored Causes of the Financial Crisis and the Lessons Yet to Be Learned.* New Haven, CT: Yale University Press.

Berg, Andrew, Ed Buffie, and Felipe Zanna. 2017. "Should We Fear the Robot Revolution? (The Correct Answer Is Yes)." Manuscript prepared for the Carnegie-Rochester NYU Conference Series.

Berger, Helge, Giovanni Dell'Ariccia, and Maurice Obstfeld. 2018. "Revisiting the Economic Case for Fiscal Union in the Euro Area." Departmental Paper, Research Department, International Monetary Fund, Washington, DC.

Berger, Helge, Thomas Dowling, Sergi Lanau, Weicheng Lian, Mico Mrkaic, Pau Rabanal, and Marzie Taheri Sanjani. 2015. "Steady as She Goes—Estimating Potential Output during Financial 'Booms and Busts'." IMF Working Paper 15/233, International Monetary Fund, Washington, DC.

Berkmen, S. Pelin, Gaston Gelos, Robert Rennhack, and James P. Walsh. 2012. "The Global Financial Crisis: Explaining

Cross-Country Differences in the Output Impact." *Journal of International Money and Finance* 31: 42–59.

Bernanke, Ben S. 2009. "Statement Regarding the Supervisory Capital Assessment Program." May 7. http://www.federalreserve.gov/newsevents/press/bcreg/bernankescap20090507.htm.

———. 2015. *The Courage to Act: A Memoir of a Crisis and Its Aftermath*. New York, NY: W. W. Norton & Company, Inc.

———. 2017. "Monetary Policy for a New Era." Prepared for conference titled "Rethinking Macroeconomic Policy," Peterson Institute for International Economics, Washington DC, October 12–13.

———. 2018. "The Real Effects of Disrupted Credit: Evidence from the Global Financial Crisis." The Per Jacobsson Foundation Lecture, Bank for International Settlements, Basel, and forthcoming in *Brookings Papers on Economic Activity*, Brookings Institution, Washington, DC.

Blanchard, Olivier, Eugenio Cerutti, and Lawrence Summers. 2015. "Inflation and Activity—Two Explorations and Their Monetary Policy Implications." NBER Working Paper 21726, National Bureau for Economic Research, Cambridge, MA.

Blanchard, Olivier, Giovanni Dell'Ariccia, and Paolo Mauro. 2010. "Rethinking Macroeconomic Policy." IMF Staff Position Note 10/03, International Monetary Fund, Washington, DC.

Blanchard, Olivier, Hamid Faruqee, and Mitali Das. 2010. "The Initial Impact of the Crisis on Emerging Market Countries." *Brooking Papers on Economic Activity* (Spring): 263–23.

Blanchard, Olivier, and Daniel Leigh. 2013. "Growth Forecast Errors and Fiscal Multipliers." *American Economic Review* 103 (3): 117–20.

Blanchard, Olivier, and Lawrence H. Summers. 2017. "Rethinking Stabilization Policy: Back to the Future." Conference titled "Rethinking Macroeconomic Policy," Peterson Institute for International Economics, Washington, DC, October 12–13.

Blinder, Alan S. 2013. *After the Music Stopped: The Financial Crisis, the Response, and the Work Ahead*. New York, NY: The Penguin Press.

Borjas, George J. 1987. "Self-Selection and the Earnings of Immigrants." *American Economic Review* 77 (4): 531–53.

Candelon, Bertrand, Alina Carare, Jean-Baptiste Hasse, and Jing Lu. 2018. "Globalization and the New Normal." IMF Working Paper 18/75, International Monetary Fund, Washington, DC.

Cerra, Valerie, Ugo Panizza, and Sweta Saxena. 2013. "International Evidence on Recovery from Recessions." *Contemporary Economic Policy* 31 (2): 424–39.

Cerra, Valerie, and Sweta Saxena. 2008. "Growth Dynamics: The Myth of Economic Recovery." *American Economic Review* 98 (1): 439–57.

———. 2017. "Booms, Crises, and Recoveries: A New Paradigm of the Business Cycle and Its Policy Implications." IMF Working Paper 17/250, International Monetary Fund, Washington, DC.

Cherlin, Andrew, Erin Cumberworth, and Christopher Morgan. 2013. "The Effects of the Great Recession on Family Structure and Fertility." *The ANNALS of the American Academy of Political and Social Science* 650: 214–31.

Chiacchio, Francesco, Georgios Petropoulos, and David Pichler. 2018. "The Impact of Industrial Robots on EU Employment and Wages: A Local Labour Market Approach." Bruegel Working Paper 02, Bruegel, Brussels.

Claessens, Stijn, Giovanni Dell'Ariccia, Deniz Igan, and Luc Laeven. 2010. "Cross-Country Experiences and Policy Implications from the Global Financial Crisis." *Economic Policy* April: 267–93.

Clark, Ximena, Timothy J. Hatton, and Jeffrey G. Williamson. 2007. "Explaining U.S. Immigration, 1971–98." *Review of Economics and Statistics* 89 (2): 359–73.

Congressional Budget Office (CBO). 2014. "Revisions to CBO's Projection of Potential Output since 2007." https://www.cbo.gov/publication/45150.

Elsby, Michael W.L., Bart Hobijn, and Aysegul Sahin. 2013. "Unemployment Dynamics in the OECD." *Review of Economics and Statistics* 95 (2): 530–48.

Enrich, David. 2010. "EU Banks Survive Stress Test." *The Wall Street Journal*, July 24. http://online.wsj.com/article/SB10001424052748703294904575384940544522582.html.

Espenshade, Thomas J. 1994. "Can Immigration Slow US Population Aging?" *Journal of Policy Analysis and Management* 13 (4): 759–68.

Fernald, John G. 2015. "Productivity and Potential Output before, during, and after the Great Recession." *NBER Macroeconomics Annual 2014* 29 (1): 1–51.

Fernandes, Marcelo, Deniz Igan, and Marcelo Pinheiro. 2015. "March Madness in Wall Street: (What) Does the Market Learn from Stress Tests?" IMF Working Paper 15/271, International Monetary Fund, Washington, DC.

Frey, Carl Benedikt, and Michael A. Osborne. 2017. "The Future of Employment: How Susceptible Are Jobs to Computerisation?" *Technological Forecasting and Social Change* 114 (C): 254–80.

Furman, Jason. 2018. "The Fiscal Response to the Great Recession: Steps Taken, Paths Rejected, and Lessons for Next Time." Brookings Institution.

Gagnon, Joseph E. 2016. "Quantitative Easing: An Underappreciated Success." Peterson Institute of International Economics Policy Brief 16–4, Peterson Institute of International Economics, Washington, DC.

Geithner, Timothy F. 2014. *Stress Test: Reflections on Financial Crises*. New York, NY: Broadway Books.

Gertler, Mark, and Simon Gilchrist. 2018. "What Happened: Financial Factors in the Great Recession." NBER Working Paper 24746, National Bureau of Economic Research, Cambridge, MA.

Giannone, Domenico, Michele Lenza, and Lucrezia Reichlin. 2011. "Market Freedom and the Global Recession." *IMF Economic Review* 59 (1): 111–35.

Goos, Maarten, and Alan Manning. 2007. "Lousy and Lovely Jobs: The Rising Polarization of Work in Britain." *The Review of Economics and Statistics* 89 (1): 118–133.

———, and Anna Salomons. 2014. "Explaining Job Polarization: Routine-Biased Technological Change and Offshoring." *American Economic Review* 104 (8): 2509–26.

Gourinchas, Pierre-Olivier, and Maurice Obstfeld. 2012. "Stories of the Twentieth Century for the Twenty-First." *American Economic Journal: Macroeconomics* 4 (1): 226–65.

Goyal, Rishi, Petya Koeva Brooks, Mahmood Pradhan, Thierry Tressel, Giovanni Dell'Ariccia, Ross Leckow, Ceyla Pazarbasioglu, and an IMF Staff Team. 2013. "A Banking Union for the Euro Area." IMF Staff Discussion Note 13/01, International Monetary Fund, Washington, DC.

Graetz, Georg, and Guy Michaels. Forthcoming. "Robots at Work." *Review of Economics and Statistics*.

Hall, Robert E. 2014. "Quantifying the Lasting Harm to the US Economy from the Financial Crisis." *NBER Macroeconomics Annual* 29: 71–128.

Hatton, Timothy J., and Jeffrey G. Williamson. 2002. "What Fundamentals Drive World Migration?" NBER Working Paper 9159, National Bureau of Economic Research, Cambridge, MA.

Hoem, Jan M. 2008. "The Impact of Public Policies on European Fertility." *Demographic Research* (19): 249–60.

Homar, Timotej, and Sweder J. G. van Wijnbergen. 2015. "On Zombie Banks and Recessions after Systemic Banking Crises: Government Intervention Matters." CEPR Discussion Paper DP10963, Centre for Economic Policy Research, London.

International Federation of Robotics (IFR). 2017. "World Robotics 2017 Industrial Robots." https://ifr.org.

International Monetary Fund (IMF). 2009. "The State of Public Finances: Outlook and Medium-Term Policies after the 2008 Crisis." Fiscal Affairs Department publication, Washington, DC.

———. 2012. "Euro Area Policies: 2012 Article IV Consultation." IMF Country Report 12/181, Washington, DC.

———. 2013a. "Euro Area Policies: 2013 Article IV Consultation—Staff Report." IMF Country Report 13/231, Washington, DC.

———. 2013b. "Greece: Ex Post Evaluation of Exceptional Access under the 2010 Stand-By Arrangement." IMF Country Report 13/156, Washington, DC.

———. 2013c. "Reassessing the Role and Modalities of Fiscal Policy in Advanced Economies." IMF Policy Paper, Washington, DC.

———. 2014. "IMF Multilateral Policy Issues Report." IMF Spillover Report, Washington, DC.

———. 2015. "Crisis Program Review." Strategy, Policy and Review Department, International Monetary Fund, Washington, DC.

Jordà, Òscar, Moritz Schularick, and Alan M. Taylor. 2016. "Sovereigns versus Banks: Credit, Crises, and Consequences." *Journal of the European Economic Association* 14 (1): 45–79.

Kahanec, Martin, and Martin Guzi. 2017. "How Immigrants Helped EU Labor Markets to Adjust during the Great Recession." *International Journal of Manpower* 38 (7): 996–1015.

Kalwij, Adriaan. 2010. "The Impact of Family Policy Expenditure on Fertility in Western Europe." *Demography* 47 (2): 503–519.

Kozlowski, Julian, Laura Veldkamp, and Venky Venkateswaran. 2017. "The Tail That Wags the Economy: Beliefs and Persistent Stagnation." NBER Working Paper 21719, National Bureau of Economic Research. Cambridge, MA.

Laeven, Luc, and Fabián Valencia. 2013. "Systemic Banking Crises Database." *IMF Economic Review* 61 (2): 225–70.

Lagarde, Christine. 2014. "The Challenge Facing the Global Economy: New Momentum to Overcome a New Mediocre." Speech at Georgetown University School of Foreign Service, Washington, DC, October 2.

———. 2016. "Decisive Action to Secure Durable Growth." Lecture at an event hosted by Bundesbank and Goethe University, Frankfurt, Germany, April 5.

Lane, Philip R., and Gian Maria Milesi-Ferretti. 2010. "The Cross-Country Incidence of the Global Crisis." IMF Working Paper 10/171, International Monetary Fund, Washington, DC.

———. 2014. "Global Imbalances and External Adjustment after the Crisis." IMF Working Paper 14/151, International Monetary Fund, Washington, DC.

———. 2017. "International Financial Integration in the Aftermath of the Global Financial Crisis." IMF Working Paper 17/115, International Monetary Fund, Washington, DC.

Lee, Jaewoo, Jonathan D. Ostry, Alessandro Prati, Luca A. Ricci, and Gian Maria Milesi-Ferretti. 2008. "Exchange Rate Assessments: CGER Methodologies, IMF Occasional Paper 261, International Monetary Fund." Washington, DC.

Lewis, Michael. 2010. *The Big Short: Inside the Doomsday Machine*. New York, NY: W. W. Norton & Company, Inc.

Lipton, David. 2018. "Trust and the Future of Multilateralism." IMF Blog.

Lowenstein, Roger. 2010. *The End of Wall Street*. New York, NY: The Penguin Press.

Mantega, Guido. 2010. International Monetary and Financial Committee, Statement by Guido Mantega, Minister of Finance, Ministerio da Fazenda, Brazil, October 9.

Mitman, Kurt. 2016. "Macroeconomic Effects of Bankruptcy and Foreclosure Policies." *American Economic Review* 106 (8): 2219–55.

Neels, Karel. 2010. "Temporal Variation in Unemployment Rates and Their Association with Tempo and Quantum of Fertility: Some Evidence for Belgium, France, and the Netherlands." Paper prepared for the session titled "Low Fertility and Its Association with Macroeconomic Trends" of the Annual Meeting of the Population Association of America.

Obstfeld, Maurice, and Kenneth Rogoff. 2009. "Global Imbalances and the Financial Crisis: Products of Common Causes." Proceedings, Federal Reserve Bank of San Francisco, October 2009.

Ong, Li Lian, and Ceyla Pazarbasioglu. 2013. "Credibility and Crisis Stress Testing." IMF Working Paper 13/178, International Monetary Fund, Washington, DC.

Organisation for Economic Co-operation and Development (OECD). 2009. *International Migration Outlook.*

Paulson, Jr., Henry H. 2013. *On the Brink: Inside the Race to Stop the Collapse of the Global Financial System.* New York, NY: Business Plus.

Perri, Fabrizio, and Vincenzo Quadrini. 2018. "International Recessions." *American Economic Review* 108 (4–5): 935–84.

Pritchett, Lant, and Lawrence H. Summers. 2013. "Asia-Phoria Meet Regression to the Mean." Proceedings, Federal Reserve Bank of San Francisco (November): 1–35.

Rajan, Raghuram G. 2010. *Fault Lines: How Hidden Fractures Still Threaten the Global Economy.* Princeton, NJ: Princeton University Press.

———. 2014. "Competitive Monetary Easing: Is It Yesterday Once More?" Remarks at the Brookings Institution, Washington, DC, April 10.

Romer, Christina D., and David H. Romer. 2018. "Phillips Lecture—Why Some Times Are Different: Macroeconomic Policy and the Aftermath of Financial Crises." *Economica* 85: 1–40.

Schanzenbach, Diane, Ryan Nunn, Lauren Bauer, and Audrey Breitwieser. 2017. "The Closing of the Jobs Gap: A Decade of Recession Recovery." Brookings Institution, The Hamilton Project, Washington, DC.

Schwartz, Carl, and Nicholas Tan. 2016. "The Australian Government Guarantee Scheme: 2008–15." Bulletin – March Quarter, Reserve Bank of Australia.

Shah, Neil. 2010. "Wait-and-See after Europe Stress Test." *The Wall Street Journal*, July 26. http://blogs.wsj.com/marketbeat/2010/07/26/wait-and-see-aftereurope-stress-test/.

Sobotka, Tomáš, Vegard Skirbekk, and Dimiter Philipov. 2011. "Economic Recession and Fertility in the Developed World." *Population and Development Review* 37 (2): 267–306.

Solt, Frederick. 2016. "The Standardized World Income Inequality Database." *Social Science Quarterly* 97 (5): 1267–281.

Sorkin, Andrew Ross. 2009. *Too Big to Fail: The Inside Story of How Wall Street and Washington Fought to Save the Financial System—and Themselves.* New York, NY: Viking Penguin.

Spargoli, Fabrizio. 2012. "Bank Recapitalization and the Information Value of a Stress Test in a Crisis." Manuscript, Universitat Pompeu Fabra.

Summers, Lawrence H. 2016. "The Age of Secular Stagnation: What It Is and What to Do about It." *Foreign Affairs*, March/April.

Sun, Yangfang, and Hui Tong. 2015. "How Does Postcrisis Bank Capital Adequacy Affect Firm Investment?" IMF Working Paper 15/145, International Monetary Fund, Washington, DC.

Thévenon, Olivier. 2011. "Family Policies in OECD Countries: A Comparative Analysis." *Population and Development Review* 37 (1): 57–87.

Thomsen, Poul. 2017. "The Euro Zone: What's Next." Speech at the *Financial Times* Investment Management Summit, London, September 28.

Timmer, Marcel. P., Erik Dietzenbacher, Bart Los, Robert Stehrer, and Gaaitzen J. de Vries. 2015. "An Illustrated User Guide to the World Input-Output Database: The Case of Global Automotive Production." *Review of International Economics* 23 (3): 575–605.

Toloui, Ramin. 2018. "Global Financial Crisis: Origins and Causes." Lectures Series on Navigating Financial Crises in the Modern Global Economy, Stanford University, Stanford, CA.

Tsangarides, Charalambos. 2012. "Crisis and Recovery: Role of the Exchange Rate Regime in Emerging Market Economies." *Journal of Macroeconomics* 34: 470–88.

Zhou, Xiaochuan. 2010. International Monetary and Financial Committee, Statement by Zhou Xiaochuan, Governor of the People's Bank of China and Governor of the IMF for China, October 9.

CHALLENGES FOR MONETARY POLICY IN EMERGING MARKETS AS GLOBAL FINANCIAL CONDITIONS NORMALIZE

Inflation in emerging market and developing economies since the mid-2000s has, on average, been low and stable. This chapter investigates whether these recent gains in inflation performance are sustainable as global financial conditions normalize. The findings are as follows: first, despite the overall stability, sizable heterogeneity in inflation performance and in variability of longer-term inflation expectations remains among emerging markets. Second, changes in longer-term inflation expectations are the main determinant of inflation, while external conditions play a more limited role, suggesting that domestic, not global, factors are the main contributor to the recent gains in inflation performance. Third, further improvements in the extent of anchoring of inflation expectations can significantly improve economic resilience to adverse external shocks in emerging markets. Anchoring reduces inflation persistence and limits the pass-through of currency depreciations to domestic prices, allowing monetary policy to focus more on smoothing fluctuations in output.

Introduction

Inflation in emerging market and developing economies (hereafter, emerging markets) has, on average, been remarkably low and stable in recent years (Figure 3.1).[1] Following large commodity price swings, inflation in most emerging markets has been quick to stabilize, and the short-lived effects of inflationary shocks have, in turn, allowed central banks in these countries to cut interest rates to fight off recessions.

As monetary policy gradually normalizes in advanced economies, the ability of emerging markets to fend off inflationary pressures is being tested

again.[2] This chapter examines whether the recent gains in inflation performance—quick stabilization after inflationary shocks—are sustainable, or represent an artifact of (potentially temporary) global factors that have put downward pressure on inflation. The answer is crucial as emerging markets craft their monetary policies to navigate the future shift in global financial conditions.

Proponents on both sides of the question can find evidence for their positions (Figure 3.2). The optimists can point to substantial supportive changes in institutional and policy frameworks (Rogoff 2004; Chapter 4 of the September 2005 *World Economic Outlook* [WEO]; Végh and Vuletin 2014; Chapter 2 of the April 2016 WEO). For example, after the Asian crisis of the late 1990s, which illustrated anew some limitations of pegged exchange rate regimes, central banks in many emerging markets adopted inflation targeting. Furthermore, as noted, their price stability endured despite sharp swings in commodity prices, the global financial crisis, and periods of strong and sustained US dollar appreciation. The policy changes, combined with real-world success, indicate that the gains in inflation performance are well rooted.

Pessimists can argue that China's integration into world trade and the broader globalization of commerce created a disinflationary environment benefiting emerging markets (Carney 2017; Auer, Levchenko, and Sauré forthcoming; Chapter 2 of the May 2018 *Regional Economic Outlook: Asia and Pacific*). They may further note that the period following the global financial crisis was characterized by historically benign external financial conditions—manifested in low US government bond yields and compressed spreads in emerging markets—that limited the number of crisis events and accompanying inflation surges in emerging markets (Chapter 2 of the April 2016 WEO).

To shed more light on these issues, this chapter first examines the above competing claims: Was the

The authors of this chapter are Rudolfs Bems (lead), Francesca Caselli, Francesco Grigoli, Bertrand Gruss, and Weicheng Lian, with contributions from Michal Andrle, Yan Carrière-Swallow, and Juan Yépez, and support from Ava Yeabin Hong, Jungjin Lee, Cynthia Nyakeri, and Jilun Xing. Comments from Rafael Portillo are gratefully acknowledged.

[1]The analysis of this chapter is largely based on 19 emerging markets: Argentina, Brazil, Bulgaria, Chile, China, Colombia, Hungary, India, Indonesia, Malaysia, Mexico, Peru, Philippines, Poland, Romania, Russia, South Africa, Thailand, and Turkey. For details on the sample selection, see Online Annex 3.1. All annexes are available online at www.imf.org/en/Publications/WEO.

[2]As advanced economies endeavor to raise interest rates from abnormal lows, currencies in emerging markets will tend to depreciate as global portfolio investments react to diminished yield differentials. The depreciation will be passed on to domestic prices.

Figure 3.1. Headline Consumer Price Index Inflation
(Percent)

Following a period of disinflation during the 1990s and early 2000s, inflation in emerging markets has remained low and stable since the mid-2000s.

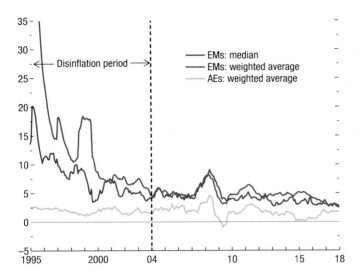

Sources: Haver Analytics; and IMF staff calculations.
Note: AEs = advanced economies; EMs = emerging markets. See Online Annex 3.1 for data sources and country coverage. Weighted average is constructed using weights of nominal GDP, expressed in US dollar terms, for 2010–12. The vertical dashed line distinguishes the disinflation period from the rest of the sample.

recent benign inflation behavior widespread among emerging markets? What was driving inflation during this episode? And have the gains in inflation been well rooted through better domestic policies, or can they be expected to wane as global conditions shift?

Analysis of these initial questions finds that, first, the improved inflation performance since the mid-2000s was indeed broad based. However, the gains have not been uniform, as some emerging markets continue to find it challenging to keep inflation low. Second, it concludes that longer-term inflation expectations have been the main factor determining inflation, compared with the considerably smaller role of external conditions. This finding suggests that domestic, not global, factors were the main contributor to the recent gains in inflation performance.[3]

---

[3]Chapter 3 of the April 2006 WEO draws similar conclusions from an analysis of the role of global factors in the disinflation episode of the 1990s and early 2000s. Focusing on advanced economies, Ihrig and others (2010) find little support for an increasing role of global factors in the inflation process, although others (see Borio and Filardo 2007) argue that the role of global factors has increased since the 1990s.

Figure 3.2. Institutional and Policy Changes, Global Shocks, and Financial Conditions

The decline and subsequent stability of inflation in emerging markets coincided with substantial improvements in institutional and policy frameworks and endured despite sharp swings in commodity prices and other large global shocks. Yet, the period was also characterized by historically benign external financial conditions.

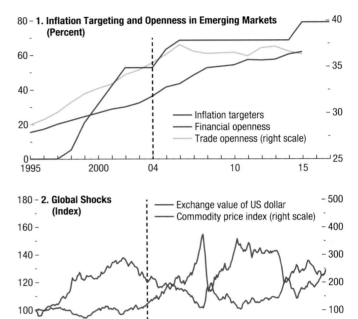

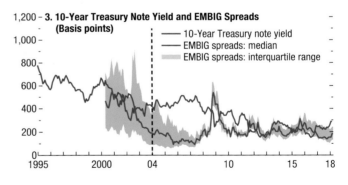

Sources: Haver Analytics; JPMorgan Emerging Market Bond Index; Lane and Milesi-Ferretti (2018); and IMF staff calculations.
Note: EMBIG = emerging market bond index global. See Online Annex 3.1 for data sources and country coverage. Inflation targeters are expressed as percent of countries in the sample. Trade openness is defined as imports in percent of GDP (five-year moving average). Financial openness is defined as the sum of foreign direct investment and portfolio equity liabilities in percent of GDP (five-year moving average). Exchange value of US dollar is the nominal broad trade-weighted exchange value of the US dollar (Jan-95=100). The commodity price index is based on prices in US dollars of a broad set of commodities (Jan-95=100). EMBIG spreads are spreads between sovereign bonds in emerging markets and comparable US Treasury bonds. The vertical dashed line distinguishes the disinflation period from the rest of the sample.

Given the importance of changes in inflation expectations in driving inflation in emerging markets, the second part of the chapter zooms in on the behavior of inflation expectations. It measures and summarizes the extent of anchoring of longer-term inflation expectations in emerging markets and studies its implications for inflation performance and the conduct of monetary policy. More specifically, the chapter addresses the following questions:

- How has the extent of anchoring of inflation expectations evolved in recent decades? How much heterogeneity in the extent of anchoring is there among emerging markets, and how does it compare with conditions in advanced economies?

- What are the implications of the extent of anchoring of inflation expectations for monetary policy cyclicality and macroeconomic resilience when facing adverse external shocks?

In examining those questions, the chapter reaches the following conclusions:

- The anchoring of inflation expectations has improved significantly over the past two decades, with the bulk of the gains taking place in the 2000s. Nonetheless, there is considerable heterogeneity in the extent of anchoring across emerging markets, as longer-term inflation expectations in several countries remain relatively volatile.

- Better-anchored inflation expectations reduce inflation persistence and limit the pass-through of currency depreciations to domestic prices. Such stability allows monetary policy to focus more on smoothing output fluctuations and improving resilience to adverse external shocks.

The chapter concludes that, amid monetary policy normalization in advanced economies, it is important for policymakers in emerging markets to consolidate and, in some cases, further improve the extent of anchoring of inflation expectations. How can the volatility of domestic inflation expectations be reduced? The empirical findings from the literature, confirmed by the evidence reported in this chapter, link the extent of anchoring to the performance of domestic fiscal and monetary policy frameworks. Fiscal sustainability is a necessary precondition for a credible nominal anchor. Similarly, a reduction in the variability of longer-term inflation expectations cannot be achieved without a credible and independent central bank that communicates its intentions in a transparent and timely manner. These recommenda-

tions remain relevant also for emerging markets with better-anchored expectations, as their commitment to inflation targets will likely be tested by the gradual monetary policy normalization in advanced economies.

Extent of Improvements in Inflation Outcomes

How broad based are the gains in inflation performance? To answer this question, this section first examines headline consumer price inflation statistics, which are available for a comprehensive set of 90 emerging market and developing economies, and then zooms in on a sample of 19 emerging markets for which more detailed inflation data are available.[4] Box 3.1 shows that the 19 sample countries, which constitute 80 percent of the GDP of all emerging market and developing economies, are broadly representative in terms of inflation trends of the comprehensive set of emerging market and developing economies.[5]

Headline consumer prices in the wider group of emerging market and developing economies, split into three broad geographical areas—Asia, Latin America, and the combination of Europe, the Middle East, and Africa—all exhibit the same pattern of convergence to lower inflation rates (Figure 3.3, panel 1). The sizable and persistent differences in inflation rates among these regions during the 1990s and early 2000s were gone by the mid-2000s. In addition, the dispersion of inflation rates across emerging market and developing economies—as measured by the distance between the 10th and 90th percentiles of the distribution—had declined substantially by the mid-2000s and has remained relatively stable since then.

The share of emerging market and developing economies with inflation rates exceeding 10 percent declined

---

[4]Country coverage, data sources, and definitions of variables are reported in Online Annex 3.1.

[5]The sample includes relatively large emerging markets but, with regard to other basic macroeconomic characteristics (income per capita, GDP growth rates, the level of financial development, and trade openness), the sample economies are comparable to the rest of emerging market and developing economies. One notable difference is that the median degree of exchange rate flexibility among the sample economies is larger than among all emerging market and developing economies. The more limited exchange rate flexibility in the broader set of emerging market and developing economies can affect inflation through channels that are less prevalent in the sample economies (see Box 3.1). However, the broader concept of inflation expectations anchoring—as studied in this chapter—is equally relevant in flexible, managed, or fixed exchange rate regimes. See Adrian, Laxton, and Obstfeld (2018) for a discussion of the challenges in managing inflation expectations under different monetary regimes.

Figure 3.3. Regional Differences and Dispersion in Headline Consumer Price Index Inflation in Emerging Market and Developing Economies
(Percent)

The gains in inflation performance among emerging market and developing economies were broad based. But 15 percent of these economies still registered double-digit inflation rates over 2004–18.

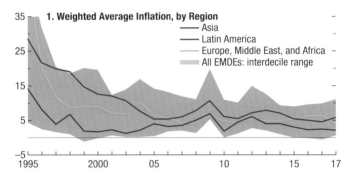

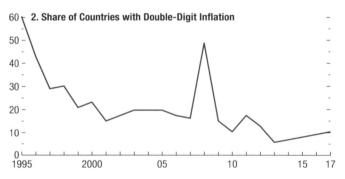

Source: IMF staff calculations.
Note: EMDEs = emerging market and developing economies. See Online Annex 3.1 for data sources and country coverage.

Figure 3.4. Other Measures of Price Inflation in Emerging Markets
(Percent)

Alternative price measures for emerging markets also indicate a sizable decline in inflation during the 1990s and early 2000s and relative price stability since the mid-2000s.

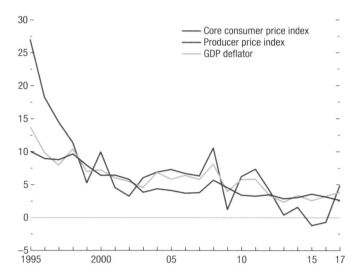

Source: IMF staff calculations.
Note: See Online Annex 3.1 for data sources and country coverage. Lines denote medians across sample emerging markets of each indicator.

dramatically from the mid-1990s until the early 2000s and stayed relatively stable thereafter (Figure 3.3, panel 2). Nonetheless, the gains in inflation behavior are not uniform—15 percent of emerging market and developing economies have had a headline inflation rate of 10 percent or more, on average, from 2004 to the first quarter of 2018. Several other economies exhibited sustained surges of inflation to double-digit rates.

Turning to other measures of price inflation, the inflation rate for so-called core consumer prices, which exclude food and energy items with more volatile prices, also declined until the mid-2000s and has remained low and stable since then (Figure 3.4).[6] The

inflation rate of producer prices fell drastically during the 1990s and has remained at relatively low levels ever since. Finally, the same pattern is exhibited by GDP deflators, which encompass the prices of all domestically produced final goods and services.

Inflation variability has been stable or declining in emerging markets since 2004 (Figure 3.5). The decline in the variability of inflation rates is not driven by exchange rate behavior, as there is no clear evidence of a decline in the variability of exchange rate movements since the late 1990s.[7] Inflation persistence also declined gradually during the sample period.[8] As with inflation rates—which are higher in emerging markets than in advanced economies—two factors suggest that emerging markets could be expected to exhibit a greater degree of inflation volatility and persistence. First, a higher share of consumption in emerging markets is devoted to food and other commodities, whose prices

---

[6]For these more detailed inflation statistics, as well as the econometric analysis that follows, the chapter focuses on the narrower sample of 19 emerging markets, defined in Online Annex 3.1.

[7]See Ilzetzki, Reinhart, and Rogoff (2017) for a discussion of changes in de facto exchange rate volatility.

[8]Inflation persistence is defined as the tendency for price shocks to elevate inflation above its long-term level for a prolonged period (see Online Annex 3.1 for details).

tend to be more volatile. And, especially regarding persistence, monetary policy institutions and frameworks in emerging markets could be less developed and thus less effective.[9] So, it is a notable commentary on the progress made in strengthening monetary policy frameworks in emerging markets that, since 2004, the volatility of inflation for a large share (but not all) of the country sample has been comparable to that in advanced economies. The persistence of inflation has also been reduced, even though it remains somewhat above the level in advanced economies.

In sum, inflation performance in emerging markets has markedly improved since the mid-2000s. The improvement is not, however, uniform across the country sample, and inflation is still generally more volatile and persistent than in advanced economies.

Determinants of Inflation in Emerging Markets

What has been driving inflation in emerging markets during the period of stable and low inflation from 2004 to the first quarter of 2018? Among other inflation determinants, this section assesses the role played by two competing forces—external price pressures and changes in longer-term inflation expectations—and gauges the overall contributions from factors of global and domestic origin.[10]

The analysis decomposes inflation into contributions from conventional determinants of inflation—the degree of economic slack, inflation expectations, and external factors—and consists of two stages.[11] The first stage estimates a Phillips curve.[12] The specification includes domestic and foreign output gaps, three-year-ahead inflation forecasts, and a measure of external price developments as explanatory factors, and allows for inflation persistence and country fixed effects. The baseline specification is estimated for a panel of sample emerging

Figure 3.5. Inflation Dynamics
(Percent)

The variability and persistence of consumer price inflation has declined significantly in emerging markets, remaining relatively low since the mid-2000s.

1. Headline Consumer Price Index Inflation

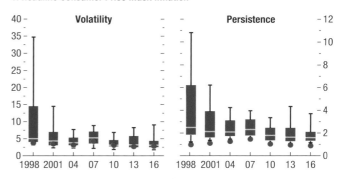

2. Core Consumer Price Index Inflation

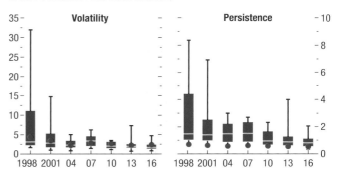

Source: IMF staff calculations.
Note: See Online Annex 3.1 for data sources and country coverage. The volatility is computed as the standard deviation of detrended (Hodrick-Prescott) inflation. Persistence denotes the standard deviation of the permanent component of inflation based on Stock and Watson (2007). The horizontal line in each box represents the median across countries; the upper and lower edges of each box show the top and bottom quartiles; and the vertical lines denote the range between the top and bottom deciles. The dots denote the average for advanced economies. *X*-axis labels indicate the start of three-year windows.

[9]See Mishkin (2007) for a discussion of how better monetary policy can contribute to a decline in inflation persistence.

[10]In line with the existing literature, longer-term inflation expectations are proxied by surveys covering professional forecasters. Some studies have documented significant differences between forecasts of households and firms and those of professional analysts (see, for instance, Mankiw, Reis, and Wolfers 2004); unfortunately, surveys covering households and firms are rarely available.

[11]See Online Annexes 3.1 and 3.2 for details.

[12]Estimates are from a hybrid variant of a standard New Keynesian Phillips curve framework. See Galí and Gertler (1999) and Galí, Gertler, and Lopez-Salido (2001, 2003) for the theoretical underpinnings. To account for the role of global factors, the analysis follows Borio and Filardo (2007); Ihrig and others (2010); and Auer, Levchenko, and Sauré (forthcoming).

markets using core inflation and quarterly data from the first quarter of 2004 to the first quarter of 2018.[13] Estimated parameters are broadly consistent with findings in the literature (Figure 3.6).

The second stage of the analysis explores the role of explanatory factors in determining actual inflation during 2004–18. The exercise is constructed in terms

[13]The chapter's main findings are unchanged for specifications using headline consumer price inflation (Online Annex 3.2). The results are robust to excluding the period of the global financial crisis or focusing the analysis on the postcrisis period.

Figure 3.6. Coefficient Estimates from the Baseline Phillips Curve Specification
(Percentage points)

Inflation expectations, domestic output gaps, and external price pressure significantly influence consumer price inflation in emerging markets.

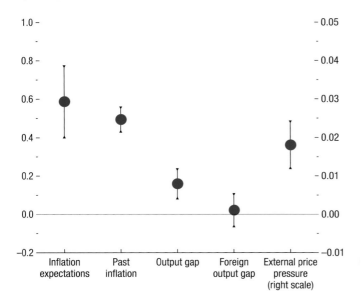

Source: IMF staff calculations.
Note: See Online Annex 3.1 for data sources and country coverage. The dots denote the estimated coefficient from a hybrid Phillips curve model (see Online Annex 3.2) and the vertical lines denote the 90 percent confidence interval.

of deviations in inflation from its target values.[14] The contribution of each explanatory factor is computed in terms of (1) average contributions to inflation *levels*, and (2) contributions to inflation *variability* at quarterly frequency, in the spirit of a variance decomposition exercise.[15]

Contributions to Inflation

The results indicate that changes in longer-term inflation expectations have been the key driver of the *level* of inflation in emerging markets, with an overall positive contribution to inflation in each of the four indicative subperiods explored (Figure 3.7, panel 1). That is, inflation expectations for the sample

[14]When a country is not an inflation targeter, its implicit target is defined as the moving average of 10-year-ahead inflation expectations.

[15]The decomposition of inflation dynamics is conducted in a manner similar to that in Yellen (2015) and Chapter 3 of the October 2016 WEO, taking into account the estimated persistence of the inflation process. See Online Annex 3.2 for details.

Figure 3.7. Contributions to Deviation of Core Inflation from Target
(Percentage points, unless noted otherwise)

Changes in longer-term inflation expectations have been the key driver of the level and variability of inflation in emerging markets, although there is substantial cross-country heterogeneity.

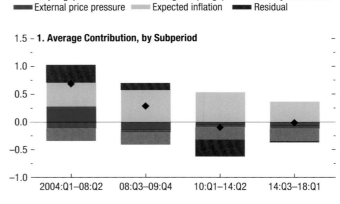

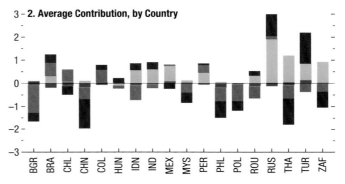

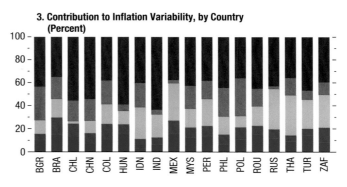

Source: IMF staff calculations.
Note: See Online Annex 3.1 for data sources and country coverage. The bars in panel 1 (panel 2) represent the simple average contribution of each factor averaged across countries (periods). The diamonds in panel 1 represent the overall deviation in inflation. Bars for contributions to inflation variability in panel 3 show the simple average of the absolute values of country-specific contributions across periods, expressed as percent of the overall deviation of core inflation from target. Data labels use International Organization for Standardization (ISO) country codes.

emerging markets, on average, exceeded the inflation target.[16] In comparison, external prices exerted a deflationary influence, but the magnitude of this effect (–0.05 percentage point annually, on average, over the sample period) was considerably smaller than that of longer-term inflation expectations (0.5 percentage point). The deflationary pressure from external prices was most pronounced during the boom that preceded the global financial crisis.

The overall deviation of inflation from the target declined gradually during 2004–14, by 0.7 percentage point.[17] This trend is partly explained by output gaps (domestic and foreign), which stimulated inflation during the boom of 2004–07 and depressed it during the bust of 2008–09, and partly by the remaining residual.

Examining the same contributions at the country level reveals that, although changes in longer-term inflation expectations are the main overall contributor to the deviations of actual inflation from target, there is noticeable cross-country heterogeneity (Figure 3.7, panel 2). The average inflationary impact of expectations is sizable for only half of the economies in the sample. In contrast, external price developments have exerted downward pressure on domestic prices for three-fourths of the economies in the sample, even though the magnitude of this contribution is small. The impact of cyclical factors is, by construction, limited when averaged over 2004–18.

Analysis of contributions to the *variability* of inflation shows that the model, on average, explains 55 percent of the deviations of inflation from target (Figure 3.7, panel 3). The results confirm the importance of fluctuations in longer-term inflation expectations around the inflation target. Inflation expectations are the largest contributing explanatory factor for four-fifths of the sample countries, explaining, on average, 20 percent of the variation in inflation. Similar to the evidence in Figure 3.7, panel 2, there is substantial heterogeneity across countries, with the share attributable to inflation expectations ranging from 2 percent to 35 percent. The results also confirm that external price movements played a more limited role in the variability in inflation rates, on average explaining 8 percent of inflation deviations. The contribution of

the foreign output gap is negligible in all decomposition results.[18]

Role of Domestic and Global Factors

The remaining task for the analysis is to assess domestic and global contributions to inflation in emerging markets. The two capture an important distinction in that only domestic factors can be influenced by policies in emerging markets, making them potentially sustainable. In contrast, foreign factors, even when deflationary, are more temporary in nature and could dissipate or reverse.

To gauge the contribution of global factors to inflation deviations from target, the analysis reinterprets results from the baseline contributions exercise in panel 3 of Figure 3.7. Fluctuations in inflation expectations and domestic output gaps are considered domestic factors, whereas external price pressure and foreign output gaps are interpreted as global factors.[19,20] Applying this definition of global factors, the contribution results for inflation variability suggest that inflation deviations from target during 2004–18 were largely determined by domestic factors, with foreign factors explaining 5–15 percent of inflation variability.

---

[16]This could reflect the public's doubts about the central bank's commitment to the inflation target, or concerns about fiscal sustainability, which may imply higher inflation in the future.

[17]This decline is consistent with the small downward trend in core consumer price inflation shown in Figure 3.4.

[18]The analysis in this section is subject to several limitations. First, the Phillips curve estimates can be affected by endogeneity issues, although the robustness exercises in Online Annex 3.2 suggest that the economic magnitude of the potential biases are relatively small. Second, the decomposition results are subject to sizable uncertainty given that 45 percent of the variability in inflation remains unexplained.

[19]The labeling of contributions as domestic and global factors warrants a cautionary note. On one hand, inflation expectations can be affected by both domestic and global factors, leading to an underestimation of the contribution of global factors. However, the baseline specification directly controls for foreign variables. Moreover, the results, when the inflation expectations variable is purged of external factors (by replacing it with the residual from a regression of inflation expectations on external price pressure, foreign output gap, and country and time fixed effects), are similar (Online Annex 3.2), indicating that inflation expectations are mostly driven by domestic factors. That said, foreign shocks that have an impact on the domestic output gap, but are not captured by changes in the foreign output gap and the external price pressure variable, can also lead to a downward bias in the estimated contribution of global factors. On the other hand, some of the fluctuations in the exchange rate embedded in the external price pressure variable can be due to domestic factors, potentially biasing the estimated contribution of foreign factors upward.

[20]Online Annex 3.2 reports results from alternative model specifications that include a broader set of foreign factors (for example, global value chain participation, external price pressure from China). Also examined is an alternative decomposition exercise that decomposes inflation levels rather than deviations from target values. Baseline results concerning domestic versus global contributions are shown to be robust to all alternative specifications.

Figure 3.8. Time Fixed Effects and Common Drivers, by Subperiod
(Percentage points)

Apart from the commodity-induced inflation surge during 2008, common factors played a limited role as drivers of inflation dynamics in emerging markets over 2004–18.

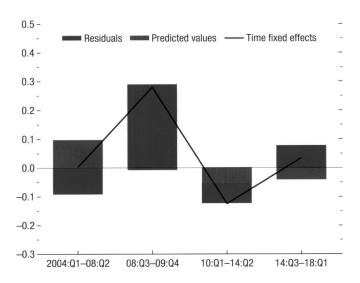

Source: IMF staff calculations.
Note: See Online Annex 3.1 for data sources and country coverage. Time fixed effects are constructed as predicted values from the regression reported in column (1) of Online Annex Table 3.2.2. Residuals are from a regression of these time fixed effects on averages of other explanatory factors included in the same first-stage regression and a constant. Time fixed effects and predicted values are subsequently normalized such that time fixed effects in 2004–18 average to zero.

Could the decrease in the average decomposition residual during 2004–14 (Figure 3.7, panel 1) signify a common source of downward pressure on inflation? To address this question, the analysis estimates a common driver of inflation across emerging markets that cannot be explained by domestic factors.[21] The approach is implemented by including time fixed effects in the model specification. Results show that the common component (that is, the time fixed effects) captures the commodity-induced inflation surge during 2008 but, for other sample subperiods, its contribution to inflation deviations from target is small in economic terms (the black line in Figure 3.8). Furthermore, the estimated time fixed effects correlate with domestic explanatory factors. Beyond these factors, the residual

provides a negligible average contribution to inflation during the post–global financial crisis period. These findings corroborate the earlier findings on the comparatively limited average impact of global factors in driving inflation in emerging markets.

Overall, the results of this section point to the centrality of fluctuations in longer-term inflation expectations in driving inflation in emerging countries, which are interpreted to be of domestic origin. Motivated by these findings, the rest of the chapter zooms in on the behavior of inflation expectations.

Anchoring of Inflation Expectations

How anchored are expectations in emerging markets? After discussing how to define and measure the degree of anchoring, this section documents the evolution of anchoring over time, the extent of its variation across the sample economies, and the influence of policy frameworks on the extent of anchoring.

Measuring Anchoring

The concept of anchored inflation expectations has no widely agreed-upon definition. The literature has, however, developed an operational or practical definition—it is a set of predictions about the behavior of inflation forecasts in economies where expectations are "anchored." Under those circumstances, expectations for inflation over a sufficiently long horizon should be centered around the explicit or implicit target and hence not react to transitory fluctuations in actual inflation or in short-term inflation expectations (Demertzis, Marcellino, and Viegi 2012; Kumar and others 2015). In addition, if the monetary framework is credible and inflation expectations are well anchored, the dispersion (range of values) of individual longer-term inflation forecasts would tend to be low (Capistrán and Ramos-Francia 2010; Dovern, Fritsche, and Slacalek 2012; Ehrmann 2015; Kumar and others 2015).

Building on these operational characteristics, the analysis uses survey-based longer-term inflation forecasts from professional forecasters to construct four complementary metrics aimed at capturing the extent of anchoring of inflation expectations:[22]

---

[21]For details of this two-stage regression specification, see notes to Figure 3.8. See Chapter 3 of the October 2017 WEO for an earlier application of this approach.

[22]Detailed definitions for each measure are provided in Online Annex 3.3.

- A summary measure of absolute deviations in inflation forecasts from a target,
- A summary measure of the variability of inflation forecasts over time,
- The dispersion of inflation forecasts across individual forecasters, and
- The sensitivity of inflation forecasts to surprises about current inflation.

In each case, a lower reading represents better anchoring of inflation expectations. Of course, each measure has advantages and shortcomings, including in terms of data coverage. Nonetheless, these four measures convey a consistent picture for each country.[23]

The Extent of Anchoring in Emerging Markets

These metrics suggest that inflation expectations have become increasingly anchored in emerging markets over the past two decades (Figure 3.9). The improvement in the extent of anchoring was particularly prominent in the early 2000s; subsequent gains have been more muted. Toward the end of the sample period, there is evidence that the extent of anchoring has worsened in a few countries. However, this recent trend is not consistent across the four anchoring metrics.

At the same time, the metrics point to substantial variation in the degree of anchoring across emerging markets (Figure 3.10). At the high end, the average level of anchoring over 2004–17 in some emerging markets was even higher than the average for a sample of 11 inflation-targeting advanced economies. But for the emerging markets in the bottom quartile (the least anchored), the average reading for each measure is between three and seven times larger than that for emerging markets in the top quartile.[24] On average, anchoring in emerging markets remains substantially weaker than in advanced economies.

The heterogeneity in the extent of anchoring is reflected in the role of inflation expectations in determining deviations of inflation from targets (Figure 3.7, panels 1 and 2). If the sample economies are split into two even groups according to how well anchored expectations were during 2004–18, the contribution of

[23]The rankings of economies, based on each metric of anchoring, correlate highly across measures, with the rank correlation between any two measures ranging from 0.56 to 0.87.

[24]The metrics also reveal that the position of economies in the ranking for anchoring has changed little over time, indicating that the extent of anchoring changes slowly (Online Annex Figure 3.3.1).

Figure 3.9. Evolution of the Degree of Anchoring of Inflation Expectations, 2000–17
(Percent)

Inflation expectations in emerging markets have become increasingly anchored over the past two decades, with most of the gains taking place prior to the mid-2000s.

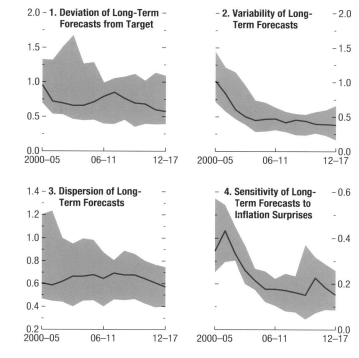

Source: IMF staff calculations.
Note: See Online Annex 3.1 for data sources and country coverage. The figure shows the evolution of the degree of anchoring of inflation expectations over six-year rolling windows. The lines denote the median across countries. The shaded areas denote interquartile ranges. The measures on the degree of anchoring of inflation expectations are defined in Online Annex 3.3. In all panels, lower values denote more-anchored inflation expectations.

changes in longer-term inflation expectations to actual inflation is substantially larger for the economies with less-anchored inflation expectations (by 0.4 percentage point annually on average) than for those with more-anchored inflation expectations.[25] The contribution of other factors to actual inflation is broadly similar across the less- and more-anchored groups.

In sum, the extent of anchoring of inflation expectations in emerging markets has improved significantly over the past few decades, but sizable differences

[25]Similarly, changes in longer-term inflation expectations account for a relatively low fraction of inflation variability in those economies with better-anchored expectations, such as Chile and Poland (Figure 3.7, panel 3).

Figure 3.10. Cross-Country Heterogeneity in Degree of Anchoring of Inflation Expectations, 2004–17
(Percent)

The extent of anchoring of inflation expectations varies markedly across emerging markets and remains substantially weaker than in advanced economies on average.

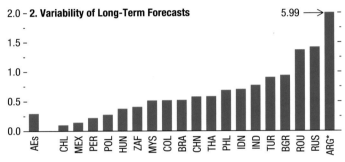

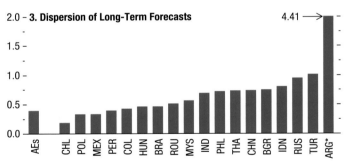

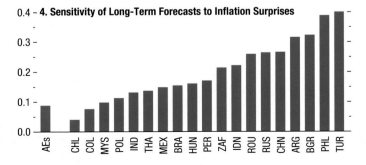

Source: IMF staff calculations.
Note: AEs = average of 11 advanced inflation targeting economies. See Online Annex 3.1 for data sources and country coverage. The figures show the average value for each anchoring measure over 2004–17. Values marked with (*) have been truncated at 2. The measures on the degree of anchoring of inflation expectations are defined in Online Annex 3.3. In all panels, lower values denote more-anchored inflation expectations. Data labels use International Organization for Standardization (ISO) country codes.

remain across emerging markets and relative to advanced economies.

Anchoring and Policy Frameworks

What explains the improvements in the anchoring of longer-term inflation expectations across emerging markets, as well as the still-sizable cross-country differences? A comprehensive study is beyond the scope of this chapter, but an exploration of the data confirms findings from the literature regarding the important role of sound monetary and fiscal frameworks in determining inflation expectations.

The literature suggests that the extent of anchoring is intimately related to the credibility of the monetary strategy (Cukierman and Meltzer 1986; King 1995).[26] A monetary policy plan will be credible if the public believes the monetary authority does not have incentives to deviate from that plan or does not need to subordinate it to other considerations, such as restoring fiscal solvency. The formation of inflation expectations thus lies at the heart of any concept of credibility. Central banks may use monetary policy to pursue multiple goals, but the credibility of the policy is typically interpreted in terms of inflation performance.

Several studies have found that adopting an inflation target and transparent public communication of monetary policy helps anchor inflation expectations in emerging and advanced economies alike.[27] The data analyzed here confirm the importance of inflation targeting and transparency in the sample of emerging markets covered in this chapter (Figure 3.11,

[26]Cukierman and Meltzer (1986) argue that the ability of the monetary authority to achieve its future objectives depends on the inflation expectations of the public, which in turn depend on the public's evaluation of the credibility of the monetary authority.
[27]Gürkaynak, Levin, and Swanson (2010) analyze the behavior of long-term forward rates on nominal and inflation-indexed bonds in Sweden, the United Kingdom, and the United States, and conclude that announcing an explicit inflation target helps anchor long-term inflation expectations. Levin, Natalucci, and Piger (2004) reach a similar conclusion for a broader sample of advanced economies. Capistrán and Ramos-Francia (2010) find that the dispersion of inflation forecasts in emerging markets tended to fall after adopting an inflation target, while Brito, Carrière-Swallow, and Gruss (2018) argue that the reduction in disagreement among forecasts that follows the adoption of inflation targeting is largely due to increased central bank transparency. Chapter 3 of the May 2018 *Regional Economic Outlook: Western Hemisphere* finds that stronger transparency frameworks and communication strategies are associated with more-anchored inflation expectations.

panel 1).[28] The cross-country variation in the degree of anchoring is related to both the maturity of an inflation targeting regime—more precisely, to the age of the regime—and to the transparency of central bank policy (as measured by Dincer and Eichengreen 2014). More broadly, central bank communication plays a key role in anchoring expectations by improving the predictability of monetary policy (Box 3.2).[29]

Regardless of the specific design of the monetary framework, sound and sustainable fiscal policy is essential for the credibility of monetary policy (see, for instance, Masson, Savastano, and Sharma 1997; Mishkin 2000; and Mishkin and Savastano 2001).[30] If public debt is perceived to be unsustainable, higher inflation will be expected. The mechanism for the expected price acceleration is the expectation of "fiscal dominance"—an eventual monetization of the debt or large devaluations of the currency. Some studies have indeed found an association between fiscal institutions and credibility on one hand and inflation performance and the anchoring of inflation expectations on the other (Combes and others 2017; Caldas Montes and Acar 2018) or a link between expected fiscal performance and inflation expectations (Celasun, Gelos, and Prati 2004). In line with these studies, the cross-country variation in the degree of anchoring in the sample covered in this chapter is positively related to the market perception about the sustainability of public debt (Figure 3.11, panel 2).[31]

Implications of Anchoring for Monetary Policy

Longer-term inflation expectations are a key driver of inflation in emerging markets, and the economies vary in the degree to which the expectations are anchored. When longer-term expectations are not well anchored,

[28]The analysis on Figure 3.11 is based on the variability of inflation forecasts, but a similar picture emerges when any of the other three anchoring metrics is used.

[29]See Al-Mashat and others (2018b) for a discussion of how central bank transparency and enhanced communication can reinforce confidence in the long-term inflation target and improve the effectiveness of the monetary policy instrument.

[30]Other factors are also likely to matter for longer-term anchoring; for instance, Mishkin and Savastano (2001) point to the importance of stringent prudential regulations and strict supervision of financial institutions to ensure that the system is capable of withstanding exchange rate fluctuations.

[31]The analysis uses asset prices to capture the market perception about the sustainability of public debt. Importantly, these measures incorporate not only concerns about the current level of public debt for intertemporal fiscal solvency, but also the expected path of future deficits.

Figure 3.11. Anchoring of Inflation Expectations and Policy Frameworks, 2004–17
(Percent, unless noted otherwise)

Sound monetary and fiscal frameworks are associated with better-anchored inflation expectations in emerging markets.

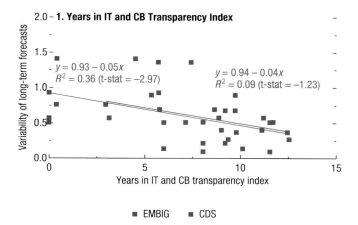

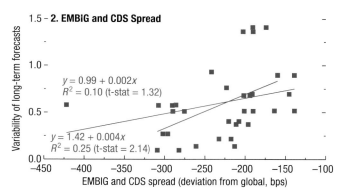

Sources: Dicer and Eichengreen (2014); JP Morgan; Thomson Reuters Datastream; and IMF staff calculations.
Note: bps = basis points; CB = central bank; CDS = credit default swap; EMBIG = emerging market bond index global; IT = inflation targeting. See Online Annex 3.1 for data sources and country coverage. EMBIG spreads and CDS spreads are the residuals from a regression on time fixed effects. For the CB transparency index, higher values indicate higher degree of transparency. Argentina is excluded from the figures as an outlier; its inclusion would further strengthen the depicted relationships.

they tend to rise with price shocks that depress economic activity and place central banks in a policy dilemma. Reacting to rising inflation expectations with tighter monetary conditions would worsen output effects, and loosening policy to boost activity would worsen inflation expectations. Hence, central banks in economies with less-anchored expectations would be less able to focus on smoothing output fluctuations.

A vast literature has explored how inflation performance differs according to variations in the monetary framework (see, for instance, Rogoff and others 2004; Ball and Sheridan 2005; and Gonçalves and Salles 2008). The approach in this section asks, instead, whether variations in the degree of anchoring of inflation expectations affect inflation performance and the trade-offs faced by monetary policy in emerging markets.[32]

In particular, the external shock represented by the ongoing normalization of monetary policy in the United States and other advanced economies may well depress activity in emerging markets while also triggering a temporary increase in inflation. This section addresses the following question: Will emerging markets with more-anchored inflation expectations be better able to fight the incipient downturn triggered by the external shock?

The approach takes the variation in the degree of anchoring among emerging markets as given, or as a characteristic that changes only slowly.[33] The analysis first adapts a conventional New Keynesian monetary model to illustrate how the extent of anchoring may influence the domestic economic impact of an external shock. Second, an event analysis uses an earlier and comparable shock—the so-called taper tantrum during the summer of 2013—to explore differences in the responses of key variables between emerging markets with more- and less-anchored inflation expectations. Finally, the analysis explores whether the ability to conduct countercyclical monetary policy in emerging markets is related to the extent of anchoring of inflation expectations.

Insights from a Monetary Model

A version of a New Keynesian monetary model is used to examine how the extent of central bank credibility can influence the impact of an external shock on domestic inflation dynamics and on the reaction of monetary policy. The shock considered is akin to a sudden stop in capital flows (Calvo 1998)

and is modeled as a temporary surge in the country risk premium.[34]

The degree of monetary policy credibility and the strength of inflation expectations anchoring significantly affect how the model economy responds to the sudden-stop shock (Figure 3.12). Regardless of the degree of credibility, the external shock induces a sharp nominal currency depreciation (not shown in Figure 3.12), which boosts actual inflation. In the economy with a more credible central bank, longer-term inflation expectations are better anchored, and inflation more quickly returns to its long-run level once the effect of the shock dissipates. The result implies a smaller exchange rate pass-through to consumer prices and lower inflation persistence.

With a shorter-lived deviation of inflation from its target, the monetary policy rate need not increase by as much in response to the adverse shock, and can return to its neutral level sooner, leading to a smaller cumulative decline in output.[35] In sum, the persistence of inflationary shocks is smaller, and monetary policy can focus more on fighting recessions when credibility is higher and expectations are better anchored, thereby increasing the economy's resilience to adverse external shocks.

The Taper Tantrum Episode

How did key macroeconomic variables in emerging markets react to the taper tantrum in the summer of 2013? The episode was based on a sudden expectation of an imminent move toward monetary normalization in the United States (via a tapering off of bond purchases by the Federal Reserve), which boosted risk premiums on debt instruments in emerging markets. Among the advantages of studying this shock are that it is related to an expectation of de facto monetary policy tightening in the advanced economies, it is well identified, and it is exogenous to emerging markets. Did the response during the taper tantrum episode differ across emerging markets according to how well anchored their inflation expectations were, as would be predicted by the model?[36]

---

[32]The approach pursued in this chapter is more closely related to Mishkin and Savastano (2001), who argue that policymakers can choose from among a wide set of monetary frameworks, but their ability to deliver price stability will ultimately be determined by their credibility, as captured in this chapter by the robustness of the public's longer-term inflation expectations.

[33]This is consistent with the evolution of anchoring in the sample. The position of economies in the ranking for anchoring has changed little over time (Online Annex 3.3).

[34]The framework follows Alichi and others (2009) and Al-Mashat and others (2018a), which extend a conventional monetary model to allow for imperfect credibility. See Online Annex 3.4 for details.

[35]The expected real interest rate also increases by less in the country with a more credible central bank.

[36]This analysis does not imply that anchoring is the ultimate driver of the differences in macroeconomic outcomes. As discussed

The empirical exercise estimates the responses of the variables of interest—the exchange rate, inflation, output, and the policy rate—to the taper tantrum shock.[37] To tease out the differential effects arising from variations in the extent of anchoring, the economies in the sample are sorted into a more-anchored and a less-anchored group, as defined in Online Annex 3.3, and responses specific to each group are estimated.[38]

In each of the two country groups, the currency depreciates on impact, as predicted by the model (Figure 3.13, panel 1). The initial depreciation is somewhat smaller in the less-anchored group, which could be an indication of "fear of floating" (see Calvo and Reinhart 2002).[39] However, after the first two months, the depreciation effect equalizes across the two groups.

The response of consumer prices suggests a very persistent and statistically significant increase in the price level for the less-anchored economies and, broadly, no consumer price impact in the more-anchored group. The differences between the two groups are statistically significant at all horizons (Figure 3.13, panel 2).

A comparison of the responses of the exchange rate and consumer prices between the two groups of countries suggests that the exchange rate pass-through during the taper tantrum event was substantially larger in countries with less-anchored inflation expectations. A systematic exploration of the exchange rate and consumer price responses across the two groups of economies confirms that the pass-through of currency depreciations is lower in economies with better-anchored inflation expectations (Figure 3.14).[40]

---

in the previous section, the varying extent of anchoring can be explained by fundamental macroeconomic factors, including the quality of fiscal and monetary policy frameworks.

[37]The estimates are produced with a local projection framework (Jordà 2005; Jordà, Schularick, and Taylor 2013). The methodology is closely related to an event study approach (see, for example, de Carvalho Filho 2011; Obstfeld 2014; and Ahmed, Coulibaly, and Zlate 2017), but controls for lags of the dependent variable.

[38]Details of the estimation strategy and a discussion of robustness checks for the results of this section are in Online Annex 3.5.

[39]As discussed further below, fear of floating could help explain weak anchoring if the central bank compromises its inflation goals to achieve exchange rate stability.

[40]See Online Annex 3.5 for details. These results are obtained from a reduced-form estimation that does not distinguish between the underlying sources of movements in the exchange rate and, therefore, need to be interpreted with caution (Forbes, Hjortsoe, and Nenova 2015). Reassuringly, however, the magnitude of the pass-through for the less-anchored countries after six months (equal to 11 percent) is comparable to the estimates obtained from the taper tantrum event exercise (14 percent), where the underlying shock is well identified. For the more-anchored countries, the magnitudes of the pass-through are 1 percent and 5 percent, respectively.

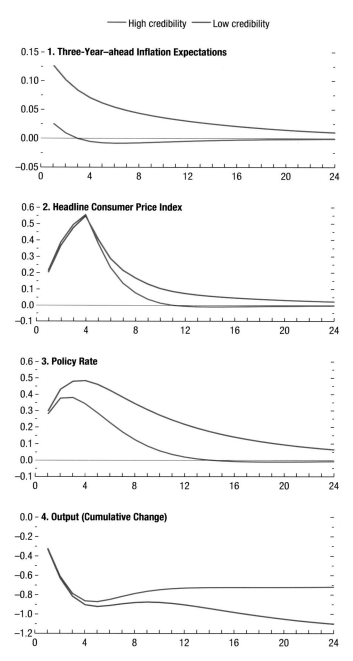

Figure 3.12. Gains from Anchoring Inflation Expectations
(Percentage points)

Model simulations suggest that when monetary policy is credible and inflation expectations are better anchored, the economy is more resilient to adverse external shocks.

—— High credibility   —— Low credibility

1. Three-Year–ahead Inflation Expectations

2. Headline Consumer Price Index

3. Policy Rate

4. Output (Cumulative Change)

Source: IMF staff calculations.
Note: The figures show impulse responses to a "sudden-stop" shock, defined as an increase in the country-specific risk premium, using a semistructural monetary model described in Online Annex 3.4. X-axis labels indicate time in quarters, with the shock occurring at time = 1.

Figure 3.13. Response to the Taper Tantrum
(Percentage points)

Economies with better-anchored inflation expectations were more resilient to the taper tantrum episode in the summer of 2013—they experienced a smaller increase in inflation and could keep monetary policy relatively more accommodative.

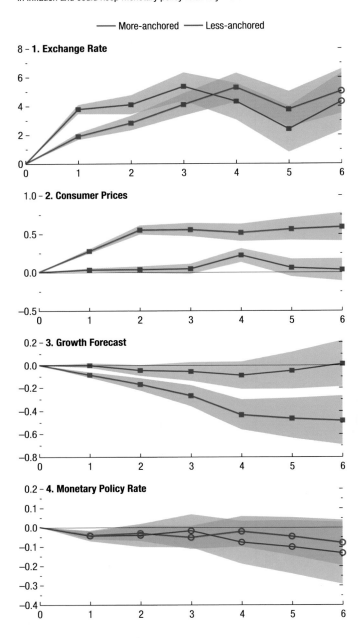

Figure 3.14. Cumulative Exchange Rate Pass-Through
(Percentage points)

The exchange rate pass-through to consumer prices is lower in economies with better-anchored inflation expectations.

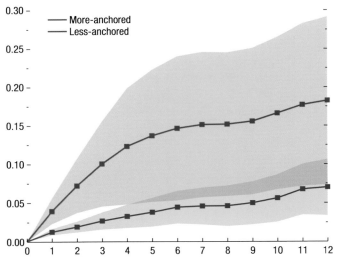

Source: IMF staff calculations.
Note: See Online Annex 3.1 for data sources and country coverage. The figure shows the cumulative impulse response of headline consumer prices to a 1 percent change in the nominal effective exchange rate (see Online Annex 3.5 for details). *X*-axis denotes time in months. The shaded area corresponds to 90 percent confidence intervals computed with Driscoll-Kraay standard errors. Solid squares (unfilled circles) for responses denote that the difference between the two responses is statistically significant (not statistically significant) at a 90 percent confidence level. The criterion to classify countries as more- and less-anchored is defined in Online Annex 3.3.

Source: IMF staff calculations.
Note: See Online Annex 3.1 for data sources and country coverage. The figures show the cumulative impulse response to the taper tantrum episode (see Online Annex 3.5 for details). An increase in the exchange rate denotes a depreciation. *X*-axis denotes time in months. The episode is defined as equal to 1 in May 2013. The shaded areas correspond to 90 percent confidence intervals computed with Driscoll-Kraay standard errors. Solid squares (unfilled circles) for responses denote that the difference between the two responses is statistically significant (not statistically significant) at a 90 percent confidence level. The criterion to classify countries as more- and less-anchored is defined in Online Annex 3.3.

These findings are consistent with several earlier studies.[41]

In terms of the monetary policy dilemma and the response of the policy rate, the less-anchored country group faced a starker trade-off between fighting inflation and countering falling growth prospects during the taper tantrum episode.[42] Although, in contrast to the more-anchored group, these countries experienced a significant fall in expected output growth, they did

[41]Taylor (2000) argues that improvements in monetary performance, as reflected in price stability and better-anchored inflation expectations, result in an endogenous reduction of exchange rate pass-through. Several studies have found evidence in line with this hypothesis, including Gagnon and Ihrig (2001), Choudhri and Hakura (2006), Edwards (2006), Mishkin and Schmidt-Hebbel (2007), Carrière-Swallow and others (2016), and Caselli and Roitman (2016).

[42]Given the monthly frequency of the estimation, the analysis proxies the response of output using one-year-ahead growth forecasts from Consensus Forecasts. An alternative exercise, using quarterly data and analyzing the reaction of actual output growth to the taper tantrum shock, shows similar results, confirming more a negative output response in less-anchored countries.

not pursue looser monetary policies. Indeed, there is no significant difference in the response of the policy rate across the two groups at any horizon.

In sum, the analysis suggests that economies with better-anchored inflation expectations were more resilient to the taper tantrum episode and were able to keep monetary policy relatively more accommodative.

Countercyclical Monetary Policy

How general are the findings of the taper tantrum episode? When output enters a cyclical decline, could the monetary authorities in countries with more-anchored inflation expectations act more countercyclically than authorities in less-anchored countries, focusing more on reducing output fluctuations?

Following Végh and Vuletin (2014) and Végh and others (2017), an examination of a simple correlation between the detrended policy rate and the output gap reveals that monetary policy in both country groups, on average, reacted countercyclically to output gap developments over the first quarter of 2004 to the first quarter of 2018 (Figure 3.15). The countercyclical response was stronger in the more-anchored group. However, such correlation-based findings can be subject to several criticisms. First, they need not be informative of the monetary policy dilemma that policymakers in emerging markets face when hit by adverse external shocks, as monetary policy tradeoffs can vary depending on the nature of the underlying shock. Second, a simple correlation does not control for other factors important to policymakers. For example, if exchange rate stability is an additional policy objective and the exchange rate is correlated with the output gap, the estimated response of the policy rate to the output gap may be biased.

To address these limitations, this section estimates a monetary policy reaction function for the emerging markets in the sample. Following Taylor (1993) and Coibion and Gorodnichenko (2012), the specification allows for inertia in monetary policy and includes the inflation rate, the output gap, and the change in the nominal effective exchange rate. The estimated coefficient on the output gap is interpreted as a measure of monetary policy countercyclicality. To assess whether the extent of anchoring influences the ability to conduct countercyclical policy, the estimation allows the coefficients in the monetary policy reaction function to differ between countries in the more- and less-anchored groups.[43]

[43]See Online Annex 3.6 for details.

Figure 3.15. Correlation between Detrended Policy Rate and Output Gap, 2004:Q1–2018:Q1
(Percent)

A simple correlation analysis suggests that over 2004–18 monetary authorities tended to react more to output gap fluctuations in economies with better-anchored inflation expectations.

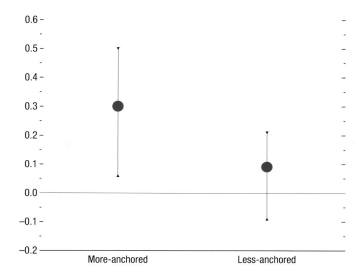

Source: IMF staff calculations.
Note: See Online Annex 3.1 for data sources and country coverage. The dots denote the median correlation across countries and the vertical lines denote the interquartile range. Monetary policy rate series have been detrended by the Hodrick-Prescott filter, following Végh and Vuletin (2014). The output gap is measured by the real-time output gap from the World Economic Outlook database if available, or by detrended real output using the Hodrick-Prescott filter. The criterion to classify countries as more- and less-anchored is defined in Online Annex 3.3.

To focus on adverse external shocks that can potentially pose a dilemma between stabilizing output and inflation, such as the one examined in the event study of the taper tantrum, two complementary identification strategies are used. First, the regression analysis is restricted to 2011–15, when emerging markets experienced a substantial slowdown in net capital inflows.[44] Second, the domestic output gap is instrumented with shocks to the global risk premium, as captured by the Chicago Board Options Exchange Volatility Index (VIX).

The results show that the output gap coefficient is smaller for less-anchored countries than for more-anchored ones for all specifications and, in two of these, the difference between the two output

[44]See Chapter 2 of the April 2016 WEO for a detailed examination of this slowdown episode and Online Annex Figure 3.6.1 for the evolution of net capital inflows to the countries in the sample.

Figure 3.16. Effects of Less-Anchored Inflation Expectations: Regression Results, 2004:Q1–2018:Q1
(Percentage points)

Model estimates suggest that monetary policy reacts more to output fluctuations and less to exchange rate developments in countries with better-anchored inflation expectations—including in periods when adverse external shocks pose a dilemma between stabilizing output and inflation.

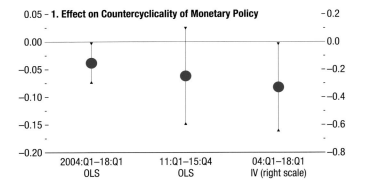

1. Effect on Countercyclicality of Monetary Policy

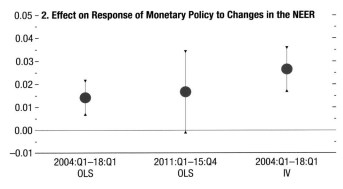

2. Effect on Response of Monetary Policy to Changes in the NEER

Source: IMF staff calculations.
Note: IV = instrumental variables; NEER = nominal effective exchange rate; OLS = ordinary least squares. See Online Annex 3.1 for data sources and country coverage. The figure shows the effect on the output gap coefficient (panel 1) and the exchange rate coefficient (panel 2) of being a less-anchored country rather than a more-anchored country from estimated monetary policy reaction functions. Each panel summarizes results from three regression specifications. Starting from the left, the first regression result refers to a full-sample OLS specification, the second regression result refers to the OLS specification in which the impact of more- or less-anchored inflation expectations is identified from the 2011:Q1–15:Q4 period only, and the third regression result refers to a full-sample instrumental variable specification (see Online Annex 3.6 for details). The criterion to classify countries as more- and less-anchored is defined in Online Annex 3.3.

gap coefficients is statistically different from zero (Figure 3.16). The results also suggest that the coefficient on the nominal effective exchange rate is larger for less-anchored countries.[45] Thus, monetary policy

in less-anchored countries not only responds less to output gap fluctuations, but it also responds more to fluctuations in the nominal effective exchange rate. Overall, these findings suggest that the ability to conduct countercyclical monetary policy in emerging markets is positively linked to the extent of anchoring of inflation expectations.[46]

Taken together, the results in this section suggest that well-anchored expectations can attenuate the monetary policy dilemma faced by emerging markets when they are hit by adverse external shocks. The inflationary impact of such shocks is smaller when inflation expectations are more anchored, allowing monetary policy to focus more on smoothing output fluctuations, thus improving the resilience of the economy.

Summary and Policy Implications

Following a period of disinflation during the 1990s and early 2000s, inflation in emerging market and developing economies has remained low and stable. This chapter examines the low and stable inflation experience in 19 emerging markets during 2004–18 to determine whether the recent gains in inflation performance are sustainable as global financial conditions normalize.

The chapter finds that, for the average sample emerging market, the gains in inflation performance have been broad based—present across alternative price measures and geographic regions, as well as in terms of both inflation levels and inflation variability. At the same time, the gains are not uniform, as some emerging markets continue to find it challenging to keep inflation low and stable in the face of capital flow reversals and exchange rate pressures. Average inflation in several sample economies remained in double-digit territory during the period under study. The main driver of deviations of inflation from target is fluctuations in longer-term inflation expectations, while the role of global factors is more limited. Zooming in on the behavior of inflation expectations reveals that the extent of expectations anchoring has improved but remains subpar in many emerging markets relative to the better-performing peers and relative to advanced economies.

---

[45]The results could indicate that fear of floating leads to less-anchored inflation expectations. But there are other possible explanations, and more research is needed before drawing strong conclusions.

[46]The findings are qualitatively robust to the exclusion of the global financial crisis period (third quarter of 2007 to the first quarter of 2009) and to alternative groupings of more-anchored and less-anchored economies.

What do these findings imply for inflation, and for economic outcomes more broadly, as global financial conditions normalize? To the extent that a tightening of global financial conditions leads to currency depreciations in emerging markets, some adjustment in relative prices and a temporary increase in their inflation rates is to be expected. But if expectations are well anchored, price stability would not be jeopardized. Indeed, the analysis shows that more-anchored inflation expectations reduce inflation persistence and limit the pass-through of currency depreciations to domestic prices, allowing monetary policy to focus more on reducing output fluctuations. Subpar levels of anchoring of longer-term inflation expectations can constrain central banks' monetary policy responses and make emerging markets more vulnerable to adverse external shocks, such as the ongoing normalization of monetary policy in the United States and other advanced economies.

In terms of policy implications, the chapter argues that domestic fiscal and monetary policy frameworks can significantly affect the performance of output and inflation in response to adverse external shocks through their impact on the extent of anchoring of inflation expectations. One important implication is that emerging markets are not simply bystanders to the forces of globalization and financial conditions in advanced economies.[47] By improving fiscal and monetary policy frameworks over the past two decades,

emerging markets have succeeded in reducing inflation to low and sustainable levels. Whether these gains will be maintained largely depends on policymakers' continued commitment to improving the long-term sustainability of fiscal frameworks, including by adopting fiscal rules, and preserving and rebuilding fiscal buffers where necessary. Equally important is their commitment to improving the credibility of central banks, which can be achieved by consolidating and enhancing their independence, as well as through improvements in timeliness, clarity, transparency, and openness in communications. In this context, it is notable that public debt has increased in emerging markets over the past decade and is projected to increase further in many of the largest economies over the next five years (see Chapter 1). Also, a number of less-anchored emerging markets have more recently come under considerable pressures from exchange rate depreciations and shorter-term inflation. These developments suggest that the past gains in inflation performance cannot be taken for granted and require continued improvements in fiscal and monetary policy frameworks.

The chapter also emphasizes that anchoring inflation expectations takes time, which suggests that policymakers in emerging markets should consolidate and further improve the extent of anchoring of inflation expectations, even when favorable economic conditions prevail. In countries where the credibility of monetary frameworks is relatively low, the emphasis should be on communicating clearly the reasons for policy actions taken in response to global developments.

---

[47]Chapter 3 of the April 2017 *Global Financial Stability Report* draws similar conclusions regarding the domestic impact of global financial conditions.

Box 3.1. Inflation Dynamics in a Wider Group of Emerging Market and Developing Economies

This box compares (1) basic macroeconomic characteristics and (2) headline inflation dynamics for a wider group of 71 emerging market and developing economies with the 19 emerging markets covered in the chapter (termed here the "sample" economies).[1] The wider set of 71 economies is separated into (1) 33 other emerging markets, and (2) 38 low-income developing countries, as defined in the *World Economic Outlook* classification, and referred to hereafter as the "other two country groups."

The 19 emerging markets covered in the chapter are among the largest emerging markets (Figure 3.1.1, panel 1). This sample is representative of the broader set of emerging markets along several dimensions, including GDP per capita and financial development (Figure 3.1.1, panels 2 and 3). Also, countries in all three groups grow at a comparable pace (Figure 3.1.1, panel 4) and exhibit similar openness to international trade over the sample period (Figure 3.1.1, panel 5). One difference is that the 19 sample economies have more flexible exchange rates, although several of them exhibit degrees of exchange rate flexibility that are comparable to those of economies in the other two country groups (Figure 3.1.1, panel 6). Greater exchange rate rigidity can contribute to higher inflation volatility for commodity exporters when facing large commodity price swings.[2] Beyond this specific set of countries, the approach pursued in the chapter emphasizes the broader concept of credible monetary policy frameworks, as captured by the extent of anchoring of inflation expectations, in delivering

The authors of this box are Francesca Caselli and Jilun Xing.

[1] The wider group includes all emerging markets and low-income developing countries not included in the core sample of 19 countries, except countries with (1) populations of fewer than 2 million people or (2) at least one episode of hyperinflation, defined as annual inflation of more than 100 percent. The selection of the core sample of 19 economies is driven by data availability. The key data constraint for inclusion in the core sample of countries is the availability of longer-term (three-year-ahead and longer) forecasts for inflation.

[2] Several countries in the "other two country groups" exhibit limited exchange rate flexibility and are heavily dependent on commodities. Under a fixed exchange rate, when commodity export prices increase, both domestic and import prices rise (given higher domestic demand, which raises nontradables prices, including distribution margins for imports), with the adjustment to the income windfall taking place through relative prices rather than the exchange rate. Conversely, periods of weak commodity export prices put downward pressure on domestic demand and prices. By contrast, under a flexible exchange rate part of the terms-of-trade movement is absorbed by the exchange rate, dampening the effect of this type of shock on inflation.

Figure 3.1.1. Comparison of Macro Characteristics across Country Groups

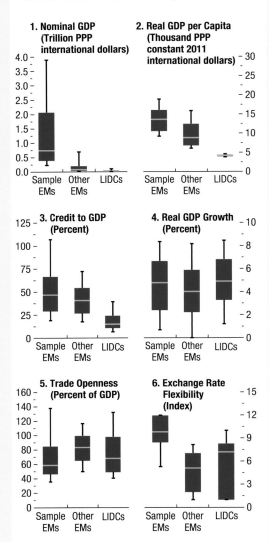

Sources: Ilzetzki, Reinhart, and Rogoff (2017); World Bank; and IMF staff calculations.
Note: EMs = emerging markets; LIDCs = low-income developing countries; PPP = purchasing power parity. See Online Annex 3.1 for data sources and country coverage. The horizontal line in each box represents the median across countries calculated over the period 2004–17; the upper and lower edges of each box show the top and bottom quartiles; and the vertical lines denote the range between the top and bottom deciles. A higher value of the exchange rate index means greater flexibility.

Box 3.1 *(continued)*

price stability over the narrower focus on the exchange rate regime.

Inflation dynamics in the wider group of other emerging markets and low-income developing countries (the "other two country groups") show broadly similar trends to that of the sample economies. Headline consumer price inflation in the other two country groups declined between the mid-1990s and the mid-2000s, and, on average, remained lower thereafter (Figure 3.1.2, panel 1). The number of countries with double-digit headline inflation also fell dramatically from the 1990s in all three groups. Less than 15 percent of the countries exhibited double-digit inflation at the end of the sample period, compared with 50–70 percent in 1995 (Figure 3.1.2, panel 2). Inflation volatility in the other two country groups also declined after 2004 (Figure 3.1.2, panel 3).

However, a focus on the post-2004 period reveals some heterogeneity across the three groups. The average inflation rates for the other emerging market and low-income developing country groups, at 7 percent and 8 percent, respectively, remain higher than those of the sample group, at 5 percent (Figure 3.1.2, panel 1). Similarly, volatility of inflation in the other two country groups remains higher than in the sample countries (Figure 3.1.2, panel 3).

What are the factors that could have contributed to higher inflation rates in the other two country groups? Compared with the sample, inflation in these two groups follows the evolution of commodity price inflation more closely (Figure 3.1.3, panel 1), pointing to stronger exposure of these economies to commodity price fluctuations. Indeed, the largest economies in the broader sample include several oil exporters, where the strength of domestic demand is heavily influenced by oil prices. The comovement of inflation with commodity prices is particularly evident in the period after 2004: headline inflation peaks along with the 2008 commodity price spike, declines during the global financial crisis, rebounds later, and finally drops again. Overall, this evidence suggests that economies in the other two country groups were not fully successful in smoothing the repeated commodity shocks they faced in the postcrisis period. Moreover, in low-income developing countries food accounts for a larger share of consumption expenditure, and higher food shares are linked to higher inflation (Figure 3.1.3, panel 2).

The greater sensitivity of inflation in the other two country groups to commodity price swings could reflect differences in the quality of the institutional and policy frameworks. For instance, Choi and

Figure 3.1.2. Inflation Dynamics
(Percent)

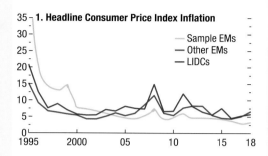

1. Headline Consumer Price Index Inflation

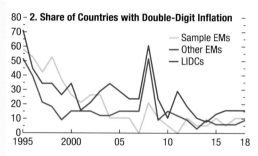

2. Share of Countries with Double-Digit Inflation

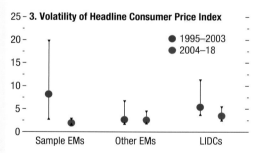

3. Volatility of Headline Consumer Price Index

Sources: Haver Analytics; and IMF staff calculations.
Note: EMs = emerging markets; LIDCs = low-income developing countries. See Online Annex 3.1 for data sources and country coverage. The lines in panel 1 denote averages weighted by nominal GDP. The weights are time invariant and computed between 2010 and 2012. The lines in panel 2 denote the share of countries with headline consumer price index greater than or equal to 10 percent. Volatility is computed as the standard deviation of headline inflation. The dots (vertical lines) in panel 3 denote the medians (interquartile ranges).

others (2018) find that, over time, a more credible monetary policy, together with reduced reliance on energy imports, lessens the impact of oil price shocks on inflation. Gelos and Ustyugova (2017) find that commodity price shocks have less persistent effects in countries with independent central banks, lower initial inflation, and better governance. Consistent with these results, central bank transparency—a proxy for

Box 3.1 *(continued)*

Figure 3.1.3. Inflation, Food Shares, and Commodity Prices
(Percent)

1. Inflation and Commodity Price Index Change

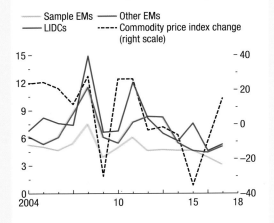

2. Inflation and Food Share in Consumption Basket

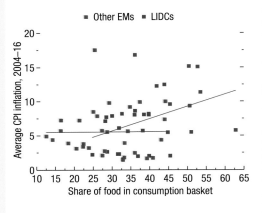

Sources: International Labour Organization; and IMF staff calculations.
Note: CPI = consumer price index; EMs = emerging markets; LIDCs = low-income developing countries. See Online Annex 3.1 for data sources and country coverage. In panel 1, the solid lines denote averages weighted by nominal GDP. The weights are time invariant and computed between 2010 and 2012. The dashed line corresponds to the change in the commodity price index (2005 = 100) of a broad set of commodities. In panel 2, the solid lines denote the fitted regression lines for each group. The slope coefficient is significant for LIDCs, but not for other EMs.

Figure 3.1.4. Central Bank Transparency
(Index)

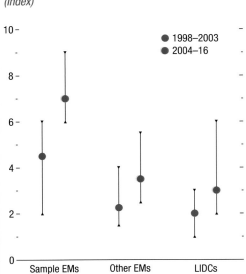

Sources: Dincer and Eichengreen (2014); and IMF staff calculations.
Note: EMs = emerging markets; LIDCs = low-income developing countries. See Online Annex 3.1 for data sources and country coverage. The dots (vertical lines) denote the medians (interquartile ranges) of each group. The transparency index ranges from 0 to 15 and reflects the sum of the scores attributed to responses to various questions about political, economic, procedural, and operational transparency. An increase represents an improvement in the index.

the quality of the monetary policy framework—in the other two country groups exhibits a slower pace of improvement and remains significantly below the levels of the sample group (Figure 3.1.4). Lack of a clear communication strategy about the inflation outlook and the presence of multiple inconsistent objectives contribute to lower transparency levels in low-income developing countries (IMF 2015). Furthermore, because economies with less transparent and credible monetary policy frameworks tend to exhibit a higher degree of exchange rate pass-through, external shocks to such economies tend to be more inflationary than for economies with better monetary frameworks (Carrière-Swallow and others 2016). Finally, sound fiscal institutions are also a precondition for credible monetary policy. Combes and others (2017), for example, find that the interaction of inflation targeting and fiscal rules has a beneficial effect on both fiscal balances and inflation.

Box 3.2. Clarity of Central Bank Communications and the Extent of Anchoring of Inflation Expectations

"Successful central bank communication efforts should make policy more predictable and market expectations of future short rates more accurate" (Blinder and others 2008).

Over the past two decades, central banks in an increasing number of emerging market and developing economies have adopted inflation targeting—a policy that sets an inflation goal and emphasizes transparency and clear communication with the public to help achieve it. The change coincided with improved anchoring of longer-term inflation expectations in many of those economies, but substantial variations in the extent of anchoring still exist. This box shows that more transparent and clear communication by the central bank can improve the anchoring of inflation expectations by reducing uncertainty about future policy actions.

One way in which the central bank can influence the anchoring of inflation expectations is by helping improve the ability of the public to anticipate its adjustments to the monetary policy rate. An empirical glimpse into the clarity and consistency of the central bank's policy rate decisions can be obtained by measuring the frequency with which central bank decisions differ from what the market expects just before the release of policy announcements. The evidence shows that achieving a high degree of monetary policy predictability has been challenging for emerging market and developing economies (Figure 3.2.1). Despite important steps taken to strengthen monetary policy frameworks during the past two decades, the predictability of policy rate actions by their central banks remains below that of more seasoned inflation-targeting central banks in advanced economies. Furthermore, the evidence shows uneven improvement over time for emerging market and developing economies.

Can poor predictability of monetary policy rate actions affect the anchoring of inflation expectations? Poor predictability may reflect a lack of public understanding about the central bank's policy strategy. Alternatively, it may indicate the public's doubt about the central bank's commitment to price stability. In either case, inflation expectations may not be anchored to the central bank's target, which has important implications for policy. In this regard, a significant relationship appears between the predictability of monetary

The authors of this box are Yan Carrière-Swallow and Juan Yépez.

Figure 3.2.1. Frequency of Monetary Policy Surprises, 2010–13 versus 2014–18
(Percent of total decisions)

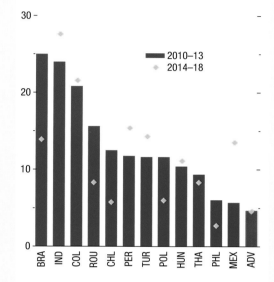

Sources: Bloomberg Finance L.P.; and IMF staff calculations.
Note: ADV = average for eight advanced economies. See Online Annex 3.1 for data sources and country coverage. Data labels use International Organization for Standardization (ISO) country codes. Surprises are the difference between the decision regarding the monetary policy rate and the average forecast among analysts surveyed by Bloomberg the day of the policy announcement.

policy and the degree of anchoring of medium-term (two-years-ahead) inflation expectations (Figure 3.2.2).

How can monetary policy be made more predictable? In general terms, predictability requires having a clear policy function that the public understands. Indeed, monetary policy is more predictable in economies where the central bank operates more transparently (Figure 3.2.3). Another characteristic of more predictable central banks is that their communication tends to be easier to understand because it uses plain language and clear sentence structures.

What can central banks do to improve transparency and the quality of their communication? Elements of best practices for transparent central banking include the announcement of a clear objective and frequent and regular publication of statements, minutes, and reports that give an account of the factors behind policy decisions and an assessment of how those factors are likely to evolve over the policy

Box 3.2 *(continued)*

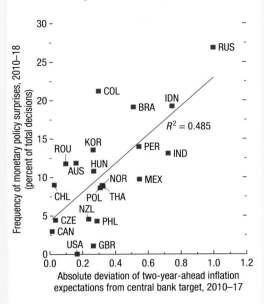

Figure 3.2.2. Monetary Policy Predictability and Anchoring of Inflation Expectations

Sources: Bloomberg Finance L.P.; Consensus Economics; and IMF staff calculations.
Note: See Online Annex 3.1 for data sources and country coverage. For the definition of monetary policy surprises see notes to Figure 3.2.1. Solid line shows the best linear fit between the variables. Data labels use International Organization for Standardization (ISO) country codes.

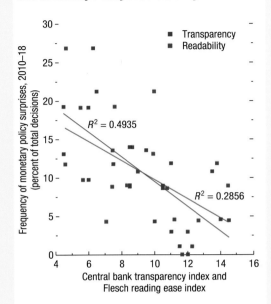

Figure 3.2.3. Central Bank Communication and Monetary Policy Predictability

Sources: Bloomberg Finance L.P.; Dincer and Eichengreen (2014); and IMF staff calculations.
Note: The Flesch reading ease (RE) index is used for central bank press releases in English, which is defined as
RE = 0.33[206.835 − (1.015 × ASL) − (84.6 × ASW)], in which ASL = average sentence length and ASW = average number of syllables per word. See Online Annex 3.1 for data sources and country coverage. Solid lines show the best linear fit between the variables. The sample includes 21 inflation-targeting economies.

horizon. Improvements along these lines over the past decade have brought the level of transparency in emerging market and developing economies much closer to the levels observed in advanced economies (Dincer and Eichengreen 2014). The Central Bank of Chile, for example, added information to the policy statements released after the meetings, such as the vote tally and the main arguments given by the members of the board.

Several countries, including Chile, Colombia, and Mexico, have also implemented reforms to their

communication strategies to increase the clarity of the information made available to the public. For instance, they have streamlined communication events to focus on medium-term developments; reduced the frequency of monetary policy meetings, aligning them with the release of the monetary policy report; and revamped the content of their policy statements, giving a richer account of the macroeconomic context and explaining why certain policy actions were taken.

References

Adrian, Tobias, Douglas Laxton, and Maurice Obstfeld. 2018. "A Robust and Adaptable Nominal Anchor." In *Advancing the Frontiers of Monetary Policy*, edited by Tobias Adrian, Douglas Laxton, and Maurice Obstfeld. Washington, DC: International Monetary Fund.

Ahmed, Shaghil, Brahima Coulibaly, and Andrei Zlate. 2017. "International Financial Spillovers to Emerging Market Economies: How Important Are Economic Fundamentals?" *Journal of International Money and Finance* 76: 133–52.

Alichi, Ali, Huigang Chen, Kevin Clinton, Charles Freedman, Marianne Johnson, Ondra Kamenik, Turgut Kışınbay, and Douglas Laxton. 2009. "Inflation Targeting under Imperfect Policy Credibility." IMF Working Paper 09/94, International Monetary Fund, Washington, DC.

Al-Mashat, Rania, Kevin Clinton, Douglas Laxton, and Hou Wang. 2018a. "India: Stabilizing Inflation." In *Advancing the Frontiers of Monetary Policy*, edited by Tobias Adrian, Douglas Laxton, and Maurice Obstfeld. Washington, DC: International Monetary Fund.

———. 2018b. "Managing Expectations." In *Advancing the Frontiers of Monetary Policy*, edited by Tobias Adrian, Douglas Laxton, and Maurice Obstfeld. Washington, DC: International Monetary Fund.

Aslam, Aqib, Natalija Novta, and Fabiano Rodrigues-Bastos. 2017. "Calculating Trade in Value Added." IMF Working Paper 17/178, International Monetary Fund, Washington, DC.

Auer, Raphael, Claudio Borio, and Andrew Filardo. 2017. "The Globalisation of Inflation: The Growing Importance of Global Value Chains." CEPR Discussion Paper 11905, Centre for Economic Policy Research, London.

Auer, Raphael, Andrei Levchenko, and Philip Sauré. Forthcoming. "International Inflation Spillovers through Input Linkages." *Review of Economics and Statistics*.

Ball, Laurence M., and Niamh Sheridan. 2005. "Does Inflation Targeting Matter?" In *The Inflation-Targeting Debate*, edited by Ben S. Bernanke and Michael Woodford. NBER Studies in Income and Wealth. Chicago: University of Chicago Press.

Blinder, Alan S., Michael Ehrmann, Marcel Fratzscher, Jacob de Haan, and David-Jan Jansen. 2008. "Central Bank Communication and Monetary Policy: A Survey of Theory and Evidence." *Journal of Economic Literature* 46 (4): 910–45.

Borio, Claudio, and Andrew Filardo. 2007. "Globalisation and Inflation: New Cross-Country Evidence on the Global Determinants of Domestic Inflation." BIS Working Paper 227, Bank for International Settlements, Basel.

Brainard, William. 1967. "Uncertainty and the Effectiveness of Policy." *American Economic Review* 57: 411–25.

Brito, Steve, Yan Carrière-Swallow, and Bertrand Gruss. 2018. "Disagreement about Future Inflation: Understanding the Benefits of Inflation Targeting and Transparency." IMF Working Paper 18/24, International Monetary Fund, Washington, DC.

Caldas Montes, Gabriel, and Tatiana Acar. 2018. "Fiscal Credibility and Disagreement in Expectations about Inflation: Evidence for Brazil." *Economics Bulletin* 38 (2): 826–43.

Calvo, Guillermo A. 1998. "Capital Flows and Capital-Market Crises: The Simple Economics of Sudden Stops." *Journal of Applied Economics* 1 (November): 35–54.

Calvo, Guillermo A., and Carmen M. Reinhart. 2002. "Fear of Floating." *Quarterly Journal of Economics* 107 (2): 379–408.

Capistrán, Carlos, and Manuel Ramos-Francia. 2010. "Does Inflation Targeting Affect the Dispersion of Inflation Expectations?" *Journal of Money, Credit and Banking* 42 (1): 113–34.

Carney, Mark. 2017. "[De]Globalization and Inflation." IMF Michel Camdessus Central Banking Lecture, Washington, DC, September 18.

Carrière-Swallow, Yan, Bertrand Gruss, Nicolás E. Magud, and Fabián Valencia. 2016. "Monetary Policy Credibility and Exchange Rate Pass-Through." IMF Working Paper 16/240, International Monetary Fund, Washington, DC.

Caselli, Francesca, and Agustin Roitman. 2016. "Non-Linear Exchange Rate Pass-Through in Emerging Markets." IMF Working Paper 16/1, International Monetary Fund, Washington, DC.

Celasun, Oya, Gaston Gelos, and Alessandro Prati. 2004. "Obstacles to Disinflation: What Is the Role of Fiscal Expectations?" *Economic Policy* 19 (40): 442–81.

Choi, Sangyup, Davide Furceri, Prakash Loungani, Saurabh Mishra, and Marcos Poplawski-Ribeiro. 2018. "Oil Prices and Inflation Dynamics: Evidence from Advanced and Developing Economies." *Journal of International Money and Finance* 82: 71–96.

Choudhri, Ehsan, and Dalia Hakura. 2006. "Exchange Rate Pass-Through to Domestic Prices: Does the Inflationary Environment Matter?" *Journal of International Money and Finance* 25 (4): 614–39.

Coibion, Olivier, and Yuriy Gorodnichenko. 2012. "Why Are Target Interest Rate Changes So Persistent?" *American Economic Journal: Macroeconomics* 4: 126–62.

Combes, Jean-Louis, Xavier Debrun, Alexandru Minea, and Rene Tapsoba. 2017. "Inflation Targeting, Fiscal Rules, and the Policy Mix: Cross-Effects and Interactions." *Economic Journal*, published online July 18.

Cukierman, Alex, and Allan Meltzer. 1986. "A Theory of Ambiguity, Credibility and Inflation under Discretion and Asymmetric Information." *Econometrica* 54 (September): 1099–128.

de Carvalho Filho, Irineu. 2011. "28 Months Later: How Inflation Targeters Outperformed Their Peers in the Great Recession." *The B.E. Journal of Macroeconomics* 1 (1): 1–46.

Demertzis, Maria, Massimiliano Marcellino, and Nicola Viegi. 2012. "A Credibility Proxy: Tracking US Monetary Developments." *The B.E. Journal of Macroeconomics* 12 (1): 1–36.

Dincer, N. Nergiz, and Barry Eichengreen. 2014. "Central Bank Transparency and Independence: Update and New Measures." *International Journal of Central Banking* 10 (1): 189–259.

Dovern, Jonas, Ulrich Fritsche, and Jiri Slacalek. 2012. "Disagreement among Forecasters in G7 Countries." *Review of Economics and Statistics* 94 (4): 1081–96.

Driscoll, John, and Aart Kraay. 1998. "Consistent Covariance Matrix Estimation with Spatially Dependent Panel Data." *Review of Economics and Statistics* 80 (4): 549–60.

Edwards, Sebastian. 2006. "The Relationship between Exchange Rates and Inflation Targeting Revisited." NBER Working Paper 12163, National Bureau of Economic Research, Cambridge, MA.

Ehrmann, Michael. 2015. "Targeting Inflation from below: How Do Inflation Expectations Behave?" *International Journal of Central Banking* 11 (4): 213–49.

Forbes, Kristin, Ida Hjortsoe, and Tsvetelina Nenova. 2015. "The Shocks Matter: Improving Our Estimates of Exchange Rate Pass-Through." Discussion Papers from Monetary Policy Committee Unit 43, Bank of England, London.

Gagnon, Joseph, and Jane E. Ihrig. 2001. "Monetary Policy and Exchange Rate Pass-Through." International Finance Discussion Paper 704, Board of Governors of the Federal Reserve System of the United States, Washington, DC.

Galí, Jordi, and Mark Gertler. 1999. "Inflation Dynamics: A Structural Econometric Analysis." *Journal of Monetary Economics* 44 (2): 195–222.

Galí, Jordi, Mark Gertler, and J. David Lopez-Salido. 2001. "European Inflation Dynamics." *European Economic Review* 45 (7): 1237–70.

Galí, Jordi, Mark Gertler, and J. David Lopez-Salido, 2003. Erratum to "European Inflation Dynamics." *European Economic Review* 47 (4): 759–60.

Gelos, Gaston, and Yulia Ustyugova. 2017. "Inflation Responses to Commodity Price Shocks—How and Why Do Countries Differ?" *Journal of International Money and Finance* 72: 28–47.

Gonçalves, Carlos, and Joao M. Salles. 2008. "Inflation Targeting in Emerging Economies: What Do the Data Say?" *Journal of Development Economics* 85 (1–2): 312–18.

Goodhart, Charles A.E. 2005. "The Monetary Policy Committee's Reaction Function: An Exercise in Estimation." *Topics in Macroeconomics* 5 (1): Article 18.

Gopinath, Gita. 2015. "The International Price System." NBER Working Paper 21646, National Bureau of Economic Research, Cambridge, MA.

Gürkaynak, Refet S., Andrew T. Levin, and Eric T. Swanson. 2010. "Does Inflation Targeting Anchor Long-Run Inflation Expectations? Evidence from Long-Term Bond Yields in the US, UK, and Sweden." *Journal of the European Economic Association* 8 (6): 1208–42

Ihrig, Jane, Steven B. Kamin, Deborah Lindner, and Jaimie Marquez. 2010. "Some Simple Tests of the Globalization and Inflation Hypothesis." *International Finance* 13 (3): 343–75.

Ilzetzki, Ethan, Carmen M. Reinhart, and Kenneth S. Rogoff. 2017. "Exchange Arrangements Entering the 21st Century: Which Anchor Will Hold?" NBER Working Paper 23134, National Bureau of Economic Research, Cambridge, MA.

Imbens, Guido W., and Joshua D. Angrist. 1994. "Identification and Estimation of Local Average Treatment Effects." *Econometrica* 62 (2): 467–75.

International Monetary Fund (IMF). 2015. "Evolving Monetary Policy Frameworks in Low-Income and Other Developing Countries—Background Paper: Country Experiences." IMF Staff Report, Washington, DC.

Jordà, Òscar. 2005. "Estimation and Inference of Impulse Responses by Local Projections." *American Economic Review* 95 (1): 161–82.

Jordà, Òscar, Moritz Schularick, and Alan M. Taylor. 2013. "When Credit Bites Back." *Journal of Money, Credit and Banking* 45: 3–28.

King, Mervyn. 1995. "Credibility and Monetary Policy: Theory and Evidence." *Scottish Journal of Political Economy* 42: 1–19.

Kumar, Saten, Hassan Afrouzi, Olivier Coibion, and Yuriy Gorodnichenko. 2015. "Inflation Targeting Does Not Anchor Inflation Expectations: Evidence from Firms in New Zealand." *Brookings Papers on Economic Activity* 46: 151–225.

Lane, Philip R., and Gian Maria Milesi-Ferretti. 2018. "The External Wealth of Nations Revisited: International Financial Integration in the Aftermath of the Global Financial Crisis." *IMF Economic Review* 66 (1): 189–222.

Levin, Andrew T., Fabio M. Natalucci, and Jeremy M. Piger. 2004. "The Macroeconomic Effects of Inflation Targeting." *Review*, Federal Reserve Bank of St. Louis, July: 51–80.

Mankiw, N.G., R. Reis, and J. Wolfers. 2004. "Disagreement about Inflation Expectations." *NBER Macroeconomics Annual 2003* 18: 209–48.

Masson, Paul R., Miguel A. Savastano, and Sunil Sharma. 1997. "The Scope for Inflation Targeting in Developing Countries." IMF Working Paper 97/130, International Monetary Fund, Washington, DC.

Mishkin, Frederic S. 2000. "Inflation Targeting in Emerging Market Countries." *American Economic Review* 90 (2): 105–9.

———. 2007. "Inflation Dynamics." *International Finance* 10 (3): 317–34.

Mishkin, Frederic S., and Miguel A. Savastano. 2001. "Monetary Policy Strategies for Latin America." *Journal of Development Economics* 66 (2): 415–44.

Mishkin, Frederic S., and Klaus Schmidt-Hebbel. 2007. "Does Inflation Targeting Make a Difference?" NBER Working Paper 12876, National Bureau of Economic Research, Cambridge, MA.

Neely, Christopher J. 2014. "Lessons from the Taper Tantrum." Economic Synopses 2, Federal Reserve Bank of St. Louis.

Obstfeld, Maurice. 2014. "Never Say Never: Commentary on a Policymaker's Reflections." *IMF Economic Review* 62 (4): 656–93.

Rogoff, Kenneth. 2004. "Globalization and Global Disinflation." In "Monetary Policy and Uncertainty: Adapting to a

Changing Economy," a symposium sponsored by the Federal Reserve Bank of Kansas City.

Rogoff, Kenneth, Aasim M. Husain, Ashoka Mody, Robin Brooks, and Nienke Oomes. 2004. "Evolution and Performance of Exchange Rate Regimes." IMF Occasional Paper 229, International Monetary Fund, Washington, DC.

Sahay, Ratna, Vivek Arora, Thanos Arvanitis, Hamid Faruqee, Papa N'Diaye, Tommaso Mancini-Griffoli, and an IMF Team. 2014. "Emerging Market Volatility: Lessons from the Taper Tantrum." IMF Staff Discussion Note 14/09, International Monetary Fund, Washington, DC.

Stock, James H., and Mark W. Watson. 2007. "Why Has US Inflation Become Harder to Forecast?" *Journal of Money, Credit and Banking* 39 (1): 3–33.

———. 2010. "Modeling Inflation after the Crisis." *Proceedings—Economic Policy Symposium—Jackson Hole, Federal Reserve Bank of Kansas City*: 173–220.

Taylor, John B. 1993. "Discretion Versus Policy Rules in Practice." *Carnegie-Rochester Conference Series on Public Policy* 39: 95–214.

———. 2000. "Low Inflation, Pass-Through, and the Pricing Power of Firms." *European Economic Review* 44 (7): 1389–408.

Végh, Carlos A., Luis Morano, Diego Friedheim, and Diego Rojas. 2017. "Between a Rock and a Hard Place: The Monetary Policy Dilemma in Latin America and the Caribbean." LAC Semiannual Report; October 2017. Washington, DC: World Bank. https://openknowledge.worldbank.org/handle/10986/28443.

Végh, Carlos A., and Guillermo Vuletin. 2014. "Overcoming the Fear of Free Falling: Monetary Policy Graduation in Emerging Markets." In *the Role of Central Banks in Financial Stability: How Has It Changed?* edited by Douglas Darrell Evanoff, Cornelia Holthausen, George G. Kaufman, and Manfred Kremer. Singapore: World Scientific Publishing.

Woodford, Michael. 2003. "Optimal Interest Rate Smoothing." *Review of Economic Studies* 70: 861–86.

Yellen, Janet L. 2015. "Inflation Dynamics and Monetary Policy." The Philip Gamble Memorial Lecture, University of Massachusetts, Amherst, September 24.

STATISTICAL APPENDIX

The Statistical Appendix presents historical data as well as projections. It comprises seven sections: Assumptions, What's New, Data and Conventions, Country Notes, Classification of Countries, Key Data Documentation, and Statistical Tables.

The assumptions underlying the estimates and projections for 2018–19 and the medium-term scenario for 2020–23 are summarized in the first section. The second section presents a brief description of the changes to the database and statistical tables since the April 2018 *World Economic Outlook* (WEO). The third section provides a general description of the data and the conventions used for calculating country group composites. The fourth section summarizes selected key information for each country. The fifth section summarizes the classification of countries in the various groups presented in the WEO. The sixth section provides information on methods and reporting standards for the member countries' national account and government finance indicators included in the report.

The last, and main, section comprises the statistical tables. (Statistical Appendix A is included here; Statistical Appendix B is available online.) Data in these tables have been compiled on the basis of information available through September 18, 2018. The figures for 2018 and beyond are shown with the same degree of precision as the historical figures solely for convenience; because they are projections, the same degree of accuracy is not to be inferred.

Assumptions

Real effective *exchange rates* for the advanced economies are assumed to remain constant at their average levels measured during the period July 17 to August 14, 2018. For 2018 and 2019, these assumptions imply average US dollar–special drawing right (SDR) conversion rates of 1.419 and 1.406, US dollar–euro conversion rates of 1.186 and 1.170, and yen–US dollar conversion rates of 109.8 and 109.3, respectively.

It is assumed that the *price of oil* will average $69.38 a barrel in 2018 and $68.76 a barrel in 2019.

Established *policies* of national authorities are assumed to be maintained. The more specific policy assumptions underlying the projections for selected economies are described in Box A1.

With regard to interest rates, it is assumed that the London interbank offered rate (LIBOR) on six-month US dollar deposits will average 2.5 percent in 2018 and 3.4 percent in 2019, that three-month euro deposits will average –0.3 percent in 2018 and –0.2 percent in 2019, and that six-month yen deposits will average 0.0 percent in 2018 and 0.1 percent in 2019.

As a reminder, in regard to the *introduction of the euro*, on December 31, 1998, the Council of the European Union decided that, effective January 1, 1999, the irrevocably fixed conversion rates between the euro and currencies of the member countries adopting the euro are as described in Box 5.4 of the October 1998 WEO:

1 euro	=	13.7603	Austrian schillings
	=	40.3399	Belgian francs
	=	0.585274	Cyprus pound[1]
	=	1.95583	Deutsche marks
	=	15.6466	Estonian krooni[2]
	=	5.94573	Finnish markkaa
	=	6.55957	French francs
	=	340.750	Greek drachmas[3]
	=	0.787564	Irish pound
	=	1,936.27	Italian lire
	=	0.702804	Latvian lat[4]
	=	3.45280	Lithuanian litas[5]
	=	40.3399	Luxembourg francs
	=	0.42930	Maltese lira[1]
	=	2.20371	Netherlands guilders
	=	200.482	Portuguese escudos
	=	30.1260	Slovak koruna[6]
	=	239.640	Slovenian tolars[7]
	=	166.386	Spanish pesetas

[1]Established on January 1, 2008.
[2]Established on January 1, 2011.
[3]Established on January 1, 2001.
[4]Established on January 1, 2014.
[5]Established on January 1, 2015.
[6]Established on January 1, 2009.
[7]Established on January 1, 2007.

See Box 5.4 of the October 1998 WEO for details on how the conversion rates were established.

What's New

- *Argentina*'s consumer prices, which were previously excluded from the group composites because of data constraints, are now included starting from 2017 onward.
- Data for *Aruba* are included in the data aggregated for the emerging market and developing economies.
- *Egypt*'s forecast data from which the nominal exchange rate assumptions are calculated that were previously excluded because the nominal exchange rate was a market-sensitive issue, are now made public.
- *Swaziland* is now called *Eswatini*.
- *Venezuela* redenominated its currency on August 20, 2018, by replacing 100,000 bolívares Fuertes (VEF) with 1 bolívar Soberano (VES). Local currency data, including the historical data, for Venezuela are expressed in the new currency beginning with the October 2018 WEO database.

Data and Conventions

Data and projections for 194 economies form the statistical basis of the WEO database. The data are maintained jointly by the IMF's Research Department and regional departments, with the latter regularly updating country projections based on consistent global assumptions.

Although national statistical agencies are the ultimate providers of historical data and definitions, international organizations are also involved in statistical issues, with the objective of harmonizing methodologies for the compilation of national statistics, including analytical frameworks, concepts, definitions, classifications, and valuation procedures used in the production of economic statistics. The WEO database reflects information from both national source agencies and international organizations.

Most countries' macroeconomic data presented in the WEO conform broadly to the 2008 version of the *System of National Accounts* (SNA). The IMF's sector statistical standards—the sixth edition of the *Balance of Payments and International Investment Position Manual* (BPM6), the *Monetary and Financial Statistics Manual and Compilation Guide* (MFSMCG), and the *Government Finance Statistics Manual 2014* (GFSM 2014)—have been or are being aligned with the SNA 2008. These standards reflect the IMF's special interest in countries' external positions, financial sector stability, and public sector fiscal positions. The process of adapting country data to the new standards begins in earnest when the manuals are released. However, full concordance with the manuals is ultimately dependent on the provision by national statistical compilers of revised country data; hence, the WEO estimates are only partially adapted to these manuals. Nonetheless, for many countries, the impact on major balances and aggregates of conversion to the updated standards will be small. Many other countries have partially adopted the latest standards and will continue implementation over a period of years.[1]

The fiscal gross and net debt data reported in the WEO are drawn from official data sources and IMF staff estimates. While attempts are made to align gross and net debt data with the definitions in the GFSM, as a result of data limitations or specific country circumstances, these data can sometimes deviate from the formal definitions. Although every effort is made to ensure the WEO data are relevant and internationally comparable, differences in both sectoral and instrument coverage mean that the data are not universally comparable. As more information becomes available, changes in either data sources or instrument coverage can give rise to data revisions that can sometimes be substantial. For clarification on the deviations in sectoral or instrument coverage, please refer to the metadata for the online WEO database.

Composite data for country groups in the WEO are either sums or weighted averages of data for individual countries. Unless noted otherwise, multiyear averages of growth rates are expressed as compound annual rates of change.[2] Arithmetically weighted averages are used for all data for the emerging market and developing economies group—except data on inflation and money growth, for which geometric averages are used. The following conventions apply:

Country group composites for exchange rates, interest rates, and growth rates of monetary aggregates are weighted by GDP converted to US dollars at market exchange rates (averaged over the preceding three years) as a share of group GDP.

Composites for other data relating to the domestic economy, whether growth rates or ratios, are weighted by GDP valued at purchasing power parity as a share of total world or group GDP.[3] Annual inflation rates are simple percentage changes from the previous years, except in the case of emerging market and developing economies, for which the rates are based on logarithmic differences.

Composites for real GDP per capita in *purchasing power parity* terms are sums of individual country data after conversion to the international dollar in the years indicated.

---

[1] Many countries are implementing the SNA 2008 or European System of National and Regional Accounts (ESA) 2010, and a few countries use versions of the SNA older than that from 1993. A similar adoption pattern is expected for the BPM6 and GFSM 2014. Please refer to Table G, which lists the statistical standards adhered to by each country.

[2] Averages for real GDP and its components, employment, inflation, factor productivity, GDP per capita, trade, and commodity prices are calculated based on the compound annual rate of change, except in the case of the unemployment rate, which is based on the simple arithmetic average.

[3] See "Revised Purchasing Power Parity Weights" in the July 2014 *WEO Update* for a summary of the revised purchasing-power-parity-based weights, as well as Box A2 of the April 2004 WEO and Annex IV of the May 1993 WEO. See also Anne-Marie Gulde and Marianne Schulze-Ghattas, "Purchasing Power Parity Based Weights for the *World Economic Outlook*," in *Staff Studies for the World Economic Outlook* (Washington, DC: International Monetary Fund, December 1993), 106–23.

Unless noted otherwise, composites for all sectors for the euro area are corrected for reporting discrepancies in intra-area transactions. Unadjusted annual GDP data are used for the euro area and for the majority of individual countries, except for Cyprus, Germany, Ireland, and Portugal, which report calendar adjusted data. For data prior to 1999, data aggregations apply 1995 European currency unit exchange rates.

Composites for fiscal data are sums of individual country data after conversion to US dollars at the average market exchange rates in the years indicated.

Composite unemployment rates and employment growth are weighted by labor force as a share of group labor force.

Composites relating to external sector statistics are sums of individual country data after conversion to US dollars at the average market exchange rates in the years indicated for balance of payments data and at end-of-year market exchange rates for debt denominated in currencies other than US dollars.

Composites of changes in foreign trade volumes and prices, however, are arithmetic averages of percent changes for individual countries weighted by the US dollar value of exports or imports as a share of total world or group exports or imports (in the preceding year).

Unless noted otherwise, group composites are computed if 90 percent or more of the share of group weights is represented.

Data refer to calendar years, except in the case of a few countries that use fiscal years; Table F lists the economies with exceptional reporting periods for national accounts and government finance data for each country.

For some countries, the figures for 2017 and earlier are based on estimates rather than actual outturns; Table G lists the latest actual outturns for the indicators in the national accounts, prices, government finance, and balance of payments indicators for each country.

Country Notes

The consumer price data for *Argentina* before December 2013 reflect the consumer price index (CPI) for the Greater Buenos Aires Area (CPI-GBA), while from December 2013 to October 2015 the data reflect the national CPI (IPCNu). The government that took office in December 2015 discontinued the IPCNu, stating that it was flawed, and released a new CPI for the Greater Buenos Aires Area on June 15, 2016 (a new national CPI has been disseminated starting in June 2017). At its November 9, 2016, meeting, the IMF Executive Board considered the new CPI series to be in line with international standards and lifted the declaration of censure issued in 2013. Given the differences in geographical coverage, weights, sampling, and methodology of these series, the average CPI inflation for 2014, 2015, and 2016,

and end-of-period inflation for 2015 and 2016 are not reported in the October 2018 WEO.

Argentina's authorities discontinued the publication of labor market data in December 2015 and released new series starting in the second quarter of 2016.

Greece's primary balance estimates for 2017 are based on preliminary excessive deficit procedure data on an accrual basis (ESA 2010) provided by the National Statistical Service as of April 23, 2018. Historical data since 2010 reflect adjustments in line with the primary balance definition under the enhanced surveillance procedure for Greece.

India's real GDP growth rates are calculated as per national accounts: for 1998 to 2011, with base year 2004/05; thereafter, with base year 2011/12.

Against the background of a civil war and weak capacities, the reliability of *Libya*'s data, especially medium-term projections, is low.

Data for *Syria* are excluded from 2011 onward because of the uncertain political situation.

Data and projections for *Turkey* represent information available as of September 11, 2018.

Projecting the economic outlook in *Venezuela*, including assessing past and current economic developments as the basis for the projections, is complicated by the lack of discussions with the authorities (the last Article IV consultation took place in 2004), long intervals in receiving data with information gaps, incomplete provision of information, and difficulties in interpreting certain reported economic indicators given economic developments. The fiscal accounts include the budgetary central government and Petróleos de Venezuela, S.A. (PDVSA), and data for 2016–23 are IMF staff estimates. Revenue includes the IMF staff's estimate of foreign exchange profits transferred from the central bank to the government (buying US dollars at the most appreciated rate and selling at more depreciated rates in a multitier exchange rate system) and excludes IMF staff's estimate of revenue from PDVSA's sale of PetroCaribe assets to the central bank. The effects of hyperinflation and the noted data gaps mean that IMF staff's projected macroeconomic indicators need to be interpreted with caution. For example, nominal GDP is estimated assuming the GDP deflator rises in line with IMF staff's projection of average inflation. Public external debt in relation to GDP is projected using IMF staff's estimate of the average exchange rate for the year. Fiscal accounts for 2010–23 correspond to the budgetary central government and PDVSA. Fiscal accounts before 2010 correspond to the budgetary central government, public enterprises (including PDVSA), Instituto Venezolano de los Seguros Sociales (IVSS - social security), and Fondo de Garantía de Depósitos y Protección Bancaria (FOGADE - deposit insurance).

Venezuela's consumer prices (CPI) are excluded from all WEO group composites.

Classification of Countries

Summary of the Country Classification

The country classification in the WEO divides the world into two major groups: advanced economies and emerging market and developing economies.[4] This classification is not based on strict criteria, economic or otherwise, and it has evolved over time. The objective is to facilitate analysis by providing a reasonably meaningful method of organizing data. Table A provides an overview of the country classification, showing the number of countries in each group by region and summarizing some key indicators of their relative size (GDP valued at purchasing power parity, total exports of goods and services, and population).

Some countries remain outside the country classification and therefore are not included in the analysis. Cuba and the Democratic People's Republic of Korea are examples of countries that are not IMF members, and their economies therefore are not monitored by the IMF.

General Features and Composition of Groups in the *World Economic Outlook* Classification

Advanced Economies

The 39 advanced economies are listed in Table B. The seven largest in terms of GDP based on market exchange rates—the United States, Japan, Germany, France, Italy, the United Kingdom, and Canada—constitute the subgroup of major advanced economies; often referred to as the Group of Seven (G7). The members of the euro area are also distinguished as a subgroup. Composite data shown in the tables for the euro area cover the current members for all years, even though the membership has increased over time.

Table C lists the member countries of the European Union, not all of which are classified as advanced economies in the WEO.

Emerging Market and Developing Economies

The group of emerging market and developing economies (155) includes all those that are not classified as advanced economies.

The regional breakdowns of emerging market and developing economies are Commonwealth of Independent States (CIS); emerging and developing Asia; emerging and developing Europe (sometimes also referred to as "central and eastern Europe"); Latin America and the Caribbean (LAC); the Middle East, North Africa, Afghanistan, and Pakistan (MENAP); and sub-Saharan Africa (SSA).

Emerging market and developing economies are also classified according to *analytical criteria*. The analytical criteria reflect the composition of export earnings and a distinction between net creditor and net debtor economies. The detailed composition of emerging market and developing economies in the regional and analytical groups is shown in Tables D and E.

The analytical criterion *source of export earnings* distinguishes between the categories fuel (Standard International Trade Classification [SITC] 3) and nonfuel and then focuses on *nonfuel primary products* (SITCs 0, 1, 2, 4, and 68). Economies are categorized into one of these groups when their main source of export earnings exceeded 50 percent of total exports on average between 2013 and 2017.[5]

The financial criteria focus on net creditor economies, net debtor economies, heavily indebted poor countries (HIPCs), and low-income developing countries (LIDCs). Economies are categorized as net debtors when their latest net international investment position, where available, was less than zero or their current account balance accumulations from 1972 (or earliest available data) to 2017 were negative. Net debtor economies are further differentiated on the basis of experience with debt servicing.

The HIPC group comprises the countries that are or have been considered by the IMF and the World Bank for participation in their debt initiative known as the HIPC Initiative, which aims to reduce the external debt burdens of all the eligible HIPCs to a "sustainable" level in a reasonably short period of time.[6] Many of these countries have already benefited from debt relief and have graduated from the initiative.

The LIDCs are countries that have per capita income levels below a certain threshold (set at $2,700 in 2016 as measured by the World Bank's Atlas method), structural features consistent with limited development and structural transformation, and insufficiently close external financial linkages to be widely seen as emerging market economies.

---

[4] As used here, the terms "country" and "economy" do not always refer to a territorial entity that is a state as understood by international law and practice. Some territorial entities included here are not states, although their statistical data are maintained on a separate and independent basis.

[5] During 2013–17, 26 economies incurred external payments arrears or entered into official or commercial bank debt-rescheduling agreements. This group is referred to as *economies with arrears and/or rescheduling during 2013–17.*

[6] See David Andrews, Anthony R. Boote, Syed S. Rizavi, and Sukwinder Singh, "Debt Relief for Low-Income Countries: The Enhanced HIPC Initiative," IMF Pamphlet Series 51 (Washington, DC: International Monetary Fund, November 1999).

Table A. Classification by World Economic Outlook Groups and Their Shares in Aggregate GDP, Exports of Goods and Services, and Population, 2017[1]
(Percent of total for group or world)

	Number of Economies	GDP Advanced Economies	World	Exports of Goods and Services Advanced Economies	World	Population Advanced Economies	World
Advanced Economies	**39**	**100.0**	**41.3**	**100.0**	**63.6**	**100.0**	**14.4**
United States		37.0	15.3	16.3	10.4	30.6	4.4
Euro Area	19	28.1	11.6	41.4	26.3	31.8	4.6
Germany		8.0	3.3	12.1	7.7	7.8	1.1
France		5.4	2.2	5.7	3.7	6.1	0.9
Italy		4.4	1.8	4.2	2.7	5.7	0.8
Spain		3.4	1.4	3.1	2.0	4.4	0.6
Japan		10.3	4.3	6.1	3.9	11.9	1.7
United Kingdom		5.5	2.3	5.5	3.5	6.2	0.9
Canada		3.4	1.4	3.5	2.2	3.4	0.5
Other Advanced Economies	16	15.7	6.5	27.2	17.3	16.0	2.3
Memorandum							
Major Advanced Economies	7	74.0	30.6	53.4	33.9	71.7	10.3

	Number of Economies	GDP Emerging Market and Developing Economies	World	Exports of Goods and Services Emerging Market and Developing Economies	World	Population Emerging Market and Developing Economies	World
Emerging Market and Developing Economies	**155**	**100.0**	**58.7**	**100.0**	**36.4**	**100.0**	**85.6**
Regional Groups							
Commonwealth of Independent States[2]	12	7.6	4.5	7.5	2.7	4.5	3.9
Russia		5.4	3.2	5.0	1.8	2.3	2.0
Emerging and Developing Asia	30	55.2	32.4	49.5	18.0	56.6	48.4
China		31.0	18.2	29.3	10.7	22.0	18.8
India		12.7	7.4	6.1	2.2	20.9	17.8
Excluding China and India	28	11.5	6.7	14.1	5.1	13.7	11.8
Emerging and Developing Europe	12	6.1	3.6	9.9	3.6	2.8	2.4
Latin America and the Caribbean	33	13.1	7.7	14.1	5.1	9.8	8.4
Brazil		4.3	2.5	3.0	1.1	3.3	2.8
Mexico		3.3	1.9	5.3	1.9	2.0	1.7
Middle East, North Africa, Afghanistan, and Pakistan	23	12.8	7.5	14.6	5.3	10.9	9.3
Middle East and North Africa	21	11.3	6.6	14.3	5.2	7.2	6.2
Sub-Saharan Africa	45	5.1	3.0	4.4	1.6	15.3	13.1
Excluding Nigeria and South Africa	43	2.6	1.5	2.6	0.9	11.5	9.8
Analytical Groups[3]							
By Source of Export Earnings							
Fuel	28	17.9	10.5	20.9	7.6	11.7	10.1
Nonfuel	126	82.1	48.2	79.1	28.8	88.3	75.5
Of Which, Primary Products	32	5.0	3.0	5.3	1.9	8.4	7.2
By External Financing Source							
Net Debtor Economies	123	49.7	29.1	45.9	16.7	66.9	57.3
Net Debtor Economies by Debt-Servicing Experience							
Economies with Arrears and/or Rescheduling during 2012–16	26	3.5	2.1	2.4	0.9	6.4	5.5
Other Groups							
Heavily Indebted Poor Countries	39	2.5	1.4	2.0	0.7	11.5	9.8
Low-Income Developing Countries	59	7.2	4.2	6.8	2.5	22.7	19.4

[1]The GDP shares are based on the purchasing-power-parity valuation of economies' GDP. The number of economies comprising each group reflects those for which data are included in the group aggregates.

[2]Georgia, Turkmenistan, and Ukraine, which are not members of the Commonwealth of Independent States, are included in this group for reasons of geography and similarity in economic structure.

[3]Syria is omitted from the source of export earnings and South Sudan and Syria are omitted from the net external position group composites because of insufficient data.

Table B. Advanced Economies by Subgroup

Major Currency Areas

United States
Euro Area
Japan

Euro Area

Austria	Greece	Netherlands
Belgium	Ireland	Portugal
Cyprus	Italy	Slovak Republic
Estonia	Latvia	Slovenia
Finland	Lithuania	Spain
France	Luxembourg	
Germany	Malta	

Major Advanced Economies

Canada	Italy	United States
France	Japan	
Germany	United Kingdom	

Other Advanced Economies

Australia	Korea	Singapore
Czech Republic	Macao SAR[2]	Sweden
Denmark	New Zealand	Switzerland
Hong Kong SAR[1]	Norway	Taiwan Province of China
Iceland	Puerto Rico	
Israel	San Marino	

[1]On July 1, 1997, Hong Kong was returned to the People's Republic of China and became a Special Administrative Region of China.
[2]On December 20, 1999, Macao was returned to the People's Republic of China and became a Special Administrative Region of China.

Table C. European Union

Austria	Germany	Poland
Belgium	Greece	Portugal
Bulgaria	Hungary	Romania
Croatia	Ireland	Slovak Republic
Cyprus	Italy	Slovenia
Czech Republic	Latvia	Spain
Denmark	Lithuania	Sweden
Estonia	Luxembourg	United Kingdom
Finland	Malta	
France	Netherlands	

Table D. Emerging Market and Developing Economies by Region and Main Source of Export Earnings

	Fuel	Nonfuel Primary Products
Commonwealth of Independent States		
	Azerbaijan	Uzbekistan
	Kazakhstan	
	Russia	
	Turkmenistan[1]	
Emerging and Developing Asia		
	Brunei Darussalam	Kiribati
	Timor-Leste	Lao P.D.R.
		Marshall Islands
		Mongolia
		Papua New Guinea
		Solomon Islands
		Tuvalu
Latin America and the Caribbean		
	Bolivia	Argentina
	Ecuador	Chile
	Trinidad and Tobago	Guyana
	Venezuela	Paraguay
		Peru
		Suriname
		Uruguay
Middle East, North Africa, Afghanistan, and Pakistan		
	Algeria	Afghanistan
	Bahrain	Mauritania
	Iran	Sudan
	Iraq	
	Kuwait	
	Libya	
	Oman	
	Qatar	
	Saudi Arabia	
	United Arab Emirates	
	Yemen	
Sub-Saharan Africa		
	Angola	Burkina Faso
	Chad	Burundi
	Republic of Congo	Central African Republic
	Equatorial Guinea	Democratic Republic of the Congo
	Gabon	Côte d'Ivoire
	Nigeria	Eritrea
	South Sudan	Guinea
		Guinea-Bissau
		Liberia
		Malawi
		Mali
		Sierra Leone
		South Africa
		Zambia

[1]Turkmenistan, which is not a member of the Commonwealth of Independent States, is included in this group for reasons of geography and similarity in economic structure.

Table E. Emerging Market and Developing Economies by Region, Net External Position, and Status as Heavily Indebted Poor Countries and Low-Income Developing Countries

	Net External Position[1]	Heavily Indebted Poor Countries[2]	Low-Income Developing Countries
Commonwealth of Independent States			
Armenia	*		
Azerbaijan	●		
Belarus	*		
Georgia[3]	*		
Kazakhstan	*		
Kyrgyz Republic	*		*
Moldova	*		*
Russia	●		
Tajikistan	*		*
Turkmenistan[3]	*		
Ukraine[3]	*		
Uzbekistan	●		*
Emerging and Developing Asia			
Bangladesh	*		*
Bhutan	*		*
Brunei Darussalam	●		
Cambodia	*		*
China	●		
Fiji	*		
India	*		
Indonesia	*		
Kiribati	●		*
Lao P.D.R.	*		*
Malaysia	*		
Maldives	*		
Marshall Islands	*		
Micronesia	●		
Mongolia	*		
Myanmar	*		*
Nauru	*		
Nepal	●		*
Palau	●		
Papua New Guinea	*		*
Philippines	*		
Samoa	*		
Solomon Islands	*		*
Sri Lanka	*		
Thailand	●		
Timor-Leste	●		*
Tonga	*		
Tuvalu	*		
Vanuatu	*		
Vietnam	*		*

	Net External Position[1]	Heavily Indebted Poor Countries[2]	Low-Income Developing Countries
Emerging and Developing Europe			
Albania	*		
Bosnia and Herzegovina	*		
Bulgaria	*		
Croatia	*		
Hungary	*		
Kosovo	*		
FYR Macedonia	*		
Montenegro	*		
Poland	*		
Romania	*		
Serbia	*		
Turkey	*		
Latin America and the Caribbean			
Antigua and Barbuda	*		
Argentina	●		
Aruba	*		
The Bahamas	*		
Barbados	*		
Belize	*		
Bolivia	*	●	
Brazil	*		
Chile	*		
Colombia	*		
Costa Rica	*		
Dominica	*		
Dominican Republic	*		
Ecuador	*		
El Salvador	*		
Grenada	*		
Guatemala	*		
Guyana	*	●	
Haiti	*	●	*
Honduras	*	●	*
Jamaica	*		
Mexico	*		
Nicaragua	*	●	*
Panama	*		
Paraguay	*		
Peru	*		
St. Kitts and Nevis	*		
St. Lucia	*		
St. Vincent and the Grenadines	*		
Suriname	*		
Trinidad and Tobago	●		
Uruguay	*		
Venezuela	●		

Table E. Emerging Market and Developing Economies by Region, Net External Position, and Status as Heavily Indebted Poor Countries and Low-Income Developing Countries *(continued)*

	Net External Position[1]	Heavily Indebted Poor Countries[2]	Low-Income Developing Countries		Net External Position[1]	Heavily Indebted Poor Countries[2]	Low-Income Developing Countries
Middle East, North Africa, Afghanistan, and Pakistan				Democratic Republic of the Congo	*	●	*
Afghanistan	●	●	*	Republic of Congo	*	●	*
Algeria	●			Côte d'Ivoire	*	●	*
Bahrain	●			Equatorial Guinea	*		
Djibouti	*		*	Eritrea	*	*	*
Egypt	*			Eswatini	●		
Iran	●			Ethiopia	*	●	*
Iraq	●			Gabon	●		
Jordan	*			The Gambia	●		
Kuwait	●			Ghana	*	●	*
Lebanon	*			Guinea	*	●	*
Libya	●			Guinea-Bissau	*	●	*
Mauritania	*	●	*	Kenya	*	●	*
Morocco	*			Lesotho	*		*
Oman	●			Liberia	*		*
Pakistan	*			Madagascar	*	●	*
Qatar	●			Malawi	*	●	*
Saudi Arabia	●			Mali	*	●	*
Somalia	*	*	*	Mauritius	*	●	*
Sudan	*	*	*	Mozambique	●		
Syria[4]	. . .			Namibia	*	●	*
Tunisia	*			Niger	*		
United Arab Emirates	●			Nigeria	*	●	*
Yemen	*		*	Rwanda	*		*
Sub-Saharan Africa				São Tomé and Príncipe	*	●	*
Angola	*			Senegal	*	●	*
Benin	*	●	*	Seychelles	*	●	*
Botswana	●			Sierra Leone	*		
Burkina Faso	*	●	*	South Africa	*	●	*
Burundi	*	●	*	South Sudan[4]	. . .		*
Cabo Verde	*			Tanzania	*	●	*
Cameroon	*	●	*	Togo	*	●	*
Central African Republic	*	●	*	Uganda	*	●	*
Chad	*	●	*	Zambia	*	●	*
Comoros	*	●	*	Zimbabwe	*		*

[1]Dot (star) indicates that the country is a net creditor (net debtor).

[2]Dot instead of star indicates that the country has reached the completion point, which allows it to receive the full debt relief committed to at the decision point.

[3]Georgia, Turkmenistan, and Ukraine, which are not members of the Commonwealth of Independent States, are included in this group for reasons of geography and similarity in economic structure.

[4]South Sudan and Syria are omitted from the net external position group composite for lack of a fully developed database.

Table F. Economies with Exceptional Reporting Periods[1]

	National Accounts	Government Finance
The Bahamas		Jul/Jun
Barbados		Apr/Mar
Belize		Apr/Mar
Bhutan	Jul/Jun	Jul/Jun
Botswana		Apr/Mar
Dominica		Jul/Jun
Egypt	Jul/Jun	Jul/Jun
Eswatini		Apr/Mar
Ethiopia	Jul/Jun	Jul/Jun
Haiti	Oct/Sep	Oct/Sep
Hong Kong SAR		Apr/Mar
India	Apr/Mar	Apr/Mar
Iran	Apr/Mar	Apr/Mar
Jamaica		Apr/Mar
Lesotho	Apr/Mar	Apr/Mar
Malawi		Jul/Jun
Marshall Islands	Oct/Sep	Oct/Sep
Mauritius		Jul/Jun
Micronesia	Oct/Sep	Oct/Sep
Myanmar	Oct/Sep	Oct/Sep
Nauru	Jul/Jun	Jul/Jun
Nepal	Aug/Jul	Aug/Jul
Pakistan	Jul/Jun	Jul/Jun
Palau	Oct/Sep	Oct/Sep
Puerto Rico	Jul/Jun	Jul/Jun
St. Lucia		Apr/Mar
Samoa	Jul/Jun	Jul/Jun
Singapore		Apr/Mar
Thailand		Oct/Sep
Trinidad and Tobago		Oct/Sep

[1]Unless noted otherwise, all data refer to calendar years.

Table G. Key Data Documentation

Country	Currency	National Accounts					Prices (CPI)	
		Historical Data Source[1]	Latest Actual Annual Data	Base Year[2]	System of National Accounts	Use of Chain-Weighted Methodology[3]	Historical Data Source[1]	Latest Actual Annual Data
Afghanistan	Afghan afghani	NSO	2016	2002/03	SNA 1993		NSO	2017
Albania	Albanian lek	IMF staff	2016	1996	SNA 1993	From 1996	NSO	2017
Algeria	Algerian dinar	NSO	2017	2001	SNA 1993	From 2005	NSO	2017
Angola	Angolan kwanza	NSO and MEP	2015	2002	ESA 1995		NSO	2015
Antigua and Barbuda	Eastern Caribbean dollar	CB	2016	2006[6]	SNA 1993		NSO	2016
Argentina	Argentine peso	NSO	2017	2004	SNA 2008		NSO	2017
Armenia	Armenian dram	NSO	2016	2005	SNA 2008		NSO	2016
Aruba	Aruban florin	NSO	2017	2000	SNA 1993	From 2000	NSO	2017
Australia	Australian dollar	NSO	2017	2015/16	SNA 2008	From 1980	NSO	2017
Austria	Euro	NSO	2017	2010	ESA 2010	From 1995	NSO	2017
Azerbaijan	Azerbaijan manat	NSO	2016	2005	SNA 1993	From 1994	NSO	2017
The Bahamas	Bahamian dollar	NSO	2016	2012	SNA 1993		NSO	2017
Bahrain	Bahrain dinar	NSO	2017	2010	SNA 2008		NSO	2017
Bangladesh	Bangladesh taka	NSO	2017	2005/06	SNA 1993		NSO	2017
Barbados	Barbados dollar	NSO and CB	2017	2010	SNA 1993		NSO	2017
Belarus	Belarusian ruble	NSO	2017	2014	SNA 2008	From 2005	NSO	2017
Belgium	Euro	CB	2017	2015	ESA 2010	From 1995	CB	2017
Belize	Belize dollar	NSO	2016	2000	SNA 1993		NSO	2016
Benin	CFA franc	NSO	2015	2007	SNA 1993		NSO	2017
Bhutan	Bhutanese ngultrum	NSO	2015/16	2000/01[6]	SNA 1993		CB	2016/17
Bolivia	Bolivian boliviano	NSO	2016	1990	SNA 2008		NSO	2017
Bosnia and Herzegovina	Bosnia convertible marka	NSO	2017	2010	ESA 2010	From 2000	NSO	2017
Botswana	Botswana pula	NSO	2017	2006	SNA 1993		NSO	2017
Brazil	Brazilian real	NSO	2017	1995	SNA 2008		NSO	2017
Brunei Darussalam	Brunei dollar	NSO and GAD	2017	2010	SNA 1993		NSO and GAD	2017
Bulgaria	Bulgarian lev	NSO	2017	2010	ESA 2010	From 1996	NSO	2017
Burkina Faso	CFA franc	NSO and MEP	2016	1999	SNA 1993		NSO	2017
Burundi	Burundi franc	NSO	2015	2005	SNA 1993		NSO	2017
Cabo Verde	Cabo Verdean escudo	NSO	2017	2007	SNA 2008	From 2011	NSO	2017
Cambodia	Cambodian riel	NSO	2017	2000	SNA 1993		NSO	2017
Cameroon	CFA franc	NSO	2016	2005	SNA 2008		NSO	2017
Canada	Canadian dollar	NSO	2017	2007	SNA 2008	From 1980	NSO	2017
Central African Republic	CFA franc	NSO	2012	2005	SNA 1993		NSO	2015
Chad	CFA franc	CB	2017	2005	...		NSO	2017
Chile	Chilean peso	CB	2017	2013[6]	SNA 2008	From 2003	NSO	2017
China	Chinese yuan	NSO	2017	2015	SNA 2008		NSO	2017
Colombia	Colombian peso	NSO	2017	2015	SNA 1993	From 2000	NSO	2017
Comoros	Comorian franc	MEP	2017	2000	...		NSO	2017
Democratic Republic of the Congo	Congolese franc	NSO	2016	2005	SNA 1993		CB	2016
Republic of Congo	CFA franc	NSO	2016	1990	SNA 1993		NSO	2017
Costa Rica	Costa Rican colón	CB	2016	2012	SNA 2008		CB	2016

Table G. Key Data Documentation (continued)

Country	Government Finance					Balance of Payments		
	Historical Data Source[1]	Latest Actual Annual Data	Statistics Manual in Use at Source	Subsectors Coverage[4]	Accounting Practice[5]	Historical Data Source[1]	Latest Actual Annual Data	Statistics Manual in Use at Source
Afghanistan	MoF	2017	2001	CG	C	NSO, MoF, and CB	2017	BPM 5
Albania	IMF staff	2016	1986	CG,LG,SS,MPC, NFPC	...	CB	2016	BPM 6
Algeria	MoF	2017	1986	CG	C	CB	2017	BPM 6
Angola	MoF	2016	2001	CG,LG	...	CB	2016	BPM 6
Antigua and Barbuda	MoF	2016	2001	CG	C	CB	2016	BPM 6
Argentina	MEP	2017	1986	CG,SG,SS	C	NSO	2017	BPM 6
Armenia	MoF	2016	2001	CG	C	CB	2016	BPM 6
Aruba	MoF	2017	2001	CG	Mixed	CB	2017	BPM 5
Australia	MoF	2016	2014	CG,SG,LG,TG	A	NSO	2017	BPM 6
Austria	NSO	2017	2001	CG,SG,LG,SS	A	CB	2017	BPM 6
Azerbaijan	MoF	2015	...	CG	C	CB	2016	BPM 6
The Bahamas	MoF	2016/17	2001	CG	C	CB	2017	BPM 5
Bahrain	MoF	2016	2001	CG	C	CB	2017	BPM 6
Bangladesh	MoF	2017	...	CG	C	CB	2017	BPM 6
Barbados	MoF	2016/17	1986	BCG	C	CB	2016	BPM 5
Belarus	MoF	2017	2001	CG,LG,SS	C	CB	2017	BPM 6
Belgium	CB	2017	ESA 2010	CG,SG,LG,SS	A	CB	2017	BPM 6
Belize	MoF	2016/17	1986	CG,MPC	Mixed	CB	2016	BPM 6
Benin	MoF	2017	1986	CG	C	CB	2016	BPM 6
Bhutan	MoF	2016/17	1986	CG	C	CB	2015/16	BPM 6
Bolivia	MoF	2016	2001	CG,LG,SS,NMPC, NFPC	C	CB	2016	BPM 6
Bosnia and Herzegovina	MoF	2017	2001	CG,SG,LG,SS	Mixed	CB	2017	BPM 6
Botswana	MoF	2017/18	1986	CG	C	CB	2017	BPM 6
Brazil	MoF	2017	2001	CG,SG,LG,SS, MPC,NFPC	C	CB	2017	BPM 6
Brunei Darussalam	MoF	2017	...	CG, BCG	C	NSO, MEP, and GAD	2017	BPM 6
Bulgaria	MoF	2017	2001	CG,LG,SS	C	CB	2017	BPM 6
Burkina Faso	MoF	2017	2001	CG	CB	CB	2016	BPM 6
Burundi	MoF	2015	2001	CG	A	CB	2016	BPM 6
Cabo Verde	MoF	2017	2001	CG	A	NSO	2017	BPM 6
Cambodia	MoF	2016	1986	CG,LG	A	CB	2017	BPM 5
Cameroon	MoF	2016	2001	CG,NFPC	C	MoF	2016	BPM 5
Canada	MoF	2017	2001	CG,SG,LG,SS,Other	A	NSO	2017	BPM 6
Central African Republic	MoF	2016	2001	CG	C	CB	2015	BPM 5
Chad	MoF	2017	1986	CG,NFPC	C	CB	2015	BPM 6
Chile	MoF	2017	2001	CG,LG	A	CB	2017	BPM 6
China	MoF	2017	...	CG,LG	C	GAD	2017	BPM 6
Colombia	MoF	2017	2001	CG,SG,LG,SS	...	CB and NSO	2017	BPM 6
Comoros	MoF	2017	1986	CG	Mixed	CB and IMF staff	2017	BPM 5
Democratic Republic of the Congo	MoF	2016	2001	CG,LG	A	CB	2016	BPM 5
Republic of Congo	MoF	2017	2001	CG	A	CB	2016	BPM 6
Costa Rica	MoF and CB	2016	1986	CG	C	CB	2016	BPM 6

Table G. Key Data Documentation *(continued)*

Country	Currency	National Accounts					Prices (CPI)	
		Historical Data Source[1]	Latest Actual Annual Data	Base Year[2]	System of National Accounts	Use of Chain-Weighted Methodology[3]	Historical Data Source[1]	Latest Actual Annual Data
Côte d'Ivoire	CFA franc	NSO	2015	2009	SNA 1993		NSO	2017
Croatia	Croatian kuna	NSO	2017	2010	ESA 2010		NSO	2017
Cyprus	Euro	NSO	2017	2005	ESA 2010	From 1995	NSO	2017
Czech Republic	Czech koruna	NSO	2017	2010	ESA 2010	From 1995	NSO	2017
Denmark	Danish krone	NSO	2017	2010	ESA 2010	From 1980	NSO	2017
Djibouti	Djibouti franc	NSO	2017	1990	SNA 1993		NSO	2017
Dominica	Eastern Caribbean dollar	NSO	2016	2006	SNA 1993		NSO	2016
Dominican Republic	Dominican peso	CB	2017	2007	SNA 2008	From 2007	CB	2017
Ecuador	US dollar	CB	2016	2007	SNA 1993		NSO and CB	2017
Egypt	Egyptian pound	MEP	2016/17	2011/12	SNA 2008		NSO	2017/18
El Salvador	US dollar	CB	2017	2005	SNA 2008		NSO	2017
Equatorial Guinea	CFA franc	MEP and CB	2016	2006	SNA 1993		MEP	2017
Eritrea	Eritrean nakfa	IMF staff	2006	2005	SNA 1993		NSO	2009
Estonia	Euro	NSO	2017	2010	ESA 2010	From 2010	NSO	2017
Eswatini	Swazi lilangeni	NSO	2016	2011	SNA 1993		NSO	2017
Ethiopia	Ethiopian birr	NSO	2016/17	2015/16	SNA 1993		NSO	2017
Fiji	Fijian dollar	NSO	2016	2011[6]	SNA 1993		NSO	2017
Finland	Euro	NSO	2017	2010	ESA 2010	From 1980	NSO	2017
France	Euro	NSO	2017	2014	ESA 2010	From 1980	NSO	2017
Gabon	CFA franc	MoF	2016	2001	SNA 1993		NSO	2017
The Gambia	Gambian dalasi	NSO	2017	2013	SNA 1993		NSO	2017
Georgia	Georgian lari	NSO	2016	2000	SNA 1993	From 1996	NSO	2017
Germany	Euro	NSO	2017	2010	ESA 2010	From 1991	NSO	2017
Ghana	Ghanaian cedi	NSO	2017	2006	SNA 1993		NSO	2017
Greece	Euro	NSO	2017	2010	ESA 2010	From 1995	NSO	2017
Grenada	Eastern Caribbean dollar	NSO	2017	2006	SNA 1993		NSO	2017
Guatemala	Guatemalan quetzal	CB	2017	2001	SNA 1993	From 2001	NSO	2017
Guinea	Guinean franc	NSO	2016	2010	SNA 1993		NSO	2017
Guinea-Bissau	CFA franc	NSO	2016	2005	SNA 1993		NSO	2017
Guyana	Guyanese dollar	NSO	2017	2006[6]	SNA 1993		NSO	2017
Haiti	Haitian gourde	NSO	2016/17	1986/87	SNA 1993		NSO	2016/17
Honduras	Honduran lempira	CB	2016	2000	SNA 1993		CB	2016
Hong Kong SAR	Hong Kong dollar	NSO	2017	2016	SNA 2008	From 1980	NSO	2017
Hungary	Hungarian forint	NSO	2017	2005	ESA 2010	From 2005	IEO	2017
Iceland	Icelandic króna	NSO	2017	2005	ESA 2010	From 1990	NSO	2017
India	Indian rupee	NSO	2017/18	2011/12	SNA 2008		NSO	2017/18
Indonesia	Indonesian rupiah	NSO	2017	2010	SNA 2008		NSO	2017
Iran	Iranian rial	CB	2016/17	2011/12	SNA 1993		CB	2016/17
Iraq	Iraqi dinar	NSO	2017	2007	SNA 1968/93		NSO	2017
Ireland	Euro	NSO	2017	2015	ESA 2010	From 1995	NSO	2017
Israel	New Israeli shekel	NSO	2017	2015	SNA 2008	From 1995	NSO	2017
Italy	Euro	NSO	2017	2010	ESA 2010	From 1980	NSO	2017
Jamaica	Jamaican dollar	NSO	2016	2007	SNA 1993		NSO	2016

Table G. Key Data Documentation *(continued)*

Country	Government Finance					Balance of Payments		
	Historical Data Source[1]	Latest Actual Annual Data	Statistics Manual in Use at Source	Subsectors Coverage[4]	Accounting Practice[5]	Historical Data Source[1]	Latest Actual Annual Data	Statistics Manual in Use at Source
Côte d'Ivoire	MoF	2017	1986	CG	A	CB	2016	BPM 6
Croatia	MoF	2017	2001	CG,LG	A	CB	2017	BPM 6
Cyprus	NSO	2017	ESA 2010	CG,LG,SS	A	CB	2017	BPM 6
Czech Republic	MoF	2016	2001	CG,LG,SS	A	NSO	2017	BPM 6
Denmark	NSO	2017	2001	CG,LG,SS	A	NSO	2017	BPM 6
Djibouti	MoF	2016	2001	CG	A	CB	2016	BPM 5
Dominica	MoF	2016/17	1986	CG	C	CB	2016	BPM 6
Dominican Republic	MoF	2017	2001	CG,SG,LG,SS, NMPC	Mixed	CB	2017	BPM 6
Ecuador	CB and MoF	2016	1986	CG,SG,LG,SS, NFPC	C	CB	2016	BPM 6
Egypt	MoF	2016/17	2001	CG,LG,SS,MPC	C	CB	2016/17	BPM 5
El Salvador	MoF and CB	2017	1986	CG,LG,SS	C	CB	2017	BPM 6
Equatorial Guinea	MoF	2016	1986	CG	C	CB	2016	BPM 5
Eritrea	MoF	2008	2001	CG	C	CB	2008	BPM 5
Estonia	MoF	2017	1986/2001	CG,LG,SS	C	CB	2017	BPM 6
Eswatini	MoF	2017/18	2001	CG	A	CB	2017	BPM 6
Ethiopia	MoF	2015/16	1986	CG,SG,LG,NFPC	C	CB	2016/17	BPM 5
Fiji	MoF	2017	1986	CG	C	CB	2017	BPM 6
Finland	MoF	2016	2001	CG,LG,SS	A	NSO	2017	BPM 6
France	NSO	2017	2001	CG,LG,SS	A	CB	2017	BPM 6
Gabon	IMF staff	2017	2001	CG	A	CB	2016	BPM 5
The Gambia	MoF	2017	1986	CG	C	CB and IMF staff	2017	BPM 5
Georgia	MoF	2017	2001	CG,LG	C	NSO and CB	2016	BPM 6
Germany	NSO	2017	2001	CG,SG,LG,SS	A	CB	2017	BPM 6
Ghana	MoF	2017	2001	CG	C	CB	2017	BPM 5
Greece	NSO	2017	2014	CG,LG,SS	A	CB	2017	BPM 6
Grenada	MoF	2017	2001	CG	CB	CB	2016	BPM 6
Guatemala	MoF	2017	2001	CG	C	CB	2017	BPM 6
Guinea	MoF	2017	2001	CG	C	CB and MEP	2017	BPM 6
Guinea-Bissau	MoF	2017	2001	CG	A	CB	2016	BPM 6
Guyana	MoF	2017	1986	CG,SS,NFPC	C	CB	2017	BPM 6
Haiti	MoF	2016/17	2001	CG	C	CB	2016/17	BPM 5
Honduras	CB and MoF	2017	2014	CG,LG,SS,Other	Mixed	CB	2015	BPM 5
Hong Kong SAR	NSO	2017/18	2001	CG	C	NSO	2017	BPM 6
Hungary	MEP and NSO	2017	ESA 2010	CG,LG,SS,NMPC	A	CB	2017	BPM 6
Iceland	NSO	2017	2001	CG,LG,SS	A	CB	2017	BPM 6
India	MoF and IMF staff	2017/18	1986	CG,SG	C	CB	2017/18	BPM 6
Indonesia	MoF	2017	2001	CG,LG	C	CB	2017	BPM 6
Iran	MoF	2016/17	2001	CG	C	CB	2016/17	BPM 5
Iraq	MoF	2017	2001	CG	C	CB	2017	BPM 6
Ireland	MoF and NSO	2017	2001	CG,LG,SS	A	NSO	2017	BPM 6
Israel	MoF and NSO	2017	2001	CG,LG,SS	…	NSO	2017	BPM 6
Italy	NSO	2017	2001	CG,LG,SS	A	NSO	2017	BPM 6
Jamaica	MoF	2016/17	1986	CG	C	CB	2016	BPM 5

Table G. Key Data Documentation *(continued)*

Country	Currency	National Accounts Historical Data Source[1]	Latest Actual Annual Data	Base Year[2]	System of National Accounts	Use of Chain-Weighted Methodology[3]	Prices (CPI) Historical Data Source[1]	Latest Actual Annual Data
Japan	Japanese yen	GAD	2017	2011	SNA 2008	From 1980	GAD	2017
Jordan	Jordanian dinar	NSO	2017	1994	SNA 1993		NSO	2017
Kazakhstan	Kazakhstani tenge	NSO	2017	2007	SNA 1993	From 1994	CB	2017
Kenya	Kenya shilling	NSO	2016	2009	SNA 2008		NSO	2017
Kiribati	Australian dollar	NSO	2016	2006	SNA 2008		NSO	2017
Korea	South Korean won	CB	2017	2010	SNA 2008	From 1980	NSO	2017
Kosovo	Euro	NSO	2017	2016	ESA 2010		NSO	2017
Kuwait	Kuwaiti dinar	MEP and NSO	2017	2010	SNA 1993		NSO and MEP	2017
Kyrgyz Republic	Kyrgyz som	NSO	2016	2005	SNA 1993		NSO	2016
Lao P.D.R.	Lao kip	NSO	2016	2012	SNA 1993		NSO	2016
Latvia	Euro	NSO	2017	2010	ESA 2010	From 1995	NSO	2017
Lebanon	Lebanese pound	NSO	2016	2010	SNA 2008	From 2010	NSO	2016/17
Lesotho	Lesotho loti	NSO	2015/16	2012/13	SNA 2008		NSO	2017
Liberia	US dollar	CB	2017	1992	SNA 1993		CB	2017
Libya	Libyan dinar	MEP	2016	2003	SNA 1993		NSO	2017
Lithuania	Euro	NSO	2017	2010	ESA 2010	From 2005	NSO	2017
Luxembourg	Euro	NSO	2017	2010	ESA 2010	From 1995	NSO	2017
Macao SAR	Macanese pataca	NSO	2017	2016	SNA 2008	From 2001	NSO	2017
FYR Macedonia	Macedonian denar	NSO	2017	2005	ESA 2010		NSO	2017
Madagascar	Malagasy ariary	NSO	2016	2000	SNA 1968		NSO	2017
Malawi	Malawian kwacha	NSO	2011	2010	SNA 2008		NSO	2017
Malaysia	Malaysian ringgit	NSO	2017	2010	SNA 2008		NSO	2017
Maldives	Maldivian rufiyaa	MoF and NSO	2017	2014	SNA 1993		CB	2017
Mali	CFA franc	NSO	2016	1999	SNA 1993		NSO	2017
Malta	Euro	NSO	2017	2010	ESA 2010	From 2000	NSO	2017
Marshall Islands	US dollar	NSO	2016/17	2003/04	SNA 1993		NSO	2016/17
Mauritania	Mauritanian ouguiya	NSO	2014	2004	SNA 1993		NSO	2017
Mauritius	Mauritian rupee	NSO	2017	2006	SNA 1993	From 1999	NSO	2017
Mexico	Mexican peso	NSO	2017	2013	SNA 2008		NSO	2017
Micronesia	US dollar	NSO	2014/15	2004	SNA 1993		NSO	2014/15
Moldova	Moldovan leu	NSO	2017	1995	SNA 1993		NSO	2017
Mongolia	Mongolian tögrög	NSO	2016	2010	SNA 1993		NSO	2016/17
Montenegro	Euro	NSO	2016	2006	ESA 2010		NSO	2016
Morocco	Moroccan dirham	NSO	2016	2007	SNA 1993	From 1998	NSO	2017
Mozambique	Mozambican metical	NSO	2017	2009	SNA 1993/ 2008		NSO	2017
Myanmar	Myanmar kyat	MEP	2016/17	2010/11	...		NSO	2017/18
Namibia	Namibia dollar	NSO	2017	2000	SNA 1993		NSO	2017
Nauru	Australian dollar	...	2015/16	2006/07	SNA 1993		NSO	2016/17
Nepal	Nepalese rupee	NSO	2017/18	2000/01	SNA 1993		CB	2017/18
Netherlands	Euro	NSO	2017	2015	ESA 2010	From 1980	NSO	2017
New Zealand	New Zealand dollar	NSO	2017	2009/10	SNA 2008	From 1987	NSO	2017
Nicaragua	Nicaraguan córdoba	CB	2017	2006	SNA 1993	From 1994	CB	2017
Niger	CFA franc	NSO	2016	2000	SNA 1993		NSO	2017
Nigeria	Nigerian naira	NSO	2017	2010	SNA 2008		NSO	2017
Norway	Norwegian krone	NSO	2017	2015	ESA 2010	From 1980	NSO	2017

Table G. Key Data Documentation *(continued)*

Country	Government Finance					Balance of Payments		
	Historical Data Source[1]	Latest Actual Annual Data	Statistics Manual in Use at Source	Subsectors Coverage[4]	Accounting Practice[5]	Historical Data Source[1]	Latest Actual Annual Data	Statistics Manual in Use at Source
Japan	GAD	2016	2014	CG,LG,SS	A	MoF	2017	BPM 6
Jordan	MoF	2017	2001	CG,NFPC	C	CB	2017	BPM 5
Kazakhstan	NSO	2017	2001	CG,LG	A	CB	2017	BPM 6
Kenya	MoF	2017	2001	CG	A	CB	2017	BPM 6
Kiribati	MoF	2016	1986	CG,LG	C	NSO	2016	BPM 6
Korea	MoF	2017	2001	CG,SS	C	CB	2017	BPM 6
Kosovo	MoF	2017	...	CG,LG	C	CB	2017	BPM 6
Kuwait	MoF	2016	1986	CG	Mixed	CB	2017	BPM 6
Kyrgyz Republic	MoF	2017	...	CG,LG,SS	C	CB	2017	BPM 5
Lao P.D.R.	MoF	2016	2001	CG	C	CB	2016	BPM 5
Latvia	MoF	2017	1986	CG,LG,SS	C	CB	2017	BPM 6
Lebanon	MoF	2017	2001	CG	Mixed	CB and IMF staff	2015	BPM 5
Lesotho	MoF	2016/17	2001	CG,LG	C	CB	2016/17	BPM 5
Liberia	MoF	2017	2001	CG	A	CB	2017	BPM 5
Libya	MoF	2017	1986	CG,SG,LG	C	CB	2017	BPM 5
Lithuania	MoF	2017	2014	CG,LG,SS	A	CB	2017	BPM 6
Luxembourg	MoF	2017	2001	CG,LG,SS	A	NSO	2017	BPM 6
Macao SAR	MoF	2016	2014	CG,SS	C	NSO	2016	BPM 6
FYR Macedonia	MoF	2017	1986	CG,SG,SS	C	CB	2017	BPM 6
Madagascar	MoF	2017	1986	CG,LG	C	CB	2017	BPM 5
Malawi	MoF	2017/18	1986	CG	C	NSO and GAD	2017	BPM 6
Malaysia	MoF	2016	2001	CG,SG,LG	C	NSO	2017	BPM 6
Maldives	MoF	2017	1986	CG	C	CB	2017	BPM 5
Mali	MoF	2016	2001	CG	Mixed	CB	2016	BPM 6
Malta	NSO	2017	2001	CG,SS	A	NSO	2017	BPM 6
Marshall Islands	MoF	2016/17	2001	CG,LG,SS	A	NSO	2016/17	BPM 6
Mauritania	MoF	2017	1986	CG	C	CB	2016	BPM 5
Mauritius	MoF	2017/18	2001	CG,LG,NFPC	C	CB	2017	BPM 6
Mexico	MoF	2017	2014	CG,SS,NMPC,NFPC	C	CB	2016	BPM 6
Micronesia	MoF	2014/15	2001	CG,SG,LG,SS	...	NSO	2014/15	BPM 5
Moldova	MoF	2016	1986	CG,LG,SS	C	CB	2016	BPM 5
Mongolia	MoF	2016	2001	CG,SG,LG,SS	C	CB	2016	BPM 6
Montenegro	MoF	2016	1986	CG,LG,SS	C	CB	2016	BPM 6
Morocco	MEP	2017	2001	CG	A	GAD	2017	BPM 6
Mozambique	MoF	2017	2001	CG,SG	Mixed	CB	2017	BPM 6
Myanmar	MoF	2016/17	...	CG,NFPC	C	IMF staff	2016/17	BPM 5
Namibia	MoF	2017	2001	CG	C	CB	2017	BPM 6
Nauru	MoF	2016/17	2001	CG	Mixed	IMF staff	2014/15	BPM 6
Nepal	MoF	2017/18	2001	CG	C	CB	2017/18	BPM 6
Netherlands	MoF	2017	2001	CG,LG,SS	A	CB	2017	BPM 6
New Zealand	MoF	2016/17	2001	CG	A	NSO	2017	BPM 6
Nicaragua	MoF	2017	1986	CG,LG,SS	C	IMF staff	2017	BPM 6
Niger	MoF	2017	1986	CG	A	CB	2017	BPM 6
Nigeria	MoF	2017	2001	CG,SG,LG	C	CB	2017	BPM 6
Norway	NSO and MoF	2016	2014	CG,LG,SS	A	NSO	2017	BPM 6

Table G. Key Data Documentation *(continued)*

Country	Currency	National Accounts					Prices (CPI)	
		Historical Data Source[1]	Latest Actual Annual Data	Base Year[2]	System of National Accounts	Use of Chain-Weighted Methodology[3]	Historical Data Source[1]	Latest Actual Annual Data
Oman	Omani rial	NSO	2017	2010	SNA 1993		NSO	2017
Pakistan	Pakistan rupee	NSO	2016/17	2005/06[6]	...		NSO	2016/17
Palau	US dollar	MoF	2016/17	2014/15	SNA 1993		MoF	2016/17
Panama	US dollar	NSO	2017	2007	SNA 1993	From 2007	NSO	2017
Papua New Guinea	Papua New Guinea kina	NSO and MoF	2015	2013	SNA 1993		NSO	2015
Paraguay	Paraguayan guaraní	CB	2017	2014	SNA 2008		CB	2017
Peru	Peruvian nuevo sol	CB	2017	2007	SNA 1993		CB	2017
Philippines	Philippine peso	NSO	2017	2000	SNA 2008		NSO	2017
Poland	Polish zloty	NSO	2017	2010	ESA 2010	From 1995	NSO	2017
Portugal	Euro	NSO	2017	2011	ESA 2010	From 1980	NSO	2017
Puerto Rico	US dollar	NSO	2016/17	1954	SNA1968		NSO	2016/17
Qatar	Qatari riyal	NSO and MEP	2016	2013	SNA 1993		NSO and MEP	2017
Romania	Romanian leu	NSO	2017	2010	ESA 2010	From 2000	NSO	2017
Russia	Russian ruble	NSO	2017	2016	SNA 2008	From 1995	NSO	2017
Rwanda	Rwandan franc	NSO	2017	2014	SNA 2008		NSO	2017
Samoa	Samoa tala	NSO	2016/17	2009/10	SNA 1993		NSO	2016/17
San Marino	Euro	NSO	2016	2007	...		NSO	2017
São Tomé and Príncipe	São Tomé and Príncipe dobra	NSO	2016	2008	SNA 1993		NSO	2017
Saudi Arabia	Saudi riyal	NSO and MEP	2017	2010	SNA 1993		NSO and MEP	2017
Senegal	CFA franc	NSO	2017	2014	SNA 1993		NSO	2017
Serbia	Serbian dinar	NSO	2016	2010	ESA 2010	From 2010	NSO	2016
Seychelles	Seychellois rupee	NSO	2016	2006	SNA 1993		NSO	2016
Sierra Leone	Sierra Leonean leone	NSO	2017	2006	SNA 1993	From 2010	NSO	2017
Singapore	Singapore dollar	NSO	2017	2010	SNA 2008		NSO	2017
Slovak Republic	Euro	NSO	2017	2010	ESA 2010	From 1997	NSO	2017
Slovenia	Euro	NSO	2017	2010	ESA 2010	From 2000	NSO	2017
Solomon Islands	Solomon Islands dollar	CB	2016	2004	SNA 1993		NSO	2017
Somalia	US dollar	CB	2016	2012	SNA 1993		CB	2014
South Africa	South African rand	NSO	2017	2010	SNA 2008		NSO	2017
South Sudan	South Sudanese pound	NSO	2017	2010	SNA 1993		NSO	2017
Spain	Euro	NSO	2017	2010	ESA 2010	From 1995	NSO	2017
Sri Lanka	Sri Lankan rupee	NSO	2017	2010	SNA 1993		NSO	2017
St. Kitts and Nevis	Eastern Caribbean dollar	NSO	2017	2006[6]	SNA 1993		NSO	2017
St. Lucia	Eastern Caribbean dollar	NSO	2017	2006	SNA 1993		NSO	2017
St. Vincent and the Grenadines	Eastern Caribbean dollar	NSO	2017	2006[6]	SNA 1993		NSO	2017
Sudan	Sudanese pound	NSO	2014	1982	SNA 1968		NSO	2017
Suriname	Surinamese dollar	NSO	2016	2007	SNA 1993		NSO	2017

Table G. Key Data Documentation *(continued)*

Country	Government Finance					Balance of Payments		
	Historical Data Source[1]	Latest Actual Annual Data	Statistics Manual in Use at Source	Subsectors Coverage[4]	Accounting Practice[5]	Historical Data Source[1]	Latest Actual Annual Data	Statistics Manual in Use at Source
Oman	MoF	2017	2001	CG	C	CB	2017	BPM 5
Pakistan	MoF	2016/17	1986	CG,SG,LG	C	CB	2016/17	BPM 6
Palau	MoF	2016/17	2001	CG	…	MoF	2016/17	BPM 6
Panama	MoF	2017	1986	CG,SG,LG,SS, NFPC	C	NSO	2017	BPM 6
Papua New Guinea	MoF	2015	1986	CG	C	CB	2015	BPM 5
Paraguay	MoF	2017	2001	CG,SG,LG,SS,MPC, NFPC	C	CB	2017	BPM 6
Peru	MoF	2017	1986	CG,SG,LG,SS	C	CB	2017	BPM 5
Philippines	MoF	2017	2001	CG,LG,SS	C	CB	2017	BPM 6
Poland	MoF and NSO	2016	ESA 2010	CG,LG,SS	A	CB	2016	BPM 6
Portugal	NSO	2017	2001	CG,LG,SS	A	CB	2017	BPM 6
Puerto Rico	MEP	2015/16	2001	…	A	…	…	…
Qatar	MoF	2017	1986	CG	C	CB and IMF staff	2017	BPM 5
Romania	MoF	2017	2001	CG,LG,SS	C	CB	2017	BPM 6
Russia	MoF	2017	2001	CG,SG,SS	Mixed	CB	2017	BPM 6
Rwanda	MoF	2016	1986	CG,LG	Mixed	CB	2017	BPM 6
Samoa	MoF	2016/17	2001	CG	A	CB	2016/17	BPM 6
San Marino	MoF	2016	…	CG	…	…	…	…
São Tomé and Príncipe	MoF and Customs	2016	2001	CG	C	CB	2016	BPM 6
Saudi Arabia	MoF	2017	2014	CG	C	CB	2017	BPM 6
Senegal	MoF	2017	2001	CG	C	CB and IMF staff	2017	BPM 6
Serbia	MoF	2016	1986/2001	CG,SG,LG,SS	C	CB	2016	BPM 6
Seychelles	MoF	2017	1986	CG,SS	C	CB	2016	BPM 6
Sierra Leone	MoF	2017	1986	CG	C	CB	2017	BPM 5
Singapore	MoF	2016/17	2001	CG	C	NSO	2017	BPM 6
Slovak Republic	NSO	2017	2001	CG,LG,SS	A	CB	2017	BPM 6
Slovenia	MoF	2017	1986	CG,SG,LG,SS	C	NSO	2017	BPM 6
Solomon Islands	MoF	2016	1986	CG	C	CB	2016	BPM 6
Somalia	MoF	2016	2001	CG	C	CB	2016	BPM 5
South Africa	MoF	2017	2001	CG,SG,SS	C	CB	2017	BPM 6
South Sudan	MoF and MEP	2017	…	CG	C	MoF, NSO, and MEP	2017	BPM 6
Spain	MoF and NSO	2017	ESA 2010	CG,SG,LG,SS	A	CB	2017	BPM 6
Sri Lanka	MoF	2017	2001	CG	C	CB	2017	BPM 5
St. Kitts and Nevis	MoF	2017	1986	CG, SG	C	CB	2016	BPM 6
St. Lucia	MoF	2017/18	1986	CG	C	CB	2016	BPM 6
St. Vincent and the Grenadines	MoF	2016	1986	CG	C	CB	2016	BPM 6
Sudan	MoF	2017	2001	CG	Mixed	CB	2017	BPM 6
Suriname	MoF	2017	1986	CG	Mixed	CB	2017	BPM 5

Table G. Key Data Documentation *(continued)*

Country	Currency	National Accounts					Prices (CPI)	
		Historical Data Source[1]	Latest Actual Annual Data	Base Year[2]	System of National Accounts	Use of Chain-Weighted Methodology[3]	Historical Data Source[1]	Latest Actual Annual Data
Sweden	Swedish krona	NSO	2017	2017	ESA 2010	From 1993	NSO	2017
Switzerland	Swiss franc	NSO	2017	2010	ESA 2010	From 1980	NSO	2017
Syria	Syrian pound	NSO	2010	2000	SNA 1993		NSO	2011
Taiwan Province of China	New Taiwan dollar	NSO	2017	2011	SNA 2008		NSO	2017
Tajikistan	Tajik somoni	NSO	2017	1995	SNA 1993		NSO	2017
Tanzania	Tanzania shilling	NSO	2016	2007	SNA 2008		NSO	2017
Thailand	Thai baht	MEP	2017	2002	SNA 1993	From 1993	MEP	2017
Timor-Leste	US dollar	MoF	2016	2015[6]	SNA 2008		NSO	2017
Togo	CFA franc	NSO	2015	2007	SNA 1993		NSO	2017
Tonga	Tongan pa'anga	CB	2017	2010	SNA 1993		CB	2017
Trinidad and Tobago	Trinidad and Tobago dollar	NSO	2017	2012	SNA 1993		NSO	2017
Tunisia	Tunisian dinar	NSO	2017	2010	SNA 1993	From 2009	NSO	2016
Turkey	Turkish lira	NSO	2017	2009	ESA 2010	From 2009	NSO	2017
Turkmenistan	New Turkmen manat	NSO	2017	2008	SNA 1993	From 2000	NSO	2017
Tuvalu	Australian dollar	PFTAC advisors	2015	2005	SNA 1993		NSO	2017
Uganda	Ugandan shilling	NSO	2016	2010	SNA 1993		CB	2016/17
Ukraine	Ukrainian hryvnia	NSO	2017	2010	SNA 2008	From 2005	NSO	2017
United Arab Emirates	U.A.E. dirham	NSO	2017	2010	SNA 2008		NSO	2017
United Kingdom	Pound sterling	NSO	2017	2016	ESA 2010	From 1980	NSO	2017
United States	US dollar	NSO	2017	2012	SNA 2008	From 1980	NSO	2017
Uruguay	Uruguayan peso	CB	2017	2005	SNA 1993		NSO	2017
Uzbekistan	Uzbek sum	NSO	2017	1995	SNA 1993		NSO	2017
Vanuatu	Vanuatu vatu	NSO	2016	2006	SNA 1993		NSO	2017
Venezuela	Venezuelan bolívar fuerte	CB	2016	1997	SNA 2008		CB	2016
Vietnam	Vietnamese dong	NSO	2017	2010	SNA 1993		NSO	2017
Yemen	Yemeni rial	IMF staff	2008	1990	SNA 1993		NSO,CB, and IMF staff	2009
Zambia	Zambian kwacha	NSO	2017	2010	SNA 2008		NSO	2017
Zimbabwe	US dollar	NSO	2015	2009	...		NSO	2016

Table G. Key Data Documentation (continued)

Country	Government Finance					Balance of Payments		
	Historical Data Source[1]	Latest Actual Annual Data	Statistics Manual in Use at Source	Subsectors Coverage[4]	Accounting Practice[5]	Historical Data Source[1]	Latest Actual Annual Data	Statistics Manual in Use at Source
Sweden	MoF	2016	2001	CG,LG,SS	A	NSO	2017	BPM 6
Switzerland	MoF	2016	2001	CG,SG,LG,SS	A	CB	2017	BPM 6
Syria	MoF	2009	1986	CG	C	CB	2009	BPM 5
Taiwan Province of China	MoF	2017	2001	CG,LG,SS	C	CB	2017	BPM 6
Tajikistan	MoF	2017	1986	CG,LG,SS	C	CB	2016	BPM 6
Tanzania	MoF	2016	1986	CG,LG	C	CB	2016	BPM 5
Thailand	MoF	2016/17	2001	CG,BCG,LG,SS	A	CB	2017	BPM 6
Timor-Leste	MoF	2017	2001	CG	C	CB	2017	BPM 6
Togo	MoF	2017	2001	CG	C	CB	2016	BPM 6
Tonga	MoF	2017	2014	CG	C	CB and NSO	2017	BPM 6
Trinidad and Tobago	MoF	2016/17	1986	CG	C	CB and NSO	2017	BPM 6
Tunisia	MoF	2016	1986	CG	C	CB	2016	BPM 5
Turkey	MoF	2017	2001	CG,LG,SS	A	CB	2017	BPM 6
Turkmenistan	MoF	2017	1986	CG,LG	C	NSO and IMF staff	2015	BPM 6
Tuvalu	MoF	2017	...	CG	Mixed	IMF staff	2012	BPM 6
Uganda	MoF	2016	2001	CG	C	CB	2016	BPM 6
Ukraine	MoF	2016	2001	CG,SG,LG,SS	C	CB	2016	BPM 6
United Arab Emirates	MoF	2017	2001	CG,BCG,SG,SS	C	CB	2017	BPM 5
United Kingdom	NSO	2017	2001	CG,LG	A	NSO	2017	BPM 6
United States	MEP	2017	2014	CG,SG,LG	A	NSO	2016	BPM 6
Uruguay	MoF	2017	1986	CG,LG,SS,MPC, NFPC	C	CB	2017	BPM 6
Uzbekistan	MoF	2016	...	CG,SG,LG,SS	C	MEP	2017	BPM 6
Vanuatu	MoF	2017	2001	CG	C	CB	2017	BPM 6
Venezuela	MoF	2013	2001	BCG,NFPC	C	CB	2016	BPM 5
Vietnam	MoF	2015	2001	CG,SG,LG	C	CB	2017	BPM 5
Yemen	MoF	2013	2001	CG,LG	C	IMF staff	2009	BPM 5
Zambia	MoF	2017	1986	CG	C	CB	2017	BPM 6
Zimbabwe	MoF	2015	1986	CG	C	CB and MoF	2016	BPM 6

Note: BPM = Balance of Payments Manual; CPI = consumer price index; ESA = European System of National Accounts; SNA = System of National Accounts.

[1]CB = central bank; Customs = Customs Authority; GAD = General Administration Department; IEO = international economic organization; MEP = Ministry of Economy, Planning, Commerce, and/or Development; MoF = Ministry of Finance and/or Treasury; NSO = National Statistics Office; PFTAC = Pacific Financial Technical Assistance Centre.

[2]National accounts base year is the period with which other periods are compared and the period for which prices appear in the denominators of the price relationships used to calculate the index.

[3]Use of chain-weighted methodology allows countries to measure GDP growth more accurately by reducing or eliminating the downward biases in volume series built on index numbers that average volume components using weights from a year in the moderately distant past.

[4]BCG = budgetary central government; CG = central government; EUA = extrabudgetary units/accounts; LG = local government; MPC = monetary public corporation, including central bank; NFPC = nonfinancial public corporation; NMPC = nonmonetary financial public corporation; SG = state government; SS = social security fund; TG = territorial governments.

[5]Accounting standard: A = accrual accounting; C = cash accounting; CB = commitments basis accounting; Mixed = combination of accrual and cash accounting.

[6]Base year is not equal to 100 because the nominal GDP is not measured in the same way as real GDP or the data are seasonally adjusted.

Box A1. Economic Policy Assumptions Underlying the Projections for Selected Economies

Fiscal Policy Assumptions

The short-term fiscal policy assumptions used in the *World Economic Outlook* (WEO) are normally based on officially announced budgets, adjusted for differences between the national authorities and the IMF staff regarding macroeconomic assumptions and projected fiscal outturns. When no official budget has been announced, projections incorporate policy measures that are judged likely to be implemented. The medium-term fiscal projections are similarly based on a judgment about the most likely path of policies. For cases in which the IMF staff has insufficient information to assess the authorities' budget intentions and prospects for policy implementation, an unchanged structural primary balance is assumed unless indicated otherwise. Specific assumptions used in regard to some of the advanced economies follow. (See also Tables B5 to B9 in the online section of the Statistical Appendix for data on fiscal net lending/borrowing and structural balances.)[1]

Argentina: Fiscal projections are based on the available information regarding budget outturn and budget plans for the federal and provincial governments, fiscal measures announced by the authorities, and the IMF staff's macroeconomic projections.

Australia: Fiscal projections are based on Australian Bureau of Statistics data, the fiscal year 2018/19 budgets of the commonwealth and states and territories, 2017/18 mid-year fiscal and economic reviews by states and territories, and the IMF staff's estimates.

Austria: Fiscal projections are based on data from Statistics Austria, the authorities' projections, and the IMF staff's estimates and projections.

Belgium: Projections are based on the 2018–21 Stability Programme and other available information

on the authorities' fiscal plans, with adjustments for the IMF staff's assumptions.

Brazil: Fiscal projections for the end of 2018 account for budget performance through May 2018, and the deficit target approved in the budget law.

Canada: Projections use the baseline forecasts in the 2018 federal budget and the latest provincial budget updates as available. The IMF staff makes some adjustments to these forecasts, including for differences in macroeconomic projections. The IMF staff's forecast also incorporates the most recent data releases from Statistics Canada's Canadian System of National Economic Accounts, including federal, provincial, and territorial budgetary outturns through the first quarter of 2018.

Chile: Projections are based on the authorities' budget projections, adjusted to reflect the IMF staff's projections for GDP and copper prices.

China: Projections assume that the pace of fiscal consolidation is likely to be more gradual, reflecting reforms to strengthen social safety nets and the social security system announced as part of the Third Plenum reform agenda.

Denmark: Estimates for 2017 are aligned with the latest official budget numbers, adjusted where appropriate for the IMF staff's macroeconomic assumptions. For 2018, the projections incorporate key features of the medium-term fiscal plan as embodied in the authorities' Convergence Programme 2017 submitted to the European Union.

France: Projections for 2018 reflect the 2018 budget law. For 2018–23, they are based on the measures in the multiyear budget and the 2018 budget laws and additional measures expected in the 2019 budget law adjusted for differences in assumptions on macro and financial variables, and revenue projections. Historical fiscal data reflect the May 2018 revisions and update of the historical fiscal accounts, debt data, and national accounts.

Germany: The IMF staff's projections for 2018 and beyond are based on the 2018 Stability Programme, revised 2018 federal budget, and data updates from the national statistical agency, adjusted for the differences in the IMF staff's macroeconomic framework and assumptions concerning revenue elasticities. The estimate of gross debt includes portfolios of impaired assets and noncore business transferred to institutions that are winding up, as well as other financial sector and EU support operations.

Greece: Fiscal projections reflect adjustments in line with the primary balance definition under the enhanced surveillance procedure for Greece.

---

[1] The output gap is actual minus potential output, as a percentage of potential output. Structural balances are expressed as a percentage of potential output. The structural balance is the actual net lending/borrowing minus the effects of cyclical output from potential output, corrected for one-time and other factors, such as asset and commodity prices and output composition effects. Changes in the structural balance consequently include effects of temporary fiscal measures, the impact of fluctuations in interest rates and debt-service costs, and other noncyclical fluctuations in net lending/borrowing. The computations of structural balances are based on the IMF staff's estimates of potential GDP and revenue and expenditure elasticities. (See Annex I of the October 1993 WEO.) Net debt is calculated as gross debt minus financial assets corresponding to debt instruments. Estimates of the output gap and of the structural balance are subject to significant margins of uncertainty.

Box A1 *(continued)*

Hong Kong Special Administrative Region: Projections are based on the authorities' medium-term fiscal projections on expenditures.

Hungary: Fiscal projections include the IMF staff's projections of the macroeconomic framework and of the impact of recent legislative measures, as well as fiscal policy plans announced in the 2018 budget.

India: Historical data are based on budgetary execution data. Projections are based on available information on the authorities' fiscal plans, with adjustments for the IMF staff's assumptions. Subnational data are incorporated with a lag of up to one year; general government data are thus finalized well after central government data. IMF and Indian presentations differ, particularly regarding divestment and license auction proceeds, net versus gross recording of revenues in certain minor categories, and some public sector lending.

Indonesia: IMF projections are based on moderate tax policy and administration reforms, fuel subsidy pricing reforms introduced since January 2015, and a gradual increase in social and capital spending over the medium term in line with fiscal space.

Ireland: Fiscal projections are based on the country's Budget 2018.

Israel: Historical data are based on Government Finance Statistics data prepared by the Central Bureau of Statistics. The central government deficit is assumed to remain at the current ceiling of 2.9 percent of GDP throughout the projection period, rather than declining in line with medium-term fiscal targets, consistent with long experience of revisions to those targets.

Italy: The IMF staff's estimates and projections are informed by the fiscal plans included in the government's 2018 budget and April 2018 Economic and Financial Document. IMF staff assumes that the automatic value-added tax hikes for next year will be canceled.

Japan: The projections include fiscal measures already announced by the government, including the consumption tax hike in October 2019.

Korea: The medium-term forecast incorporates the medium-term path for public spending announced by the government.

Mexico: Fiscal projections for 2018 are broadly in line with the approved budget; projections for 2019 onward assume compliance with rules established in the Fiscal Responsibility Law.

Netherlands: Fiscal projections for 2017–23 are based on the authorities' Bureau for Economic Policy Analysis budget projections, after differences in macroeconomic assumptions are adjusted for. Historical data were revised following the June 2014 Central Bureau of Statistics release of revised macro data because of the adoption of ESA 2010 and the revisions of data sources.

New Zealand: Fiscal projections are based on the fiscal year 2018/19 budget and 2017 Half-Year Economic and Fiscal Update, and the IMF staff's estimates.

Portugal: The projections for the current year are based on the authorities' approved budget, adjusted to reflect the IMF staff's macroeconomic forecast. Projections thereafter are based on the assumption of unchanged policies.

Puerto Rico: Fiscal projections are based on the Puerto Rico Fiscal and Economic Growth Plans (FEGPs), which were prepared in April and updated in August of 2018, and is pending certification by the Oversight Board. In line with assumptions of this plan, IMF projections assume federal aid for rebuilding after Hurricane Maria devastated the island in September 2017. The projections also assume revenue losses from the following: elimination of federal funding for the Affordable Care Act starting in 2018 for Puerto Rico; elimination of federal tax incentives starting in 2018 that had neutralized the effects of Puerto Rico's Act 154 on foreign firms; and the effects of the Tax Cuts and Job Act, which reduce tax advantages of US firms producing in Puerto Rico. Given sizable policy uncertainty, some FEGP and IMF assumptions may differ, in particular those relating to the effects of the corporate tax reform, tax compliance, and tax adjustments (fees and rates); reduction of subsidies and expenses, freezing of payroll operational costs, and improvement of mobility; and increasing health care efficiency. On the expenditure side, measures include extension of Act 66, which freezes much government spending, through 2020; reduction of operating costs; decreases in government subsidies; and spending cuts in education. Although IMF policy assumptions are similar to those in the FEGP scenario with full measures, the IMF's projections of fiscal revenues, expenditures, and balance are different from FEGP's. This stems from two main differences in methodologies: first, while IMF projections are on an accrual basis, FEGP's are on a cash basis. Second, the IMF and FEGP make very different macroeconomic assumptions. Third, the IMF's projections are on a calendar year basis while FEGP's are on a fiscal year basis.

Russia: Projections for 2018–21 are the IMF staff's estimates, based on the authorities' budget. Projections

Box A1 *(continued)*

for 2022–23 are based on the new oil price rule, with adjustments by the IMF staff.

Saudi Arabia: Staff baseline projections of total government revenues reflect the impact of announced policies in the 2018 Budget. Oil revenues are based on WEO baseline oil prices and the assumption that Saudi Arabia continues to meet its commitments under the OPEC+ agreement. Expenditure projections take the 2018 budget as a starting point and reflect staff estimates of the effects of the latest changes in policies and economic developments. Expenditures in 2018 include allowances and other measures announced in the Royal Decree for one year in January 2018.

Singapore: For fiscal year 2018/19, projections are based on budget numbers. For the rest of the projection period, the IMF staff assumes unchanged policies.

South Africa: Fiscal projections are based on the 2018 Budget. Nontax revenue excludes transactions in financial assets and liabilities, as they involve primarily revenues associated with realized exchange rate valuation gains from the holding of foreign currency deposits, sale of assets, and conceptually similar items.

Spain: For 2018 and beyond, fiscal projections are based on the information specified in the government's 2018 Stability Programme and on the IMF staff's macroeconomic projections.

Sweden: Fiscal projections account for the authorities' projections based on the 2018 Spring Budget. The impact of cyclical developments on the fiscal accounts is calculated using the Organisation for Economic Co-operation and Development's 2005 elasticity to take into account output and employment gaps.

Switzerland: The projections assume that fiscal policy is adjusted as necessary to keep fiscal balances in line with the requirements of Switzerland's fiscal rules.

Turkey: The fiscal projections for 2018 are based on the authorities' Medium Term Programme 2018–20, with adjustments for additionally announced fiscal measures and the IMF staff's higher inflation forecast. For the medium term, the fiscal projections assume a more gradual fiscal consolidation than envisaged in the Medium Term Programme.

United Kingdom: Fiscal projections are based on the country's November 2017 Budget and the March 2018 update, with expenditure projections based on the budgeted nominal values and with revenue projections adjusted for differences between the IMF staff's forecasts of macroeconomic variables (such as GDP growth and inflation) and the forecasts of these variables assumed in

the authorities' fiscal projections. The IMF staff's data exclude public sector banks and the effect of transferring assets from the Royal Mail Pension Plan to the public sector in April 2012. Real government consumption and investment are part of the real GDP path, which, according to the IMF staff, may or may not be the same as projected by the UK Office for Budget Responsibility.

United States: Fiscal projections are based on the August update to the April 2018 Congressional Budget Office baseline, adjusted for the IMF staff's policy and macroeconomic assumptions. Projections incorporate the effects of tax reform (Tax Cuts and Jobs Act, signed into law end of 2017) as well as the Bipartisan Budget Act of 2018 passed in February 2018. Finally, fiscal projections are adjusted to reflect the IMF staff's forecasts for key macroeconomic and financial variables and different accounting treatment of financial sector support and defined-benefit pension plans, and are converted to a general government basis. Data are compiled using SNA 2008, and when translated into government finance statistics, this is in accordance with the *Government Finance Statistics Manual 2014*. Because of data limitations, most series begin in 2001.

Monetary Policy Assumptions

Monetary policy assumptions are based on the established policy framework in each country. In most cases, this implies a nonaccommodative stance over the business cycle: official interest rates will increase when economic indicators suggest that inflation will rise above its acceptable rate or range; they will decrease when indicators suggest inflation will not exceed the acceptable rate or range, that output growth is below its potential rate, and that the margin of slack in the economy is significant. On this basis, the London interbank offered rate on six-month US dollar deposits is assumed to average 2.5 percent in 2018 and 3.4 percent in 2019 (see Table 1.1). The rate on three-month euro deposits is assumed to average –0.3 percent in 2018 and –0.2 percent in 2019. The interest rate on six-month Japanese yen deposits is assumed to average 0.0 percent in 2018 and 0.1 percent in 2019.

Argentina: Monetary policy assumptions are consistent with gradual disinflation of the economy to a single digit.

Australia: Monetary policy assumptions are in line with market expectations.

Box A1 *(continued)*

Brazil: Monetary policy assumptions are consistent with gradual convergence of inflation toward the middle of the target range.

Canada: Monetary policy assumptions are in line with market expectations.

China: Monetary policy is expected to tighten with a gradual rise in the interest rate.

Denmark: The monetary policy is to maintain the peg to the euro.

Euro area: Monetary policy assumptions for euro area member countries are in line with market expectations.

Hong Kong Special Administrative Region: The IMF staff assumes that the currency board system remains intact.

India: The policy (interest) rate assumption is consistent with an inflation rate within the Reserve Bank of India's targeted band. Consistent with IMF staff's estimates of natural rate of inflation and an inflation-forecast targeting policy rule, an additional increase of policy rate (25–50 basis points) is needed.

Indonesia: Monetary policy assumptions are in line with the maintenance of inflation within the central bank's targeted band.

Japan: Monetary policy assumptions are in line with market expectations.

Korea: Monetary policy assumptions are in line with market expectations.

Mexico: Monetary policy assumptions are consistent with attaining the inflation target.

Russia: Monetary projections assume that the Central Bank of Russia will complete the transition to a neutral stance at a slower pace given upside risks to the inflation outlook.

Saudi Arabia: Monetary policy projections are based on the continuation of the exchange rate peg to the US dollar.

Singapore: Broad money is projected to grow in line with the projected growth in nominal GDP.

South Africa: Monetary policy will remain neutral.

Sweden: Monetary projections are in line with Riksbank projections.

Switzerland: The projections assume no change in the policy rate in 2018–19.

Turkey: The outlook for monetary and financial conditions assumes no changes to the current policy stance.

United Kingdom: The short-term interest rate path is based on market interest rate expectations.

United States: The IMF staff expects continued gradual normalization of the federal funds target rate over the medium term, in line with the broader macroeconomic outlook.

List of Tables

Output

Inflation

Financial Policies

Foreign Trade

Current Account Transactions

Balance of Payments and External Financing

Flow of Funds

Medium-Term Baseline Scenario

Table A1. Summary of World Output[1]
(Annual percent change)

	Average 2000–09	2010	2011	2012	2013	2014	2015	2016	2017	Projections 2018	2019	2023
World	**3.9**	**5.4**	**4.3**	**3.5**	**3.5**	**3.6**	**3.5**	**3.3**	**3.7**	**3.7**	**3.7**	**3.6**
Advanced Economies	**1.8**	**3.1**	**1.7**	**1.2**	**1.4**	**2.1**	**2.3**	**1.7**	**2.3**	**2.4**	**2.1**	**1.5**
United States	1.9	2.6	1.6	2.2	1.8	2.5	2.9	1.6	2.2	2.9	2.5	1.4
Euro Area	1.4	2.1	1.6	−0.9	−0.2	1.4	2.1	1.9	2.4	2.0	1.9	1.4
Japan	0.5	4.2	−0.1	1.5	2.0	0.4	1.4	1.0	1.7	1.1	0.9	0.5
Other Advanced Economies[2]	2.8	4.6	3.0	1.9	2.4	2.9	2.1	2.1	2.6	2.4	2.2	2.1
Emerging Market and Developing Economies	**6.1**	**7.4**	**6.4**	**5.3**	**5.1**	**4.7**	**4.3**	**4.4**	**4.7**	**4.7**	**4.7**	**4.8**
Regional Groups												
Commonwealth of Independent States[3]	5.9	4.6	5.3	3.7	2.5	1.1	−1.9	0.4	2.1	2.3	2.4	2.1
Emerging and Developing Asia	8.1	9.6	7.9	7.0	6.9	6.8	6.8	6.5	6.5	6.5	6.3	6.1
Emerging and Developing Europe	4.0	4.3	6.6	2.5	4.9	3.9	4.7	3.3	6.0	3.8	2.0	2.7
Latin America and the Caribbean	3.0	6.1	4.6	2.9	2.9	1.3	0.3	−0.6	1.3	1.2	2.2	2.9
Middle East, North Africa, Afghanistan, and Pakistan	5.2	4.6	4.4	4.8	2.6	2.9	2.5	5.1	2.2	2.4	2.7	3.0
Middle East and North Africa	5.2	4.8	4.5	4.9	2.4	2.7	2.4	5.2	1.8	2.0	2.5	3.0
Sub-Saharan Africa	5.6	7.1	5.1	4.6	5.2	5.1	3.3	1.4	2.7	3.1	3.8	4.1
Memorandum												
European Union	1.7	2.0	1.8	−0.3	0.3	1.9	2.4	2.0	2.7	2.2	2.0	1.6
Low-Income Developing Countries	6.3	7.4	5.1	4.6	6.1	6.1	4.7	3.6	4.7	4.7	5.2	5.4
Analytical Groups												
By Source of Export Earnings												
Fuel	5.7	5.1	5.2	5.0	2.6	2.2	0.3	1.9	0.9	1.2	1.9	2.0
Nonfuel	6.2	8.0	6.7	5.4	5.7	5.3	5.2	4.9	5.6	5.4	5.2	5.3
Of Which, Primary Products	3.8	6.8	4.9	2.3	4.2	2.1	2.8	1.7	2.8	1.6	2.1	3.6
By External Financing Source												
Net Debtor Economies	4.9	6.9	5.4	4.2	4.8	4.6	4.2	3.8	4.7	4.8	4.8	5.2
Net Debtor Economies by Debt-Servicing Experience												
Economies with Arrears and/or Rescheduling during 2013–17	4.7	4.2	2.7	1.5	3.2	1.9	1.0	2.8	3.2	3.9	4.4	5.0
Memorandum												
Median Growth Rate												
Advanced Economies	2.4	2.3	1.9	1.0	1.5	2.5	2.0	2.2	2.9	2.8	2.5	1.9
Emerging Market and Developing Economies	4.5	4.6	4.7	4.2	4.3	3.8	3.3	3.2	3.4	3.5	3.7	3.7
Low-Income Developing Countries	5.0	6.4	6.1	5.1	5.3	4.8	3.9	4.2	4.5	4.0	4.8	5.0
Output per Capita[4]												
Advanced Economies	1.1	2.5	1.1	0.7	0.9	1.6	1.7	1.2	1.9	1.9	1.7	1.1
Emerging Market and Developing Economies	4.4	5.9	4.9	3.6	3.6	3.2	2.8	2.9	3.2	3.3	3.3	3.6
Low-Income Developing Countries	3.7	5.0	3.5	1.6	3.7	3.8	2.3	1.2	2.4	2.4	3.0	3.2
World Growth Rate Based on Market Exchange Rates	**2.6**	**4.1**	**3.1**	**2.5**	**2.6**	**2.8**	**2.8**	**2.5**	**3.2**	**3.2**	**3.1**	**2.8**
Value of World Output (billions of US dollars)												
At Market Exchange Rates	46,626	66,011	73,230	74,619	76,750	78,832	74,602	75,653	80,051	84,835	88,081	108,712
At Purchasing Power Parities	66,722	89,402	95,018	99,891	105,088	110,805	115,729	120,693	127,489	135,236	143,089	177,424

[1]Real GDP.
[2]Excludes the United States, euro area countries, and Japan.
[3]Georgia, Turkmenistan, and Ukraine, which are not members of the Commonwealth of Independent States, are included in this group for reasons of geography and similarity in economic structure.
[4]Output per capita is in international currency at purchasing power parity.

Table A2. Advanced Economies: Real GDP and Total Domestic Demand[1]

(Annual percent change)

	Average 2000–09	2010	2011	2012	2013	2014	2015	2016	2017	Projections 2018	Projections 2019	Projections 2023	Fourth Quarter[2] 2017:Q4	Fourth Quarter[2] Projections 2018:Q4	Fourth Quarter[2] Projections 2019:Q4
Real GDP															
Advanced Economies	**1.8**	**3.1**	**1.7**	**1.2**	**1.4**	**2.1**	**2.3**	**1.7**	**2.3**	**2.4**	**2.1**	**1.5**	**2.5**	**2.3**	**1.9**
United States	1.9	2.6	1.6	2.2	1.8	2.5	2.9	1.6	2.2	2.9	2.5	1.4	2.5	3.1	2.3
Euro Area	1.4	2.1	1.6	−0.9	−0.2	1.4	2.1	1.9	2.4	2.0	1.9	1.4	2.7	1.7	1.9
Germany	0.8	3.9	3.7	0.7	0.6	2.2	1.5	2.2	2.5	1.9	1.9	1.2	2.8	1.9	1.6
France	1.4	1.9	2.2	0.3	0.6	1.0	1.0	1.1	2.3	1.6	1.6	1.6	2.8	1.3	1.7
Italy	0.5	1.7	0.6	−2.8	−1.7	0.1	1.0	0.9	1.5	1.2	1.0	0.7	1.6	0.8	1.3
Spain	2.7	0.0	−1.0	−2.9	−1.7	1.4	3.6	3.2	3.0	2.7	2.2	1.7	3.0	2.5	2.1
Netherlands	1.6	1.3	1.5	−1.0	−0.1	1.4	2.0	2.2	2.9	2.8	2.6	1.8	3.1	2.4	2.6
Belgium	1.7	2.7	1.8	0.2	0.2	1.3	1.4	1.4	1.7	1.5	1.5	1.5	1.9	1.6	1.3
Austria	1.7	1.8	2.9	0.7	0.0	0.8	1.1	1.5	3.0	2.8	2.2	1.4	3.5	1.8	2.6
Greece	2.7	−5.5	−9.1	−7.3	−3.2	0.7	−0.3	−0.2	1.4	2.0	2.4	1.2	2.0	2.2	2.5
Portugal	0.9	1.9	−1.8	−4.0	−1.1	0.9	1.8	1.6	2.7	2.3	1.8	1.4	2.4	2.4	1.2
Ireland	3.6	1.9	3.7	0.2	1.3	8.7	25.0	4.9	7.2	4.7	4.0	2.8	5.4	0.3	6.3
Finland	2.0	3.0	2.6	−1.4	−0.8	−0.6	0.1	2.5	2.8	2.6	1.8	1.2	2.6	2.7	1.4
Slovak Republic	4.5	5.0	2.8	1.7	1.5	2.8	3.9	3.3	3.4	3.9	4.1	3.4	3.6	4.2	4.2
Lithuania	4.6	1.6	6.0	3.8	3.5	3.5	2.0	2.3	3.9	3.5	2.9	2.0	3.8	3.1	3.0
Slovenia	2.9	1.2	0.6	−2.7	−1.1	3.0	2.3	3.1	5.0	4.5	3.4	2.1	6.0	3.6	3.3
Luxembourg	3.0	4.9	2.5	−0.4	3.7	5.8	2.9	3.1	2.3	4.0	3.5	3.0	1.8	3.5	4.5
Latvia	4.7	−3.9	6.4	4.0	2.4	1.9	3.0	2.2	4.5	3.7	3.3	3.0	4.8	2.5	4.3
Estonia	4.1	2.3	7.6	4.3	1.9	2.9	1.7	2.1	4.9	3.7	3.2	2.9	5.1	3.5	2.3
Cyprus	3.5	1.3	0.3	−3.1	−5.9	−1.4	2.0	3.4	3.9	4.0	4.2	2.4	4.0	4.2	3.9
Malta	1.6	3.5	1.3	2.7	4.6	8.2	9.5	5.2	6.7	5.7	4.6	3.2	5.6	6.7	3.6
Japan	0.5	4.2	−0.1	1.5	2.0	0.4	1.4	1.0	1.7	1.1	0.9	0.5	2.0	1.0	−0.3
United Kingdom	1.8	1.7	1.6	1.4	2.0	2.9	2.3	1.8	1.7	1.4	1.5	1.6	1.3	1.5	1.4
Korea	4.7	6.5	3.7	2.3	2.9	3.3	2.8	2.9	3.1	2.8	2.6	2.6	2.8	3.2	2.3
Canada	2.1	3.1	3.1	1.7	2.5	2.9	1.0	1.4	3.0	2.1	2.0	1.6	3.0	2.1	1.9
Australia	3.1	2.4	2.7	3.9	2.2	2.6	2.5	2.6	2.2	3.2	2.8	2.6	2.4	3.2	2.8
Taiwan Province of China	3.8	10.6	3.8	2.1	2.2	4.0	0.8	1.4	2.9	2.7	2.4	1.9	3.4	1.9	2.1
Switzerland	1.9	2.9	1.8	1.0	1.9	2.5	1.3	1.6	1.7	3.0	1.8	1.7	2.6	2.6	1.7
Sweden	2.0	6.0	2.7	−0.3	1.2	2.6	4.5	2.7	2.1	2.4	2.2	1.9	2.7	1.9	2.6
Singapore	5.2	15.2	6.4	4.1	5.1	3.9	2.2	2.4	3.6	2.9	2.5	2.6	3.6	1.9	2.6
Hong Kong SAR	4.2	6.8	4.8	1.7	3.1	2.8	2.4	2.2	3.8	3.8	2.9	3.1	3.3	3.4	3.3
Norway	1.8	0.7	1.0	2.7	1.0	2.0	2.0	1.1	1.9	2.1	2.1	1.8	1.6	2.7	1.6
Czech Republic	3.4	2.3	1.8	−0.8	−0.5	2.7	5.3	2.5	4.3	3.1	3.0	2.5	5.0	3.2	2.5
Israel	3.5	5.5	5.2	2.2	4.2	3.5	2.6	4.0	3.3	3.6	3.5	3.0	3.1	3.4	3.5
Denmark	1.0	1.9	1.3	0.2	0.9	1.6	1.6	2.0	2.3	2.0	1.9	1.7	1.3	3.2	2.2
New Zealand	2.9	2.0	1.9	2.5	2.2	3.2	4.2	4.1	3.0	3.1	3.0	2.5	3.2	3.1	3.0
Puerto Rico	1.0	−0.4	−0.4	0.0	−0.3	−1.2	−1.0	−1.3	−2.4	−2.3	−1.1	−0.8	. . .	. . .	. . .
Macao SAR	. . .	25.3	21.7	9.2	11.2	−1.2	−21.6	−0.9	9.1	6.3	6.3	4.2	. . .	. . .	. . .
Iceland	3.5	−3.4	1.9	1.3	4.1	2.1	4.5	7.4	4.0	3.7	2.9	2.5	1.9	2.9	4.7
San Marino	. . .	−4.8	−9.3	−7.6	−3.2	−0.9	0.6	2.2	1.9	1.4	1.0	0.8	. . .	. . .	. . .
Memorandum															
Major Advanced Economies	1.4	2.8	1.6	1.4	1.5	1.9	2.1	1.5	2.1	2.2	2.0	1.2	2.3	2.2	1.7
Real Total Domestic Demand															
Advanced Economies	**1.7**	**2.9**	**1.4**	**0.8**	**1.1**	**2.1**	**2.6**	**1.9**	**2.3**	**2.4**	**2.4**	**1.5**	**2.3**	**2.6**	**2.1**
United States	1.9	3.0	1.5	2.2	1.6	2.6	3.6	1.8	2.5	3.1	3.2	1.2	2.6	3.5	2.8
Euro Area	1.3	1.5	0.7	−2.4	−0.6	1.3	2.4	2.3	1.7	2.0	1.9	1.5	1.3	2.4	1.6
Germany	0.3	2.9	3.0	−0.8	1.0	1.6	1.4	3.0	2.2	2.0	2.1	1.4	1.9	2.3	1.8
France	1.7	2.1	2.1	−0.4	0.7	1.5	1.5	1.6	2.2	1.3	1.6	1.6	2.1	1.8	1.3
Italy	0.7	2.0	−0.6	−5.6	−2.6	0.2	1.5	1.1	1.4	1.4	1.2	0.7	1.2	1.1	1.7
Spain	2.9	−0.5	−3.1	−5.1	−3.2	2.0	4.0	2.6	2.9	2.8	2.0	1.5	3.3	2.7	1.7
Japan	0.2	2.4	0.7	2.3	2.4	0.4	1.0	0.4	1.2	0.9	1.1	0.5	1.8	0.9	−0.4
United Kingdom	2.0	2.0	−0.2	1.8	2.1	3.2	2.3	2.4	1.3	1.3	1.3	1.6	0.6	1.6	1.4
Canada	2.8	5.1	3.4	2.0	2.1	1.7	0.1	0.9	3.8	2.4	1.3	1.5	4.9	1.4	1.2
Other Advanced Economies[3]	2.9	6.1	3.1	2.0	1.5	2.7	2.4	2.2	3.3	2.9	2.6	2.5	3.7	2.6	3.2
Memorandum															
Major Advanced Economies	1.4	2.8	1.4	1.2	1.4	2.0	2.4	1.7	2.1	2.3	2.3	1.2	2.3	2.5	1.9

[1]In this and other tables, when countries are not listed alphabetically, they are ordered on the basis of economic size.
[2]From the fourth quarter of the preceding year.
[3]Excludes the G7 (Canada, France, Germany, Italy, Japan, United Kingdom, United States) and euro area countries.

Table A3. Advanced Economies: Components of Real GDP

(Annual percent change)

	Averages		2010	2011	2012	2013	2014	2015	2016	2017	Projections	
	2000–09	2010–19									2018	2019
Private Consumer Expenditure												
Advanced Economies	**2.1**	**1.8**	**1.8**	**1.1**	**0.9**	**1.2**	**1.8**	**2.5**	**2.2**	**2.2**	**2.1**	**2.0**
United States	2.4	2.4	1.7	1.9	1.5	1.5	2.9	3.7	2.7	2.5	2.8	2.4
Euro Area	1.4	0.8	0.8	0.0	−1.2	−0.6	0.9	1.8	2.0	1.6	1.5	1.6
Germany	0.7	1.3	0.3	1.4	1.4	0.8	1.1	1.6	1.9	2.0	1.6	1.6
France	2.0	1.0	1.9	0.6	−0.4	0.5	0.8	1.5	2.1	1.0	0.9	1.4
Italy	0.6	0.2	1.2	0.0	−4.0	−2.4	0.2	1.9	1.4	1.4	1.0	1.2
Spain	2.5	0.5	0.3	−2.4	−3.5	−3.1	1.5	3.0	2.8	2.5	2.2	1.8
Japan	0.8	0.8	2.4	−0.4	2.0	2.4	−0.9	0.0	0.1	1.0	0.6	0.8
United Kingdom	2.2	1.5	0.7	−0.7	1.5	1.8	2.0	2.6	3.1	1.8	1.1	1.2
Canada	3.2	2.3	3.6	2.3	1.9	2.6	2.6	2.2	2.3	3.4	1.7	0.7
Other Advanced Economies[1]	3.1	2.7	3.8	3.0	2.2	2.3	2.4	2.7	2.5	2.7	2.8	2.6
Memorandum												
Major Advanced Economies	1.8	1.7	1.7	1.1	1.1	1.3	1.8	2.5	2.2	2.1	2.0	1.8
Public Consumption												
Advanced Economies	**2.3**	**0.8**	**0.9**	**−0.6**	**−0.1**	**−0.1**	**0.5**	**1.7**	**1.9**	**0.8**	**1.6**	**2.0**
United States	2.2	0.0	0.1	−3.0	−1.5	−1.9	−0.8	1.7	1.5	−0.1	1.1	2.7
Euro Area	2.0	0.8	0.8	−0.1	−0.3	0.3	0.7	1.3	1.9	1.1	1.2	1.2
Germany	1.2	1.8	1.3	0.9	1.1	1.3	1.6	2.9	4.0	1.6	1.4	2.0
France	1.7	1.2	1.3	1.1	1.6	1.5	1.3	1.0	1.4	1.3	1.0	0.3
Italy	1.3	−0.2	0.6	−1.8	−1.4	−0.3	−0.7	−0.6	0.6	0.1	0.4	0.8
Spain	5.1	0.1	1.5	−0.3	−4.7	−2.1	−0.3	2.1	1.0	1.9	1.5	1.0
Japan	1.7	1.2	1.9	1.9	1.7	1.5	0.5	1.5	1.3	0.4	0.5	1.1
United Kingdom	2.9	0.8	0.3	0.1	1.2	−0.2	2.2	1.4	0.8	−0.1	1.3	0.9
Canada	2.6	1.4	2.3	1.3	0.7	−0.7	0.5	1.6	2.2	2.3	2.4	1.5
Other Advanced Economies[1]	2.9	2.6	2.7	1.6	1.9	2.3	2.4	2.6	3.4	2.2	3.9	2.6
Memorandum												
Major Advanced Economies	2.0	0.6	0.7	−1.1	−0.2	−0.5	0.1	1.6	1.6	0.4	1.1	1.9
Gross Fixed Capital Formation												
Advanced Economies	**0.8**	**3.0**	**2.0**	**3.2**	**2.6**	**1.7**	**3.4**	**3.1**	**2.1**	**3.6**	**4.1**	**4.1**
United States	0.4	4.3	2.2	4.6	6.9	3.6	4.9	3.3	1.7	4.0	5.6	6.0
Euro Area	0.9	1.5	−0.4	1.5	−3.4	−2.3	1.6	4.8	3.9	2.5	4.1	3.5
Germany	−0.4	3.0	5.0	7.4	−0.1	−1.2	3.9	1.1	3.3	3.6	3.3	3.5
France	1.6	1.8	2.1	2.0	0.2	−0.8	0.0	1.0	2.8	4.5	2.9	3.2
Italy	0.8	−0.8	−0.5	−1.9	−9.3	−6.6	−2.3	2.1	3.2	3.8	3.6	1.1
Spain	2.4	0.3	−4.9	−6.9	−8.6	−3.4	4.7	6.7	2.9	4.8	5.6	3.6
Japan	−2.0	2.0	−1.6	1.7	3.5	4.9	3.1	1.7	1.1	2.5	1.9	1.2
United Kingdom	0.2	3.2	4.1	2.6	2.1	3.4	7.2	3.4	2.3	3.4	0.9	2.5
Canada	3.1	2.5	11.4	4.6	4.9	1.3	2.4	−5.2	−2.9	2.8	3.7	2.6
Other Advanced Economies[1]	2.8	3.2	5.9	4.1	3.0	2.5	2.5	1.9	2.3	3.8	2.8	3.0
Memorandum												
Major Advanced Economies	0.2	3.2	2.3	3.7	3.7	2.2	3.8	2.2	1.8	3.7	4.1	4.2

Table A3. Advanced Economies: Components of Real GDP *(continued)*
(Annual percent change)

	Averages		2010	2011	2012	2013	2014	2015	2016	2017	Projections	
	2000–09	2010–19									2018	2019
Final Domestic Demand												
Advanced Economies	**1.8**	**1.9**	**1.7**	**1.3**	**1.1**	**1.1**	**2.0**	**2.5**	**2.2**	**2.2**	**2.5**	**2.4**
United States	2.0	2.4	1.6	1.6	2.0	1.3	2.8	3.3	2.3	2.5	3.2	3.2
Euro Area	1.4	1.0	0.5	0.3	−1.5	−0.8	1.0	2.3	2.4	1.7	2.0	2.0
Germany	0.5	1.8	1.4	2.5	1.0	0.5	1.8	1.8	2.6	2.3	1.9	2.1
France	1.8	1.2	1.8	1.0	0.2	0.5	0.8	1.3	2.1	1.8	1.4	1.5
Italy	0.8	−0.1	0.7	−0.8	−4.5	−2.8	−0.4	1.4	1.5	1.5	1.4	1.1
Spain	2.9	0.4	−0.7	−3.0	−4.8	−3.0	1.8	3.5	2.6	2.8	2.8	2.0
Japan	0.3	1.2	1.4	0.5	2.3	2.8	0.2	0.7	0.6	1.2	1.0	1.1
United Kingdom	2.0	1.6	1.1	0.0	1.6	1.7	2.9	2.5	2.5	1.7	1.1	1.4
Canada	3.0	2.2	5.0	2.6	2.4	1.6	2.1	0.3	1.1	3.0	2.3	1.3
Other Advanced Economies[1]	3.0	2.8	4.1	3.0	2.3	2.4	2.5	2.5	2.6	2.9	2.9	2.7
Memorandum												
Major Advanced Economies	1.5	1.8	1.6	1.3	1.4	1.2	1.9	2.3	2.0	2.1	2.3	2.3
Stock Building[2]												
Advanced Economies	**−0.1**	**0.1**	**1.2**	**0.2**	**−0.2**	**0.0**	**0.1**	**0.1**	**−0.3**	**0.0**	**0.0**	**0.0**
United States	−0.2	0.1	1.4	−0.1	0.2	0.2	−0.1	0.3	−0.5	0.0	−0.1	0.0
Euro Area	−0.1	0.1	0.9	0.5	−0.9	0.2	0.3	0.0	0.0	0.0	0.0	0.0
Germany	−0.2	0.1	1.4	0.5	−1.7	0.5	−0.2	−0.3	0.3	−0.1	0.1	0.0
France	−0.1	0.2	0.3	1.1	−0.6	0.2	0.8	0.2	−0.5	0.4	0.0	0.0
Italy	−0.1	0.1	1.3	0.2	−1.1	0.2	0.6	0.1	−0.4	−0.1	0.0	0.0
Spain	0.0	0.0	0.2	−0.1	−0.2	−0.3	0.2	0.4	0.0	0.1	0.1	0.0
Japan	0.0	0.1	1.0	0.2	0.0	−0.4	0.1	0.3	−0.2	−0.1	0.1	0.0
United Kingdom	−0.1	0.1	1.0	−0.2	0.2	0.2	0.7	−0.2	−0.1	−0.5	0.1	−0.1
Canada	0.0	0.1	0.1	0.7	−0.3	0.5	−0.4	−0.2	−0.2	0.8	0.1	0.0
Other Advanced Economies[1]	−0.1	0.1	1.9	0.2	−0.3	−0.8	0.2	0.0	−0.3	0.2	0.0	−0.1
Memorandum												
Major Advanced Economies	−0.1	0.1	1.2	0.2	−0.2	0.2	0.1	0.1	−0.3	0.0	0.0	0.0
Foreign Balance[2]												
Advanced Economies	**0.1**	**0.0**	**0.1**	**0.3**	**0.4**	**0.3**	**0.0**	**−0.3**	**−0.2**	**0.1**	**−0.1**	**−0.2**
United States	−0.1	−0.3	−0.5	0.0	0.0	0.2	−0.3	−0.8	−0.3	−0.3	−0.3	−0.8
Euro Area	0.1	0.4	0.6	0.9	1.5	0.3	0.1	−0.2	−0.3	0.8	0.1	0.0
Germany	0.5	0.4	1.1	0.9	1.4	−0.3	0.7	0.2	−0.6	0.3	0.0	−0.1
France	−0.3	−0.1	−0.2	0.1	0.7	−0.1	−0.5	−0.4	−0.5	0.1	0.2	0.0
Italy	−0.2	0.3	−0.3	1.2	2.8	0.8	−0.1	−0.5	−0.3	0.1	−0.2	−0.1
Spain	−0.2	0.6	0.5	2.1	2.2	1.5	−0.5	−0.3	0.8	0.1	−0.1	0.2
Japan	0.1	0.1	1.6	−0.9	−0.8	−0.4	0.0	0.3	0.6	0.5	0.1	0.0
United Kingdom	−0.1	−0.1	−0.7	1.5	−0.4	−0.5	−0.4	−0.3	−0.7	0.6	0.1	0.1
Canada	−0.8	−0.1	−2.1	−0.3	−0.4	0.3	1.1	0.9	0.7	−0.9	−0.4	0.7
Other Advanced Economies[1]	0.6	0.2	0.0	0.5	0.5	0.9	0.4	−0.2	0.0	−0.5	0.1	0.1
Memorandum												
Major Advanced Economies	0.0	−0.1	−0.1	0.1	0.2	0.0	−0.1	−0.4	−0.2	0.0	−0.1	−0.4

[1]Excludes the G7 (Canada, France, Germany, Italy, Japan, United Kingdom, United States) and euro area countries.
[2]Changes expressed as percent of GDP in the preceding period.

Table A4. Emerging Market and Developing Economies: Real GDP

(Annual percent change)

	Average 2000–09	2010	2011	2012	2013	2014	2015	2016	2017	Projections 2018	2019	2023
Commonwealth of Independent States[1,2]	**5.9**	**4.6**	**5.3**	**3.7**	**2.5**	**1.1**	**−1.9**	**0.4**	**2.1**	**2.3**	**2.4**	**2.1**
Russia	5.4	4.5	5.1	3.7	1.8	0.7	−2.5	−0.2	1.5	1.7	1.8	1.2
Excluding Russia	7.5	5.0	6.0	3.6	4.2	1.9	−0.6	2.0	3.6	3.9	3.6	4.1
Armenia	8.5	2.2	4.7	7.1	3.3	3.6	3.3	0.3	7.5	6.0	4.8	4.5
Azerbaijan	14.6	4.6	−1.6	2.1	5.9	2.7	0.6	−3.1	0.1	1.3	3.6	2.0
Belarus	7.2	7.8	5.5	1.7	1.0	1.7	−3.8	−2.5	2.4	4.0	3.1	2.0
Georgia	5.9	6.2	7.2	6.4	3.4	4.6	2.9	2.8	5.0	5.5	4.8	5.2
Kazakhstan	8.5	7.3	7.5	5.0	6.0	4.3	1.2	1.1	4.0	3.7	3.1	4.6
Kyrgyz Republic	4.6	−0.5	6.0	−0.1	10.9	4.0	3.9	4.3	4.6	2.8	4.5	2.4
Moldova	4.6	7.1	6.8	−0.7	9.4	4.8	−0.4	4.3	4.5	3.8	3.8	3.8
Tajikistan	8.2	6.5	7.4	7.5	7.4	6.7	6.0	6.9	7.1	5.0	5.0	4.0
Turkmenistan	14.2	9.2	14.7	11.1	10.2	10.3	6.5	6.2	6.5	6.2	5.6	5.7
Ukraine[3]	4.5	0.3	5.5	0.2	0.0	−6.6	−9.8	2.4	2.5	3.5	2.7	3.4
Uzbekistan	6.4	8.5	8.3	8.2	8.0	8.0	7.9	7.8	5.3	5.0	5.0	6.0
Emerging and Developing Asia	**8.1**	**9.6**	**7.9**	**7.0**	**6.9**	**6.8**	**6.8**	**6.5**	**6.5**	**6.5**	**6.3**	**6.1**
Bangladesh	5.8	6.0	6.5	6.3	6.0	6.3	6.8	7.2	7.4	7.3	7.1	7.0
Bhutan	8.2	9.3	9.7	6.4	3.6	4.0	6.2	7.3	7.4	5.8	4.8	7.5
Brunei Darussalam	1.4	2.7	3.7	0.9	−2.1	−2.5	−0.4	−2.5	1.3	2.3	5.1	3.9
Cambodia	8.4	6.0	7.1	7.3	7.4	7.1	7.0	7.0	6.9	6.9	6.8	6.0
China	10.3	10.6	9.5	7.9	7.8	7.3	6.9	6.7	6.9	6.6	6.2	5.6
Fiji	0.9	3.0	2.7	1.4	4.7	5.6	3.8	0.7	3.0	3.2	3.4	3.2
India[4]	6.9	10.3	6.6	5.5	6.4	7.4	8.2	7.1	6.7	7.3	7.4	7.7
Indonesia	5.3	6.4	6.2	6.0	5.6	5.0	4.9	5.0	5.1	5.1	5.1	5.4
Kiribati	1.4	−0.9	1.6	4.6	4.3	−0.6	10.3	1.1	3.1	2.3	2.4	1.8
Lao P.D.R.	7.0	8.0	8.0	7.8	8.0	7.6	7.3	7.0	6.9	6.8	7.0	6.8
Malaysia	4.7	7.5	5.3	5.5	4.7	6.0	5.1	4.2	5.9	4.7	4.6	4.8
Maldives	6.3	7.1	8.4	2.3	7.1	7.6	2.2	4.5	4.8	4.7	5.0	5.4
Marshall Islands	2.0	0.5	3.0	2.8	−0.5	−0.6	2.0	3.6	2.5	2.3	2.2	1.2
Micronesia	0.5	3.3	1.0	−1.7	−3.0	−2.5	3.9	2.9	2.0	1.4	0.9	0.6
Mongolia	5.6	7.3	17.3	12.3	11.6	7.9	2.4	1.2	5.1	6.2	6.3	5.7
Myanmar	11.1	5.3	5.6	7.3	8.4	8.0	7.0	5.9	6.8	6.4	6.8	7.2
Nauru	. . .	13.6	11.7	10.1	34.2	36.5	2.8	10.4	4.0	−2.4	−1.0	1.7
Nepal	4.1	4.8	3.4	4.8	4.1	6.0	3.3	0.6	7.9	6.3	5.0	4.3
Palau	. . .	−0.9	6.3	3.9	−1.6	2.7	10.1	0.0	−3.7	0.8	2.2	2.0
Papua New Guinea	2.8	10.1	1.1	4.6	3.8	15.4	5.3	1.6	2.5	−1.1	3.8	3.8
Philippines	4.4	7.6	3.7	6.7	7.1	6.1	6.1	6.9	6.7	6.5	6.6	6.9
Samoa	3.2	−2.0	5.6	0.4	−1.9	1.2	1.6	7.1	2.5	1.8	3.2	2.2
Solomon Islands	1.2	6.8	13.2	4.6	3.0	2.3	2.5	3.5	3.5	3.4	2.9	2.8
Sri Lanka	5.1	8.0	8.4	9.1	3.4	5.0	5.0	4.5	3.3	3.7	4.3	5.0
Thailand	4.3	7.5	0.8	7.2	2.7	1.0	3.0	3.3	3.9	4.6	3.9	3.6
Timor-Leste[5]	. . .	8.5	7.7	5.5	2.5	4.1	4.0	5.3	−4.6	0.8	5.0	4.8
Tonga	1.1	3.2	1.8	−1.1	−0.6	2.9	3.5	4.2	2.5	2.9	5.5	1.8
Tuvalu	. . .	−3.1	7.9	−3.8	4.6	1.3	9.1	3.0	3.2	4.3	4.1	3.9
Vanuatu	3.3	1.6	1.2	1.8	2.0	2.3	0.2	3.5	4.2	3.8	3.5	3.0
Vietnam	6.9	6.4	6.2	5.2	5.4	6.0	6.7	6.2	6.8	6.6	6.5	6.5
Emerging and Developing Europe	**4.0**	**4.3**	**6.6**	**2.5**	**4.9**	**3.9**	**4.7**	**3.3**	**6.0**	**3.8**	**2.0**	**2.7**
Albania	5.9	3.7	2.5	1.4	1.0	1.8	2.2	3.4	3.8	4.0	3.7	4.0
Bosnia and Herzegovina	4.2	0.8	0.9	−0.7	2.4	1.1	3.1	3.2	3.0	3.2	3.5	4.0
Bulgaria	5.0	1.3	1.9	0.0	0.9	1.3	3.6	3.9	3.6	3.6	3.1	2.8
Croatia	3.0	−1.5	−0.3	−2.3	−0.5	−0.1	2.4	3.5	2.8	2.8	2.6	2.1
Hungary	2.4	0.7	1.7	−1.6	2.1	4.2	3.4	2.2	4.0	4.0	3.3	2.2
Kosovo	. . .	3.3	4.4	2.8	3.4	1.2	4.1	4.1	3.7	4.0	4.0	4.0
FYR Macedonia	3.1	3.4	2.3	−0.5	2.9	3.6	3.9	2.9	0.0	1.6	2.6	3.4
Montenegro	. . .	2.7	3.2	−2.7	3.5	1.8	3.4	2.9	4.3	3.7	2.5	3.0
Poland	3.9	3.6	5.0	1.6	1.4	3.3	3.8	3.0	4.6	4.4	3.5	2.8
Romania	4.8	−2.8	2.0	1.2	3.5	3.4	3.9	4.8	6.9	4.0	3.4	3.1
Serbia	5.1	0.6	1.4	−1.0	2.6	−1.8	0.8	2.8	1.9	4.0	3.5	4.0
Turkey	3.8	8.5	11.1	4.8	8.5	5.2	6.1	3.2	7.4	3.5	0.4	2.6

Table A4. Emerging Market and Developing Economies: Real GDP (continued)

(Annual percent change)

	Average 2000–09	2010	2011	2012	2013	2014	2015	2016	2017	Projections 2018	2019	2023
Latin America and the Caribbean	**3.0**	**6.1**	**4.6**	**2.9**	**2.9**	**1.3**	**0.3**	**−0.6**	**1.3**	**1.2**	**2.2**	**2.9**
Antigua and Barbuda	2.8	−7.2	−2.1	3.5	−0.1	5.1	4.1	5.3	2.8	3.5	3.0	2.0
Argentina	2.3	10.1	6.0	−1.0	2.4	−2.5	2.7	−1.8	2.9	−2.6	−1.6	3.2
Aruba	0.3	−3.3	3.5	−1.4	4.2	0.9	−0.4	−0.1	1.2	1.1	1.0	1.2
The Bahamas	1.0	1.5	0.6	3.1	−0.4	−0.1	1.0	−1.7	1.4	2.3	2.1	1.5
Barbados	1.4	−2.2	−0.8	−0.1	−1.4	−0.2	2.2	2.3	−0.2	−0.5	−0.1	1.8
Belize	4.9	3.3	2.1	3.7	0.7	4.0	3.8	−0.5	0.8	1.8	2.0	1.7
Bolivia	3.7	4.1	5.2	5.1	6.8	5.5	4.9	4.3	4.2	4.3	4.2	3.7
Brazil	3.4	7.5	4.0	1.9	3.0	0.5	−3.5	−3.5	1.0	1.4	2.4	2.2
Chile	4.2	5.8	6.1	5.3	4.1	1.8	2.3	1.3	1.5	4.0	3.4	3.0
Colombia	3.9	4.3	7.4	3.9	4.6	4.7	3.0	2.0	1.8	2.8	3.6	3.5
Costa Rica	4.2	5.0	4.3	4.8	2.3	3.5	3.6	4.2	3.3	3.3	3.3	3.4
Dominica	2.6	0.7	−0.2	−1.1	0.8	4.2	−3.7	2.6	−4.7	−14.1	9.4	1.5
Dominican Republic	4.2	8.3	3.1	2.7	4.9	7.6	7.0	6.6	4.6	6.4	5.0	5.1
Ecuador	3.9	3.5	7.9	5.6	4.9	3.8	0.1	−1.2	2.4	1.1	0.7	1.8
El Salvador	1.5	2.1	3.8	2.8	2.4	2.0	2.4	2.6	2.3	2.5	2.3	2.2
Grenada	2.3	−0.5	0.8	−1.2	2.4	7.3	6.4	3.7	5.1	3.6	3.6	2.7
Guatemala	3.3	2.9	4.2	3.0	3.7	4.2	4.1	3.1	2.8	2.8	3.4	3.5
Guyana	1.8	4.4	5.4	5.0	5.0	3.9	3.1	3.4	2.1	3.4	4.8	27.9
Haiti	0.8	−5.5	5.5	2.9	4.2	2.8	1.2	1.5	1.2	2.0	2.5	3.0
Honduras	4.5	3.7	3.8	4.1	2.8	3.1	3.8	3.8	4.8	3.5	3.6	3.7
Jamaica	0.9	−1.4	1.4	−0.5	0.2	0.6	0.9	1.5	0.7	1.2	1.5	2.2
Mexico	1.4	5.1	3.7	3.6	1.4	2.8	3.3	2.9	2.0	2.2	2.5	3.0
Nicaragua	2.9	4.4	6.3	6.5	4.9	4.8	4.8	4.7	4.9	−4.0	−1.0	4.2
Panama	5.5	5.8	11.8	9.2	6.6	6.0	5.8	5.0	5.4	4.6	6.8	5.5
Paraguay	2.3	11.1	4.2	−0.5	8.4	4.9	3.1	4.3	4.8	4.4	4.2	4.1
Peru	5.0	8.5	6.5	6.0	5.8	2.4	3.3	4.0	2.5	4.1	4.1	4.0
St. Kitts and Nevis	3.2	−2.9	−0.8	−0.8	6.6	9.5	2.7	2.9	2.1	2.7	3.5	2.7
St. Lucia	2.2	−1.6	0.6	0.2	0.3	3.6	−0.9	3.4	3.0	3.4	3.6	1.5
St. Vincent and the Grenadines	3.1	−2.3	0.2	1.3	2.5	0.2	0.8	0.8	0.7	2.0	2.3	2.5
Suriname	4.5	5.2	5.8	2.7	2.9	0.3	−2.6	−5.1	1.9	2.0	2.2	3.0
Trinidad and Tobago	6.0	3.5	−0.2	−1.8	2.7	−1.2	1.7	−6.1	−2.6	1.0	0.9	2.2
Uruguay	2.2	7.8	5.2	3.5	4.6	3.2	0.4	1.7	2.7	2.0	3.2	3.0
Venezuela	3.7	−1.5	4.2	5.6	1.3	−3.9	−6.2	−16.5	−14.0	−18.0	−5.0	−1.5
Middle East, North Africa, Afghanistan, and Pakistan	**5.2**	**4.6**	**4.4**	**4.8**	**2.6**	**2.9**	**2.5**	**5.1**	**2.2**	**2.4**	**2.7**	**3.0**
Afghanistan	. . .	8.4	6.5	14.0	5.7	2.7	1.0	2.2	2.7	2.3	3.0	5.0
Algeria	3.9	3.6	2.8	3.4	2.8	3.8	3.7	3.2	1.4	2.5	2.7	0.5
Bahrain	5.6	4.3	2.0	3.7	5.4	4.4	2.9	3.5	3.8	3.2	2.6	2.6
Djibouti	3.2	4.1	7.3	4.8	5.0	6.0	6.5	6.5	6.7	6.7	6.7	6.0
Egypt	5.0	5.1	1.8	2.2	3.3	2.9	4.4	4.3	4.2	5.3	5.5	6.0
Iran	4.8	5.7	3.1	−7.7	−0.3	3.2	−1.6	12.5	3.7	−1.5	−3.6	2.3
Iraq	10.9	6.4	7.5	13.9	7.6	0.7	2.5	13.1	−2.1	1.5	6.5	2.2
Jordan	6.5	2.3	2.6	2.7	2.8	3.1	2.4	2.0	2.0	2.3	2.5	3.0
Kuwait	5.3	−2.4	10.9	7.9	0.4	0.6	−1.0	2.2	−3.3	2.3	4.1	2.9
Lebanon	5.0	8.0	0.9	2.8	2.7	2.0	0.2	1.7	1.5	1.0	1.4	2.9
Libya[4]	4.2	3.2	−66.7	124.7	−36.8	−53.0	−13.0	−7.4	64.0	10.9	10.8	1.5
Mauritania	4.3	4.8	4.7	5.8	6.1	5.6	0.4	1.8	3.5	2.5	5.2	5.3
Morocco	4.8	3.8	5.2	3.0	4.5	2.7	4.5	1.1	4.1	3.2	3.2	4.5
Oman	3.5	2.0	2.6	9.1	5.1	1.4	4.7	5.0	−0.9	1.9	5.0	1.5
Pakistan	4.7	2.6	3.6	3.8	3.7	4.1	4.1	4.6	5.4	5.8	4.0	3.0
Qatar	12.1	18.1	13.4	4.7	4.4	4.0	3.7	2.1	1.6	2.7	2.8	2.7
Saudi Arabia	3.4	5.0	10.0	5.4	2.7	3.7	4.1	1.7	−0.9	2.2	2.4	2.3
Somalia	. . .	. . .	. . .	1.2	1.4	0.4	3.9	4.4	2.3	3.1	3.5	3.5
Sudan[6]	5.7	1.4	−2.4	−17.9	3.7	4.8	1.3	3.0	1.4	−2.3	−1.9	0.4
Syria[7]	4.4	3.4	. . .	. . .	. . .	. . .	. . .	. . .	. . .	. . .	. . .	. . .
Tunisia	4.3	3.5	−1.9	4.0	2.9	3.0	1.2	1.1	2.0	2.4	2.9	4.2
United Arab Emirates	4.9	1.6	6.9	4.5	5.1	4.4	5.1	3.0	0.8	2.9	3.7	2.9
Yemen	4.1	7.7	−12.7	2.4	4.8	−0.2	−16.7	−13.6	−5.9	−2.6	14.7	6.6

Table A4. Emerging Market and Developing Economies: Real GDP *(continued)*

(Annual percent change)

	Average 2000–09	2010	2011	2012	2013	2014	2015	2016	2017	Projections 2018	2019	2023
Sub-Saharan Africa	**5.6**	**7.1**	**5.1**	**4.6**	**5.2**	**5.1**	**3.3**	**1.4**	**2.7**	**3.1**	**3.8**	**4.1**
Angola	8.6	4.9	3.5	8.5	5.0	4.8	0.9	−2.6	−2.5	−0.1	3.1	3.8
Benin	4.2	2.1	3.0	4.8	7.2	6.4	2.1	4.0	5.6	6.0	6.3	6.1
Botswana	3.4	8.6	6.0	4.5	11.3	4.1	−1.7	4.3	2.4	4.6	3.6	5.5
Burkina Faso	5.3	8.4	6.6	6.5	5.8	4.3	3.9	5.9	6.4	5.9	6.0	5.3
Burundi	3.4	5.1	4.0	4.4	5.9	4.5	−4.0	−1.0	0.0	0.1	0.4	0.5
Cabo Verde	6.0	1.5	4.0	1.1	0.8	0.6	1.0	4.7	4.0	4.3	4.0	4.0
Cameroon	3.9	3.4	4.1	4.5	5.4	5.9	5.7	4.6	3.5	3.8	4.4	5.4
Central African Republic	1.0	3.0	3.3	4.1	−36.7	1.0	4.8	4.5	4.3	4.3	5.0	5.0
Chad	8.3	13.6	0.1	8.8	5.8	6.9	1.8	−6.4	−3.1	3.5	3.6	4.2
Comoros	2.0	2.1	2.2	3.0	3.5	2.0	1.0	2.2	2.7	2.8	2.8	3.3
Democratic Republic of the Congo	3.1	7.1	6.9	7.1	8.5	9.5	6.9	2.4	3.4	3.8	4.1	4.7
Republic of Congo	4.6	8.7	3.4	3.8	3.3	6.8	2.6	−2.8	−3.1	2.0	3.7	0.4
Côte d'Ivoire	0.7	2.0	−4.2	10.1	9.3	8.8	8.8	8.3	7.8	7.4	7.0	6.5
Equatorial Guinea	25.3	−8.9	6.5	8.3	−4.1	0.4	−9.1	−8.6	−3.2	−7.7	−2.6	3.4
Eritrea	−0.7	2.2	8.7	7.0	4.6	2.9	2.6	1.9	5.0	4.2	3.8	4.3
Eswatini	3.3	3.8	2.2	4.7	6.4	1.9	0.4	1.4	1.6	1.3	0.4	2.0
Ethiopia	8.4	10.6	11.4	8.7	9.9	10.3	10.4	8.0	10.9	7.5	8.5	7.5
Gabon	0.6	6.3	7.1	5.3	5.5	4.4	3.9	2.1	0.5	2.0	3.4	4.5
The Gambia	3.7	6.5	−4.3	5.6	4.8	−0.9	5.9	0.4	4.6	5.4	5.4	4.8
Ghana	5.4	7.9	14.0	9.3	7.3	4.0	3.8	3.7	8.4	6.3	7.6	5.1
Guinea	2.9	4.2	5.6	5.9	3.9	3.7	3.8	10.5	8.2	5.8	5.9	5.0
Guinea-Bissau	2.0	4.6	8.1	−1.7	3.3	1.0	6.1	6.3	5.9	4.5	5.0	5.0
Kenya	3.4	8.4	6.1	4.6	5.9	5.4	5.7	5.9	4.9	6.0	6.1	6.0
Lesotho	3.7	6.3	6.7	4.9	2.2	3.0	2.5	3.1	−1.6	0.8	1.2	1.3
Liberia	. . .	6.4	7.7	8.4	8.8	0.7	0.0	−1.6	2.5	3.0	4.5	5.3
Madagascar	3.0	0.3	1.5	3.0	2.3	3.3	3.1	4.2	4.2	5.0	5.4	4.9
Malawi	4.2	6.9	4.9	1.9	5.2	5.7	2.9	2.3	4.0	3.3	4.7	6.5
Mali	5.2	5.4	3.2	−0.8	2.3	7.1	6.2	5.8	5.4	5.1	4.8	4.8
Mauritius	4.4	4.4	4.1	3.5	3.4	3.7	3.6	3.8	3.8	3.9	4.0	4.0
Mozambique	7.6	6.7	7.1	7.2	7.1	7.4	6.6	3.8	3.7	3.5	4.0	11.1
Namibia	3.8	6.0	5.1	5.1	5.6	6.4	6.1	0.7	−0.8	1.1	3.1	3.4
Niger	4.3	8.4	2.2	11.8	5.3	7.5	4.3	4.9	4.9	5.3	5.4	6.0
Nigeria	8.3	11.3	4.9	4.3	5.4	6.3	2.7	−1.6	0.8	1.9	2.3	2.4
Rwanda	8.3	7.3	7.8	8.8	4.7	7.6	8.9	6.0	6.1	7.2	7.8	7.5
São Tomé and Príncipe	4.5	6.7	4.4	3.1	4.8	6.5	3.8	4.2	3.9	4.0	4.5	5.0
Senegal	4.0	3.6	1.5	5.1	2.8	6.6	6.4	6.2	7.2	7.0	6.7	6.4
Seychelles	1.9	5.9	5.4	3.7	6.0	4.5	4.9	4.5	5.3	3.6	3.3	3.3
Sierra Leone	8.7	5.3	6.3	15.2	20.7	4.6	−20.5	6.3	3.7	3.7	5.5	4.6
South Africa	3.6	3.0	3.3	2.2	2.5	1.8	1.3	0.6	1.3	0.8	1.4	1.8
South Sudan	. . .	. . .	. . .	−52.4	29.3	2.9	−0.2	−13.9	−5.1	−3.2	−4.6	−5.8
Tanzania	6.2	6.4	7.9	5.1	7.3	7.0	7.0	7.0	6.0	5.8	6.6	6.4
Togo	1.5	6.1	6.4	6.5	6.1	5.9	5.7	5.1	4.4	4.7	5.0	5.4
Uganda	7.5	7.7	6.8	2.2	4.7	4.6	5.7	2.3	4.8	5.9	6.1	6.5
Zambia	6.8	10.3	5.6	7.6	5.1	4.7	2.9	3.8	3.4	3.8	4.5	4.5
Zimbabwe[8]	−6.1	15.4	16.3	13.6	5.3	2.8	1.4	0.7	3.7	3.6	4.2	5.0

[1]Data for some countries refer to real net material product (NMP) or are estimates based on NMP. The figures should be interpreted only as indicative of broad orders of magnitude because reliable, comparable data are not generally available. In particular, the growth of output of new private enterprises of the informal economy is not fully reflected in the recent figures.
[2]Georgia, Turkmenistan, and Ukraine, which are not members of the Commonwealth of Independent States, are included in this group for reasons of geography and similarity in economic structure.
[3]Data are based on the 2008 System of National Accounts. The revised national accounts data are available beginning in 2000 and exclude Crimea and Sevastopol from 2010 onward.
[4]See country-specific notes for India and Libya in the "Country Notes" section of the Statistical Appendix.
[5]In this table only, the data for Timor-Leste are based on non-oil GDP.
[6]Data for 2011 exclude South Sudan after July 9. Data for 2012 and onward pertain to the current Sudan.
[7]Data for Syria are excluded for 2011 onward owing to the uncertain political situation.
[8]The Zimbabwe dollar ceased circulating in early 2009. Data are based on IMF staff estimates of price and exchange rate developments in US dollars. IMF staff estimates of US dollar values may differ from authorities' estimates. Real GDP is in constant 2009 prices.

Table A5. Summary of Inflation
(Percent)

	Average 2000–09	2010	2011	2012	2013	2014	2015	2016	2017	Projections 2018	2019	2023
GDP Deflators												
Advanced Economies	**1.8**	**0.9**	**1.3**	**1.3**	**1.3**	**1.4**	**1.3**	**0.9**	**1.4**	**1.8**	**1.8**	**1.9**
United States	2.2	1.2	2.1	1.9	1.8	1.9	1.1	1.1	1.9	2.3	2.1	1.9
Euro Area	2.0	0.7	1.0	1.3	1.2	0.9	1.4	0.7	1.1	1.5	1.6	2.0
Japan	−1.1	−1.9	−1.7	−0.8	−0.3	1.7	2.1	0.3	−0.2	0.8	1.5	1.0
Other Advanced Economies[1]	2.1	2.0	2.0	1.2	1.4	1.3	1.0	1.2	1.9	1.7	1.7	1.9
Consumer Prices												
Advanced Economies	**2.0**	**1.5**	**2.7**	**2.0**	**1.4**	**1.4**	**0.3**	**0.8**	**1.7**	**2.0**	**1.9**	**2.0**
United States	2.6	1.6	3.1	2.1	1.5	1.6	0.1	1.3	2.1	2.4	2.1	2.2
Euro Area[2]	2.1	1.6	2.7	2.5	1.3	0.4	0.0	0.2	1.5	1.7	1.7	2.1
Japan	−0.3	−0.7	−0.3	−0.1	0.3	2.8	0.8	−0.1	0.5	1.2	1.3	1.3
Other Advanced Economies[1]	2.1	2.4	3.3	2.1	1.7	1.5	0.5	0.9	1.8	2.0	1.9	2.0
Emerging Market and Developing Economies[3]	**6.8**	**5.6**	**7.1**	**5.8**	**5.5**	**4.7**	**4.7**	**4.2**	**4.3**	**5.0**	**5.2**	**4.1**
Regional Groups												
Commonwealth of Independent States[4]	13.7	7.2	9.8	6.2	6.5	8.1	15.5	8.3	5.5	4.5	5.7	4.5
Emerging and Developing Asia	4.0	5.1	6.5	4.6	4.6	3.4	2.7	2.8	2.4	3.0	3.2	3.3
Emerging and Developing Europe	12.7	5.7	5.4	6.1	4.5	4.1	3.2	3.2	6.2	8.3	9.0	7.2
Latin America and the Caribbean	6.2	4.2	5.2	4.6	4.6	4.9	5.5	5.6	6.0	6.1	5.9	3.5
Middle East, North Africa, Afghanistan, and Pakistan	6.7	6.6	9.3	9.8	9.2	6.7	5.4	4.7	6.4	10.8	10.2	6.0
Middle East and North Africa	6.6	6.3	8.8	9.7	9.4	6.5	5.5	4.9	6.7	11.8	10.6	6.2
Sub-Saharan Africa	10.7	8.1	9.3	9.2	6.5	6.3	6.9	11.2	11.0	8.6	8.5	7.6
Memorandum												
European Union	2.5	2.0	3.1	2.6	1.5	0.5	0.0	0.2	1.7	1.9	1.9	2.1
Low-Income Developing Countries	9.7	9.2	11.7	9.9	8.0	7.1	6.9	8.6	9.6	9.5	8.8	7.8
Analytical Groups												
By Source of Export Earnings												
Fuel	10.3	6.7	8.6	8.0	8.1	6.4	8.6	6.9	5.4	7.5	8.3	5.7
Nonfuel	5.9	5.3	6.7	5.3	4.9	4.2	3.8	3.7	4.0	4.6	4.6	3.9
Of Which, Primary Products[5]	6.8	4.7	6.2	6.5	6.2	6.5	4.9	6.0	11.4	13.3	12.5	6.2
By External Financing Source												
Net Debtor Economies	8.0	6.8	7.7	7.0	6.3	5.8	5.6	5.3	5.7	5.9	5.8	4.7
Net Debtor Economies by Debt-Servicing Experience												
Economies with Arrears and/or Rescheduling during 2013–17	8.9	9.5	10.3	7.9	6.7	10.1	13.8	8.5	16.8	16.7	11.9	7.8
Memorandum												
Median Inflation Rate												
Advanced Economies	2.3	1.9	3.2	2.6	1.4	0.7	0.1	0.6	1.6	1.8	1.8	2.0
Emerging Market and Developing Economies[3]	5.2	4.1	5.4	4.5	3.8	3.1	2.7	2.7	3.3	3.6	3.7	3.0

[1]Excludes the United States, euro area countries, and Japan.
[2]Based on Eurostat's harmonized index of consumer prices.
[3]Excludes Venezuela but includes Argentina starting from 2017 onward. See country-specific notes for Argentina and Venezuela in the "Country Notes" section of the Statistical Appendix.
[4]Georgia, Turkmenistan, and Ukraine, which are not members of the Commonwealth of Independent States, are included in this group for reasons of geography and similarity in economic structure.
[5]Includes Argentina starting from 2017 onward. See country-specific note for Argentina in the "Country Notes" section of the Statistical Appendix.

Table A6. Advanced Economies: Consumer Prices[1]

(Annual percent change)

	Average 2000–09	2010	2011	2012	2013	2014	2015	2016	2017	Projections 2018	Projections 2019	Projections 2023	End of Period[2] 2017	End of Period[2] Projections 2018	End of Period[2] Projections 2019
Advanced Economies	**2.0**	**1.5**	**2.7**	**2.0**	**1.4**	**1.4**	**0.3**	**0.8**	**1.7**	**2.0**	**1.9**	**2.0**	**1.7**	**1.9**	**2.0**
United States	2.6	1.6	3.1	2.1	1.5	1.6	0.1	1.3	2.1	2.4	2.1	2.2	2.2	2.1	2.3
Euro Area[3]	2.1	1.6	2.7	2.5	1.3	0.4	0.0	0.2	1.5	1.7	1.7	2.1	1.4	1.9	1.7
Germany	1.6	1.2	2.5	2.1	1.6	0.8	0.1	0.4	1.7	1.8	1.8	2.6	1.6	1.8	1.9
France	1.9	1.7	2.3	2.2	1.0	0.6	0.1	0.3	1.2	1.9	1.8	1.9	1.3	1.6	2.2
Italy	2.3	1.6	2.9	3.3	1.2	0.2	0.1	−0.1	1.3	1.3	1.4	1.7	1.0	1.9	1.4
Spain	3.0	1.8	3.2	2.4	1.4	−0.1	−0.5	−0.2	2.0	1.8	1.8	1.9	1.1	2.2	1.7
Netherlands	2.3	0.9	2.5	2.8	2.6	0.3	0.2	0.1	1.3	1.4	1.6	2.1	1.2	1.5	1.7
Belgium	2.1	2.3	3.4	2.6	1.2	0.5	0.6	1.8	2.2	2.2	1.8	2.0	2.1	1.9	1.6
Austria	1.9	1.7	3.5	2.6	2.1	1.5	0.8	1.0	2.2	2.0	2.1	2.0	2.3	1.9	2.1
Greece	3.2	4.7	3.1	1.0	−0.9	−1.4	−1.1	0.0	1.1	0.7	1.2	1.8	1.0	0.9	1.3
Portugal	2.6	1.4	3.6	2.8	0.4	−0.2	0.5	0.6	1.6	1.7	1.6	2.1	1.6	4.7	−2.5
Ireland	2.9	−1.6	1.2	1.9	0.6	0.3	0.0	−0.2	0.3	0.7	1.2	2.0	−0.1	1.8	1.3
Finland	1.8	1.7	3.3	3.2	2.2	1.2	−0.2	0.4	0.8	1.2	1.7	2.0	0.5	1.6	1.7
Slovak Republic	5.2	0.7	4.1	3.7	1.5	−0.1	−0.3	−0.5	1.3	2.6	2.2	2.0	2.0	2.8	2.0
Lithuania	3.0	1.2	4.1	3.2	1.2	0.2	−0.7	0.7	3.7	2.5	2.2	2.5	3.8	2.2	2.2
Slovenia	4.9	1.8	1.8	2.6	1.8	0.2	−0.5	−0.1	1.4	2.1	2.0	2.0	1.7	2.1	2.0
Luxembourg	2.7	2.8	3.7	2.9	1.7	0.7	0.1	0.0	2.1	1.5	1.8	2.0	1.5	0.7	3.7
Latvia	5.8	−1.2	4.2	2.3	0.0	0.7	0.2	0.1	2.9	2.7	2.4	2.3	2.2	2.7	2.4
Estonia	4.3	2.7	5.1	4.2	3.2	0.5	0.1	0.8	3.7	3.0	2.5	2.1	3.8	3.0	2.5
Cyprus	2.6	2.6	3.5	3.1	0.4	−0.3	−1.5	−1.2	0.7	0.8	1.8	2.0	−0.4	2.4	2.0
Malta	2.5	2.0	2.5	3.2	1.0	0.8	1.2	0.9	1.3	1.8	2.1	2.0	1.3	2.1	2.1
Japan	−0.3	−0.7	−0.3	−0.1	0.3	2.8	0.8	−0.1	0.5	1.2	1.3	1.3	0.6	1.4	1.7
United Kingdom	1.8	3.3	4.5	2.8	2.6	1.5	0.0	0.7	2.7	2.5	2.2	2.0	3.0	2.3	2.1
Korea	3.1	2.9	4.0	2.2	1.3	1.3	0.7	1.0	1.9	1.5	1.8	2.0	1.5	1.6	1.9
Canada	2.1	1.8	2.9	1.5	0.9	1.9	1.1	1.4	1.6	2.6	2.2	2.0	1.8	2.7	2.1
Australia	3.2	2.9	3.3	1.7	2.5	2.5	1.5	1.3	2.0	2.2	2.3	2.5	2.0	2.2	2.4
Taiwan Province of China	0.9	1.1	1.4	1.6	1.0	1.3	−0.6	1.0	1.1	1.5	1.3	2.0	1.2	1.5	1.3
Switzerland	1.0	0.7	0.2	−0.7	−0.2	0.0	−1.1	−0.4	0.5	1.1	1.4	1.0	0.9	1.4	1.1
Sweden	1.9	1.9	1.4	0.9	0.4	0.2	0.7	1.1	1.9	1.9	1.7	2.0	1.8	2.0	1.6
Singapore	1.5	2.8	5.2	4.6	2.4	1.0	−0.5	−0.5	0.6	1.0	1.4	1.3	0.4	2.0	1.3
Hong Kong SAR	−0.2	2.3	5.3	4.1	4.3	4.4	3.0	2.4	1.5	2.3	2.1	2.5	1.5	2.3	2.1
Norway	2.1	2.4	1.3	0.7	2.1	2.0	2.2	3.6	1.9	1.9	2.0	2.0	1.6	1.8	2.0
Czech Republic	2.8	1.5	1.9	3.3	1.4	0.3	0.3	0.7	2.4	2.3	2.3	2.0	2.4	2.6	2.1
Israel	2.0	2.7	3.5	1.7	1.5	0.5	−0.6	−0.5	0.2	0.9	1.3	2.0	0.4	1.2	1.5
Denmark	2.1	2.3	2.8	2.4	0.8	0.6	0.5	0.3	1.1	1.4	1.7	2.0	1.0	1.6	1.8
New Zealand	2.7	2.3	4.1	1.0	1.1	1.2	0.3	0.6	1.9	1.4	1.7	2.0	1.6	1.6	1.9
Puerto Rico	2.8	2.5	2.9	1.3	1.1	0.6	−0.8	−0.3	1.8	2.7	1.2	1.2	1.2	2.7	1.2
Macao SAR	...	2.8	5.8	6.1	5.5	6.0	4.6	2.4	1.2	2.2	2.4	2.8	2.0	2.2	2.4
Iceland	6.2	5.4	4.0	5.2	3.9	2.0	1.6	1.7	1.8	2.5	2.6	2.5	1.9	2.6	2.6
San Marino	...	2.6	2.0	2.8	1.6	1.1	0.1	0.6	1.0	1.5	1.6	1.8	1.0	1.5	1.6
Memorandum															
Major Advanced Economies	1.9	1.4	2.6	1.9	1.3	1.5	0.3	0.8	1.8	2.1	1.9	2.0	1.8	2.0	2.1

[1]Movements in consumer prices are shown as annual averages.
[2]Monthly year-over-year changes and, for several countries, on a quarterly basis.
[3]Based on Eurostat's harmonized index of consumer prices.

Table A7. Emerging Market and Developing Economies: Consumer Prices[1]
(Annual percent change)

	Average 2000–09	2010	2011	2012	2013	2014	2015	2016	2017	Projections 2018	Projections 2019	Projections 2023	End of Period[2] 2017	End of Period[2] Projections 2018	End of Period[2] Projections 2019
Commonwealth of Independent States[3],[4]	**13.7**	**7.2**	**9.8**	**6.2**	**6.5**	**8.1**	**15.5**	**8.3**	**5.5**	**4.5**	**5.7**	**4.5**	**4.7**	**4.8**	**6.0**
Russia	13.9	6.9	8.4	5.1	6.8	7.8	15.5	7.1	3.7	2.8	5.1	4.6	2.5	3.6	5.7
Excluding Russia	13.3	8.1	13.3	9.2	5.7	8.8	15.5	11.3	9.9	8.6	7.0	4.4	10.1	7.9	6.4
Armenia	3.6	7.3	7.7	2.5	5.8	3.0	3.7	−1.4	0.9	3.0	4.4	4.0	2.7	4.7	4.2
Azerbaijan	7.0	5.7	7.8	1.1	2.5	1.5	4.1	12.6	13.0	3.5	3.3	3.0	10.0	3.5	3.3
Belarus	31.6	7.7	53.2	59.2	18.3	18.1	13.5	11.8	6.0	5.5	5.5	5.0	4.6	5.5	5.5
Georgia	7.3	7.1	8.5	−0.9	−0.5	3.1	4.0	2.1	6.0	2.8	2.7	3.0	6.7	2.5	3.0
Kazakhstan	9.2	7.1	8.3	5.1	5.8	6.7	6.7	14.6	7.4	6.4	5.6	2.1	7.1	6.0	5.2
Kyrgyz Republic	8.5	8.0	16.6	2.8	6.6	7.5	6.5	0.4	3.2	2.9	4.6	5.0	3.7	4.1	5.0
Moldova	11.7	7.4	7.6	4.6	4.6	5.1	9.6	6.4	6.6	3.6	4.9	5.0	7.3	3.0	5.7
Tajikistan	16.0	6.5	12.4	5.8	5.0	6.1	5.8	5.9	7.3	5.8	5.5	6.0	6.7	5.0	6.0
Turkmenistan	7.6	4.4	5.3	5.3	6.8	6.0	7.4	3.6	8.0	9.4	8.2	6.0	10.4	9.4	8.2
Ukraine[5]	12.9	9.4	8.0	0.6	−0.3	12.1	48.7	13.9	14.4	10.9	7.3	5.2	13.7	9.0	6.2
Uzbekistan	15.8	12.3	12.4	11.9	11.7	9.1	8.5	8.0	12.5	19.2	14.9	7.6	18.9	17.5	13.1
Emerging and Developing Asia	**4.0**	**5.1**	**6.5**	**4.6**	**4.6**	**3.4**	**2.7**	**2.8**	**2.4**	**3.0**	**3.2**	**3.3**	**2.8**	**3.4**	**3.0**
Bangladesh	5.6	9.4	11.5	6.2	7.5	7.0	6.2	5.7	5.6	6.0	6.1	5.5	5.7	5.8	6.1
Bhutan	4.8	5.7	7.3	9.3	11.3	9.5	7.6	7.6	5.8	4.6	4.9	4.7	3.0	4.5	4.6
Brunei Darussalam	0.6	0.2	0.1	0.1	0.4	−0.2	−0.4	−0.7	−0.2	0.4	0.5	0.5	0.0	0.5	0.5
Cambodia	4.6	4.0	5.5	2.9	3.0	3.9	1.2	3.0	2.9	3.3	3.3	3.0	2.2	3.5	3.2
China	1.8	3.3	5.4	2.6	2.6	2.0	1.4	2.0	1.6	2.2	2.4	3.0	1.8	2.5	2.3
Fiji	3.4	3.7	7.3	3.4	2.9	0.5	1.4	3.9	3.4	3.9	3.2	3.0	2.8	4.5	3.0
India	5.8	9.5	9.5	10.0	9.4	5.8	4.9	4.5	3.6	4.7	4.9	4.0	4.6	5.1	3.9
Indonesia	8.5	5.1	5.3	4.0	6.4	6.4	6.4	3.5	3.8	3.4	3.8	3.0	3.6	3.6	4.0
Kiribati	3.5	−3.9	1.5	−3.0	−1.5	2.1	0.6	1.9	0.4	2.5	2.5	2.5	2.5	2.5	2.5
Lao P.D.R.	7.8	6.0	7.6	4.3	6.4	4.1	1.3	1.6	0.8	0.9	4.5	3.1	0.1	2.6	2.9
Malaysia	2.2	1.7	3.2	1.7	2.1	3.1	2.1	2.1	3.8	1.0	2.3	2.3	3.5	3.0	2.5
Maldives	3.2	6.2	11.3	10.9	3.8	2.1	1.9	0.8	2.3	1.7	2.7	2.3	2.2	2.0	2.1
Marshall Islands	. . .	1.8	5.4	4.3	1.9	1.1	−2.2	−1.5	0.0	1.4	1.5	2.0	0.0	1.4	1.5
Micronesia	3.1	3.7	4.1	6.3	2.2	0.7	−0.2	0.5	0.5	2.0	2.0	2.0	0.5	2.0	2.0
Mongolia	8.9	10.3	7.7	15.0	8.6	12.9	5.9	0.5	4.6	7.6	8.0	6.8	7.2	8.0	8.1
Myanmar	18.9	8.2	2.8	2.8	5.7	5.1	10.0	6.8	4.0	6.0	5.8	5.4	5.4	6.3	5.9
Nauru	. . .	−2.0	−3.4	0.3	−1.1	0.3	9.8	8.2	5.1	3.8	2.5	2.0	1.6	3.0	2.8
Nepal	5.5	9.6	9.6	8.3	9.9	9.0	7.2	9.9	4.5	4.2	5.0	5.5	2.7	4.6	5.6
Palau	. . .	1.4	4.7	3.6	3.4	4.1	0.9	−1.0	0.9	2.5	2.3	2.0	0.5	2.5	2.3
Papua New Guinea	7.5	5.1	4.4	4.5	5.0	5.2	6.0	6.7	5.4	4.2	3.8	3.8	4.7	4.2	3.8
Philippines	5.2	4.1	4.8	3.0	2.6	3.6	0.7	1.3	2.9	4.9	4.0	3.0	2.9	5.2	3.7
Samoa	5.7	−0.2	2.9	6.2	−0.2	−1.2	1.9	0.1	1.3	3.4	3.0	3.0	1.0	3.0	2.9
Solomon Islands	9.1	1.0	7.4	5.9	5.4	5.2	−0.6	0.5	0.5	1.0	1.6	4.2	2.1	3.4	3.3
Sri Lanka	9.7	6.2	6.7	7.5	6.9	2.8	2.2	4.0	6.5	4.8	4.8	4.9	7.1	4.7	4.8
Thailand	2.4	3.3	3.8	3.0	2.2	1.9	−0.9	0.2	0.7	0.9	0.9	2.0	0.8	0.5	1.1
Timor-Leste	. . .	5.2	13.2	10.9	9.5	0.7	0.6	−1.3	0.6	1.8	2.7	4.0	0.8	2.5	2.8
Tonga	8.0	3.5	6.3	1.1	2.1	1.2	−1.1	2.6	7.4	5.2	5.3	2.5	5.6	9.4	1.5
Tuvalu	. . .	−1.9	0.5	1.4	2.0	1.1	3.1	3.5	4.1	4.2	3.7	2.9	4.4	4.0	3.4
Vanuatu	2.9	2.8	0.9	1.3	1.5	0.8	2.5	0.8	3.1	4.8	3.4	3.0	3.3	4.6	3.4
Vietnam	6.5	9.2	18.7	9.1	6.6	4.1	0.6	2.7	3.5	3.8	4.0	4.0	2.6	4.0	4.0
Emerging and Developing Europe	**12.7**	**5.7**	**5.4**	**6.1**	**4.5**	**4.1**	**3.2**	**3.2**	**6.2**	**8.3**	**9.0**	**7.2**	**6.8**	**10.5**	**8.5**
Albania	2.7	3.6	3.4	2.0	1.9	1.6	1.9	1.3	2.0	2.3	2.8	3.0	1.8	2.5	2.9
Bosnia and Herzegovina	2.4	2.2	3.7	2.1	−0.1	−0.9	−1.0	−1.1	1.2	1.4	1.6	2.0	1.6	1.7	1.8
Bulgaria[6]	6.7	3.0	3.4	2.4	0.4	−1.6	−1.1	−1.3	1.2	2.6	2.3	2.3	1.8	3.0	2.3
Croatia	3.2	1.0	2.3	3.4	2.2	−0.2	−0.5	−1.1	1.1	1.6	1.5	1.8	1.2	1.3	1.5
Hungary	6.1	4.9	3.9	5.7	1.7	−0.2	−0.1	0.4	2.4	2.8	3.3	3.0	2.1	3.1	3.1
Kosovo	. . .	3.5	7.3	2.5	1.8	0.4	−0.5	0.3	1.5	0.8	2.1	2.2	0.5	2.4	2.0
FYR Macedonia	2.6	1.5	3.9	3.3	2.8	−0.3	−0.3	−0.2	1.4	1.8	2.0	2.2	2.4	2.0	2.0
Montenegro	10.1	0.4	3.5	4.1	2.2	−0.7	1.5	−0.3	2.4	2.8	2.0	2.0	1.9	2.9	1.9
Poland	3.5	2.6	4.3	3.7	0.9	0.0	−0.9	−0.6	2.0	2.0	2.8	2.5	2.1	2.3	2.9
Romania	15.7	6.1	5.8	3.3	4.0	1.1	−0.6	−1.6	1.3	4.7	2.7	2.5	3.3	3.5	2.8
Serbia	20.2	6.1	11.1	7.3	7.7	2.1	1.4	1.1	3.1	2.1	2.3	3.0	3.0	2.4	2.5
Turkey	21.7	8.6	6.5	8.9	7.5	8.9	7.7	7.8	11.1	15.0	16.7	13.0	11.9	20.0	15.5

Table A7. Emerging Market and Developing Economies: Consumer Prices[1] (continued)

(Annual percent change)

	Average 2000–09	2010	2011	2012	2013	2014	2015	2016	2017	Projections 2018	Projections 2019	2023	End of Period[2] 2017	End of Period[2] Projections 2018	End of Period[2] Projections 2019
Latin America and the Caribbean[7]	**6.2**	**4.2**	**5.2**	**4.6**	**4.6**	**4.9**	**5.5**	**5.6**	**6.0**	**6.1**	**5.9**	**3.5**	**5.9**	**6.8**	**4.9**
Antigua and Barbuda	1.8	3.4	3.5	3.4	1.1	1.1	1.0	−0.5	2.5	1.4	2.0	2.0	2.8	2.0	2.0
Argentina[8]	8.4	10.5	9.8	10.0	10.6	...	...	...	25.7	31.8	31.7	4.9	24.8	40.5	20.2
Aruba	3.6	2.1	4.4	0.6	−2.4	0.4	0.5	−0.9	−0.5	1.0	1.5	2.1	−0.3	0.5	1.6
The Bahamas	2.3	1.6	3.1	1.9	0.4	1.2	1.9	−0.3	1.4	2.5	2.9	2.1	2.0	3.0	2.8
Barbados	3.7	5.8	9.4	4.5	1.8	1.8	−1.1	1.5	4.4	4.2	0.8	2.3	6.6	0.0	1.4
Belize	2.5	0.9	1.7	1.2	0.5	1.2	−0.9	0.7	1.1	1.3	1.9	1.7	1.1	1.6	2.1
Bolivia	4.8	2.5	9.9	4.5	5.7	5.8	4.1	3.6	2.8	3.2	4.2	4.5	2.7	3.7	4.5
Brazil	6.9	5.0	6.6	5.4	6.2	6.3	9.0	8.7	3.4	3.7	4.2	4.0	2.9	4.2	4.2
Chile	3.5	1.4	3.3	3.0	1.9	4.4	4.3	3.8	2.2	2.4	3.0	3.0	2.3	2.9	3.0
Colombia	6.3	2.3	3.4	3.2	2.0	2.9	5.0	7.5	4.3	3.2	3.4	3.0	4.1	3.1	3.0
Costa Rica	10.9	5.7	4.9	4.5	5.2	4.5	0.8	0.0	1.6	2.4	2.6	3.0	2.6	2.2	3.0
Dominica	2.0	2.8	1.1	1.4	0.0	0.8	−0.8	0.0	0.6	1.4	1.6	1.6	1.4	1.4	1.8
Dominican Republic	12.2	6.3	8.5	3.7	4.8	3.0	0.8	1.6	3.3	4.3	4.2	4.0	4.2	4.1	4.1
Ecuador	15.3	3.6	4.5	5.1	2.7	3.6	4.0	1.7	0.4	−0.2	0.5	1.2	−0.2	0.7	0.1
El Salvador	3.5	1.2	5.1	1.7	0.8	1.1	−0.7	0.6	1.0	1.2	1.8	2.0	2.0	1.4	2.0
Grenada	2.8	3.4	3.0	2.4	0.0	−1.0	−0.6	1.7	0.9	2.6	1.8	2.0	0.5	3.0	1.9
Guatemala	7.0	3.9	6.2	3.8	4.3	3.4	2.4	4.4	4.4	3.7	3.9	4.0	5.7	3.2	3.9
Guyana	6.1	4.3	4.4	2.4	1.9	0.7	−0.9	0.8	2.0	1.3	2.9	3.3	1.5	2.2	3.0
Haiti	14.8	4.1	7.4	6.8	6.8	3.9	7.5	13.4	14.7	13.3	11.6	5.5	15.4	13.0	10.0
Honduras	8.2	4.7	6.8	5.2	5.2	6.1	3.2	2.7	3.9	4.4	4.5	4.0	4.7	4.7	4.5
Jamaica	10.9	12.6	7.5	6.9	9.4	8.3	3.7	2.3	4.4	3.4	4.2	5.0	5.2	3.5	5.0
Mexico	5.2	4.2	3.4	4.1	3.8	4.0	2.7	2.8	6.0	4.8	3.6	3.0	6.8	4.3	3.1
Nicaragua	8.9	5.5	8.1	7.2	7.1	6.0	4.0	3.5	3.9	5.9	8.0	7.0	5.7	7.0	7.0
Panama	2.4	3.5	5.9	5.7	4.0	2.6	0.1	0.7	0.9	2.0	2.4	2.0	0.5	2.0	2.4
Paraguay	8.2	4.6	8.2	3.7	2.7	5.0	3.1	4.1	3.6	4.2	4.0	4.0	4.5	4.1	4.0
Peru	2.6	1.5	3.4	3.7	2.8	3.2	3.5	3.6	2.8	1.4	2.0	2.0	1.4	2.4	2.0
St. Kitts and Nevis	3.4	0.9	5.8	0.8	1.1	0.2	−2.3	−0.3	0.0	1.4	2.0	2.0	0.8	2.0	2.0
St. Lucia	2.8	3.3	2.8	4.2	1.5	3.5	−1.0	−3.1	0.1	1.9	1.9	1.5	2.2	2.0	1.5
St. Vincent and the Grenadines	2.9	0.8	3.2	2.6	0.8	0.2	−1.7	−0.2	2.2	2.4	2.0	2.0	3.0	2.0	2.0
Suriname	15.3	6.9	17.7	5.0	1.9	3.4	6.9	55.5	22.0	7.8	6.0	3.4	9.3	6.8	6.0
Trinidad and Tobago	6.3	10.5	5.1	9.3	5.2	5.7	4.7	3.1	1.9	2.3	3.1	3.8	1.3	2.3	3.1
Uruguay	8.5	6.7	8.1	8.1	8.6	8.9	8.7	9.6	6.2	7.6	6.7	6.1	6.6	7.9	6.5
Venezuela[8]	20.8	28.2	26.1	21.1	43.5	57.3	111.8	254.4	1,087.5	1,370,000.0	10,000,000.0	10,000,000.0	2,818.2	2,500,000.0	10,000,000.0
Middle East, North Africa, Afghanistan, and Pakistan	**6.7**	**6.6**	**9.3**	**9.8**	**9.2**	**6.7**	**5.4**	**4.7**	**6.4**	**10.8**	**10.2**	**6.0**	**7.1**	**13.0**	**9.0**
Afghanistan	...	2.2	11.8	6.4	7.4	4.7	−0.7	4.4	5.0	3.0	4.0	5.0	3.0	3.0	4.0
Algeria	3.2	3.9	4.5	8.9	3.3	2.9	4.8	6.4	5.6	6.5	6.7	12.0	4.9	9.0	4.8
Bahrain	1.6	2.0	−0.4	2.8	3.3	2.7	1.8	2.8	1.4	3.0	4.8	1.5	1.4	2.9	4.3
Djibouti	3.4	4.0	5.1	3.7	2.4	2.9	2.1	2.7	0.7	1.0	2.5	2.5	−1.0	1.5	2.5
Egypt	7.0	11.7	11.1	8.6	6.9	10.1	11.0	10.2	23.5	20.9	14.0	7.0	29.8	14.4	11.1
Iran	14.7	12.3	21.5	30.6	34.7	15.6	11.9	9.1	9.6	29.6	34.1	12.0	8.3	47.8	27.7
Iraq	...	2.4	5.6	6.1	1.9	2.2	1.4	0.5	0.1	2.0	2.0	2.0	0.2	2.0	2.0
Jordan	3.6	4.8	4.2	4.5	4.8	2.9	−0.9	−0.8	3.3	4.5	2.3	2.5	3.2	4.2	2.5
Kuwait	2.9	4.5	4.9	3.2	2.7	3.1	3.7	3.5	1.5	0.8	3.0	2.7	1.5	0.8	3.0
Lebanon	2.4	4.0	5.0	6.6	4.8	1.9	−3.7	−0.8	4.5	6.5	3.5	2.4	5.0	5.4	2.4
Libya[8]	−0.1	2.5	15.9	6.1	2.6	2.4	9.8	25.9	28.5	28.1	17.9	12.3	34.0	23.7	13.4
Mauritania	6.2	6.3	5.7	4.9	4.1	3.8	0.5	1.5	2.3	3.8	3.9	4.2	1.2	4.1	3.9
Morocco	1.9	1.0	0.9	1.3	1.9	0.4	1.5	1.6	0.8	2.4	1.4	2.0	1.9	2.4	1.4
Oman	2.5	3.3	4.0	2.9	1.2	1.0	0.1	1.1	1.6	1.5	3.2	3.0	1.6	1.5	3.2
Pakistan	7.5	10.1	13.7	11.0	7.4	8.6	4.5	2.9	4.1	3.9	7.5	5.0	3.9	5.2	7.7
Qatar	5.5	−2.4	2.0	1.8	3.2	3.4	1.8	2.7	0.4	3.7	3.5	2.0	...	...	...
Saudi Arabia	1.6	3.8	3.8	2.9	3.5	2.2	1.3	2.0	−0.9	2.6	2.0	2.1	−1.1	2.6	2.0
Somalia	...	...	...	...	...	...	...	...	...	...	...	...	5.3	2.8	2.5
Sudan[9]	10.2	13.0	18.1	35.6	36.5	36.9	16.9	17.8	32.4	61.8	49.2	61.1	25.2	64.3	56.8
Syria[10]	4.8	4.4	...	...	...	...	...	...	...	...	...	...	...	...	...
Tunisia	3.2	4.4	3.5	5.1	5.8	4.9	4.9	3.7	5.3	8.1	7.5	4.0	6.4	8.9	6.8
United Arab Emirates	5.5	0.9	0.9	0.7	1.1	2.3	4.1	1.6	2.0	3.5	1.9	1.9	2.0	3.5	1.9
Yemen	10.9	11.2	19.5	9.9	11.0	8.2	12.0	−12.6	24.7	41.8	20.0	5.0	53.5	30.0	10.0

Table A7. Emerging Market and Developing Economies: Consumer Prices[1] *(continued)*
(Annual percent change)

	Average 2000–09	2010	2011	2012	2013	2014	2015	2016	2017	Projections 2018	Projections 2019	Projections 2023	End of Period[2] 2017	End of Period[2] Projections 2018	End of Period[2] Projections 2019
Sub-Saharan Africa	**10.7**	**8.1**	**9.3**	**9.2**	**6.5**	**6.3**	**6.9**	**11.2**	**11.0**	**8.6**	**8.5**	**7.6**	**10.1**	**8.8**	**8.2**
Angola	62.4	14.5	13.5	10.3	8.8	7.3	9.2	30.7	29.8	20.5	15.8	6.5	23.7	20.0	12.0
Benin	3.2	2.2	2.7	6.7	1.0	−1.1	0.3	−0.8	0.1	2.3	2.3	1.9	3.0	1.7	2.8
Botswana	8.7	6.9	8.5	7.5	5.9	4.4	3.1	2.8	3.3	3.8	3.9	4.0	3.2	4.4	3.6
Burkina Faso	2.8	−0.6	2.8	3.8	0.5	−0.3	0.9	−0.2	0.4	2.0	2.0	2.0	2.1	2.0	2.0
Burundi	10.7	6.5	9.6	18.2	7.9	4.4	5.6	5.5	16.6	1.2	7.3	9.0	10.5	5.3	9.0
Cabo Verde	2.0	2.1	4.5	2.5	1.5	−0.2	0.1	−1.4	0.8	1.0	1.6	2.0	0.3	1.0	1.6
Cameroon	2.6	1.3	2.9	2.4	2.1	1.9	2.7	0.9	0.6	1.0	1.1	2.0	0.8	1.0	1.1
Central African Republic	3.4	1.5	1.2	5.9	6.6	11.6	4.5	4.6	4.1	4.0	3.4	3.0	4.2	3.6	3.4
Chad	3.5	−2.1	1.9	7.7	0.2	1.7	6.8	−1.1	−0.9	2.1	2.6	3.0	7.2	−2.3	5.4
Comoros	4.4	3.9	2.2	5.9	1.6	1.3	2.0	1.8	1.0	2.0	2.0	2.0	2.9	6.2	2.8
Democratic Republic of the Congo	61.5	23.5	14.9	0.9	0.9	1.2	1.0	18.2	41.5	23.0	13.5	4.9	55.0	20.0	14.8
Republic of Congo	2.9	0.4	1.8	5.0	4.6	0.9	3.2	3.2	0.5	1.2	2.0	3.0	1.8	2.1	2.4
Côte d'Ivoire	3.0	1.4	4.9	1.3	2.6	0.4	1.2	0.7	0.8	1.7	2.0	2.0	1.1	2.0	2.0
Equatorial Guinea	5.6	5.3	4.8	3.4	3.2	4.3	1.7	1.4	0.7	0.9	1.4	3.0	−0.2	1.3	1.5
Eritrea	18.7	11.2	3.9	6.0	6.5	10.0	9.0	9.0	9.0	9.0	9.0	9.0	9.0	9.0	9.0
Eswatini	7.9	4.5	6.1	8.9	5.6	5.7	5.0	7.8	6.2	5.0	5.3	5.5	4.7	5.5	4.9
Ethiopia	10.3	8.1	33.2	24.1	8.1	7.4	10.1	7.3	9.9	12.7	9.5	8.0	13.6	10.5	8.0
Gabon	1.1	1.4	1.3	2.7	0.5	4.5	−0.1	2.1	2.7	2.8	2.5	2.5	1.1	2.8	2.5
The Gambia	6.6	5.0	4.8	4.6	5.2	6.3	6.8	7.2	8.0	6.2	5.3	4.8	6.9	5.5	5.0
Ghana	17.7	6.7	7.7	7.1	11.7	15.5	17.2	17.5	12.4	9.5	8.0	6.0	11.8	8.0	8.0
Guinea	15.1	15.5	21.4	15.2	11.9	9.7	8.2	8.2	8.9	8.2	8.0	7.8	9.5	8.0	8.0
Guinea-Bissau	3.0	1.1	5.1	2.1	0.8	−1.0	1.5	1.5	1.1	2.0	2.2	2.8	−1.3	2.0	2.3
Kenya	7.3	4.3	14.0	9.4	5.7	6.9	6.6	6.3	8.0	5.0	5.6	5.0	4.5	6.9	5.0
Lesotho	7.3	3.3	6.0	5.5	5.0	4.6	4.3	6.2	5.3	6.3	5.3	5.0	4.9	7.0	5.0
Liberia	9.8	7.3	8.5	6.8	7.6	9.9	7.7	8.8	12.4	21.3	24.5	8.5	13.9	27.0	22.0
Madagascar	10.4	9.2	9.5	5.7	5.8	6.1	7.4	6.7	8.3	7.8	7.2	5.0	9.0	7.7	6.4
Malawi	10.1	7.4	7.6	21.3	28.3	23.8	21.9	21.7	12.2	9.2	8.4	5.0	7.1	9.0	7.8
Mali	2.5	1.3	3.1	5.3	−0.6	0.9	1.4	−1.8	1.8	2.5	2.1	2.2	1.1	2.0	2.1
Mauritius	5.9	2.9	6.5	3.9	3.5	3.2	1.3	1.0	3.7	5.1	4.5	3.7	4.2	5.9	4.7
Mozambique	10.5	12.7	10.4	2.1	4.2	2.3	2.4	19.2	15.3	6.0	5.7	5.0	7.2	6.5	5.5
Namibia	7.6	4.9	5.0	6.7	5.6	5.3	3.4	6.7	6.1	3.5	5.8	5.8	5.2	2.9	5.8
Niger	3.1	−2.8	2.9	0.5	2.3	−0.9	1.0	0.2	2.4	3.9	2.0	2.0	4.8	2.4	2.0
Nigeria	12.3	13.7	10.8	12.2	8.5	8.0	9.0	15.7	16.5	12.4	13.5	14.5	15.4	12.9	13.0
Rwanda	8.1	2.3	5.7	6.3	4.2	1.8	2.5	5.7	4.8	3.3	5.5	5.0	0.7	5.0	6.0
São Tomé and Príncipe	15.9	13.3	14.3	10.6	8.1	7.0	5.3	5.4	5.7	6.8	5.5	3.0	7.7	6.0	5.0
Senegal	2.0	1.2	3.4	1.4	0.7	−1.1	0.1	0.8	1.3	0.4	0.9	1.5	−0.7	0.8	1.7
Seychelles	8.6	−2.4	2.6	7.1	4.3	1.4	4.0	−1.0	2.9	4.4	3.7	3.0	3.5	5.2	3.8
Sierra Leone	7.4	7.9	6.1	6.6	5.5	4.6	6.7	10.9	18.2	15.6	13.1	8.7	15.3	15.0	13.0
South Africa	6.0	4.3	5.0	5.6	5.8	6.1	4.6	6.3	5.3	4.8	5.3	5.5	4.7	5.3	5.3
South Sudan	...	...	...	45.1	0.0	1.7	52.8	379.8	187.9	106.4	91.4	48.5	117.7	99.4	92.7
Tanzania	6.5	7.2	12.7	16.0	7.9	6.1	5.6	5.2	5.3	3.8	4.7	5.0	4.0	4.3	5.0
Togo	3.0	1.4	3.6	2.6	1.8	0.2	1.8	0.9	−0.7	0.4	1.2	2.0	−1.6	1.5	2.0
Uganda	6.4	3.7	15.0	12.7	4.9	3.1	5.4	5.5	5.6	3.8	4.2	5.0	3.3	4.3	4.5
Zambia	17.2	8.5	8.7	6.6	7.0	7.8	10.1	17.9	6.6	8.5	8.2	8.0	6.1	8.5	8.0
Zimbabwe[11]	−5.5	3.0	3.5	3.7	1.6	−0.2	−2.4	−1.6	0.9	3.9	9.6	3.9	3.5	6.3	10.9

[1]Movements in consumer prices are shown as annual averages.
[2]Monthly year-over-year changes and, for several countries, on a quarterly basis.
[3]For many countries, inflation for the earlier years is measured on the basis of a retail price index. Consumer price index (CPI) inflation data with broader and more up-to-date coverage are typically used for more recent years.
[4]Georgia, Turkmenistan, and Ukraine, which are not members of the Commonwealth of Independent States, are included in the group for reasons of geography and similarity in economic structure.
[5]Starting in 2014 data exclude Crimea and Sevastopol.
[6]Based on Eurostat's harmonized index of consumer prices.
[7]Excludes Venezuela but includes Argentina starting from 2017 onward.
[8]See country-specific notes for Argentina, Libya, and Venezuela in the "Country Notes" section of the Statistical Appendix.
[9]Data for 2011 exclude South Sudan after July 9. Data for 2012 and onward pertain to the current Sudan.
[10]Data for Syria are excluded for 2011 onward owing to the uncertain political situation.
[11]The Zimbabwe dollar ceased circulating in early 2009. Data are based on IMF staff estimates of price and exchange rate developments in US dollars. IMF staff estimates of US dollar values may differ from authorities' estimates.

Table A8. Major Advanced Economies: General Government Fiscal Balances and Debt[1]
(Percent of GDP unless noted otherwise)

	Average 2000–09	2012	2013	2014	2015	2016	2017	Projections 2018	2019	2023
Major Advanced Economies										
Net Lending/Borrowing	−4.0	−6.3	−4.1	−3.4	−2.8	−3.1	−3.0	−3.2	−3.3	−2.9
Output Gap[2]	0.0	−2.0	−1.7	−1.3	−0.6	−0.6	0.0	0.6	1.0	0.6
Structural Balance[2]	−3.8	−5.2	−3.7	−3.0	−2.7	−3.1	−3.0	−3.5	−3.7	−3.2
United States										
Net Lending/Borrowing[3]	−4.2	−7.6	−4.1	−3.7	−3.2	−3.9	−3.8	−4.7	−5.0	−4.5
Output Gap[2]	0.2	−2.3	−1.9	−1.2	−0.1	−0.2	0.2	1.1	1.6	0.9
Structural Balance[2]	−3.7	−6.1	−4.0	−3.4	−3.2	−3.9	−4.0	−5.1	−5.6	−4.8
Net Debt	45.3	80.3	80.8	80.4	80.1	81.2	78.8	77.7	77.9	83.7
Gross Debt	65.4	103.3	104.9	104.6	104.8	106.8	105.2	106.1	107.8	117.0
Euro Area										
Net Lending/Borrowing	−2.5	−3.7	−3.0	−2.5	−2.0	−1.5	−0.9	−0.6	−0.6	−0.9
Output Gap[2]	0.7	−1.8	−2.6	−2.3	−1.7	−1.2	−0.2	0.3	0.6	0.4
Structural Balance[2]	−3.0	−2.2	−1.3	−1.1	−1.0	−0.8	−0.7	−0.7	−1.0	−1.2
Net Debt	55.2	72.1	74.6	74.8	73.8	73.7	71.8	69.5	67.7	61.8
Gross Debt	68.8	89.6	91.5	91.7	89.8	88.8	86.6	84.4	82.0	74.5
Germany										
Net Lending/Borrowing	−2.2	0.0	−0.1	0.6	0.8	0.9	1.0	1.5	1.5	0.8
Output Gap[2]	−0.3	0.5	−0.3	0.1	0.1	0.2	0.9	1.2	1.4	0.7
Structural Balance[2]	−2.2	−0.1	0.2	0.9	0.8	1.0	0.9	1.0	0.7	0.4
Net Debt	52.3	58.4	57.6	54.1	51.1	48.2	44.9	41.5	38.3	29.4
Gross Debt	63.9	79.8	77.5	74.6	70.9	67.9	63.9	59.8	56.0	44.6
France										
Net Lending/Borrowing	−3.2	−5.0	−4.1	−3.9	−3.6	−3.6	−2.6	−2.6	−2.8	−2.8
Output Gap[2]	0.5	−0.6	−0.9	−0.9	−0.9	−0.9	0.0	0.1	0.3	0.3
Structural Balance[2]	−3.6	−4.5	−3.4	−3.3	−2.9	−2.8	−2.5	−2.4	−2.8	−3.0
Net Debt	56.7	80.0	83.0	85.5	86.4	87.5	87.5	87.4	87.2	84.6
Gross Debt	65.6	90.6	93.4	94.9	95.6	96.6	96.8	96.7	96.5	93.9
Italy										
Net Lending/Borrowing	−3.3	−2.9	−2.9	−3.0	−2.6	−2.5	−2.3	−1.7	−1.7	−2.2
Output Gap[2]	0.1	−2.8	−4.1	−4.1	−3.2	−2.6	−1.5	−0.8	−0.3	0.0
Structural Balance[2,4]	−4.0	−1.5	−0.6	−1.0	−0.7	−1.3	−1.6	−1.3	−1.5	−2.2
Net Debt	94.9	111.6	116.7	118.8	119.5	119.5	119.5	118.3	117.0	114.4
Gross Debt	103.2	123.4	129.0	131.8	131.5	132.0	131.8	130.3	128.7	125.1
Japan										
Net Lending/Borrowing	−6.3	−8.6	−7.9	−5.6	−3.8	−3.7	−4.3	−3.7	−2.8	−2.0
Output Gap[2]	−1.3	−3.7	−2.2	−2.6	−2.0	−1.8	−0.8	−0.3	0.1	0.0
Structural Balance[2]	−5.9	−7.4	−7.3	−5.3	−4.2	−4.1	−4.1	−3.6	−2.8	−2.0
Net Debt	93.6	146.7	146.4	148.5	147.6	152.8	154.9	155.7	154.8	153.8
Gross Debt[5]	168.9	229.0	232.5	236.1	231.3	235.6	237.6	238.2	236.6	235.4
United Kingdom										
Net Lending/Borrowing	−3.0	−7.6	−5.3	−5.4	−4.2	−2.9	−1.8	−2.0	−1.7	−0.8
Output Gap[2]	0.9	−2.0	−1.8	−0.7	−0.1	−0.1	0.0	0.0	0.0	0.0
Structural Balance[2]	−3.7	−6.0	−3.9	−4.6	−4.0	−2.9	−1.8	−2.0	−1.7	−0.8
Net Debt	36.7	75.5	76.8	78.8	79.3	78.8	77.9	78.0	77.6	74.5
Gross Debt	41.6	84.1	85.2	87.0	87.9	87.9	87.5	87.4	87.2	84.0
Canada										
Net Lending/Borrowing	0.5	−2.5	−1.5	0.2	−0.1	−1.1	−1.1	−1.2	−1.1	−0.9
Output Gap[2]	0.5	−0.5	0.0	0.8	−0.2	−0.9	0.1	0.2	0.3	0.0
Structural Balance[2]	0.2	−2.3	−1.5	−0.5	0.0	−0.7	−1.2	−1.4	−1.3	−0.9
Net Debt[6]	31.3	28.3	29.3	28.0	27.7	28.5	27.7	27.7	27.2	25.3
Gross Debt	74.6	84.8	85.8	85.0	90.5	91.1	89.7	87.3	84.7	76.6

Note: The methodology and specific assumptions for each country are discussed in Box A1. The country group composites for fiscal data are calculated as the sum of the US dollar values for the relevant individual countries.

[1]Debt data refer to the end of the year and are not always comparable across countries. Gross and net debt levels reported by national statistical agencies for countries that have adopted the System of National Accounts (SNA) 2008 (Australia, Canada, Hong Kong SAR, United States) are adjusted to exclude unfunded pension liabilities of government employees' defined-benefit pension plans. Fiscal data for the aggregated major advanced economies and the United States start in 2001, and the average for the aggregate and the United States is therefore for the period 2001–07.

[2]Percent of potential GDP.

[3]Figures reported by the national statistical agency are adjusted to exclude items related to the accrual-basis accounting of government employees' defined-benefit pension plans.

[4]Excludes one-time measures based on the authorities' data and, if unavailable, on receipts from the sale of assets.

[5]Nonconsolidated basis.

[6]Includes equity shares.

Table A9. Summary of World Trade Volumes and Prices
(Annual percent change)

| | Averages | | 2010 | 2011 | 2012 | 2013 | 2014 | 2015 | 2016 | 2017 | Projections | |
	2000–09	2010–19									2018	2019
Trade in Goods and Services												
World Trade[1]												
Volume	5.0	4.8	12.5	7.2	3.0	3.6	3.8	2.8	2.2	5.2	4.2	4.0
Price Deflator												
In US Dollars	3.4	0.3	5.5	11.0	−1.7	−0.7	−1.8	−13.2	−4.1	4.2	5.4	0.4
In SDRs	2.1	1.2	6.6	7.3	1.3	0.1	−1.7	−5.8	−3.5	4.5	2.9	1.3
Volume of Trade												
Exports												
Advanced Economies	3.9	4.4	12.1	6.1	2.9	3.2	3.9	3.8	1.8	4.4	3.4	3.1
Emerging Market and Developing Economies	8.0	5.5	13.8	8.9	3.5	4.7	3.2	1.6	3.0	6.9	4.7	4.8
Imports												
Advanced Economies	3.6	4.4	11.6	5.3	1.7	2.5	3.9	4.8	2.4	4.2	3.7	4.0
Emerging Market and Developing Economies	9.1	5.8	14.2	11.6	5.3	5.1	4.2	−0.9	1.8	7.0	6.0	4.8
Terms of Trade												
Advanced Economies	−0.2	0.1	−0.8	−1.5	−0.7	0.9	0.3	1.9	1.0	−0.2	−0.1	0.1
Emerging Market and Developing Economies	1.4	0.1	1.7	4.0	0.6	−0.6	−0.6	−4.3	−1.4	0.6	1.6	−0.2
Trade in Goods												
World Trade[1]												
Volume	4.9	4.8	14.4	7.4	2.8	3.2	2.9	2.0	2.1	5.4	4.4	4.1
Price Deflator												
In US Dollars	3.3	0.3	6.5	12.2	−1.9	−1.2	−2.3	−14.2	−4.9	5.0	5.8	0.3
In SDRs	2.0	1.2	7.6	8.4	1.1	−0.4	−2.3	−6.9	−4.2	5.2	3.3	1.2
World Trade Prices in US Dollars[2]												
Manufactures	1.7	0.3	2.2	4.1	2.7	−3.0	−0.5	−2.3	−5.2	1.7	2.5	1.6
Oil	13.1	1.1	27.9	31.6	1.0	−0.9	−7.5	−47.2	−15.7	23.3	31.4	−0.9
Nonfuel Primary Commodities	5.3	1.2	26.7	18.1	−10.2	−1.5	−3.9	−17.6	−1.5	6.8	2.7	−0.7
Food	5.5	1.3	12.3	20.5	−2.9	0.4	−4.1	−17.4	2.7	2.2	2.3	1.7
Beverages	5.2	−1.2	14.1	16.6	−18.6	−11.9	20.7	−3.1	−5.0	−9.3	−5.7	−2.7
Agricultural Raw Materials	0.1	2.1	33.2	22.7	−12.7	1.6	2.0	−13.5	−5.7	2.3	1.5	−1.5
Metal	9.4	0.8	48.2	13.5	−16.8	−4.3	−10.1	−23.0	−5.4	22.2	5.3	−3.6
World Trade Prices in SDRs[2]												
Manufactures	0.5	1.3	3.2	0.6	5.9	−2.2	−0.4	6.1	−4.6	1.9	0.2	2.5
Oil	11.8	2.0	29.3	27.2	4.1	−0.1	−7.5	−42.7	−15.1	23.6	28.3	0.1
Nonfuel Primary Commodities	4.1	2.1	28.0	14.2	−7.4	−0.7	−3.9	−10.5	−0.9	7.0	0.3	0.3
Food	4.2	2.3	13.5	16.5	0.1	1.2	−4.1	−10.3	3.4	2.5	0.0	2.7
Beverages	4.0	−0.3	15.3	12.7	−16.1	−11.2	20.8	5.2	−4.4	−9.0	−7.9	−1.8
Agricultural Raw Materials	−1.1	3.1	34.6	18.5	−10.0	2.4	2.0	−6.1	−5.1	2.5	−0.8	−0.6
Metal	8.1	1.8	49.8	9.7	−14.3	−3.5	−10.1	−16.4	−4.8	22.5	2.9	−2.7
World Trade Prices in Euros[2]												
Manufactures	−1.0	2.1	7.2	−0.7	11.2	−6.1	−0.5	17.0	−4.9	−0.4	−2.4	2.9
Oil	10.2	2.9	34.3	25.5	9.3	−4.1	−7.6	−36.8	−15.4	20.8	25.1	0.4
Nonfuel Primary Commodities	2.6	2.9	32.9	12.7	−2.8	−4.6	−4.0	−1.3	−1.3	4.6	−2.3	0.6
Food	2.7	3.1	17.9	14.9	5.1	−2.8	−4.2	−1.1	3.0	0.2	−2.6	3.1
Beverages	2.5	0.5	19.8	11.2	−11.9	−14.7	20.7	16.1	−4.8	−11.1	−10.2	−1.4
Agricultural Raw Materials	−2.6	3.9	39.8	17.0	−5.5	−1.7	1.9	3.6	−5.5	0.2	−3.4	−0.2
Metal	6.6	2.6	55.5	8.3	−10.0	−7.3	−10.2	−7.8	−5.1	19.8	0.2	−2.3

Table A9. Summary of World Trade Volumes and Prices (continued)

(Annual percent change)

	Averages										Projections	
	2000–09	2010–19	2010	2011	2012	2013	2014	2015	2016	2017	2018	2019
Trade in Goods												
Volume of Trade												
Exports												
Advanced Economies	3.6	4.4	14.4	6.3	2.6	2.6	3.1	2.7	1.5	4.2	3.6	3.1
Emerging Market and Developing Economies	7.9	5.4	15.4	7.8	3.8	4.6	2.6	1.2	2.9	6.6	4.5	4.7
Fuel Exporters	5.1	2.3	6.2	5.7	2.7	2.0	−0.2	3.4	2.2	0.7	−0.4	1.3
Nonfuel Exporters	9.0	6.4	19.1	8.7	4.3	5.8	3.8	0.4	3.1	8.1	5.8	5.7
Imports												
Advanced Economies	3.4	4.4	13.3	6.0	1.1	2.0	3.3	3.4	2.3	4.7	4.2	4.3
Emerging Market and Developing Economies	9.1	5.8	15.4	11.3	5.1	4.7	2.5	−0.8	2.2	7.2	6.3	4.8
Fuel Exporters	11.0	2.7	7.8	11.8	8.5	3.7	1.0	−7.5	−5.2	2.9	4.6	0.6
Nonfuel Exporters	8.7	6.4	17.3	11.2	4.4	4.9	2.9	0.7	3.7	8.1	6.6	5.5
Price Deflators in SDRs												
Exports												
Advanced Economies	1.3	1.0	4.7	6.1	−0.4	0.3	−1.8	−6.0	−2.1	4.7	3.4	1.3
Emerging Market and Developing Economies	4.6	1.8	12.3	13.1	3.1	−1.2	−3.1	−8.9	−7.3	6.6	4.1	1.1
Fuel Exporters	9.0	1.8	21.9	25.7	4.4	−2.5	−6.9	−30.1	−13.5	16.6	16.0	0.8
Nonfuel Exporters	2.8	1.6	8.6	8.1	2.4	−0.6	−1.4	−0.7	−5.5	4.1	1.0	1.1
Imports												
Advanced Economies	1.6	0.9	6.1	8.0	0.7	−0.5	−2.0	−7.8	−3.5	4.6	3.2	1.2
Emerging Market and Developing Economies	2.7	1.6	11.1	8.2	2.5	−0.7	−2.6	−4.5	−5.7	5.6	2.6	1.3
Fuel Exporters	3.3	1.5	8.5	6.4	3.2	0.0	−2.3	−3.1	−3.8	3.3	1.4	1.7
Nonfuel Exporters	2.6	1.7	11.7	8.6	2.4	−0.9	−2.7	−4.9	−6.1	6.0	2.8	1.3
Terms of Trade												
Advanced Economies	−0.3	0.1	−1.3	−1.8	−1.1	0.9	0.2	2.0	1.4	0.1	0.3	0.1
Emerging Market and Developing Economies	1.8	0.1	1.2	4.5	0.5	−0.5	−0.4	−4.5	−1.7	1.0	1.5	−0.3
Regional Groups												
Commonwealth of Independent States[3]	3.6	0.5	12.7	20.9	1.6	−6.6	−1.9	−22.0	−13.5	10.7	12.3	−1.1
Emerging and Developing Asia	−0.9	−0.1	−6.6	−2.7	1.4	1.1	2.5	8.7	0.1	−3.4	−1.6	0.5
Emerging and Developing Europe	1.6	−0.8	−5.4	0.0	−1.1	2.1	0.9	−0.4	0.6	−2.8	−1.2	−0.3
Latin America and the Caribbean	2.3	0.0	7.2	5.2	−1.8	−1.3	−2.4	−9.0	1.2	4.5	−1.0	−1.7
Middle East, North Africa, Afghanistan, and												
Pakistan	5.0	−0.1	8.5	12.7	−0.1	−0.1	−4.6	−25.8	−6.2	10.0	11.5	−0.7
Middle East and North Africa	5.3	−0.1	8.4	12.9	0.5	−0.1	−4.7	−26.5	−6.8	10.3	11.9	−0.5
Sub-Saharan Africa	3.6	0.9	12.3	12.3	−1.4	−2.0	−3.3	−15.4	−0.1	7.0	4.0	−1.4
Analytical Groups												
By Source of Export Earnings												
Fuel	5.6	0.4	12.4	18.1	1.2	−2.5	−4.7	−27.9	−10.1	12.9	14.4	−0.9
Nonfuel	0.3	0.0	−2.8	−0.5	0.1	0.3	1.3	4.4	0.6	−1.8	−1.7	−0.1
Memorandum												
World Exports in Billions of US Dollars												
Goods and Services	12,367	22,609	18,728	22,307	22,608	23,323	23,749	21,097	20,692	22,713	24,921	25,947
Goods	9,794	17,666	14,900	17,929	18,130	18,546	18,629	16,200	15,732	17,400	19,208	19,985
Average Oil Price[4]	13.1	1.1	27.9	31.6	1.0	−0.9	−7.5	−47.2	−15.7	23.3	31.4	−0.9
In US Dollars a Barrel	49.17	77.29	79.03	104.01	105.01	104.07	96.25	50.79	42.84	52.81	69.38	68.76
Export Unit Value of Manufactures[5]	1.7	0.3	2.2	4.1	2.7	−3.0	−0.5	−2.3	−5.2	1.7	2.5	1.6

[1]Average of annual percent change for world exports and imports.

[2]As represented, respectively, by the export unit value index for manufactures of the advanced economies and accounting for 83 percent of the advanced economies' trade (export of goods) weights; the average of UK Brent, Dubai Fateh, and West Texas Intermediate crude oil prices; and the average of world market prices for nonfuel primary commodities weighted by their 2002–04 shares in world commodity exports.

[3]Georgia, Turkmenistan, and Ukraine, which are not members of the Commonwealth of Independent States, are included in this group for reasons of geography and similarity in economic structure.

[4]Percent change of average of UK Brent, Dubai Fateh, and West Texas Intermediate crude oil prices.

[5]Percent change for manufactures exported by the advanced economies.

Table A10. Summary of Current Account Balances
(Billions of US dollars)

	2010	2011	2012	2013	2014	2015	2016	2017	2018	2019	2023
									Projections		
Advanced Economies	**−1.7**	**−35.9**	**23.3**	**218.9**	**244.7**	**299.0**	**333.7**	**439.8**	**380.4**	**259.8**	**219.1**
United States	−431.3	−445.7	−426.8	−348.8	−365.2	−407.8	−432.9	−449.1	−515.7	−652.1	−809.6
Euro Area	−7.7	−12.4	174.1	293.1	331.8	377.1	429.4	436.5	417.9	407.3	439.0
Germany	192.3	229.7	248.9	252.5	291.0	301.2	297.5	291.0	326.9	323.6	359.2
France	−16.7	−24.6	−25.9	−14.3	−27.3	−9.0	−18.5	−14.8	−25.6	−19.9	−3.3
Italy	−72.6	−68.3	−7.0	21.3	41.3	27.8	47.6	53.4	41.3	33.6	18.8
Spain	−56.2	−47.4	−3.1	20.7	14.9	13.5	23.8	24.7	16.6	17.3	25.4
Japan	221.0	129.8	59.7	45.9	36.8	136.4	194.9	196.1	183.7	196.2	245.0
United Kingdom	−82.9	−51.6	−100.9	−141.9	−149.6	−142.4	−139.3	−99.2	−99.2	−90.3	−93.0
Canada	−58.2	−49.6	−65.7	−59.4	−43.2	−55.9	−49.3	−48.8	−52.2	−45.6	−48.0
Other Advanced Economies[1]	283.4	266.0	272.2	347.5	360.4	366.6	348.3	356.8	370.4	367.2	394.3
Emerging Market and Developing Economies	**278.5**	**375.8**	**355.3**	**178.7**	**173.9**	**−58.3**	**−72.8**	**−14.0**	**−7.4**	**−4.2**	**−340.8**
Regional Groups											
Commonwealth of Independent States[2]	68.9	107.3	67.5	17.9	57.6	53.1	0.8	23.5	86.4	73.9	49.7
Russia	67.5	97.3	71.3	33.4	57.5	67.7	24.4	35.4	97.1	85.6	61.0
Excluding Russia	1.4	10.0	−3.8	−15.5	0.1	−14.6	−23.6	−12.0	−10.7	−11.7	−11.3
Emerging and Developing Asia	232.6	97.4	121.2	99.3	231.8	312.1	228.7	151.2	28.2	32.3	−104.8
China	237.8	136.1	215.4	148.2	236.0	304.2	202.2	164.9	97.5	98.4	17.5
India	−47.9	−78.2	−87.8	−32.3	−26.8	−22.1	−14.4	−48.7	−80.4	−74.0	−112.3
ASEAN-5[3]	45.4	49.6	6.3	−3.5	22.5	30.9	43.2	45.9	31.2	26.0	3.2
Emerging and Developing Europe	−86.8	−119.4	−81.8	−71.9	−59.7	−35.2	−32.7	−49.4	−53.2	−26.1	−49.4
Latin America and the Caribbean	−96.0	−111.6	−136.7	−163.4	−184.9	−173.3	−95.0	−82.1	−85.6	−92.9	−127.1
Brazil	−75.8	−77.0	−74.2	−74.8	−104.2	−59.4	−23.5	−9.8	−24.8	−30.9	−44.7
Mexico	−5.2	−12.5	−18.6	−31.0	−24.0	−29.8	−23.3	−19.4	−15.3	−16.0	−24.0
Middle East, North Africa, Afghanistan, and Pakistan	170.2	410.7	411.8	332.5	191.8	−123.1	−119.5	−21.4	62.9	67.3	−27.6
Sub-Saharan Africa	−10.4	−8.7	−26.7	−35.7	−62.6	−91.8	−55.1	−35.8	−46.1	−58.8	−81.6
South Africa	−5.6	−9.2	−20.3	−21.2	−17.8	−14.6	−8.2	−8.6	−12.1	−13.5	−16.5
Analytical Groups											
By Source of Export Earnings											
Fuel	309.5	619.9	597.0	465.5	311.6	−78.1	−76.5	74.8	228.7	220.6	99.0
Nonfuel	−29.4	−244.0	−241.7	−286.7	−137.7	19.8	3.7	−88.8	−236.1	−224.8	−439.8
Of Which, Primary Products	−11.5	−28.6	−64.6	−82.9	−55.4	−62.5	−41.3	−55.3	−55.5	−57.2	−63.3
By External Financing Source											
Net Debtor Economies	−262.6	−348.5	−401.9	−374.5	−369.8	−339.9	−257.9	−276.3	−351.7	−340.9	−457.2
Net Debtor Economies by Debt-Servicing Experience											
Economies with Arrears and/or Rescheduling during 2013–17	−23.3	−37.0	−55.0	−54.4	−39.2	−49.0	−52.7	−44.2	−40.1	−44.5	−59.1
Memorandum											
World	**276.7**	**339.9**	**378.6**	**397.6**	**418.7**	**240.6**	**260.8**	**425.8**	**373.0**	**255.6**	**−121.7**
European Union	−9.4	77.0	206.6	287.1	304.4	310.8	324.9	433.3	429.0	424.4	459.6
Low-Income Developing Countries	−16.6	−22.8	−32.8	−39.7	−43.9	−77.5	−42.5	−35.5	−53.8	−65.0	−88.4
Middle East and North Africa	169.7	405.8	414.3	335.0	193.7	−120.9	−116.1	−9.9	80.1	83.0	−1.2

Table A10. Summary of Current Account Balances *(continued)*
(Percent of GDP)

	2010	2011	2012	2013	2014	2015	2016	2017	Projections 2018	Projections 2019	Projections 2023
Advanced Economies	**0.0**	**−0.1**	**0.1**	**0.5**	**0.5**	**0.7**	**0.7**	**0.9**	**0.7**	**0.5**	**0.4**
United States	−2.9	−2.9	−2.6	−2.1	−2.1	−2.2	−2.3	−2.3	−2.5	−3.0	−3.3
Euro Area	−0.1	−0.1	1.4	2.2	2.5	3.2	3.6	3.5	3.0	2.9	2.6
Germany	5.6	6.1	7.0	6.7	7.5	8.9	8.5	7.9	8.1	7.9	7.3
France	−0.6	−0.9	−1.0	−0.5	−1.0	−0.4	−0.8	−0.6	−0.9	−0.7	−0.1
Italy	−3.4	−3.0	−0.3	1.0	1.9	1.5	2.6	2.8	2.0	1.6	0.8
Spain	−3.9	−3.2	−0.2	1.5	1.1	1.1	1.9	1.9	1.2	1.2	1.4
Japan	3.9	2.1	1.0	0.9	0.8	3.1	3.9	4.0	3.6	3.8	4.1
United Kingdom	−3.4	−2.0	−3.8	−5.1	−4.9	−4.9	−5.2	−3.8	−3.5	−3.2	−2.9
Canada	−3.6	−2.8	−3.6	−3.2	−2.4	−3.6	−3.2	−2.9	−3.0	−2.5	−2.1
Other Advanced Economies[1]	5.0	4.1	4.1	5.1	5.2	5.8	5.4	5.1	5.0	4.8	4.3
Emerging Market and Developing Economies	**1.2**	**1.4**	**1.3**	**0.6**	**0.6**	**−0.2**	**−0.2**	**0.0**	**0.0**	**0.0**	**−0.7**
Regional Groups											
Commonwealth of Independent States[2]	3.2	4.0	2.4	0.6	2.1	2.8	0.0	1.1	4.1	3.3	1.9
Russia	4.1	4.7	3.2	1.5	2.8	4.9	1.9	2.2	6.2	5.2	3.4
Excluding Russia	0.3	1.7	−0.6	−2.2	0.0	−2.7	−5.1	−2.4	−1.9	−2.0	−1.5
Emerging and Developing Asia	2.4	0.8	0.9	0.7	1.5	2.0	1.4	0.9	0.1	0.2	−0.4
China	3.9	1.8	2.5	1.5	2.2	2.7	1.8	1.4	0.7	0.7	0.1
India	−2.8	−4.3	−4.8	−1.7	−1.3	−1.1	−0.6	−1.9	−3.0	−2.5	−2.6
ASEAN-5[3]	2.7	2.6	0.3	−0.2	1.1	1.5	2.0	2.0	1.3	1.0	0.1
Emerging and Developing Europe	−5.0	−6.3	−4.4	−3.6	−2.9	−1.9	−1.8	−2.6	−2.8	−1.4	−1.9
Latin America and the Caribbean	−1.9	−1.9	−2.3	−2.7	−3.1	−3.3	−1.9	−1.5	−1.6	−1.8	−2.0
Brazil	−3.4	−2.9	−3.0	−3.0	−4.2	−3.3	−1.3	−0.5	−1.3	−1.6	−1.9
Mexico	−0.5	−1.1	−1.5	−2.4	−1.8	−2.5	−2.2	−1.7	−1.3	−1.3	−1.6
Middle East, North Africa, Afghanistan, and Pakistan	6.1	12.7	12.5	9.8	5.5	−4.0	−3.9	−0.7	1.8	1.9	−0.6
Sub-Saharan Africa	−0.8	−0.6	−1.7	−2.2	−3.6	−6.0	−3.9	−2.3	−2.8	−3.4	−3.4
South Africa	−1.5	−2.2	−5.1	−5.8	−5.1	−4.6	−2.8	−2.5	−3.2	−3.5	−3.6
Analytical Groups											
By Source of Export Earnings											
Fuel	6.4	10.5	9.6	7.3	5.0	−1.6	−1.7	1.5	4.3	4.1	1.5
Nonfuel	−0.2	−1.2	−1.1	−1.2	−0.6	0.1	0.0	−0.3	−0.8	−0.8	−1.1
Of Which, Primary Products	−0.8	−1.7	−3.5	−4.4	−3.0	−3.4	−2.4	−2.9	−3.0	−3.1	−2.8
By External Financing Source											
Net Debtor Economies	−2.3	−2.7	−3.1	−2.7	−2.6	−2.7	−2.0	−2.0	−2.5	−2.3	−2.3
Net Debtor Economies by Debt-Servicing Experience											
Economies with Arrears and/or Rescheduling during 2013–17	−3.4	−4.8	−6.7	−6.2	−4.5	−5.7	−6.2	−5.7	−4.9	−4.9	−4.9
Memorandum											
World	**0.4**	**0.5**	**0.5**	**0.5**	**0.5**	**0.3**	**0.3**	**0.5**	**0.4**	**0.3**	**−0.1**
European Union	−0.1	0.4	1.2	1.6	1.6	1.9	2.0	2.5	2.3	2.2	2.0
Low-Income Developing Countries	−1.3	−1.5	−2.0	−2.2	−2.3	−4.2	−2.4	−1.9	−2.7	−3.0	−2.9
Middle East and North Africa	6.6	13.5	13.5	10.7	6.0	−4.3	−4.2	−0.3	2.6	2.6	0.0

Table A10. Summary of Current Account Balances *(continued)*
(Percent of exports of goods and services)

	2010	2011	2012	2013	2014	2015	2016	2017	Projections 2018	Projections 2019	Projections 2023
Advanced Economies	**0.0**	**−0.3**	**0.2**	**1.5**	**1.6**	**2.2**	**2.5**	**3.0**	**2.4**	**1.6**	**1.1**
United States	−23.3	−21.0	−19.2	−15.2	−15.4	−18.0	−19.5	−19.1	−20.4	−24.9	−27.8
Euro Area	−0.3	−0.4	5.4	8.6	9.3	11.7	13.3	12.3	. . .	. . .	. . .
Germany	13.3	13.6	15.3	14.8	16.3	19.0	18.5	16.7	17.3	16.5	15.0
France	−2.3	−3.0	−3.2	−1.7	−3.1	−1.2	−2.4	−1.8	−2.9	−2.1	−0.3
Italy	−13.5	−11.1	−1.2	3.5	6.5	5.1	8.6	8.8	6.2	4.9	2.4
Spain	−15.3	−11.0	−0.8	4.7	3.3	3.4	5.8	5.5	3.4	3.4	3.9
Japan	25.4	13.9	6.5	5.5	4.3	17.4	24.0	22.4	19.5	20.3	23.6
United Kingdom	−12.0	−6.4	−12.6	−17.3	−17.5	−17.9	−18.5	−12.5	−11.7	−10.7	−10.2
Canada	−12.4	−9.1	−11.9	−10.7	−7.6	−11.4	−10.4	−9.5	−9.6	−8.0	−7.1
Other Advanced Economies[1]	8.6	6.8	6.8	8.4	8.7	9.9	9.6	9.1	8.7	8.3	7.4
Emerging Market and Developing											
Economies	**4.0**	**4.5**	**3.9**	**2.0**	**2.2**	**−0.6**	**−0.9**	**−0.2**	**−0.1**	**−0.1**	**−2.9**
Regional Groups											
Commonwealth of Independent States[2]	10.3	12.1	7.4	2.0	6.8	9.0	0.2	3.8	11.6	9.7	5.9
Russia	15.3	17.0	12.1	5.6	10.2	17.2	7.3	8.6	19.5	16.9	11.2
Excluding Russia	0.6	3.2	−1.2	−5.1	0.0	−7.5	−13.6	−5.8	−4.4	−4.6	−3.8
Emerging and Developing Asia	8.3	2.8	3.3	2.6	5.8	8.2	6.2	3.7	0.6	0.7	−1.8
China	14.8	6.8	9.9	6.3	9.6	12.9	9.2	6.8	3.7	3.6	0.6
India	−12.6	−17.2	−19.4	−6.9	−5.6	−5.3	−3.2	−9.7	−14.4	−12.0	−12.8
ASEAN-5[3]	6.1	5.5	0.7	−0.4	2.3	3.4	4.7	4.4	2.7	2.1	0.2
Emerging and Developing Europe	−14.8	−17.2	−11.8	−9.7	−7.6	−5.0	−4.5	−6.1	−5.8	−2.7	−4.0
Latin America and the Caribbean	−9.6	−9.0	−10.7	−12.9	−14.9	−16.0	−9.0	−7.0	−6.8	−7.1	−7.9
Brazil	−32.7	−26.3	−26.4	−26.8	−39.5	−26.5	−10.8	−3.9	−9.2	−11.1	−13.7
Mexico	−1.7	−3.4	−4.8	−7.8	−5.7	−7.4	−5.8	−4.4	−3.2	−3.1	−3.7
Middle East, North Africa, Afghanistan, and											
Pakistan	13.6	26.8	24.3	20.9	13.7	−9.9	−10.6	−2.0	4.5	4.6	−1.8
Sub-Saharan Africa	−2.7	−1.8	−5.6	−7.4	−13.8	−26.6	−17.5	−9.7	−11.0	−13.4	−15.8
South Africa	−5.2	−7.3	−17.3	−18.7	−16.1	−15.2	−9.1	−8.3	−11.0	−12.0	−12.5
Analytical Groups											
By Source of Export Earnings											
Fuel	16.5	25.3	22.6	18.4	13.8	−4.2	−4.9	4.2	11.2	10.7	4.8
Nonfuel	−0.6	−4.2	−4.0	−4.5	−2.1	0.3	0.1	−1.4	−3.3	−3.0	−4.6
Of Which, Primary Products	−2.9	−5.9	−13.5	−17.6	−12.1	−16.0	−10.7	−12.6	−11.8	−11.7	−10.6
By External Financing Source											
Net Debtor Economies	−8.7	−9.5	−10.8	−9.8	−9.6	−10.0	−7.7	−7.3	−8.3	−7.5	−7.7
Net Debtor Economies by											
Debt-Servicing Experience											
Economies with Arrears and/or											
Rescheduling during 2013–17	−10.9	−14.7	−22.1	−21.9	−16.9	−25.4	−30.0	−22.3	−17.5	−17.8	−18.5
Memorandum											
World	**1.4**	**1.5**	**1.6**	**1.7**	**1.8**	**1.2**	**1.3**	**1.9**	**1.5**	**1.0**	**−0.4**
European Union	−0.1	1.0	2.8	3.7	3.8	4.3	4.5	5.5	4.9	4.7	4.2
Low-Income Developing Countries	−4.5	−4.8	−6.8	−7.7	−8.3	−16.2	−8.9	−6.3	−8.3	−9.1	−8.4
Middle East and North Africa	13.9	27.1	25.0	21.5	14.1	−10.0	−10.6	−1.1	5.8	5.9	0.0

[1]Excludes the G7 (Canada, France, Germany, Italy, Japan, United Kingdom, United States) and euro area countries.
[2]Georgia, Turkmenistan, and Ukraine, which are not members of the Commonwealth of Independent States, are included in this group for reasons of geography and similarity in economic structure.
[3]Indonesia, Malaysia, Philippines, Thailand, Vietnam.

Table A11. Advanced Economies: Balance on Current Account
(Percent of GDP)

	2010	2011	2012	2013	2014	2015	2016	2017	Projections 2018	2019	2023
Advanced Economies	**0.0**	**−0.1**	**0.1**	**0.5**	**0.5**	**0.7**	**0.7**	**0.9**	**0.7**	**0.5**	**0.4**
United States	−2.9	−2.9	−2.6	−2.1	−2.1	−2.2	−2.3	−2.3	−2.5	−3.0	−3.3
Euro Area[1]	−0.1	−0.1	1.4	2.2	2.5	3.2	3.6	3.5	3.0	2.9	2.6
Germany	5.6	6.1	7.0	6.7	7.5	8.9	8.5	7.9	8.1	7.9	7.3
France	−0.6	−0.9	−1.0	−0.5	−1.0	−0.4	−0.8	−0.6	−0.9	−0.7	−0.1
Italy	−3.4	−3.0	−0.3	1.0	1.9	1.5	2.6	2.8	2.0	1.6	0.8
Spain	−3.9	−3.2	−0.2	1.5	1.1	1.1	1.9	1.9	1.2	1.2	1.4
Netherlands	7.3	9.0	10.7	9.7	8.5	6.3	8.0	10.5	9.9	9.7	8.3
Belgium	1.8	−1.1	−0.1	−0.3	−0.9	−0.1	0.1	−0.2	0.1	−0.1	0.2
Austria	2.9	1.6	1.5	1.9	2.5	1.9	2.1	1.9	2.2	1.8	2.0
Greece	−11.4	−10.0	−3.8	−2.0	−1.6	−0.2	−1.1	−0.8	−0.8	−0.4	0.0
Portugal	−10.1	−6.0	−1.8	1.6	0.1	0.1	0.6	0.5	0.0	−0.3	−1.5
Ireland	−1.2	−1.6	−2.6	1.5	1.1	4.4	−4.2	8.5	7.4	6.7	5.0
Finland	1.1	−1.7	−2.3	−1.9	−1.5	−0.9	−0.3	0.7	0.9	0.9	1.1
Slovak Republic	−4.7	−5.0	0.9	1.9	1.1	−1.7	−1.5	−2.1	−1.8	−0.9	0.2
Lithuania	−1.3	−4.5	−1.4	0.8	3.2	−2.8	−1.1	0.8	0.3	0.0	−2.3
Slovenia	−0.1	0.2	2.1	4.4	5.8	4.5	5.5	7.1	6.3	5.5	2.6
Luxembourg	6.7	6.0	5.6	5.5	5.2	5.1	5.1	5.0	4.9	4.8	4.6
Latvia	2.0	−3.2	−3.6	−2.7	−1.7	−0.5	1.4	−0.8	−2.0	−2.6	−3.4
Estonia	1.8	1.3	−1.9	0.5	0.3	2.0	1.9	3.1	2.2	1.1	−2.4
Cyprus	−11.3	−4.1	−6.0	−4.9	−4.3	−1.5	−4.9	−6.7	−3.1	−5.2	−3.6
Malta	−4.7	−0.2	1.7	2.7	8.8	4.5	7.0	13.6	11.6	11.1	10.6
Japan	3.9	2.1	1.0	0.9	0.8	3.1	3.9	4.0	3.6	3.8	4.1
United Kingdom	−3.4	−2.0	−3.8	−5.1	−4.9	−4.9	−5.2	−3.8	−3.5	−3.2	−2.9
Korea	2.6	1.6	4.2	6.2	6.0	7.7	7.0	5.1	5.0	4.7	4.1
Canada	−3.6	−2.8	−3.6	−3.2	−2.4	−3.6	−3.2	−2.9	−3.0	−2.5	−2.1
Australia	−3.7	−3.1	−4.3	−3.4	−3.1	−4.6	−3.3	−2.6	−2.8	−3.1	−2.7
Taiwan Province of China	8.3	7.8	8.9	10.0	11.5	14.2	13.7	14.5	13.8	13.6	10.5
Switzerland	14.8	7.9	10.3	11.3	8.5	10.8	9.4	9.8	10.2	9.8	9.3
Sweden	6.0	5.6	5.6	5.2	4.5	4.5	4.3	3.3	2.6	2.8	3.0
Singapore	23.4	22.1	17.0	16.5	18.7	18.6	19.0	18.8	18.5	18.3	15.9
Hong Kong SAR	7.0	5.6	1.6	1.5	1.4	3.3	4.0	4.3	3.4	3.1	3.4
Norway	10.9	12.4	12.5	10.3	10.5	7.9	3.8	5.5	7.8	7.8	7.1
Czech Republic	−3.6	−2.1	−1.6	−0.5	0.2	0.2	1.6	1.1	−0.4	−0.9	−1.9
Israel	3.9	2.1	0.5	3.0	4.4	5.3	3.8	2.9	2.3	2.3	2.9
Denmark	6.6	6.6	6.3	7.8	8.9	8.8	7.3	7.6	7.7	7.5	6.3
New Zealand	−2.3	−2.8	−3.9	−3.2	−3.2	−3.1	−2.3	−2.7	−3.6	−3.8	−3.8
Puerto Rico	...	...	...	...	...	...	...	...	...	...	...
Macao SAR	39.4	40.9	39.3	40.2	34.2	25.3	27.0	33.3	35.9	38.1	41.0
Iceland	−6.4	−5.1	−3.8	5.8	3.9	5.2	7.5	3.5	2.4	2.0	2.2
San Marino	...	...	...	...	...	...	...	...	...	...	...
Memorandum											
Major Advanced Economies	−0.8	−0.8	−0.9	−0.7	−0.6	−0.4	−0.3	−0.2	−0.4	−0.6	−0.7
Euro Area[2]	0.5	0.8	2.3	2.8	3.0	3.4	3.4	3.8	3.6	3.5	3.2

[1]Data corrected for reporting discrepancies in intra-area transactions.
[2]Data calculated as the sum of the balances of individual euro area countries.

Table A12. Emerging Market and Developing Economies: Balance on Current Account
(Percent of GDP)

	2010	2011	2012	2013	2014	2015	2016	2017	Projections 2018	Projections 2019	Projections 2023
Commonwealth of Independent States[1]	**3.2**	**4.0**	**2.4**	**0.6**	**2.1**	**2.8**	**0.0**	**1.1**	**4.1**	**3.3**	**1.9**
Russia	4.1	4.7	3.2	1.5	2.8	4.9	1.9	2.2	6.2	5.2	3.4
Excluding Russia	0.3	1.7	−0.6	−2.2	0.0	−2.7	−5.1	−2.4	−1.9	−2.0	−1.5
Armenia	−13.6	−10.4	−10.0	−7.3	−7.6	−2.6	−2.3	−2.8	−3.8	−3.8	−4.7
Azerbaijan	28.4	26.0	21.4	16.6	13.9	−0.4	−3.6	4.1	6.6	8.1	9.6
Belarus	−14.5	−8.2	−2.8	−10.0	−6.6	−3.3	−3.5	−1.7	−2.5	−4.2	−2.0
Georgia	−10.3	−12.8	−11.7	−5.8	−10.7	−12.0	−12.8	−8.9	−10.5	−10.2	−8.6
Kazakhstan	0.9	5.3	0.5	0.5	2.8	−2.8	−6.5	−3.4	−0.2	0.2	0.6
Kyrgyz Republic	−2.2	−2.9	3.7	−13.3	−16.0	−16.0	−11.6	−4.0	−12.3	−11.8	−12.6
Moldova	−6.4	−10.0	−6.5	−4.2	−4.5	−4.9	−3.4	−6.3	−7.4	−6.3	−5.7
Tajikistan	−9.6	−7.3	−9.2	−7.8	−2.8	−6.0	−5.2	−0.5	−4.7	−4.3	−3.3
Turkmenistan	−12.9	−0.8	−0.9	−7.3	−6.1	−15.6	−19.9	−11.5	−8.2	−6.4	−5.9
Ukraine[2]	−2.2	−6.3	−8.1	−9.2	−3.9	1.7	−1.5	−1.9	−3.1	−3.9	−3.1
Uzbekistan	7.0	5.7	1.2	2.8	1.7	0.7	0.6	3.5	−0.5	−1.5	−2.6
Emerging and Developing Asia	**2.4**	**0.8**	**0.9**	**0.7**	**1.5**	**2.0**	**1.4**	**0.9**	**0.1**	**0.2**	**−0.4**
Bangladesh	0.4	−1.0	0.7	1.2	1.3	1.9	0.6	−2.0	−3.2	−2.7	−0.9
Bhutan	−22.2	−29.8	−21.4	−25.4	−26.4	−28.3	−29.4	−22.8	−22.8	−15.0	2.9
Brunei Darussalam	36.6	34.7	29.8	20.9	31.9	16.7	12.9	16.7	7.8	17.4	15.7
Cambodia	−14.9	−11.9	−14.0	−13.4	−10.1	−9.0	−8.6	−8.5	−10.8	−10.6	−7.0
China	3.9	1.8	2.5	1.5	2.2	2.7	1.8	1.4	0.7	0.7	0.1
Fiji	−4.5	−5.1	−1.4	−9.7	−6.2	−2.2	−2.9	−5.7	−4.7	−4.0	−3.3
India	−2.8	−4.3	−4.8	−1.7	−1.3	−1.1	−0.6	−1.9	−3.0	−2.5	−2.6
Indonesia	0.7	0.2	−2.7	−3.2	−3.1	−2.0	−1.8	−1.7	−2.4	−2.4	−2.2
Kiribati	−2.2	−13.1	−4.4	8.3	25.0	46.7	19.4	9.0	16.9	7.1	−15.7
Lao P.D.R.	−16.5	−15.3	−26.0	−28.4	−20.0	−18.0	−13.0	−12.1	−13.9	−12.3	−8.7
Malaysia	10.1	10.9	5.2	3.5	4.4	3.0	2.4	3.0	2.9	2.3	1.7
Maldives	−7.3	−14.8	−6.6	−4.3	−3.2	−7.4	−24.5	−19.5	−18.2	−15.2	−9.5
Marshall Islands	−17.8	−2.1	−6.2	−9.2	−1.2	15.0	7.6	−0.3	−0.6	−1.0	−3.1
Micronesia	−15.4	−18.8	−13.4	−10.1	1.2	4.2	3.3	3.6	3.2	3.1	3.2
Mongolia	−13.0	−26.5	−27.4	−25.4	−11.3	−4.0	−6.3	−10.4	−8.3	−10.8	0.7
Myanmar	−1.1	−1.8	−4.0	−4.9	−2.2	−5.1	−3.9	−4.3	−5.3	−5.7	−5.8
Nauru	46.3	26.1	38.1	18.8	−13.5	−9.5	1.7	4.1	−7.7	−7.5	−6.0
Nepal	−2.4	−1.0	4.8	3.3	4.5	5.0	6.3	−0.4	−8.2	−6.3	−3.4
Palau	−9.3	−11.5	−11.5	−12.0	−15.2	−7.7	−11.7	−18.1	−17.5	−17.2	−13.3
Papua New Guinea	−20.4	−24.0	−36.1	−30.8	1.3	12.0	24.1	24.5	23.4	23.6	19.9
Philippines	3.6	2.5	2.8	4.2	3.8	2.5	−0.4	−0.8	−1.5	−1.5	−1.3
Samoa	−6.7	−6.9	−9.0	−1.7	−8.1	−3.1	−4.7	−2.3	−3.1	−4.5	−4.5
Solomon Islands	−32.9	−8.3	1.7	−3.4	−4.3	−3.0	−3.9	−4.2	−6.4	−8.3	−6.8
Sri Lanka	−1.9	−7.1	−5.8	−3.4	−2.5	−2.3	−2.1	−2.6	−2.9	−2.7	−2.1
Thailand	3.4	2.5	−0.4	−1.2	3.7	8.0	11.7	11.2	9.1	8.1	4.2
Timor-Leste	39.7	39.1	39.7	42.3	27.0	6.6	−21.6	−10.2	−1.2	−2.6	−12.6
Tonga	−18.5	−13.2	−7.9	−11.5	−14.7	−12.0	−6.9	−11.6	−17.1	−14.1	−6.3
Tuvalu	−12.0	−37.1	18.2	−6.6	2.9	−52.8	23.2	4.2	3.5	−2.0	−11.3
Vanuatu	−5.9	−7.8	−6.5	−3.3	2.4	−10.7	−4.6	−1.5	−8.5	−7.6	−6.4
Vietnam	−3.8	0.2	6.0	4.5	4.9	−0.1	2.9	2.5	2.2	2.0	1.5
Emerging and Developing Europe	**−5.0**	**−6.3**	**−4.4**	**−3.6**	**−2.9**	**−1.9**	**−1.8**	**−2.6**	**−2.8**	**−1.4**	**−1.9**
Albania	−11.3	−13.2	−10.1	−9.3	−10.8	−8.6	−7.6	−6.9	−7.1	−6.6	−6.2
Bosnia and Herzegovina	−6.1	−9.5	−8.7	−5.3	−7.4	−5.4	−4.9	−4.8	−6.0	−6.6	−5.0
Bulgaria	−1.7	0.3	−0.9	1.3	0.1	0.0	2.3	4.5	2.4	1.6	0.1
Croatia	−1.1	−0.7	−0.1	0.9	2.0	4.5	2.6	3.9	2.7	2.3	0.5
Hungary	0.3	0.7	1.8	3.8	1.5	3.5	6.0	3.2	2.3	2.1	1.0
Kosovo	−11.7	−12.7	−5.8	−3.4	−6.9	−8.6	−7.9	−6.6	−7.2	−6.6	−5.2
FYR Macedonia	−2.0	−2.5	−3.2	−1.6	−0.5	−2.0	−2.7	−1.3	−1.1	−1.6	−2.6
Montenegro	−20.3	−14.8	−15.3	−11.4	−12.4	−11.0	−16.2	−16.3	−16.8	−16.0	−8.3
Poland	−5.4	−5.2	−3.7	−1.3	−2.1	−0.6	−0.3	0.3	−0.8	−1.3	−1.5
Romania	−5.1	−5.0	−4.8	−1.1	−0.7	−1.2	−2.1	−3.4	−3.5	−3.4	−3.0
Serbia	−6.4	−8.6	−11.5	−6.1	−6.0	−4.7	−3.1	−5.7	−5.7	−5.6	−4.1
Turkey	−5.8	−8.9	−5.5	−6.7	−4.7	−3.7	−3.8	−5.6	−5.7	−1.4	−2.4

Table A12. Emerging Market and Developing Economies: Balance on Current Account *(continued)*
(Percent of GDP)

	2010	2011	2012	2013	2014	2015	2016	2017	Projections 2018	2019	2023
Latin America and the Caribbean	**−1.9**	**−1.9**	**−2.3**	**−2.7**	**−3.1**	**−3.3**	**−1.9**	**−1.5**	**−1.6**	**−1.8**	**−2.0**
Antigua and Barbuda	. . .	. . .	. . .	. . .	2.0	6.8	0.2	−7.3	−13.8	−4.4	−2.1
Argentina	−0.4	−1.0	−0.4	−2.1	−1.6	−2.7	−2.7	−4.9	−3.7	−3.2	−3.5
Aruba	−19.4	−10.5	3.5	−12.9	−5.2	4.1	5.0	0.8	1.1	0.7	0.8
The Bahamas	−7.9	−10.9	−14.3	−14.3	−20.0	−13.7	−7.3	−15.7	−12.7	−8.0	−3.3
Barbados	−5.6	−11.8	−8.5	−8.4	−9.2	−6.1	−4.3	−3.8	−3.1	−3.4	−2.7
Belize	−2.9	−1.1	−1.2	−4.5	−7.8	−9.8	−9.0	−7.7	−6.0	−5.8	−5.0
Bolivia	3.9	0.3	7.2	3.4	1.7	−5.8	−5.6	−6.3	−5.2	−5.1	−4.7
Brazil	−3.4	−2.9	−3.0	−3.0	−4.2	−3.3	−1.3	−0.5	−1.3	−1.6	−1.9
Chile	1.4	−1.6	−3.9	−4.0	−1.7	−2.3	−1.4	−1.5	−2.5	−2.7	−1.8
Colombia	−3.1	−2.9	−3.1	−3.3	−5.2	−6.3	−4.3	−3.3	−2.4	−2.4	−2.4
Costa Rica	−3.2	−5.3	−5.1	−4.8	−4.8	−3.5	−2.3	−2.9	−3.3	−3.5	−4.5
Dominica	. . .	. . .	. . .	. . .	−7.1	−1.9	0.8	−12.5	−32.7	−23.4	−12.6
Dominican Republic	−7.5	−7.5	−6.5	−4.1	−3.3	−1.9	−1.1	−0.2	−1.6	−2.1	−2.7
Ecuador	−2.3	−0.5	−0.2	−1.0	−0.5	−2.1	1.4	−0.3	−0.5	0.7	1.2
El Salvador	−2.9	−5.5	−5.8	−6.9	−5.4	−3.2	−2.1	−2.0	−3.9	−4.3	−4.7
Grenada	. . .	. . .	. . .	. . .	−4.4	−3.8	−3.2	−6.8	−7.5	−7.5	−6.8
Guatemala	−1.4	−3.4	−2.6	−2.5	−2.1	−0.2	1.5	1.5	1.0	0.4	−1.2
Guyana	−8.4	−12.2	−11.3	−13.3	−9.5	−5.1	0.4	−6.7	−6.1	−4.3	40.7
Haiti	−1.5	−4.3	−5.7	−6.6	−8.5	−3.1	−1.0	−4.0	−4.0	−2.9	−2.7
Honduras	−4.3	−8.0	−8.5	−9.5	−6.9	−4.7	−2.7	−1.7	−3.2	−3.4	−3.8
Jamaica	−8.0	−12.2	−11.1	−9.2	−7.5	−3.2	−2.7	−4.6	−4.9	−4.2	−1.2
Mexico	−0.5	−1.1	−1.5	−2.4	−1.8	−2.5	−2.2	−1.7	−1.3	−1.3	−1.6
Nicaragua	−8.9	−11.9	−10.7	−10.9	−7.1	−9.1	−7.5	−5.0	−6.2	−6.4	−6.8
Panama	−10.3	−12.6	−10.0	−9.4	−13.1	−7.9	−5.5	−4.9	−7.0	−6.1	−5.1
Paraguay	0.2	0.6	−0.9	1.6	−0.1	−0.8	1.2	−0.8	−1.3	−0.9	−0.2
Peru	−2.4	−1.8	−2.8	−4.6	−4.4	−4.8	−2.7	−1.1	−1.8	−2.2	−2.1
St. Kitts and Nevis	. . .	. . .	. . .	. . .	−4.5	−9.1	−10.7	−10.1	−9.9	−15.8	−16.0
St. Lucia	. . .	. . .	. . .	. . .	3.4	6.9	−1.9	1.3	−1.6	−3.0	−1.8
St. Vincent and the Grenadines	. . .	. . .	. . .	. . .	−25.7	−14.9	−15.8	−14.8	−13.3	−12.3	−9.1
Suriname	14.9	9.8	3.3	−3.8	−7.9	−16.3	−5.2	−0.1	−3.3	−2.4	−0.9
Trinidad and Tobago	18.5	16.9	13.0	20.1	14.7	7.6	−2.9	10.2	10.7	7.3	5.1
Uruguay	. . .	. . .	−4.0	−3.6	−3.2	−1.0	0.8	1.5	0.9	0.2	−1.3
Venezuela	1.9	4.9	0.8	2.0	2.3	−6.6	−1.6	2.0	6.1	4.0	0.0
Middle East, North Africa, Afghanistan, and Pakistan	**6.1**	**12.7**	**12.5**	**9.8**	**5.5**	**−4.0**	**−3.9**	**−0.7**	**1.8**	**1.9**	**−0.6**
Afghanistan	29.4	26.6	10.9	0.3	5.8	2.9	7.3	5.0	5.1	0.8	−5.2
Algeria	7.5	9.9	5.9	0.4	−4.4	−16.4	−16.5	−13.2	−9.0	−7.9	−3.0
Bahrain	3.0	8.8	8.4	7.4	4.6	−2.4	−4.6	−4.5	−2.5	−2.3	−3.6
Djibouti	2.8	−13.1	−18.8	−23.3	−25.1	−31.8	−9.4	−13.8	−14.3	−14.8	−9.3
Egypt	−1.9	−2.5	−3.6	−2.2	−0.9	−3.7	−6.0	−6.3	−2.6	−2.4	−1.2
Iran	4.2	10.4	6.0	6.7	3.2	0.3	4.0	2.2	1.3	0.3	−0.4
Iraq	1.6	10.9	5.1	1.1	2.6	−6.5	−7.8	2.3	6.9	3.1	−4.9
Jordan	−7.1	−10.3	−15.2	−10.4	−7.3	−9.1	−9.5	−10.6	−9.6	−8.6	−6.3
Kuwait	31.8	42.9	45.5	40.3	33.4	3.5	−4.6	5.9	11.3	11.0	4.4
Lebanon	−20.2	−15.2	−23.6	−26.1	−26.0	−18.3	−21.7	−22.8	−25.6	−25.5	−21.3
Libya[3]	21.1	9.9	29.9	0.0	−78.4	−54.4	−24.7	8.4	1.5	2.9	−1.3
Mauritania	−8.2	−5.0	−24.1	−22.0	−27.3	−19.8	−15.1	−14.4	−16.0	−17.2	−6.5
Morocco	−4.4	−7.6	−9.3	−7.6	−5.9	−2.1	−4.2	−3.6	−4.3	−4.5	−2.3
Oman	8.6	13.0	10.2	6.6	5.2	−15.9	−18.7	−15.2	−3.3	−0.5	−4.4
Pakistan	−2.2	0.1	−2.1	−1.1	−1.3	−1.0	−1.7	−4.1	−5.9	−5.3	−6.1
Qatar	19.1	31.1	33.2	30.4	24.0	8.5	−5.5	3.8	4.8	6.6	6.6
Saudi Arabia	12.6	23.6	22.4	18.1	9.8	−8.7	−3.7	2.2	8.4	8.8	2.4
Somalia	. . .	. . .	. . .	−3.4	−5.2	−4.7	−6.3	−6.6	−6.3	−5.7	−6.4
Sudan[4]	−2.6	−4.0	−12.8	−11.0	−5.8	−8.3	−7.6	−10.5	−14.2	−13.1	−10.4
Syria[5]	−2.8	. . .	. . .	. . .	. . .	. . .	. . .	. . .	. . .	. . .	. . .
Tunisia	−4.8	−7.4	−8.3	−8.4	−9.1	−8.9	−8.8	−10.5	−9.6	−8.5	−6.0
United Arab Emirates	4.2	12.6	19.7	19.0	13.5	4.9	3.7	6.9	7.2	7.5	4.2
Yemen	−3.4	−3.0	−1.7	−3.1	−1.7	−6.2	−5.1	−4.0	−9.3	−7.4	−7.4

Table A12. Emerging Market and Developing Economies: Balance on Current Account (continued)
(Percent of GDP)

	2010	2011	2012	2013	2014	2015	2016	2017	Projections 2018	2019	2023
Sub-Saharan Africa	**−0.8**	**−0.6**	**−1.7**	**−2.2**	**−3.6**	**−6.0**	**−3.9**	**−2.3**	**−2.8**	**−3.4**	**−3.4**
Angola	9.0	11.7	10.8	6.1	−2.6	−8.8	−4.8	−1.0	−2.1	−1.9	−0.7
Benin	−8.2	−7.3	−7.4	−7.4	−8.6	−9.0	−9.4	−11.1	−10.6	−8.9	−6.5
Botswana	−2.8	3.1	0.3	8.9	15.4	7.8	13.7	12.3	8.7	7.7	10.0
Burkina Faso	−2.2	−4.0	−6.7	−11.3	−8.1	−8.5	−7.2	−8.1	−8.6	−7.6	−6.3
Burundi	−12.2	−14.4	−18.6	−19.3	−18.5	−17.7	−13.1	−12.3	−13.4	−12.6	−9.5
Cabo Verde	−12.4	−16.3	−12.6	−4.9	−9.1	−3.2	−2.4	−6.2	−9.1	−10.0	−8.9
Cameroon	−2.5	−2.7	−3.3	−3.6	−4.0	−3.8	−3.2	−2.7	−3.2	−3.0	−3.0
Central African Republic	−10.2	−7.6	−6.5	−3.3	−14.8	−9.7	−5.5	−8.4	−8.9	−8.4	−5.3
Chad	−8.5	−5.8	−7.8	−9.1	−8.9	−13.6	−9.2	−5.7	−4.2	−5.5	−4.3
Comoros	−0.4	−6.0	−5.5	−7.0	−6.3	−0.4	−7.4	−4.1	−9.2	−10.1	−8.8
Democratic Republic of the Congo	−10.5	−5.2	−4.6	−5.0	−4.6	−3.7	−3.1	−0.5	0.0	−1.8	−2.9
Republic of Congo	7.3	14.0	17.7	13.8	1.4	−54.1	−73.6	−12.9	9.1	12.4	−5.1
Côte d'Ivoire	1.9	10.4	−1.2	−1.4	1.4	−0.6	−1.1	−4.6	−4.6	−4.2	−2.8
Equatorial Guinea	−20.2	−5.7	−1.1	−2.4	−4.3	−16.2	−12.9	−5.9	−3.1	−3.6	−6.0
Eritrea	−6.1	3.2	2.7	3.6	4.0	−1.4	−2.1	−2.4	−1.6	−2.3	−2.7
Eswatini	−8.7	1.0	12.5	18.7	21.2	26.1	17.2	13.7	10.3	9.8	14.0
Ethiopia	−1.4	−2.5	−6.9	−5.9	−6.4	−10.2	−9.0	−8.1	−6.2	−6.2	−4.4
Gabon	14.9	24.0	17.9	7.3	7.6	−5.6	−9.9	−4.9	−1.6	−0.5	3.7
The Gambia	−9.5	−7.5	−4.5	−6.8	−7.2	−9.8	−5.9	−13.1	−12.5	−13.6	−11.8
Ghana	−8.6	−9.0	−11.7	−11.9	−9.5	−7.7	−6.7	−4.5	−4.1	−4.0	−3.6
Guinea	−6.4	−18.4	−20.0	−12.5	−13.4	−12.5	−31.1	−6.9	−21.2	−16.4	−10.9
Guinea-Bissau	−13.5	−1.3	−8.4	−4.6	0.5	1.9	1.3	−2.0	−3.6	−4.1	−3.1
Kenya	−5.9	−9.2	−8.4	−8.8	−10.4	−6.7	−5.2	−6.3	−5.6	−5.3	−4.1
Lesotho	−8.9	−13.4	−8.4	−5.1	−4.8	−3.9	−8.2	−3.7	−6.0	−12.5	−6.9
Liberia	−17.6	−12.8	−11.4	−17.0	−19.4	−20.8	−14.1	−19.1	−18.3	−21.4	−20.6
Madagascar	−10.2	−7.0	−7.6	−5.9	−0.3	−1.9	0.6	−0.3	−2.2	−3.4	−4.4
Malawi	−8.6	−8.6	−9.2	−8.4	−8.3	−9.4	−13.6	−9.5	−9.3	−8.1	−7.6
Mali	−10.7	−5.1	−2.2	−2.9	−4.7	−5.3	−7.2	−5.8	−7.2	−7.8	−7.1
Mauritius	−10.0	−13.5	−7.1	−6.2	−5.6	−4.8	−4.3	−6.6	−8.2	−10.4	−4.0
Mozambique	−16.1	−25.3	−44.7	−42.9	−38.2	−40.3	−39.3	−22.4	−18.2	−44.7	−105.8
Namibia	−3.5	−3.0	−5.7	−4.0	−10.8	−12.4	−13.8	−3.3	−6.0	−7.6	−5.5
Niger	−19.8	−25.1	−16.1	−16.8	−15.4	−20.5	−15.7	−14.1	−16.2	−18.3	−12.1
Nigeria	3.6	2.6	3.8	3.7	0.2	−3.2	0.7	2.8	2.0	1.0	0.1
Rwanda	−7.2	−7.4	−11.2	−8.7	−10.3	−14.5	−15.8	−6.8	−8.9	−9.4	−5.3
São Tomé and Príncipe	−22.9	−27.7	−21.9	−15.2	−21.9	−13.0	−6.5	−8.2	−7.0	−10.2	−7.4
Senegal	−3.5	−6.5	−8.7	−8.2	−7.0	−5.4	−4.0	−7.3	−7.7	−7.1	−6.1
Seychelles	−19.4	−23.0	−21.1	−11.9	−23.1	−18.6	−20.1	−20.5	−18.4	−18.0	−17.0
Sierra Leone	−22.7	−65.0	−31.8	−17.5	−18.2	−17.4	−2.3	−11.3	−13.4	−14.1	−9.3
South Africa	−1.5	−2.2	−5.1	−5.8	−5.1	−4.6	−2.8	−2.5	−3.2	−3.5	−3.6
South Sudan	. . .	18.2	−15.9	−3.9	−1.5	−7.1	1.3	−5.0	−8.8	2.7	−1.8
Tanzania	−7.7	−10.8	−11.6	−10.6	−10.1	−8.4	−4.5	−2.8	−4.3	−5.5	−4.5
Togo	−5.8	−7.8	−7.6	−13.2	−10.0	−11.0	−9.3	−8.0	−9.2	−8.0	−5.9
Uganda	−8.0	−9.9	−6.8	−7.1	−8.1	−7.1	−2.9	−4.6	−6.9	−8.9	−3.6
Zambia	7.5	4.7	5.4	−0.6	2.1	−3.9	−4.5	−3.9	−4.0	−3.4	−1.8
Zimbabwe[6]	−14.3	−20.1	−13.1	−16.6	−14.2	−9.5	−3.4	−4.1	−5.8	−5.6	−5.0

[1]Georgia, Turkmenistan, and Ukraine, which are not members of the Commonwealth of Independent States, are included in this group for reasons of geography and similarity in economic structure.
[2]Starting in 2014 data exclude Crimea and Sevastopol.
[3]See country-specific note for Libya in the "Country Notes" section of the Statistical Appendix.
[4]Data for 2011 exclude South Sudan after July 9. Data for 2012 and onward pertain to the current Sudan.
[5]Data for Syria are excluded for 2011 onward owing to the uncertain political situation.
[6]The Zimbabwe dollar ceased circulating in early 2009. Data are based on IMF staff estimates of price and exchange rate developments in US dollars. IMF staff estimates of US dollar values may differ from authorities' estimates.

Table A13. Summary of Financial Account Balances

(Billions of US dollars)

	2010	2011	2012	2013	2014	2015	2016	2017	Projections 2018	Projections 2019
Advanced Economies										
Financial Account Balance	−123.6	−260.6	−149.4	229.5	363.3	349.7	436.4	512.0	337.0	269.6
Direct Investment, Net	340.7	358.9	111.9	154.3	235.9	69.5	−146.5	292.9	−28.6	156.0
Portfolio Investment, Net	−969.0	−1,111.5	−246.3	−540.9	71.8	175.9	505.1	151.3	389.5	125.3
Financial Derivatives, Net	−114.1	−6.4	−98.3	73.9	−11.5	−107.6	14.5	−13.9	1.8	−18.8
Other Investment, Net	265.8	148.9	−189.9	389.2	−67.8	−14.8	−116.6	−167.2	−110.0	−66.4
Change in Reserves	352.9	349.8	273.2	153.1	134.9	226.7	179.7	248.9	84.0	73.5
United States										
Financial Account Balance	−446.4	−526.0	−448.2	−400.3	−297.3	−325.9	−385.1	−331.9	−567.1	−643.2
Direct Investment, Net	85.8	173.1	126.9	104.7	135.7	−202.0	−181.5	24.4	−341.3	−171.2
Portfolio Investment, Net	−620.8	−226.3	−498.3	−30.7	−114.9	−53.5	−195.1	−212.5	−170.4	−398.7
Financial Derivatives, Net	−14.1	−35.0	7.1	2.2	−54.3	−27.0	7.8	23.1	23.4	16.8
Other Investment, Net	100.9	−453.7	−88.4	−473.4	−260.1	−37.1	−18.4	−165.2	−78.8	−90.1
Change in Reserves	1.8	15.9	4.5	−3.1	−3.6	−6.3	2.1	−1.7	0.0	0.0
Euro Area										
Financial Account Balance	−16.9	−40.9	184.3	443.7	350.9	296.5	384.1	467.7	. . .	. . .
Direct Investment, Net	82.3	124.9	59.4	23.8	90.3	276.1	187.0	49.7	. . .	. . .
Portfolio Investment, Net	−81.4	−383.3	−175.8	−156.9	40.8	79.7	552.5	355.7	. . .	. . .
Financial Derivatives, Net	−4.4	5.5	38.9	42.1	66.2	96.6	19.6	28.7	. . .	. . .
Other Investment, Net	−27.1	197.7	242.9	528.5	147.8	−167.7	−392.4	35.1	. . .	. . .
Change in Reserves	13.7	14.3	19.0	6.2	5.8	11.8	17.4	−1.5	. . .	. . .
Germany										
Financial Account Balance	123.7	167.7	194.3	300.0	317.8	264.9	284.3	316.3	326.9	323.6
Direct Investment, Net	60.6	10.3	33.6	26.0	95.3	74.8	33.2	47.1	59.5	50.7
Portfolio Investment, Net	154.1	−51.4	66.8	209.6	177.7	213.5	228.8	228.1	253.4	247.9
Financial Derivatives, Net	17.6	39.8	30.9	31.8	43.3	29.0	35.8	10.3	28.5	26.1
Other Investment, Net	−110.7	165.1	61.1	31.4	4.8	−49.9	−15.4	32.3	−14.4	−1.1
Change in Reserves	2.1	3.9	1.7	1.2	−3.3	−2.4	1.9	−1.5	0.0	0.0
France										
Financial Account Balance	−1.6	−78.6	−48.0	−19.2	−10.3	−0.8	−14.4	−36.0	−24.3	−18.6
Direct Investment, Net	34.3	19.8	19.4	−13.9	47.2	7.9	28.1	8.3	13.2	17.6
Portfolio Investment, Net	−155.0	−335.1	−50.6	−79.3	−23.8	43.2	23.8	22.4	34.4	43.1
Financial Derivatives, Net	−4.1	−19.4	−18.4	−22.3	−31.8	14.5	−17.6	−1.4	−8.7	−16.3
Other Investment, Net	115.5	263.8	−3.6	98.2	−2.9	−74.2	−51.1	−61.9	−65.8	−65.6
Change in Reserves	7.7	−7.7	5.2	−1.9	1.0	8.0	2.5	−3.4	2.6	2.6
Italy										
Financial Account Balance	−107.1	−79.9	−4.1	29.0	68.5	39.1	72.4	53.3	43.4	35.7
Direct Investment, Net	21.3	17.2	6.8	0.9	3.1	2.7	−4.5	−12.7	2.6	3.0
Portfolio Investment, Net	62.5	25.6	−22.4	−5.4	5.5	108.2	176.5	111.1	72.2	28.7
Financial Derivatives, Net	6.6	−10.1	7.5	4.0	−4.8	2.6	−3.3	−6.5	−2.7	−0.6
Other Investment, Net	−198.9	−113.9	2.1	27.5	65.9	−75.0	−95.1	−41.7	−28.7	4.6
Change in Reserves	1.4	1.3	1.9	2.0	−1.3	0.6	−1.3	3.0	0.0	0.0

Table A13. Summary of Financial Account Balances *(continued)*
(Billions of US dollars)

	2010	2011	2012	2013	2014	2015	2016	2017	Projections 2018	Projections 2019
Spain										
Financial Account Balance	−58.9	−43.4	0.5	41.6	14.8	23.1	27.9	27.3	19.8	20.6
Direct Investment, Net	−1.9	12.8	−27.2	−24.6	8.6	31.0	18.5	22.9	19.9	20.3
Portfolio Investment, Net	−46.6	43.1	53.7	−83.6	−12.1	10.2	55.1	26.3	6.7	6.2
Financial Derivatives, Net	−11.4	2.9	−10.7	1.4	1.7	−1.1	−2.9	−2.5	0.0	0.0
Other Investment, Net	0.0	−116.2	−18.2	147.8	11.5	−22.6	−51.8	−23.4	−6.7	−5.9
Change in Reserves	1.1	13.9	2.8	0.7	5.1	5.6	9.1	4.1	0.0	0.0
Japan										
Financial Account Balance	247.3	158.4	53.9	−4.3	58.9	180.9	263.7	158.0	180.4	193.0
Direct Investment, Net	72.5	117.8	117.5	144.7	118.6	133.3	134.4	149.7	132.5	144.6
Portfolio Investment, Net	147.9	−162.9	28.8	−280.6	−42.2	131.5	276.5	−53.5	−47.0	−44.0
Financial Derivatives, Net	−11.9	−17.1	6.7	58.1	34.0	17.7	−16.1	30.5	31.7	32.6
Other Investment, Net	−5.5	43.4	−61.1	34.8	−60.1	−106.7	−125.4	7.7	52.8	48.8
Change in Reserves	44.3	177.3	−37.9	38.7	8.5	5.1	−5.7	23.6	10.5	11.0
United Kingdom										
Financial Account Balance	−108.1	−43.3	−92.6	−132.5	−154.2	−142.6	−145.8	−77.9	−101.7	−92.6
Direct Investment, Net	−10.1	53.4	−34.8	−11.2	−176.1	−106.0	−219.5	81.7	64.6	53.4
Portfolio Investment, Net	−201.0	−215.5	275.0	−284.2	16.4	−201.8	−195.4	−86.3	0.0	0.0
Financial Derivatives, Net	−69.3	7.4	−65.8	63.4	31.2	−128.6	29.3	12.7	1.8	−8.4
Other Investment, Net	162.9	103.4	−279.1	91.8	−37.5	261.6	231.0	−94.8	−180.5	−150.7
Change in Reserves	9.4	7.9	12.1	7.8	11.7	32.2	8.8	8.8	12.4	13.2
Canada										
Financial Account Balance	−58.3	−49.4	−62.7	−56.9	−42.2	−57.8	−51.5	−40.0	−52.2	−45.6
Direct Investment, Net	6.3	12.5	12.8	−12.0	1.3	22.2	36.3	54.4	30.2	28.3
Portfolio Investment, Net	−109.9	−104.3	−63.8	−27.1	−32.9	−44.8	−119.2	−81.0	−62.7	−66.6
Financial Derivatives, Net	. . .	. . .	. . .	. . .	. . .	. . .	. . .	. . .	. . .	. . .
Other Investment, Net	41.4	34.3	−13.4	−22.5	−15.9	−43.8	25.8	−14.2	−19.8	−7.2
Change in Reserves	3.9	8.1	1.7	4.7	5.3	8.5	5.6	0.8	0.0	0.0
Other Advanced Economies[1]										
Financial Account Balance	283.8	284.7	256.3	375.4	352.3	303.7	337.9	342.6	372.5	360.6
Direct Investment, Net	93.5	−6.5	−34.8	26.3	−7.3	−108.1	−79.0	−52.7	−47.0	−24.8
Portfolio Investment, Net	−57.1	46.8	148.7	138.4	180.7	333.5	275.2	163.4	203.2	208.0
Financial Derivatives, Net	−15.2	31.1	−28.3	−33.5	−23.5	−14.2	−0.8	−29.6	−40.4	−37.1
Other Investment, Net	−16.8	88.5	−104.0	143.1	96.0	−83.4	−8.6	43.8	202.0	172.2
Change in Reserves	279.3	125.1	274.7	101.3	106.3	175.9	151.0	217.7	54.6	42.2
Emerging Market and Developing Economies										
Financial Account Balance	150.3	239.6	119.4	33.9	15.9	−275.3	−420.7	−257.0	23.6	33.9
Direct Investment, Net	−456.7	−530.6	−486.7	−480.2	−416.6	−340.5	−271.5	−343.6	−326.1	−323.9
Portfolio Investment, Net	−223.7	−145.4	−234.4	−155.7	−113.2	114.5	−46.3	−174.8	−31.0	−19.4
Financial Derivatives, Net	. . .	. . .	. . .	. . .	. . .	. . .	. . .	. . .	. . .	. . .
Other Investment, Net	−18.8	163.2	399.0	83.0	409.4	460.1	385.6	95.4	370.7	321.2
Change in Reserves	848.4	747.0	442.3	590.9	128.8	−513.7	−476.8	162.7	10.7	56.0

Table A13. Summary of Financial Account Balances *(continued)*
(Billions of US dollars)

	2010	2011	2012	2013	2014	2015	2016	2017	Projections 2018	Projections 2019
Regional Groups										
Commonwealth of Independent States[2]										
Financial Account Balance	87.4	103.0	62.6	2.6	12.2	53.9	3.7	29.1	88.2	76.1
Direct Investment, Net	−8.5	−15.2	−27.6	−3.6	19.2	0.6	−34.3	−1.6	2.6	1.9
Portfolio Investment, Net	−14.2	17.9	3.5	−0.2	28.8	12.0	−2.4	−17.4	−0.6	−2.9
Financial Derivatives, Net	...	...	...	...	...	...	...	...	...	...
Other Investment, Net	36.0	64.3	44.4	27.5	73.0	38.8	29.9	18.8	19.9	9.3
Change in Reserves	72.4	34.2	40.9	−21.5	−114.1	−4.9	10.1	28.8	66.0	67.5
Emerging and Developing Asia										
Financial Account Balance	146.5	65.7	7.4	31.7	150.4	87.1	−31.6	−91.2	30.5	41.3
Direct Investment, Net	−225.0	−277.3	−222.0	−273.2	−203.4	−139.8	−26.9	−145.2	−137.9	−128.9
Portfolio Investment, Net	−93.3	−58.0	−115.5	−64.7	−123.9	82.3	31.5	−45.9	14.2	−16.8
Financial Derivatives, Net	0.2	−0.3	1.5	−2.0	0.8	−1.3	−10.0	2.6	2.0	2.0
Other Investment, Net	−97.3	−28.6	207.4	−78.7	281.3	462.4	356.6	−98.2	234.5	238.1
Change in Reserves	562.9	431.7	139.2	451.3	196.2	−316.1	−381.9	196.5	−80.7	−52.7
Emerging and Developing Europe										
Financial Account Balance	−89.2	−107.2	−66.7	−62.7	−44.0	−9.9	−14.3	−45.7	−35.8	−16.8
Direct Investment, Net	−26.8	−39.9	−27.7	−26.5	−32.8	−35.0	−30.7	−24.7	−32.2	−27.9
Portfolio Investment, Net	−45.8	−53.5	−70.2	−40.0	−19.3	24.6	−4.2	−24.0	5.4	−0.6
Financial Derivatives, Net	0.0	1.6	−3.0	−1.4	0.3	−1.8	0.1	−3.2	−0.7	−0.9
Other Investment, Net	−52.4	−30.1	6.4	−13.3	8.0	12.8	−2.9	18.0	−1.0	15.0
Change in Reserves	35.9	14.6	27.8	18.5	−0.2	−10.4	23.5	−11.7	−7.3	−2.3
Latin America and the Caribbean										
Financial Account Balance	−115.1	−126.6	−146.5	−188.3	−205.3	−192.5	−102.5	−90.4	−84.4	−91.3
Direct Investment, Net	−111.3	−145.1	−149.2	−145.3	−141.0	−134.7	−130.9	−137.3	−128.3	−123.1
Portfolio Investment, Net	−95.9	−106.9	−80.9	−101.2	−109.6	−59.0	−51.5	−39.0	−8.8	−2.9
Financial Derivatives, Net	0.7	5.5	2.5	1.8	4.4	1.2	−1.1	4.7	0.6	0.7
Other Investment, Net	0.3	11.8	21.9	44.8	1.8	28.7	60.1	63.5	60.8	35.2
Change in Reserves	91.0	108.1	59.1	11.7	39.1	−28.9	20.9	17.5	−8.7	−1.2
Middle East, North Africa, Afghanistan, and Pakistan										
Financial Account Balance	127.1	320.6	284.1	304.4	180.5	−134.5	−207.8	−21.0	62.5	75.0
Direct Investment, Net	−48.1	−20.5	−25.5	−7.9	−28.9	0.5	−7.4	−6.6	4.2	1.6
Portfolio Investment, Net	26.0	74.4	57.0	72.5	132.6	69.8	−6.4	−27.1	−23.7	9.4
Financial Derivatives, Net	...	...	...	...	...	...	...	...	...	...
Other Investment, Net	63.5	128.3	98.4	112.0	61.0	−65.6	−55.0	93.7	50.9	23.5
Change in Reserves	85.9	137.8	154.3	128.1	16.3	−138.9	−138.5	−80.7	31.2	40.7
Sub-Saharan Africa										
Financial Account Balance	−6.4	−15.8	−21.6	−53.7	−78.0	−79.4	−68.3	−37.8	−37.5	−50.4
Direct Investment, Net	−37.0	−32.7	−34.6	−23.6	−29.6	−32.1	−41.2	−28.2	−34.5	−47.5
Portfolio Investment, Net	−0.4	−19.3	−28.4	−22.0	−21.8	−15.2	−13.3	−21.5	−17.6	−5.6
Financial Derivatives, Net	−0.2	−1.7	−1.7	−0.8	−1.5	−0.4	0.9	0.3	−0.2	−0.2
Other Investment, Net	31.2	17.5	20.5	−9.3	−15.8	−17.0	−3.0	−0.2	5.7	0.1
Change in Reserves	0.3	20.7	21.0	2.8	−8.5	−14.4	−10.8	12.1	10.3	4.0

Table A13. Summary of Financial Account Balances *(continued)*
(Billions of US dollars)

	2010	2011	2012	2013	2014	2015	2016	2017	Projections 2018	2019
Analytical Groups										
By Source of Export Earnings										
Fuel										
Financial Account Balance	250.8	511.8	445.7	376.1	226.2	−85.8	−158.5	67.2	226.7	223.2
Direct Investment, Net	−32.5	−24.0	−29.3	13.0	5.4	6.9	−29.3	11.7	21.6	15.8
Portfolio Investment, Net	20.4	88.9	50.2	79.1	164.6	80.9	−9.3	−38.9	−14.4	3.0
Financial Derivatives, Net	...	...	...	...	...	...	...	...	...	...
Other Investment, Net	146.0	250.3	188.7	183.5	157.7	8.5	34.4	147.4	116.4	89.5
Change in Reserves	115.1	194.7	234.5	100.2	−106.5	−189.7	−154.6	−53.5	102.5	114.3
Nonfuel										
Financial Account Balance	−99.0	−272.2	−326.3	−342.2	−210.3	−189.5	−262.2	−324.2	−203.1	−189.3
Direct Investment, Net	−422.0	−506.6	−457.4	−493.2	−422.0	−347.4	−242.2	−355.4	−347.7	−339.7
Portfolio Investment, Net	−244.1	−234.3	−284.7	−234.8	−277.7	33.5	−37.0	−135.9	−16.6	−22.3
Financial Derivatives, Net	0.7	5.8	−0.9	−2.4	3.9	−2.2	−10.0	4.3	1.8	1.5
Other Investment, Net	−164.4	−87.1	210.4	−100.5	251.7	451.6	351.2	−52.0	254.3	231.6
Change in Reserves	732.2	552.3	207.7	490.7	235.3	−324.0	−322.1	216.2	−91.8	−58.3
By External Financing Source										
Net Debtor Economies										
Financial Account Balance	−269.1	−365.7	−398.1	−402.7	−390.8	−309.8	−272.7	−289.0	−320.4	−306.2
Direct Investment, Net	−212.8	−281.7	−275.7	−265.1	−288.1	−289.7	−306.7	−293.4	−305.3	−320.0
Portfolio Investment, Net	−221.5	−182.6	−215.9	−179.6	−198.4	−50.2	−49.4	−108.0	−17.5	−31.1
Financial Derivatives, Net	...	...	...	...	...	...	...	...	...	...
Other Investment, Net	−54.3	−78.7	−31.1	−27.3	−13.8	36.3	18.9	28.2	31.8	15.1
Change in Reserves	219.3	175.2	127.4	73.2	104.6	−4.3	77.5	81.2	−28.7	29.5
Net Debtor Economies by Debt-Servicing Experience										
Economies with Arrears and/or Rescheduling during 2013-17										
Financial Account Balance	0.9	−28.3	−46.3	−48.2	−31.9	−41.9	−54.3	−38.8	−33.0	−34.1
Direct Investment, Net	−20.3	−20.8	−27.4	−24.1	−19.9	−25.5	−26.2	−24.9	−25.8	−32.1
Portfolio Investment, Net	−11.1	0.8	−1.7	−10.5	−4.1	1.9	−1.0	−23.0	−21.0	−2.7
Financial Derivatives, Net	...	...	...	...	...	...	...	...	...	...
Other Investment, Net	7.3	2.1	−5.7	−16.8	0.0	−24.9	−23.7	8.8	8.0	−1.6
Change in Reserves	25.3	−9.8	−13.3	4.1	−7.0	7.3	−2.1	0.8	7.2	3.6
Memorandum										
World										
Financial Account Balance	26.6	−21.0	−30.0	263.4	379.1	74.4	15.7	255.1	360.6	303.5

Note: The estimates in this table are based on individual countries' national accounts and balance of payments statistics. Country group composites are calculated as the sum of the US dollar values for the relevant individual countries. Some group aggregates for the financial derivatives are not shown because of incomplete data. Projections for the euro area are not available because of data constraints.

[1] Excludes the G7 (Canada, France, Germany, Italy, Japan, United Kingdom, United States) and euro area countries.

[2] Georgia, Turkmenistan, and Ukraine, which are not members of the Commonwealth of Independent States, are included in this group for reasons of geography and similarity in economic structure.

Table A14. Summary of Net Lending and Borrowing
(Percent of GDP)

	Averages								Projections		
	2000–09	2004–11	2012	2013	2014	2015	2016	2017	2018	2019	Average 2020–23
Advanced Economies											
Net Lending and Borrowing	−0.8	−0.7	0.1	0.5	0.5	0.6	0.7	0.9	0.8	0.5	0.4
Current Account Balance	−0.9	−0.7	0.1	0.5	0.5	0.7	0.7	0.9	0.7	0.5	0.4
Savings	22.0	21.5	21.7	21.9	22.5	22.7	22.2	22.8	22.8	22.9	23.0
Investment	22.7	22.2	21.2	21.1	21.4	21.5	21.3	21.6	22.0	22.4	22.7
Capital Account Balance	0.0	0.0	0.0	0.0	0.0	0.0	0.0	0.0	0.0	0.0	0.0
United States											
Net Lending and Borrowing	−4.5	−4.3	−2.6	−2.1	−2.1	−2.2	−2.3	−2.2	−2.5	−3.0	−3.2
Current Account Balance	−4.5	−4.3	−2.6	−2.1	−2.1	−2.2	−2.3	−2.3	−2.5	−3.0	−3.3
Savings	17.8	16.7	18.7	19.2	20.3	20.1	18.6	18.9	18.8	18.7	18.8
Investment	22.0	21.1	20.0	20.4	20.8	21.0	20.3	20.6	21.1	21.8	22.1
Capital Account Balance	0.0	0.0	0.0	0.0	0.0	0.0	0.0	0.1	0.0	0.0	0.1
Euro Area											
Net Lending and Borrowing	−0.1	0.0	1.5	2.4	2.6	3.1	3.6	3.3	. . .	. . .	. . .
Current Account Balance	−0.2	−0.1	1.4	2.2	2.5	3.2	3.6	3.5	3.0	2.9	2.8
Savings	22.8	22.7	22.3	22.4	22.9	23.7	24.1	24.7	24.9	25.1	25.4
Investment	22.5	22.2	20.0	19.6	19.9	20.3	20.7	20.8	21.3	21.6	22.0
Capital Account Balance	0.1	0.1	0.1	0.2	0.1	−0.1	0.0	−0.2	. . .	. . .	. . .
Germany											
Net Lending and Borrowing	3.4	5.5	7.0	6.7	7.6	8.9	8.6	7.9	8.1	7.9	7.5
Current Account Balance	3.4	5.6	7.0	6.7	7.5	8.9	8.5	7.9	8.1	7.9	7.5
Savings	23.7	25.3	26.3	26.2	27.1	28.1	28.2	28.0	28.5	28.7	28.9
Investment	20.3	19.8	19.3	19.5	19.6	19.2	19.7	20.1	20.4	20.8	21.4
Capital Account Balance	0.0	0.0	0.0	0.0	0.1	0.0	0.1	0.0	0.0	0.0	0.0
France											
Net Lending and Borrowing	1.0	0.0	−1.1	−0.5	−1.0	−0.4	−0.7	−0.5	−0.9	−0.7	−0.3
Current Account Balance	1.0	−0.1	−1.0	−0.5	−1.0	−0.4	−0.8	−0.6	−0.9	−0.7	−0.3
Savings	23.4	22.7	21.7	21.8	21.8	22.3	21.9	22.9	22.7	22.9	23.4
Investment	22.4	22.8	22.6	22.3	22.7	22.7	22.7	23.5	23.7	23.6	23.7
Capital Account Balance	0.0	0.0	−0.2	0.0	−0.1	0.0	0.1	0.0	0.0	0.0	0.0
Italy											
Net Lending and Borrowing	−0.8	−1.8	−0.1	1.0	2.1	1.7	2.4	2.7	2.1	1.7	1.2
Current Account Balance	−0.9	−1.9	−0.3	1.0	1.9	1.5	2.6	2.8	2.0	1.6	1.1
Savings	20.2	19.2	17.5	18.0	19.0	18.8	19.7	20.3	20.1	19.9	19.4
Investment	21.1	21.1	17.9	17.0	17.0	17.3	17.1	17.5	18.1	18.4	18.3
Capital Account Balance	0.1	0.1	0.2	0.0	0.2	0.2	−0.2	−0.1	0.1	0.1	0.1
Spain											
Net Lending and Borrowing	−5.5	−6.0	0.3	2.2	1.6	1.8	2.2	2.1	1.4	1.4	1.6
Current Account Balance	−6.2	−6.5	−0.2	1.5	1.1	1.1	1.9	1.9	1.2	1.2	1.4
Savings	22.2	21.1	19.8	20.2	20.5	21.5	22.4	23.0	22.9	23.1	23.4
Investment	28.3	27.6	20.0	18.7	19.5	20.4	20.5	21.1	21.8	22.0	22.0
Capital Account Balance	0.7	0.5	0.5	0.6	0.5	0.7	0.2	0.2	0.2	0.2	0.2
Japan											
Net Lending and Borrowing	3.1	3.4	0.9	0.7	0.7	3.1	3.8	4.0	3.6	3.7	4.1
Current Account Balance	3.2	3.4	1.0	0.9	0.8	3.1	3.9	4.0	3.6	3.8	4.1
Savings	27.9	26.9	23.6	24.1	24.7	27.1	27.5	28.0	28.1	28.4	28.7
Investment	24.7	23.5	22.7	23.2	23.9	24.0	23.6	24.0	24.5	24.6	24.5
Capital Account Balance	−0.1	−0.1	0.0	−0.1	0.0	−0.1	−0.1	−0.1	−0.1	−0.1	−0.1
United Kingdom											
Net Lending and Borrowing	−2.8	−3.0	−3.8	−5.2	−5.0	−5.0	−5.3	−3.9	−3.6	−3.3	−3.0
Current Account Balance	−2.8	−3.0	−3.8	−5.1	−4.9	−4.9	−5.2	−3.8	−3.5	−3.2	−2.9
Savings	14.7	13.7	12.1	11.1	12.3	12.3	12.0	13.6	13.7	14.0	14.7
Investment	17.5	16.7	15.9	16.2	17.3	17.2	17.3	17.4	17.2	17.2	17.7
Capital Account Balance	0.0	0.0	0.0	−0.1	−0.1	−0.1	−0.1	−0.1	−0.1	−0.1	−0.1

Table A14. Summary of Net Lending and Borrowing *(continued)*
(Percent of GDP)

	Averages								Projections		
	2000–09	2004–11	2012	2013	2014	2015	2016	2017	2018	2019	Average 2020–23
Canada											
Net Lending and Borrowing	1.1	−0.4	−3.6	−3.2	−2.4	−3.6	−3.2	−3.0	−3.0	−2.5	−2.1
Current Account Balance	1.1	−0.4	−3.6	−3.2	−2.4	−3.6	−3.2	−2.9	−3.0	−2.5	−2.1
Savings	23.0	22.8	21.3	21.7	22.5	20.5	20.0	20.8	20.8	21.5	22.2
Investment	21.9	23.2	24.9	24.9	24.9	24.1	23.2	23.7	23.8	24.0	24.3
Capital Account Balance	0.0	0.0	0.0	0.0	0.0	0.0	0.0	0.0	0.0	0.0	0.0
Other Advanced Economies[1]											
Net Lending and Borrowing	3.8	4.1	4.1	5.2	5.1	5.4	5.5	5.0	5.0	4.8	4.4
Current Account Balance	3.8	4.1	4.1	5.1	5.2	5.8	5.4	5.1	5.0	4.8	4.5
Savings	29.7	30.3	30.2	30.3	30.5	30.8	30.1	30.5	30.6	30.5	30.0
Investment	25.6	25.9	26.0	25.1	25.2	24.8	24.7	25.3	25.5	25.6	25.4
Capital Account Balance	−0.1	0.0	0.0	0.1	−0.1	−0.4	0.1	−0.2	0.0	−0.1	−0.1
Emerging Market and Developing Economies											
Net Lending and Borrowing	2.6	2.8	1.3	0.7	0.6	0.0	−0.2	0.0	0.1	0.1	−0.4
Current Account Balance	2.5	2.8	1.3	0.6	0.6	−0.2	−0.2	0.0	0.0	0.0	−0.5
Savings	29.5	32.2	33.5	32.8	33.0	32.7	32.0	32.2	32.7	32.6	32.1
Investment	27.3	29.6	32.4	32.4	32.6	32.9	32.2	32.2	32.8	32.8	32.7
Capital Account Balance	0.1	0.2	0.1	0.1	0.0	0.1	0.1	0.1	0.1	0.1	0.1
Regional Groups											
Commonwealth of Independent States[2]											
Net Lending and Borrowing	6.0	4.8	2.2	0.6	0.6	2.8	0.0	1.2	4.1	3.3	2.3
Current Account Balance	6.5	5.1	2.4	0.6	2.1	2.8	0.0	1.1	4.1	3.3	2.3
Savings	27.4	27.1	27.1	24.3	25.1	26.0	24.8	25.8	26.3	26.7	26.6
Investment	21.1	22.0	24.7	23.6	22.9	22.8	24.3	24.5	22.0	23.2	24.2
Capital Account Balance	−0.5	−0.3	−0.2	0.0	−1.5	0.0	0.0	0.0	0.0	0.0	0.0
Emerging and Developing Asia											
Net Lending and Borrowing	3.7	3.9	1.0	0.8	1.6	2.0	1.4	0.9	0.2	0.2	−0.1
Current Account Balance	3.6	3.8	0.9	0.7	1.5	2.0	1.4	0.9	0.1	0.2	−0.1
Savings	38.4	42.4	43.7	43.0	43.6	42.4	41.1	40.7	40.3	39.9	38.9
Investment	35.2	38.8	42.6	42.3	42.0	40.4	39.7	39.9	40.1	39.8	39.0
Capital Account Balance	0.1	0.1	0.1	0.1	0.0	0.0	0.0	0.0	0.0	0.0	0.0
Emerging and Developing Europe											
Net Lending and Borrowing	−4.5	−5.3	−3.4	−2.5	−1.7	−0.6	−1.1	−1.9	−2.0	−0.5	−1.1
Current Account Balance	−4.8	−5.8	−4.4	−3.6	−2.9	−1.9	−1.8	−2.6	−2.8	−1.4	−1.8
Savings	19.7	19.9	20.5	21.5	22.1	22.9	22.4	23.0	22.7	22.2	21.3
Investment	24.2	25.7	24.9	25.0	24.9	24.7	24.1	25.5	25.4	23.7	23.0
Capital Account Balance	0.3	0.5	0.9	1.1	1.3	1.3	0.6	0.6	0.8	0.9	0.7
Latin America and the Caribbean											
Net Lending and Borrowing	−0.1	−0.1	−2.3	−2.7	−3.1	−3.3	−1.9	−1.5	−1.6	−1.7	−1.9
Current Account Balance	−0.2	−0.2	−2.3	−2.7	−3.1	−3.3	−1.9	−1.5	−1.6	−1.8	−1.9
Savings	20.3	21.3	20.0	19.3	17.9	18.2	17.5	17.9	18.0	17.9	18.4
Investment	20.4	21.3	22.4	22.3	21.6	21.8	19.3	19.0	20.0	20.7	21.5
Capital Account Balance	0.1	0.1	0.0	0.1	0.0	0.0	0.0	0.0	0.0	0.0	0.0
Middle East, North Africa, Afghanistan, and Pakistan											
Net Lending and Borrowing	7.8	9.5	12.0	10.0	6.3	−3.6	−3.7	−0.7	2.0	2.0	0.1
Current Account Balance	8.3	10.1	12.5	9.8	5.5	−4.0	−3.9	−0.7	1.8	1.9	0.0
Savings	34.6	37.3	38.0	36.2	32.9	25.0	24.7	26.5	29.7	29.4	27.0
Investment	27.0	28.0	25.9	25.9	26.7	28.3	27.6	26.8	27.2	26.6	25.9
Capital Account Balance	0.1	0.1	0.0	0.0	0.2	0.0	0.0	0.1	0.1	0.1	0.1
Sub-Saharan Africa											
Net Lending and Borrowing	1.9	2.3	−0.6	−1.7	−3.3	−5.6	−3.4	−1.9	−2.4	−3.0	−3.1
Current Account Balance	0.7	0.9	−1.7	−2.2	−3.6	−6.0	−3.9	−2.3	−2.8	−3.4	−3.4
Savings	20.2	21.5	19.5	18.7	18.8	16.7	17.4	19.0	17.8	17.6	17.9
Investment	19.7	20.6	21.0	20.9	22.0	22.0	20.8	21.1	20.5	20.9	21.2
Capital Account Balance	1.2	1.5	1.1	0.4	0.4	0.4	0.4	0.4	0.4	0.4	0.3

Table A14. Summary of Net Lending and Borrowing *(continued)*
(Percent of GDP)

	Averages								Projections		
	2000–09	2004–11	2012	2013	2014	2015	2016	2017	2018	2019	Average 2020–23
Analytical Groups											
By Source of Export Earnings											
Fuel											
Net Lending and Borrowing	9.1	10.0	9.3	7.4	4.7	−1.5	−1.6	1.4	4.4	4.1	2.3
Current Account Balance	9.6	10.4	9.6	7.3	5.0	−1.6	−1.7	1.5	4.3	4.1	2.2
Savings	33.9	35.0	34.6	32.0	30.2	26.6	25.4	27.4	29.7	29.5	27.5
Investment	24.7	25.0	25.4	24.9	25.3	28.2	26.5	25.6	24.8	24.7	24.5
Capital Account Balance	−0.1	0.0	−0.1	0.0	−0.6	−0.1	0.0	0.0	0.1	0.1	0.0
Nonfuel											
Net Lending and Borrowing	0.8	0.8	−0.9	−1.0	−0.4	0.3	0.1	−0.2	−0.7	−0.6	−0.8
Current Account Balance	0.6	0.6	−1.1	−1.2	−0.6	0.1	0.0	−0.3	−0.8	−0.8	−0.9
Savings	28.4	31.4	33.2	33.1	33.7	33.9	33.2	33.1	33.3	33.2	32.8
Investment	28.0	30.9	34.2	34.2	34.2	33.7	33.1	33.4	34.2	34.2	34.0
Capital Account Balance	0.2	0.2	0.2	0.2	0.2	0.2	0.1	0.1	0.1	0.1	0.1
By External Financing Source											
Net Debtor Economies											
Net Lending and Borrowing	−0.7	−1.1	−2.7	−2.4	−2.3	−2.3	−1.8	−1.8	−2.3	−2.1	−2.1
Current Account Balance	−1.1	−1.4	−3.1	−2.7	−2.6	−2.7	−2.0	−2.0	−2.5	−2.3	−2.3
Savings	22.3	23.6	23.1	22.5	22.5	22.0	22.2	22.5	22.4	22.7	23.2
Investment	23.6	25.2	26.1	25.2	25.1	24.6	24.1	24.5	24.8	24.9	25.5
Capital Account Balance	0.3	0.4	0.3	0.3	0.3	0.3	0.2	0.2	0.2	0.2	0.2
Net Debtor Economies by Debt-Servicing Experience											
Economies with Arrears and/or Rescheduling during 2013–17											
Net Lending and Borrowing	−0.4	−1.7	−6.1	−6.0	−4.1	−5.4	−6.1	−5.4	−4.6	−4.6	−4.7
Current Account Balance	−0.9	−2.3	−6.7	−6.2	−4.5	−5.7	−6.2	−5.7	−4.9	−4.9	−4.9
Savings	20.2	20.1	14.5	13.1	14.1	12.5	12.6	13.9	14.8	15.3	16.8
Investment	21.7	22.3	20.7	19.2	18.6	17.7	18.3	18.9	19.3	19.9	21.3
Capital Account Balance	0.5	0.6	0.6	0.3	0.4	0.3	0.1	0.3	0.2	0.3	0.2
Memorandum											
World											
Net Lending and Borrowing	0.0	0.3	0.5	0.6	0.6	0.4	0.4	0.5	0.5	0.3	0.1
Current Account Balance	0.0	0.3	0.5	0.5	0.5	0.3	0.3	0.5	0.4	0.3	0.0
Savings	23.9	24.7	26.2	26.2	26.7	26.7	26.0	26.5	26.7	26.8	26.8
Investment	23.9	24.4	25.4	25.5	25.8	26.0	25.5	25.8	26.2	26.5	26.8
Capital Account Balance	0.1	0.1	0.1	0.1	0.0	0.0	0.0	0.0	0.1	0.1	0.1

Note: The estimates in this table are based on individual countries' national accounts and balance of payments statistics. Country group composites are calculated as the sum of the US dollar values for the relevant individual countries. This differs from the calculations in the April 2005 and earlier issues of the *World Economic Outlook*, in which the composites were weighted by GDP valued at purchasing power parities as a share of total world GDP. The estimates of gross national savings and investment (or gross capital formation) are from individual countries' national accounts statistics. The estimates of the current account balance, the capital account balance, and the financial account balance (or net lending/net borrowing) are from the balance of payments statistics. The link between domestic transactions and transactions with the rest of the world can be expressed as accounting identities. Savings (S) minus investment (I) is equal to the current account balance (CAB) (S – I = CAB). Also, net lending/net borrowing (NLB) is the sum of the current account balance and the capital account balance (KAB) (NLB = CAB + KAB). In practice, these identities do not hold exactly; imbalances result from imperfections in source data and compilation as well as from asymmetries in group composition due to data availability.

[1]Excludes the G7 (Canada, France, Germany, Italy, Japan, United Kingdom, United States) and euro area countries.
[2]Georgia, Turkmenistan, and Ukraine, which are not members of the Commonwealth of Independent States, are included in this group for reasons of geography and similarity in economic structure.

Table A15. Summary of World Medium-Term Baseline Scenario

	Averages		2016	2017	Projections			
					2018	2019	Averages	
	2000–09	2010–19					2016–19	2020–23
	Annual Percent Change							
World Real GDP	**3.9**	**3.8**	**3.3**	**3.7**	**3.7**	**3.7**	**3.6**	**3.6**
Advanced Economies	1.8	2.0	1.7	2.3	2.4	2.1	2.1	1.6
Emerging Market and Developing Economies	6.1	5.2	4.4	4.7	4.7	4.7	4.6	4.9
Memorandum								
Potential Output								
Major Advanced Economies	1.9	1.3	1.5	1.5	1.6	1.6	1.6	1.5
World Trade, Volume[1]	**5.0**	**4.8**	**2.2**	**5.2**	**4.2**	**4.0**	**3.9**	**3.8**
Imports								
Advanced Economies	3.6	4.4	2.4	4.2	3.7	4.0	3.6	3.2
Emerging Market and Developing Economies	9.1	5.8	1.8	7.0	6.0	4.8	4.9	5.3
Exports								
Advanced Economies	3.9	4.4	1.8	4.4	3.4	3.1	3.1	3.2
Emerging Market and Developing Economies	8.0	5.5	3.0	6.9	4.7	4.8	4.8	4.6
Terms of Trade								
Advanced Economies	−0.2	0.1	1.0	−0.2	−0.1	0.1	0.2	0.0
Emerging Market and Developing Economies	1.4	0.1	−1.4	0.6	1.6	−0.2	0.1	−0.1
World Prices in US Dollars								
Manufactures	1.7	0.3	−5.2	1.7	2.5	1.6	0.1	0.1
Oil	13.1	1.1	−15.7	23.3	31.4	−0.9	7.9	−3.2
Nonfuel Primary Commodities	5.3	1.2	−1.5	6.8	2.7	−0.7	1.7	0.2
Consumer Prices								
Advanced Economies	2.0	1.6	0.8	1.7	2.0	1.9	1.6	2.0
Emerging Market and Developing Economies	6.8	5.2	4.2	4.3	5.0	5.2	4.7	4.3
Interest Rates	*Percent*							
Real Six-Month LIBOR[2]	1.2	−0.6	0.0	−0.4	0.2	1.1	0.2	1.5
World Real Long-Term Interest Rate[3]	2.1	0.5	0.4	−0.2	−0.1	0.5	0.2	0.9
Current Account Balances	*Percent of GDP*							
Advanced Economies	−0.9	0.4	0.7	0.9	0.7	0.5	0.7	0.4
Emerging Market and Developing Economies	2.5	0.5	−0.2	0.0	0.0	0.0	−0.1	−0.5
Total External Debt								
Emerging Market and Developing Economies	31.1	28.3	29.7	30.1	29.9	29.8	29.9	27.9
Debt Service								
Emerging Market and Developing Economies	9.3	10.0	10.7	9.8	10.4	10.4	10.3	9.8

[1]Data refer to trade in goods and services.
[2]London interbank offered rate on US dollar deposits minus percent change in US GDP deflator.
[3]GDP-weighted average of 10-year (or nearest-maturity) government bond rates for Canada, France, Germany, Italy, Japan, the United Kingdom, and the United States.

WORLD ECONOMIC OUTLOOK
SELECTED TOPICS

World Economic Outlook Archives

I. Methodology—Aggregation, Modeling, and Forecasting

II. Historical Surveys

III. Economic Growth—Sources and Patterns

IV. Inflation and Deflation and Commodity Markets

V. Fiscal Policy

VI. Monetary Policy, Financial Markets, and Flow of Funds

VII. Labor Markets, Poverty, and Inequality

VIII. Exchange Rate Issues

IX. External Payments, Trade, Capital Movements, and Foreign Debt

IMF EXECUTIVE BOARD DISCUSSION OF THE OUTLOOK, OCTOBER 2018

The following remarks were made by the Chair at the conclusion of the Executive Board's discussion of the Fiscal Monitor, Global Financial Stability Report, and World Economic Outlook on September 20, 2018.

Executive Directors broadly shared the assessment of global economic prospects and risks. They observed that the global expansion, while remaining strong, has lost some momentum and growth may have plateaued in some major economies. Prospects increasingly diverge among countries, reflecting differences in policy stances and the combined impact of tighter financial conditions, rising trade barriers, higher oil prices, and increased geopolitical tensions. Beyond 2019, growth in most advanced economies is expected to be held back by slow labor force growth and weak labor productivity. In emerging market and developing economies, growth is projected to remain relatively robust, although income convergence toward advanced economy levels would likely be less favorable for countries undergoing substantial fiscal adjustment, economic transformation, or conflicts.

Directors generally agreed that near-term risks to the global outlook have recently shifted to the downside and some have partially materialized. Trade barriers have risen, with adverse consequences for investment and growth. Financial conditions in most emerging market and developing countries have tightened since mid-April. Capital flows to some of these countries have declined, reflecting weak fundamentals, higher political risks, and/or U.S. monetary policy normalization. While financial conditions in advanced economies remain broadly accommodative, an inflation surprise could lead to an abrupt tightening of monetary policy and to an intensification of market pressures across a broader range of countries. In addition, most Directors saw as key risks a further escalation of trade tensions, a rise in political and policy uncertainties, and growing inequality. Meanwhile, high debt levels limit the room for maneuver in many countries.

Most Directors considered that the recent intensification of trade tensions and the potential for further escalation pose a substantial risk to global growth and welfare. They noted that unilateral trade actions and retaliatory measures could disrupt global supply chains, weaken investor confidence, and undermine broader multilateral cooperation at a time when it is urgently needed to address shared challenges. They therefore urged all countries to adopt a cooperative approach to promote growth in goods and services trade, reduce trade costs, resolve disagreements without raising tariff and nontariff barriers, and modernize the rules-based multilateral trading system. The possibility of an outcome in which trade issues could be resolved in a positive way was also pointed out. Directors noted that persistent large external imbalances continue to call for sustained efforts, mindful of countries' cyclical positions, to increase domestic growth potential in surplus countries and to raise supply or rein in demand in deficit countries.

Given a narrowing window of opportunity, Directors underscored the urgency of policy measures to sustain the expansion, strengthen resilience, and raise medium-term growth prospects. They encouraged countries to rebuild fiscal buffers where needed, and implement growth-friendly measures calibrated to avoid procyclicality and the risk of sharp drags on activity. Directors agreed that, where inflation is below target, continued monetary accommodation remains appropriate. Where inflation is close to or above target, monetary support should be withdrawn in a gradual, data-dependent, and well-communicated manner. Directors emphasized the critical role of structural reforms in boosting potential output, ensuring that gains are widely shared, and improving safety nets—including to protect those vulnerable to structural change.

Most Directors shared the assessment that near-term risks to financial stability have increased while medium-term risks remain elevated. They highlighted, in particular, the buildup of financial vulnerabilities over the past few years of very accommodative financial conditions, including high and rising public and corporate debt, and stretched asset valuations in some major markets. Addressing these vulnerabilities remains an important priority for many countries. For some countries, priorities include cleaning up bank balance sheets, improving corporate governance, and addressing risks from the sovereign-bank nexus, although a number of Directors felt that regulatory issues pertaining to sovereign exposures would best be left to the remit of the Basel Committee on Banking Supervision, which is the standard-setting body on the matter for a number of member countries. Directors also stressed the importance of completing and fully implementing the regulatory reform agenda, and of avoiding a rollback of reforms that have contributed to a more resilient financial system ten years after the global financial crisis.

Directors agreed that financial regulators and supervisors should remain vigilant about potential threats to financial stability and stand ready to act. They called for special attention to liquidity conditions and new risks, including those related to cybersecurity, financial technology, and other institutions or activities outside the perimeter of prudential regulation. These require policymakers to further develop policy tools, including macroprudential policies, and deploy them proactively as needed, as well as enhance coordination across borders.

Directors stressed that, as monetary policy normalization proceeds in advanced economies, emerging market and developing economies need to prepare for an environment of tighter financial conditions and higher volatility. Countries need to tackle their vulnerabilities and enhance resilience with an appropriate mix of fiscal, monetary, exchange rate, and prudential policies. In certain circumstances, capital flow management measures may be appropriate but not as a substitute for macroeconomic adjustment. Directors observed that markets have so far differentiated among emerging market and developing economies based on

their fundamentals and idiosyncratic factors. In this context, they underlined the importance of maintaining credible policy and institutional frameworks, strengthening governance, and improving human and physical capital. Directors noted that the current environment highlights the need for the Fund to offer granular, tailored policy advice and stand ready to provide financial support to its members as needed.

Directors underscored that priorities for low-income developing countries include building resilience, lifting potential growth, improving inclusiveness, and making progress toward the 2030 Sustainable Development Goals, while commodity exporters should also prioritize economic diversification. Stronger efforts are needed to create room for development expenditure, through broadening the tax base, improving revenue administration, and prioritizing spending on health, education, and infrastructure, while cutting wasteful subsidies. Directors also called for urgent action to contain debt vulnerabilities, which are rising in many countries. They stressed that both debtors and creditors share a responsibility for ensuring sustainable financing practices and enhancing debt transparency.

Directors agreed that public sector balance sheet analysis provides a useful tool to analyze public finances. By revealing the full scale of public assets in addition to debt and nondebt liabilities, it helps governments identify risks and manage both assets and liabilities, potentially reducing borrowing costs and raising returns on assets. Directors noted that the long-term intertemporal analysis is particularly relevant in aging societies. They also saw the benefits of the added transparency in enriching the policy debate. At the same time, Directors acknowledged that the balance sheet approach still has limitations, notably data quality and differences in accounting practices hindering cross-country comparisons, and thus it should be used with caveats to complement traditional fiscal analysis.

Highlights from IMF Publications

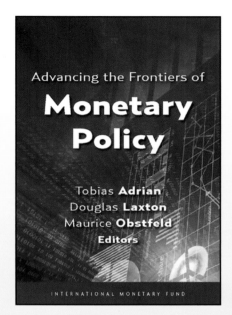

Advancing the Frontiers of Monetary Policy

$30. English. Paperback
ISBN 978-1-48432-594-0. 296pp.

The ASEAN Way: Sustaining Growth and Stability

$25. English. Paperback
ISBN 978-1-51355-890-5. 308pp.

Finance & Development Magazine

$29 annual subscription fee.
Free to developing countries.
English ISSN 0145-1707

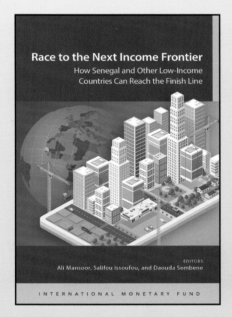

Race to the Next Income Frontier

$40. English. Paperback
ISBN 978-14843-0313-9. 430pp.

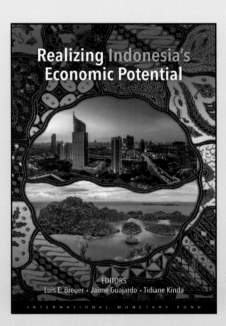

Realizing Indonesia's Economic Potential

$30. English. Paperback
ISBN 978-1-48433-714-1. 336pp.

Modernizing China: Investing in Soft Infrastructure

$38. English. Paperback
ISBN 978-1-51353-994-2. 388pp.

To order, visit bookstore.imf.org/weo1018